'*Jyotish: The Art of Vedic Astrology* by Andrew Mason is a refreshing new look at an ancient system of astrology. Written with humility, humour and hints of deep insight, this book is a welcome change from other books on Jyotish. The personal stories and experiences in the book help to bring an often-obscure system of astrology into modern times. The section on medical astrology and astrological remedies is especially appreciated, and will certainly help a number of readers.'

    – Vaidya Ātreya Smith, Director, European Institute of Vedic Studies and author of Ayurvedic Nutrition *and* Ayurvedic Healing for Women

'Andrew Mason brings a fresh, new, and serious voice to the current array of books on Vedic astrology. From his time spent in Sri Lanka he brings a unique slant on remedial measures and medical astrology – his real passion. Copious illustrations and tables plus extensive footnotes and bibliography enhance all sections of this book, including those on Jyotish fundamentals. Mason presents the planets throughout in their sequence in the Planetary Cabinet, departing from the Vedic classical norm.'

    – Edith Hathaway, Vedic Astrologer and author of In Search of Destiny

Jyotish

by the same author

Rasa Shāstra
The Hidden Art of Medical Alchemy
ISBN 978 1 84819 107 5
eISBN 978 0 85701 088 9

Vedic Palmistry
Hastā Rekha Shāstra
ISBN 978 1 84819 350 5
eISBN 978 0 85701 309 5

Jyotish

The Art of Vedic Astrology

ANDREW MASON

Foreword by James Braha

SINGING
DRAGON

LONDON AND PHILADELPHIA

First published in 2017
by Singing Dragon
an imprint of Jessica Kingsley Publishers
73 Collier Street
London N1 9BE, UK
and
400 Market Street, Suite 400
Philadelphia, PA 19106, USA

www.singingdragon.com

Library of Congress Cataloging in Publication Data
Names: Mason, Andrew (Ayurvedic therapist), author.
Title: Jyotish : the art of Vedic astrology / Andrew Mason.
Description: Philadelphia : Jessica Kingsley Publishers, 2017. | Includes
index.
Identifiers: LCCN 2017010655 (print) | LCCN 2016048161 (ebook) | ISBN
9781848192102 | ISBN 9780857011602 (ebook)
Subjects: LCSH: Hindu astrology.
Classification: LCC BF1714.H5 M36 2017 (ebook) | LCC BF1714.H5 (print) | DDC
133.5/9445--dc23

British Library Cataloguing in Publication Data
A CIP catalogue record for this book is available from the British Library

ISBN 978 1 84819 210 2
eISBN 978 0 85701 160 2

Printed and bound in Great Britain

Dedicated to my wife Atsuko
and daughter Himiko

CONTENTS

PART II: RASHIS, THE ZODIAC AND THE SYMBOLISM OF THE TWELVE SIGNS

PART III: MEDICAL ASTROLOGY AND ĀYURVEDA

PART IV: THE MOON AND ITS LUNAR MANSIONS

PART V: THE PROPITIATION OF PLANETS AND REMEDIAL MEASURES

FOREWORD

For scholarly astrologers, *Jyotish: The Art of Vedic Astrology* is one of the most important books of the last four decades. It is an encyclopaedic text providing the origins of the myriad body of ancient Indian astrological techniques, and a real contribution to our field. It is enormously detailed and spectacularly researched. This is a book that will thrill academic-minded Vedic astrologers who want to dig deeper into every facet of the miraculous star language.

Anyone expecting an ordinary introductory book will, I dare say, be disappointed. And, in any case, there are now enough introductory texts written by both Westerners and Easterners to satisfy all tastes. The material you are about to read is not ordinary because Andrew Mason is as far from an ordinary astrologer as anyone I have ever met. He is passionate about metaphysics, determined in his ways, and driven to find the truth and historical accuracy of all astrological material.

Unlike the focus of my work and writing, which has been generally to determine which techniques work the best and which fall short so we can produce the most accurate horoscope readings possible, Andrew wants to discover the roots and very basis of all astrological knowledge. What, for example, are the origins of gemstones as remedial measures, and when were gems first mentioned in ancient texts? What is the basis for planetary Upayes (healing methods)? How are planetary yagyas performed, and are they more powerful than talismans, yantras or other methods? Which ancient texts appear most trustworthy, and are their statements borne out by direct observations of the skies? What does *Sûrya Siddhânta* say and why? What did Varāhamihira conclude?

Andrew, to be frank, is very nearly a questioning machine who has actually had to learn to manage his unrelenting curiosity and drive for answers in order not to offend teachers and mentors. From Andrew's view, no astrological knowledge or technique should be blindly accepted without some solid historical basis and proven logic – or at least before given serious deliberation. This has not always sat well with Andrew's teachers, for many different reasons. But it is this intense drive that is responsible for the detailed and intricate information you are about to read, and the reason Andrew addresses so many issues – mathematical, technical and theoretical – that are so often ignored or treated superficially by others.

Upon first reading this book, I called Andrew to discuss what was, for me, an overwhelming amount of detailed, technical material. I asked whether he felt he might have included too much information. To my surprise, his response concerned his fear that he had 'short-changed the reader by not including enough!' Therein, of course, lies the beauty of this text for those who want to delve deeper than ever before. Not only is there an enormous amount of information, the work is detailed and meticulous.

Like many astrologers, Andrew came upon the star language in a roundabout way. In his twenties, he was plagued with a painful injury and spent 12 years seeking a cure. This led him to Āyurveda, the Hindu healthcare method that incorporates Jyotish, which grabbed him so profoundly that he opted to study in Śrī Laṅkā on a one-year internship, longer than the three-month requirement. Eventually, as happens to many Āyurvedic students, a fascination with astrology took hold and never let go.

This book is divided into five major sections, and I would love to point to the best, most fascinating, one. The task, however, is impossible. Every section is more intricate and insightful than the next. When asked for his opinion, Andrew said he favours the section on Upayes, healing methods. As he explained, 'Everyone has aspects of their horoscopes that are challenging. What good is Jyotish if it doesn't provide cures and ameliorations?' I agree completely, and have argued for decades that too many Westerners practicing Vedic Astrology ignore or downplay astrological Upayes. But, to the question of which part of this book is best, the answer must be based on each reader's particular interest. Because, as you will soon see, each section is like a book unto itself.

To say that the field of Jyotish is vast is an understatement, especially in Eastern astrology, where there are techniques, methodologies and systems that one could easily study beyond the length of one lifetime. To make matters worse, disagreements, complexities and conundrums abound. In India, at the front of many temples sit two lions, as if guarding the door. The lions are said to represent the two issues which stop disciples from what the temple has to offer – God. The two issues are doubt (that God exists) and paradox (that which appears contradictory or impossible and yet is true). If one intends to approach anywhere near a mastery of Jyotish, he or she absolutely must embrace paradox, and make peace with a significant level of confusion.

The first problem occurs when an astrologer tries to analyse the charts of twins who are born within seconds, or a minute or two, of each other.

The horoscopes are near exactly the same (including, quite often, the major Varga charts – Navamsha D-9 and Dasamsha D-10) yet the two lives are dramatically different. The careers diverge, one twin divorces while the other is happily married, one is extroverted, the other somewhat shy, and so on (I am aware that some astrologers cite the Shastiamsha (D-60) Varga chart as significant for twins, but the D-60 has absolutely nothing to do with career or marriage, to name only two major life conditions). We know from experience that astrology works. So, what gives?

The next problem occurs about five to ten years into our practice, when, if we are truly honest with ourselves and diligent in our work, we come to realise that no one astrological feature works 100 per cent of the time, no matter how definitive the indication. I am referring to planets in their highest degree of exaltation, without afflictions or bad aspects from other planets, giving mediocre or poor results rather than what they should produce. Or very badly aspected planets that once in a great while produce quite positive effects. I am not, to be clear, unaware that certain features of a horoscope can unduly influence the tenor of an entire horoscope, thus rendering other features less effective. We all know that if Saturn, for example, sits on the ascendant or tightly aspects many planets, the whole chart is affected and the person may fail to realise many of the positive features. Nor am I ignoring horoscope-altering techniques such as Neechabhanga and other important yogas. Those are obvious explanations. I am addressing relatively ordinary horoscopes where a profoundly positive or profoundly negative indication simply falls completely flat. In over 35 years of practice, I have witnessed this odd and rare phenomena a few too many times. Quite simply, there is not one definitively powerful positive or negative feature in all of astrology that, if we are honest, we have not seen utterly fail at least a few times. Why does this happen?

Next comes the issue of different astrological systems sometimes contradicting each other or indicating dramatically different outcomes. In the fall of 1992, about three or four months before my second marriage, an interesting thing happened. Using the most popular and widely used Jyotish system, Parasara, I could not find any indications whatsoever of my upcoming wedding. Nor could I find any such indications in my Western horoscope transits or progressions. Yet, I was sure I would marry. One day the phone rang and my friend Richard Houck, author of several Hindu astrology books and someone who also used Western solar, primary and lunar progressions, called to tell me to stop making wedding plans because there was positively nothing indicating marriage! The call was shocking because Rick had a wonderful predictive track record. He lived near Washington, DC and consistently predicted political elections accurately.

He also had a thriving professional astrology business, and actually rectified the horoscope of every single client he ever worked for. If several major events did not occur in the client's life at the time the horoscope indicated, he would back up the birth time or move it forward until the chart fit. If rectifying the birth time required a big time change to produce accuracy, he refused to read the chart until the person did more research on their birth data.

When Rick made his declaration of no marriage, I replied, 'I know, Rick. I can't find marriage in my Hindu or Western chart. But I am getting married.' 'No, you're not,' he said, while laughing. Well, the marriage occurred on schedule and 24 years later is still going strong, thank you very much. Later that year, about nine or ten months after my wedding, I taught at the Vedic Astrology Conference in California. There I met K.N. Rao, who gave a workshop on the Jaimini astrological system. I asked him if marriage showed up in my horoscope in 1993 within the Jaimini system and he replied, 'Yes, yes. It is right here.' At first, sceptic that I am, I had my doubts. But as I studied, it became obvious that he was not lying. In October 1991, at the age of 40, I entered Libra dasa. Libra is the sign of relationships and in my chart Libra holds Mercury, the marriage indicator within my Jaimini horoscope (the marriage indicator is called Dara Kāraka, and is the planet in the lowest degree of all the planets. Mercury is in the 3rd degree of my chart, lower than all others). As soon as Libra dasa started, I began the strongest relationship in more than a decade, and within 15 months we married.

These are but a few of the complexities, conundrums and paradoxes in our field. Which brings us to the most critical and controversial astrological issue of all, the all-important Ayanāmśa. The Ayanāmśa, described fully in Chapter 1 – and in more detail than I have ever seen – is the calculation that allows astrologers to determine when the coincidence of the two zodiacs, the tropical (based on the spring equinox) and the sidereal (based on fixed stars), last occurred. It is generally accepted that this event happened somewhere between 200 and 550 AD. This 350-year discrepancy, unfortunately, can cause a horoscope error of up to approximately 5°. Aside from causing ascendants of many horoscopes to change signs, the dasas and bhukti dates become radically altered.

Disagreements about which date and calculation to use have been so prevalent over the centuries that in 1952 the Government of India commissioned seven academics, one of whom (N.C. Lahiri) also had some prior knowledge of astrology, to come up with a decisive figure that the government would sanction. The result, after three years of research, became what is called the Lahiri Ayanāmśa. And it is now the most popular, widely accepted calculation by astrologers.

Andrew reports that researching the Ayanāmśa issue is akin to opening a Pandora's box of epic proportions. The deeper he delved, the more technical and historical problems he found – from all the proposed Ayanāmśa figures. To mention a few issues: al-Bīrūnī (the 10th-century AD Islamic scholar), travelling in India, noted that astrologers' and astronomers' identification of certain key stars (used to plot zodiacal increments) varied from region to region. Next, what appear to be singular points of light are sometimes two stars which, when viewed at great distance, appear as one. Then, while some ancient texts appear to be aware of the precession of equinoxes, others do not. Further, many of the centuries-old texts we use today appear to have been periodically rewritten over the centuries, with some authors adding their own thoughts and views without acknowledgement. As if all this is not enough, it seems that the rate of precession is not constant, and by all accounts has sped up in the last 2000 years. This little-known phenomena, according to Andrew, is not well understood. If so, delineating an accurate Ayanāmśa is, for all practical purposes, impossible. Pandora's box indeed.

Andrew suggests that perhaps the clearest remaining textbook description of Ayanāmśa may be given in *Sûrya Siddhânta* (written sometime within the 4th century AD) and confirmed by Varāhamihira in his *Pañca Siddhântika* (5th century AD). This figure, properly referred to as Revatipakṣa, was also followed by the respected astrologer Shil Ponde. In Chapter 1 of his book *Hindu Astrology* (1939), he suggests an Ayanāmśa based on Revatipakṣa, this appearing to be the most historically relevant in his era.

Andrew makes a strong astronomical case for Ponde's calculation, and it is easy to accept that Indian astrologers may have used this Ayanāmśa because it was promoted in *Sûrya Siddhânta*, one of the most respected and trustworthy ancient texts. This I do not doubt.

The problem, however, is that, as a practising astrologer for over 30 years, the only Ayanāmśas that have worked for me have been Lahiri's and (occasionally) Krishnamurthi's. These two Ayanāmśas are extremely close to each other (within 5 or 6 seconds) and therefore produce horoscopes with near-exact ascendant degrees. The dasa bhukti periods and sub-periods starting points using Krishnamurthi, however, start approximately 20–45 days earlier (depending on whether one is born in a short dasa or a long one) than when employing Lahiri's figure. These three to six weeks are of course quite significant when predicting the dates of events that appear in one's horoscope. And this is the main reason that many astrologers spend time and effort testing whether the Lahiri Ayanāmśa works better than Krishnamurthi's.

The calculation of Ayanāmśa favoured by Shil Ponde, on the other hand, produces horoscopes that vary from Lahiri by more than 3°. This is a relatively huge horoscope discrepancy that causes many Lahiri-based ascendants and planets to change signs. Also, when using Shil Ponde's calculation, the dasa bhukti starting dates occur between two and five years earlier than Lahiri's. A person born in a short period, such as Mars, Sun, Ketu or Moon, begins his or her dasas approximately two years earlier when using Shil Ponde versus Lahiri, while a person born in a long dasa, such as Rāhu, Jupiter, Venus, Mercury or Saturn, begins his or her dasas about four or five years earlier with Shil Ponde.

Astrologers who use a Revatipakṣa Ayanāmśa (per Shil Ponde) argue, of course, that they use it not just for historical reasons, but because it produces the greatest horoscope accuracy – both with ascendants and dasa bhuktis. Those who use Lahiri, of course, give the same reason. They say it works best! To quote Andrew, 'Let the games begin.'

My advice to astrologers using a different Ayanāmśa than what is advocated in this book is to remain open-minded and avoid passing judgement. Hard as it is to admit, what matters most are the results each astrologer produces for his or her clients, not which techniques and calculations are most perfect. In the same way that people rarely change their political or religious beliefs, it is doubtful that astrologers using an Ayanāmśa that has worked well for them will change. Disconcerting as all this may seem, it is quite possible – dare I say probable – that two astrologers using different Ayanāmśa could both produce largely accurate results, or at least provide great help to their clients.

Most seasoned astrologers I have met consider Jyotish to be an art/ science; a field that is part empirical and scientific, and part intuitive or psychic. Indeed, when studying with my Indian mentors decades ago, I distinctly remember times when they made very accurate statements about my friends and family (whose horoscopes we analysed nightly) that made no astrological sense. Several times, I saw my mentors make accurate statements they seemed to pull from the ethers! When I asked for their reasoning in these cases I remained decidedly unconvinced by their answers.

Also, consider some age-old divination systems such as the I-Ching and Tarot cards, both of which have been uncannily accurate many times throughout my life (not always, but quite often I have found no predictive technique or system to be perfect). It has never made one whit of sense to me how throwing three coins in the air six times and then reading their textbook meanings could produce anything worthwhile. And how could ascribing meanings to 78 playing cards and then shuffling them and placing them in a certain order possibly predict the future? Well…in my experience, they have. They do.

Interestingly, while all Tarot decks give the same meanings to all cards, there is one odd variation. In many decks, the #8 card represents justice and the #11 card indicates strength, while in other decks the meanings are reversed. Does this mean that one reader gets accurate results and the other fails? No. For the reader using the #8 card as justice, his or her clients will draw the #8 when justice energy is arising. The clients of Tarot readers who consider the #11 card to represent justice will draw the #11 card when the same energy arises. This, like it or not, is simply the nature of oracles and predictive arts. To anyone who believes that astrology is strictly empirical and scientific, the Ayanāmśa dilemma will be profoundly disturbing.

I am, and have always been, an experience-based astrologer, who cares little for authoritative teachings and scriptural texts and so on, unless they produce predictive accuracy. Those who have read my second Jyotish book (*Art and Practice of Ancient Hindu Astrology*, written in 2001) know how adamant I am about any traditional techniques I have found lacking. I have never, for example, found Vargottama planets to produce anything special, as they are supposed to. Neechabhanga Rajayoga, in my practice, works in about 10 to 20 per cent of cases, enough to be essentially worthless, because even the best astrologers only produce about 70 to 80 per cent accuracy. As for Western astrology solar return charts (known as Varshaphal in Jyotish), I found them to be completely ineffective even before learning Jyotish. One of the earliest questions I asked my first Indian mentor, R. Santhanam, was about this technique. I was heartened that his words matched my experience: 'They are useless and baseless' (no offence to readers who use Solar Returns, I am aware of how many astrologers swear by them).

Nevertheless, in spite of my disagreements with many scriptural teachings and respected authorities, and in spite of basing my practice entirely on techniques that work for me, I remain open to different views. Indeed, throughout a lifetime of professional practice, I have gone back every so many years to re-visit the techniques mentioned above (and others) that I determined decades ago do not work. I do this because it is always possible that, with added experience and wisdom, my views could change. I also do it because I consider mental flexibility, open-mindedness and passionate curiosity the most important qualities any astrologer can have.

During my first five or ten years in astrology, what fascinated me most was how a group of symbols on a page could so reveal a person's life.

The more time passed, however, the more my fascination changed to the question of why certain very seemingly clear astrological conditions in some horoscopes do not produce the effects they should.

Albert Einstein proclaimed that the reason he could produce mathematical, scientific results that eluded others was that he was comfortable wading in confusion until clarity might, hopefully, arise. To my mind, those who run from confusion, especially in our case from the all-important Ayanāmśa conundrum, get what they deserve – superficial experience, superficial results.

Had anyone told me that in 2017 I would be reviewing the Revatipakṣa Ayanāmśa to see if it worked because a strong historical and technical case had been made for it, I would have assumed they were crazy. I concluded decades ago, based on horoscope research, that this calculation was all but absurd. All these years later, I still find it produces significantly inaccurate results. But, I can say for sure that after reading this book what I have learned about historical 'astronomical observations' and its comparisons to Lahiri's and Krishnamurthi's will keep me pondering the issue for years to come. For that, I say bravo to Andrew Mason. And bravo for the care, dedication and seriousness he has put into this book!

James Braha
Vedic Astrologer and author of Ancient Hindu Astrology
for the Modern Western Astrologer *and* The Art
and Practice of Ancient Hindu Astrology

ACKNOWLEDGEMENTS

The author would like to extend his appreciation to the following people, without whom this book could not have been written.

My sincere thanks go to:
Dr Andrew Foss, Gordon Brennan, Linda Day, Gary Gomes, Udaya Danndunnage, Dominik and Dagmar Wujastyk, Christèle Barois, Ilona Kędzia, Robert Ray, Alan Oken, Roy Gillett, Danny Cavanaugh, Chris Lawson, Philip Weeks, Jane Adams, Robert A. Bartlett, Sato Tamotsu, Professor Hari Shankara Sharma and Victoria Peters.

With special thanks to:
James Braha, Andrew Kirk, Ernst Wilhelm, Vaidya Ātreya Smith, Edith Hathaway, Dr Gishanthi Arambepola, Dr Mauroof Athique, Meulin Athique, Dr Venkata Narayana Joshi, Jessica Kingsley and Singing Dragon.

ॐ सुमुखश्चैक दन्तश्च कपिलो गजकर्णकः लम्बोदरश्च
वक्रिटो विघ्न नाशो गणाधिपिः धूम्रकेतुर्गणाध्यक्षो
भालचन्द्रो गजाननः द्वादशैतानि नामानि यः पठेत्
शृणुयादप विद्यारम्भे विवाहेच प्रवेशे निर्गमे तथा
संग्रामे संकटंचैव विघ्नसतसय न जायते

Translation: *Beautiful-faced (sumukha), elephant-faced (gajānana), bearing one tusk (ekadanta), reddish in hue (kapila), having elephant ears (gajakarṇaka), large-bellied (lambodara), terrifying and formidable (vikaṭa), remover of obstacles (vighnanāśa), commander of the celestial army (gaṇādhipa), organiser of its troops (gaṇādhyakṣa), of smoky complexion (dhūmraketu) and adorning the moon upon his forehead (bhālacandra). He who would recite his twelve names, or should hear them upon commencement of study, weddings, on entering and departing or facing battle, will surely overcome all obstacles.*

INTRODUCTION

I.1 ANCIENT TECHNOLOGIES

The gods of the Sun[1] and Moon[2] are often portrayed in attendance to The Medicine Buddha.[3] Worship within the temple of the Medicine Buddha is said to be good for study of medicine and health. Shingon Mikkyō considers the Medicine Buddha to be secretive and hidden (mystical). He illuminates (like the Sun and Moon) only those that are worthy – yet his hand is outstretched showing he grants boons. Atharva Veda describes the removal of sickness via the use of this deity's mantra and a certain black wood.

The Gods of Shingon Mikkyō by Sato Tamotsu

Although a number of 'occult' sciences remain intact into the 21st century, many have been lost or driven into semi-obscurity. Much of what is today called pseudo-science or ancient superstition had in the past important practical application. These ancient technologies were often melting pots of observable phenomena and ritual that when combined could be used to coerce Providence or the Fates to manifest a favourable outcome.

In the past there were quite literally necromancers, rain-makers, oracles, magicians and geomancers. Those skilled in these arts were consulted in all manner of undertakings, such as healthcare, childbirth, attainment of wealth, victory in war, love and longevity; and – most importantly – foreknowledge of events. In a world of uncertainty, the honouring and propitiation of nature and its emissaries (such as planets) were believed to answer the querent – if one was skilled enough to interpret their answers.

To the western mindset a term such as 'ancient technology' appears a little paradoxical, as it is mostly assumed that the ancients lived in a kind of ignorant bliss, only improving their situation with the advent of modern industrialised society. This myth is quickly dispelled by spending an afternoon roaming the galleries of any major museum and studying its exhibits. Closer analysis of cultural antiquity quickly reveals how little daily existence has really changed. Technologies employed in former eras were (in some ways) just as ingenious as those of our current time. Although deprived of iPhones, combustion engines and atom bombs,[4] the ancients were able to combine surprising levels of sophistication, functionality and exquisite artistry[5] – all of this from the most basic and most abundant of materials.

Knowledge is quite literally power, so technologies were at times held in check through the initiation[6] process – knowledge transferable only through the master/disciple relationship. Such practices often included detailed instruction in the art of astronomy, martial arts, medicine, surgery, metallurgy, chemistry, geomancy and more. Astrology was one such important technology, eventually fused with alchemy, herbalism and geomancy – its remit touching every part of human existence.

I.2 ASTR-OLOGY

Some of mankind's earliest religious works pay tribute to the stars, the Sun and the Moon. Astr-ology[7] (in one form or another) is to be found in all ancient cultures. From occident[8] to orient, the worship of planetary gods often presided over a nation's prosperity and fertility.

Today many of the world's 'developed' countries rest in a state of indifference toward astrology and, just to add complexity to an already elusive subject, the east–west interpretations of this subject diverged some 1500 years ago,[9] having gone their separate ways over the course of time.

Though essentially rooted in the same star-pool, alternative astrological schools (such as Greek, Roman, Persian and later Arabic[10]) imprinted their own interpretations upon the constellations and planets, eventually culminating in what today could be called Western Astrology. This specialisation of astrology was largely precipitated by different cultural beliefs – however, dislocation of the western zodiac was caused by a phenomenon known as precession, a technical term used to describe the Sun's apparent backward movement through the signs of the zodiac. Observable only over long periods, precession was perhaps understood by Indian astronomers (by inference) but is more broadly accepted as an earlier Greek discovery.[11]

Meticulous cataloguing of the Sun's position along the ecliptic revealed it to be in a state of slow precession, shifting its stellar background at a rate of approximately 50 arc seconds yearly. Over a period of some 2160 years[12] this creeping motion traverses a full zodiacal sign (30°). Over the course of 25,920 years the Sun completes an entire lap of the zodiac. Any use of compensatory calculations allowing for this solar motion is said to favour a sidereal zodiac, that is to say, it is based upon the fixity of stars, preserving a secure reference point from which to commence the zodiac. Conversely, calculation based on the Sun's current position (at the spring equinox), marking the zodiac's starting point, is said to favour a tropical zodiac, or – to put it another way – an astrology that is eternally tied to Earthly seasons.[13]

In light of the powerful and unique symbology associated with each of the twelve constellations (within which reside the zodiacal signs), it seems unlikely that a transitory zero degree would endure as a popular means of astrological calculation. This in effect leads to the displacement of one sign every 2160 years, eventually usurping all signs during one full precessionary cycle, also termed 'A Great Year'. During this great year the Sun is effectively framed against *every* constellation and at every point is held to represent 0° Aries. Any system of astrological measurement that adheres to this methodology is based upon a tropical zodiac that gives precedence to the declination of the Sun – a kind of 'Solar-ology', if you will.

In our current century, discontinuity of sign and constellation is not so great, but for future generations the gap will inexorably widen. Tropical astrology has long acknowledged this fact, working now with an abstract zodiac that moves independently of the stars. It should also be noted here that, in its favour, the tropical model does provide a commonly agreed exactness of tropical degree as well as dispensing with the need to recalculate any accrued degrees of precession, which as we will see in Part I is far from being agreed upon.

In contrast to a tropical model, Jyotish is a sidereal astrology that aligns itself to the actual stars and therefore requires constant adjustment to counter the slow march of precession. Ayanāṃśa[14] (the name given to its corrective value) may be applied to any tropical computation to rectify the stellar background to reflect its true state, for any time or date in question.

Astrology is a highly resilient and adaptive system (whichever variation one finds most favourable), managing to stay current to the needs of successive generations. Experimentation of techniques, particularly by those who favour the tropical model, has seen a strong infusion of Jyotish in the last decade. This in part has come from numerous written works on Jyotish by accomplished western astrologers, or those who have sought to enrich their predictive skills by integrating Jyotish.

Typically, many new Vedic recruits are drawn to the use of its lunar Nakshatras (see Chapter 26). Although there are rich lunar interpretations in oriental astrology,[15] these are also to be found in the western tradition – although an intimate knowledge of their use and indications has withered over the centuries.[16]

I.3 JYOTISH

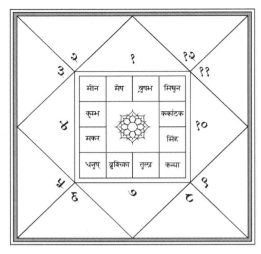

Jyotish might be translated as 'science of starlight' (or 'knowledge of starlight'). India's traditional astrology is but one of a number of profound Vedic sciences attempting to deal with the true nature of existence. There are references to various types of celestial phenomena, including planets and stars within the pages of the *Vedas*[17] (India's oldest writings). Whilst some of these texts detail astute astronomical observations, others delve deeply into the very fabric of the universe, often through the medium of astrology. Vedic texts make little distinction between astrology and astronomy, seeing each as an integral part of the whole. By providing a means to divine future events, honour the gods or confer appropriate times to perform sacrificial offerings, Jyotish often incurs the epithet 'the eyes of the *Vedas*'; that is, a means by which we are able to see and comprehend what the *Vedas* attempt to reveal.

Any would-be student hungry for Vedic knowledge is first confronted by a study of its various limbs, known as Shadaṅgas. These six limbs are likened to parts of a living organism called *Vedapuruṣa*, each indispensable for the maintenance of the whole and each intimately connected. These are delineated as: eyes (Jyotish/vision), nose (Shiksha/phonetics), mouth (Vyakarana/word), ears (Nirukta/sound), hands (Kalpa/tactile) and feet (Chhanda/movement), all being essential components for any deeper understanding of its pansophy.

Like many aspects of Vedic wisdom, each part can be subjected to a series of subdivisions to further attenuate its focus. In the case of Jyotish it too is subjected to a series of subdivisions,[18] described below.

Gola (observational astronomy)

A detailed study of spherical geometry, planets, stars, zodiacal signs and ecliptic. Gola[19] primarily concerns itself with the accurate measurement and cataloguing of astronomical bodies with reference to the ecliptic and equatorial plane. It also concerns itself with retrograde planets, eclipse prediction and lunar nodes, planetary motion, comets, asteroids, sunspots and the variation of stellar luminosity. It also concerns itself with the construction of such devices that aid in the pursuit of these observations.

Gaṇita (calculation)

A subdivision of Gola forming the bedrock of calculation techniques contained in various Siddhântic material. Gaṇita is expressed through advanced mathematical formulae enabling an accurate prediction of celestial motion including: solar ingress of signs, rising and setting solar timetables, solstices, equinoxes, eclipses, calculation of ephemerides and calendars (both solar and lunar) and the positions of planets for the casting of horoscopes (Jataka).

Jataka/Horā (natal astrology)

Calculation of a horoscope using the person's birth time and location. Jataka represents what most would recognise as astrology, that is, analysis of the heavens tied to one's birth data. Jataka predicts probable life-events, relative to planetary placements, subdivisional charts (Vargas) or dasha periods (timing), and so on. Jataka is also an assessment of inherent, acquired or collective karma and the remedial techniques thereof, best suited to alleviate an individual's suffering.

Prasna (questioning)

Also known as *horary astrology*, deals specifically with asking questions. *Prasna* means 'questioning'. Prasna charts are usually erected at their moment of occurrence, or the time of the question is duly noted and consulted thereafter. The information contained in this snapshot of the heavens is then deciphered to answer the querent. Some astrologers may employ prasna charts if the birth data submitted is in question or the birth horoscope seems overly confusing or contradictory.

Mhurta (timing of events)

Also known as *electional astrology*, *Mhurta* means 'moment'.[20] This popular branch of Jyotish may be used to elect all manner of daily and yearly religious and social undertakings – from the laying of a foundation stone to a marriage. Mhurta is popular with some Āyurvedic pharmacies, both for the manufacturing and prescribing of medicines (Mhurta helping attune a remedy to specific ailment). Mhurta also helps elect an auspicious moment to attract the attention of a specific deity when hoping for a particular outcome.

Nimitta (omenology)

Perhaps one of the most interesting yet least accessible levels[21] of Jyotish. It interprets portents on a minute-to-minute basis. A number of classic astrological works recount favourable or unfavourable omens delivered by such diverse messengers as flocking birds, baying hounds, wandering camels, ravens and the cries of a peacock. Omens were also forecast by the hue or obscuration of the luminaries (Sun and Moon). Other celestial events included lightning, meteors, eclipses and sunspots.

Jyotish refers to the planets[22] as *grahas*, a word meaning to 'grasp' or 'seize'. To the ancients these nine celestial wanderers were considered primary dispensers of Earthly karma.[23] Individually these were: Sun (Sûrya), Moon (Chandra), Mercury (Budha), Venus (Shukra), Mars (Kuja), Jupiter (Brihaspati) and Saturn (Shani). In addition to the seven visible planets, two non-luminous planets were also considered, Rāhu and Ketu, referring to the north and south nodes of the Moon (see Chapter 24).

The Earth (and ultimately mankind) was perceived as occupying the epicentre of creation, with the stars, Moon and other planets revolving about us in their sequential distances. From closest to furthest these were Moon, Mercury, Venus, Sun, Mars, Jupiter, Saturn and finally the Nakshatras (stars). The spherical mass of the Earth was buoyed up on *Earthly air* known as *Bhūvā*yu, suspended like a ball of iron between magnets while the planets were fastened about the pole star and driven eastwards on the *pravaha wind*.

This charting of the planets against their starry backdrop set the scene for great cosmic theatre, whose observation and decipherment proved an important tool with which to unlock the mysteries of the universe as well as gaining insights into an individual's destiny. Through the medium of astrology it became possible to discern dosha (physical constitution), caste (social status), longevity, career, wealth and most importantly life purpose, known as *dharma*. India's Rishis, or enlightened ones, were able to interpret the movements of the planets and stars into an art form, which might then be applied to all aspects of human existence.

Much like its sister sciences (Āyurveda, Yoga or Vāstu), Jyotish is a resplendent archive of carefully catalogued information, infused with elaborate ritual, mathematics and eloquent language. Any or all attempts to absorb the entirety of this astrological system might stretch into multiple lifetimes. As one convert from Western Astrology once jokingly put it to me, 'You might comfortably squeeze the entirety of Western Astrology into a match box and set it afloat upon the ocean of Vedic Astrology.' The book you now hold in your hands contents itself with being a primer that seeks only to introduce and popularise India's premier science.

One of the best ways to study Jyotish is to become intimate with the planets, to understand their personalities, life-lessons and personal histories/planetary ages.[24] Learning their stories allows each of them to converse with you. Once embraced, the planets take on a life of their own, no longer just glyphs inscribed within a geometric framework (the horoscope). Their positioning (for better or worse) and interactions start to offer up a wealth of information.

I.4 OVERVIEW

There remain innumerable ways to disseminate astrological knowledge, every teacher having their own methodology or expertise. One of my early tutors, also one with a strong mathematical inclination, used a simple counting strategy that ran roughly along the lines of:

1. individual planets

2. polarities, masculine/feminine, benefic/malefic, etc.

3. modes of sign expression, movable, fixed or dual

4. primary elements in astrology, Air, Fire, Water and Earth

and so on.

This book uses a similar tiered system, slowly building upon the information given in each section.

In Part I we 'set up shop' and consider some important prerequisites, one of which is the commencement of the zodiac (a controversial topic in itself but a highly important consideration). Here we take a closer look at the corrective calculation known as Ayanāṃśa. From here I introduce each of the planets through a series of planetary portraits, casting each as players in a grand celestial court and wherever possible trying to integrate the bedrock of this science, its rich and diverse mythologies.

Part II introduces the zodiac and the symbolism of the twelve signs, known as *Rashi*. We also consider the construction of horoscopes, some of the most popular designs, their application and strengths. Part II also looks at domification (or astrological houses) and the most popular method of dividing their space. This section also includes a study of significations (called Kārakas) for the twelve houses, as well as their combinations. This Part also dwells on the retrograde motion of planets, as well as the effects of solar combustion and planetary war.

Part III introduces medical astrology and its interaction with Āyurveda, India's 'complete' and indigenous medical system. Here connections between planet and constitution (known as dosha) are explored along with character portraits of *tridosha* (Vāta, Pitta and Kapha), better known as the guardians of health. This Part also examines the science of taste and the impact of strengthened or weakened planets, their effects on metabolism and tissues, and so on. It also includes the use of divisional charts (called Vargas), planetary periods known as *dashas* and, finally, Dṛṣṭi (planetary aspects), the line of sight between the planets.

Part IV deals almost exclusivity to the Moon and its lunar mansions (known as Nakshatras). Jyotish considers Moon a 'special planet' and, as our nearest and dearest celestial companion, this entire section is given over to its motion, occultation, eclipsing lunar nodes and daily sojourn in the embraces of its 27 lunar brides.

Part V is dedicated to the propitiation of planets and remedial measures. Known as Upayes, we consider the use of yantra, gemstones, rudrākṣa beads, ceremonial offerings (pooja) and fire rituals, known as ahuti. We also explore Bali/Shanti Karma, elaborate planetary ceremonies performed in Śrī Laṅkā that aim to deflect the negative emissions of planets known as *graha-apala*.

There is no right or wrong way to learn Jyotish, there is only learning. With practice, experimentation and a little determination, Jyotish will start to reveal itself to you – becoming a kind of second nature. Any investment made in its deeper symbology will always reward. Its initial complexities, however daunting, *will* (over time) coalesce and harmonise, facilitating an open dialogue with the planets.

We begin therefore with a story – set in an age of seers, whose talents in the divination arts were unparalleled and unquestioned.

Legend of Varāhamihira

If the Sun should blacken its countenance or be variegated in colour, if animals and birds should fearfully howl toward the fall of the night, then death can be expected. If the Sun should be the colour of blood in the mid-heaven or should appear the deepest red, as if engulfed by a dust storm – then the reigning prince shall die.

Brihat Saṃhitā[25] by Varāhamihira

King Vikramāditya[26] of Ujjayinī[27] summoned his Navaratnā[28] enquiring as to the fate of his soon to be born son. The learned sages arrived at court from their places of study and prepared to face and answer their king. Mihira (court astrologer) having directed his observation to the planets, who were after all most auspicious for such revelations, was also among the entourage.

Now assembled, each delivered a unanimous verdict: 'Excellency,' each chorused, 'I have considered your request in great earnestness in order that I might give answer to your question. It is therefore with deep regret that I inform you of an ill-fate which awaits the child: upon his sixteenth year of life, he will perish.'

Rising to his feet with graven look the king demanded the details of this fate. Why he asked, had such a curse fallen upon the royal household. Lowering their heads the sages replied, 'Though we cannot say what sequence of events will lead to his death, we all agree the youth will meet his end by the assault of a wild beast.'

Knowing his advisors to be beyond reproach and implicitly trusting their collective wisdom, the king had no choice but to accept their verdict. The palace, he knew, bordered a wilderness from which did on occasion present some danger in the form of prowling animals. The royal court also enjoyed hunting in this wilderness; perhaps it was to be on one such foray that his son would meet his end?

He was about to dismiss the entourage when Mihira stepped forward and added, 'Your majesty, I do not contradict these findings but would add that this beast will be a wild boar. Be aware, however, there can be no protection against the animal for the hand of fate aids it with supernatural qualities, striking without warning amidst a storm.'

The king gravely acknowledged these words, pondering his child's cruel and yet ironic fate – to be slain by their royal insignia, which was that of a ferocious looking wild boar.[29]

The child grew and relished life at court, never restricted in his movements and greatly enjoying any foray into the wilderness to hunt. He was never observed to flinch in the face of danger.

It had long ago been decided that the youth's fate be kept from him. If, reasoned the king, he was to be killed by a wild boar, he must live out his life unburdened by that knowledge.

Years passed and the prediction was somewhat forgotten, but as his sixteenth birthday drew near the predictions of the Navaratnā again returned to haunt the king, who now began a day and night vigil over the youth. If, reasoned the king, I were to keep the boy from harm's way, perhaps he might be spared. With this thought in mind he slowly began to restrict the movement of the prince, curtailing any events which might bring his son within striking distance of the wilderness. In the remaining days before his sixteenth birthday the king ordered the boy confined to the palace, having no contact with the outside world.

On the day of his son's sixteenth birthday the king received word a large boar had been sighted near the palace, close to the wilderness edge. Suspecting this to be the supernatural agent, come to claim his son, the king rode out to meet the beast, hoping to slay the animal. Before leaving, the king gave instruction that the boy be guarded at all times and forbidden to leave his room.

After searching in vain for the animal, the king returned to the palace only to be met with a great commotion. Hurriedly ascending to the rooms occupied by the prince he found his son dead, lying upon the terrace, impaled by a decorative lance that had hung upon the wall. Closer examination of its wooden shaft showed its end carved into the royal insignia – a ferocious wild boar.

Questioning the terrified attendants, they told how the signal of the king's return had prompted the youth to run out onto the terrace to welcome his return. At that very moment a fierce wind shook the palace, dislodging the lance, which had fallen and impaled the youth. Later, in honour of his stunning prediction, Mihira was awarded the title Varāhamihira (Varāha meaning boar), a title which persists to this day.

The son of Ādityadāsa,[30] Varāhamihira,[31] is historically honoured as scientist, astronomer, mathematician, author and, of course, astrologer. Little remains known of the man himself or his true origins, and like so many historical characters there is much disagreement over the accuracy of events surrounding his life.

As an author he is known to have written on a wide variety of subjects including: pilgrimages (tīrtha/yātrā), military campaigns (bṛhadyātrā), marriage (vivāhapaṭala), mathematics (karaṇa) and of course Jataka (natal astrology). His surviving *Pañca Siddhântikâ* (five astronomical canons[32]) has been dated in the region of AD 450–570 and remains an important compendium on early Indian Astronomy. Mihira's residence in Ujjayinī (Ujjain) is almost universally accepted, especially in regard to his famed mathematical school which later to become an important Indian cultural centre that prospered under his patronage. Mihira is often quoted as saying, 'There is no better boat than a horoscope to help a man cross the troubled seas of life.'

NOTES

1. Also known as Nikko Bosatsu or Sûryaprabha.
2. Also known as Gatten or Chandraprabha.
3. Also known as Yakushiji Nyorai, master of healing in Mahāyāna Buddhism.
4. The Indian classic *Mahabharat* describes weapons known as *Brahmā-astras* and *Agneya-astras*, which when taken in the context of a nuclear explosion seem eerily similar in their devastating effects, including radiation sickness. The *Agnī Purana* mentions *Dhupa* (projectiles/flying weapons) and the use of *Visvasaghati*, a mixture of metal oxides, carbon, oils, waxes, turpentine and other organic materials producing a highly volatile substance akin to modern-day napalm.
5. Two such examples include: the bronze cast chariots and horses of Emperor Qin Shi Huang Di, unearthed in China in 1980. These examples are perhaps the largest ever found and are not only highly decorative and detailed but are also functional. Although these half life-scale replicas were apparently ornamental, both are comprised of over seven thousand separately carved and cast pieces. These parts include skilful mechanical jointing and flattened sheet sections of 1–4mm in thickness. A second example would be the *Daibutsu* in the Tōdai-ji Temple, Nara Prefecture (Japan). Completed in AD 750 this 50-feet-high giant is considered one of the largest Buddha statues of its kind and is believed to have consumed the nation's entire copper/tin reserves during construction. Weighing in at a staggering 250 tons (minus base), its gold finishing swallowed over 200 kilos of liquid mercury during its final fire-gilding.
6. Much of humanity was thought to reside in a dim collective morass and so shielded from potentially dangerous knowledge, i.e. 'too much light can damage weak eyes'.
7. Astr = stars and ology = the study thereof.

8. May AD 330 saw the founding of Constantinople, Constantine himself presiding over an entourage of pagan/Christian priests, who under the instruction of astrologers renamed Byzantium Constantinople.

9. The coincidence of sidereal and tropical zodiacs, thought to be within the range of AD 285–576. Shil Ponde's calculation offers a possible congruence around the year AD 522.

10. Those using a twelve-fold division of the zodiac. During the Islamic incursion into North India, Tajik/Tāzig (Iranian for Arab) techniques may have been re-imported into Jyotish; these techniques are still favoured in some Vargas (divisional charts).

11. Hipparchus of Nicaea (150 BC) suggested an Ayanāṃśa value of 'no less than 36" yearly'.

12. This value is based upon a total processionary cycle of 25,920 years.

13. Earth's seasons (solstices and equinox) are tied to our orbit about the Sun. Due to the phenomena of precession, the planet's nutation slowly shifts the apparent position of the Sun backward against the stars at each of these juncture points.

14. Ayana = solstice and amsha = portion.

15. Worship of the twenty-eight asterisms (and other heavenly bodies) played a significant role in the Esoteric Buddhism founded in China. For more information see Brill (2013).

16. Use of Arabic Lunar Mansions in alchemy gained some ground during the renaissance for electional astrology. Today they are little used by astrologers in the west. For more information see Bartlett (2008).

17. The origins of Jyotish Shāstra are commonly attributed to a number of sutras in *Kāuçika Sūtra* (Atharva Veda); these early references to the planets, Nakshatras and other celestial phenomena appear mainly in the form of Mhurta (electional astrology) but are nonetheless prolific.

18. The Saṃhitā (science) of astronomy is sometimes presented as Karaṇa: planetary calculation only, Siddhānta/Tantra: planetary positions and the structure of the universe, etc., Jataka/Horā: individual horoscopes and later Tājik: celestial timing and the study of fortuitous events.

19. Might also be termed the mapping (geography) of space just as Bhūgola is the mapping or geography of Earth.

20. More specifically, Mhurta = 48 minutes.

21. Nimitta requires skilled guidance by one already proficient in this form of divination.

22. From the Greek πλανηται = wanderers.

23. Parasara recounts how nine aspects of the god Vishnu incarnated into each of the grahas. To the Sun, lord Rama; to the Moon, Krishna; to Mars, Narasimha; to Mercury, the Buddha; to Jupiter, Vamana; to Venus, Parashurama; to Saturn, Kurma; to Rāhu, Varāha; and to Ketu, Matsya.

24. See Kirk (2013).

25. Saṃhitā = a collection/an authoritative work.

26. Hero, warrior and semi-mythical Emperor/King heralding from India's 'golden age'. Vikramāditya is commonly agreed to be Chandragupta II (late 4th to early 5th century CE).

27. Ujjayini City is situated in the modern-day state of Madhya Pradesh (India). Ujjayini was taken as prime meridian for the calculation of solar/luna positioning.

28. Navaratnā, literally meaning 'nine jewels', in this instance nine wise and learned men: Varāhamihira (astrologer), Dhanvantarī (Āyurvedic Physician), Kālidāsa (poet), Vetālabhaṭṭa (scientist/philosopher), Saṅku (map maker/geographer), Ghaṭakarpara (architect), Vararuchi (Sanskrit scholar), Amarasiṃha (poet/author) and Kṣapaṇaka (Jain scholar).

29. The royal insignia is believed to represent *Varaha* (the third avatar of Vishnu) who rescued the submerged Earth from below the primal waters.

30. Devotee of the Sun and honoured as the source of all his Earthly knowledge.

31. Historically; Varāhamihira is thought to have lived between the years 450–570 CE; his ethnicity of Persian decent. The Islamic historian and scholar al-Bīrūnī (Abû Raiḥân), c.973–1048, notes *Pañca Siddhântikâ* to have been composed five hundred years prior to his own time, somewhat corroborating these dates. Varāhamihira (a polymath) is credited with a number of important written works including: *Pañca Siddhântikâ* (astronomy), *Brihat Jātaka* (astrology) and *Brihat Saṃhitā* (natural earth sciences).

32. A compendium of astrological information obtained from Indian, Greek, Roman and Persian sources, these Siddhānta (texts) being: *Paitāmaha, Romaka, Vāsishṭha, Pauliśa* and *Sûrya*.

PART I

SETTING UP SHOP

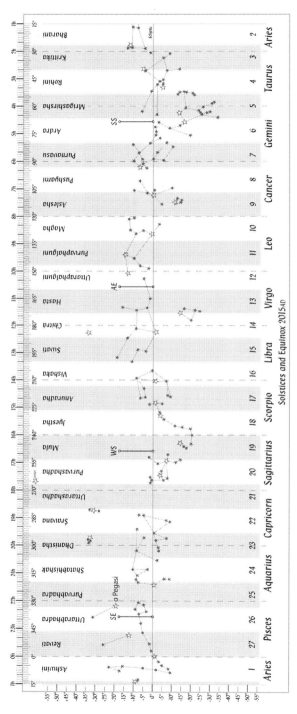

Zodiacal belt key: Central horizontal line = ecliptic, large white stars = Yogatārā, alternating vertical bands = 27 Nakshatras. SE = spring equinox, SS = summer solstice, AE = autumnal equinox and WS = winter solstice. As of 2015 the spring equinox is approximately 9° 16′ Pisces; its closest Yogatārā is α Pegasi in Purvabhadra Nakshatra.

1

AYANĀMŚA

A few years back I ran into an old colleague and we got talking amongst other things about Jyotish. Knowing his great enthusiasm for astrology I enquired if he'd come across anything new and exciting. Immediately he began to download a whole barrage of statistics, techniques and other assorted goodies. Pausing briefly, he unexpectedly said the word *Ayanāmśa*. Having more than a passing interest I asked him to expand on the topic, intrigued to hear his comments.

He went on to explain that as a longstanding member of a Vedic Astrological Association, he'd recently returned from its annual get-together. The weekend event had been a mixture of lectures by both home-grown and international speakers. The event had also been a chance to stock up on books, CDs, magazines and demos of the latest Jyotish software.

The final afternoon, he explained, had offered back-to-back lectures titled *11th House of Gain* or *The Question of Ayanāmśa*. Greatly intrigued by the sound of the Ayanāmśa lecture, my friend had then made his way toward the appropriate lecture hall, only to be mowed down by a mass of charging delegates speeding toward the adjacent lecture. Recovering from this surge of bodies (heading in the opposite direction), he peered nervously into the room, wondering if he was to be the only one crossing its threshold.

Upon entrance he was relieved to see a handful of Ayanāmśa devotees sprawled along the front row, trying uncomfortably to make the room seem a little more occupied than it was. He then went on to give me a great synopsis of the whole presentation as related by its speaker, saying, 'I found the whole thing pretty remarkable; it brought up in my mind a great number of misgivings. Toward the close of the discussion I really started to wonder how I'd ever missed its profundity. After all, it is value that determines all end results, yet curiously it hardly seems to get a mention.'

He continued, chuckling, 'I guess it just goes to show where some folks are with Jyotish, tripping over the fundamentals like Ayanāmśa to get a profitable seat in the 11th House. Seems to me to be a perfect example of "me-ing" taking precedence over "be-ing", at least in the world of some Jyotish acolytes.'

1.1 INTRODUCTION TO AYANĀMŚA

At one time, the Sun's southward course commenced on his reaching the middle of Aslesha (the ninth lunar constellation) and its northward course on its reaching the beginning of Dhanistha the twenty-third constellation (the Delphin of European Astronomers). This must have been the case as we find it recorded in ancient books.

Brihat Saṃhitā by Varāhamihira

In this chapter I have tried to distil the salient points of Ayanāṃśa into a greatly simplified form that hopefully enlightens the reader to the 'rhino in the room', draped with a lace tablecloth.

As the following is a bit technical, the reader is urged to ponder the diagrams and accompanying text – but above all remain calm. If the points discussed do not resonate immediately, simply return to this chapter at regular intervals and reacquaint yourself with its various concepts. Some of the topics discussed may at times appear contradictory, complex and even detrimental to the precepts of astrology; however, during compilation I felt I should provide a balanced appraisal wherever possible.

All of the following sections are therefore best considered pieces of an elaborate puzzle that *float* individually or, when taken in totality, lock neatly together, helping one to become cognisant of the subject's importance.

1.2 LET THE GAMES BEGIN

Many Vedic and some western sidereal astrologers are first confronted with the word *Ayanāṃśa* upon installation of their newly acquired software, momentarily hesitating as to which option they should click next. In some cases this rather troublesome decision is made for you by the software as it neatly and unobtrusively instals its default values. The default and most endorsed *Ayanāṃśa* for most Vedic Astrology software is that proposed by the Indian Calendar Reform Committee or CRC, called Chitrāpaksha/Lahiri Ayanāṃśa with an epoch value of 23° 15' and an annual precessionary rate of 50.28 (as of 1 January 1950). Although some software allows for a little tinkering, by and large the Ayanāṃśa edit facility is far less likely to suffer from excess wear and tear.

So what is all this Ayanāṃśa business, and why have I dedicated a whole chapter to this subject? Well, Ayanāṃśa *is* a fundamental cornerstone, if not one of the most historically interesting aspects of Vedic Astrology, and as such I felt a little space should be afforded it.

One tentative translation of Ayanāṃśa[1] might be 'a measurement' (amsha) of the solstices (ayana) *or* the value that marks the difference between the solar (tropical) zodiac and the sidereal[2] (starry) zodiac.

At first glance it seems best to just 'go with the flow' using default settings, but once you've disengaged your autopilot and asked yourself why the default is the default, Pandora's Box pops open and the fun begins.

Many, in truth, turn back long before reaching this point, and in fairness this is understandable as the initial allure of astrology, that is, its planets, signs and houses, is far more attractive than the gearwheels and cogs that hide unseen within the mechanism.

Additionally, you may also find that Ayanāṃśa values are one of the most incendiary topics amongst Jyotishi – but, if nothing else, are a useful barometer with which to gauge the liberality of your astrological company.

Some astrologers, like my colleague at the start of this chapter, feel quite comfortable about raising their misgivings over popular Ayanāṃśa values – while others refrain from any experimentation, feeling content with endorsed values. There are those who feel that the whole issue has been satisfactorily resolved and that any further experimentation is ill-advised or, worse, folly. As one astrological colleague related to me after installing newly acquired software: 'I found Ayanāṃśa editing pretty restrictive – in fact, borderline impossible.' Somewhat perturbed, he contacted the programmer to vent his frustrations only to be told: 'Adjustment of Ayanāṃśa is superfluous and anyone wishing to do so is probably on an ego trip.' Of course, the reply was framed in a polite manner.

A well-respected astrologer I discussed this issue with told me he'd personally known a number of astro-colleagues who'd spend a decent amount of time tinkering with different values – and while modern authors afforded little space to the subject in their books, there of course remained deep interest in the subject.

Whatever your particular take on this issue, the following attempts to present a number of components that constitute the Ayanāṃśa paradox, with our first visit paid to the solar zodiac and lunar Nakshatras.

1.3 RĀSHICAKRA, NAKSHATRAS AND YOGATÂRÂ

Again Brahmā, of subdued passions, divided a circle invented by himself into 12 equal parts naming it the Rasi-vritta and the same circle into 27 parts, naming it the Nakshatra-vritta.

Sûrya Siddhântikâ

The zodiac or *Rāshicakra* comprises twelve signs called *Rashis*, these being Mesha (Aries), Vrishaba (Taurus), Mithuna (Gemini), Karkata (Cancer), Simha (Leo), Kanya (Virgo), Tula (Libra), Vrishchika (Scorpio), Dhanus (Sagittarius), Makara (Capricorn), Kumbha (Aquarius) and Meena (Pisces). To each, 30° of the heavens is allotted and so divided.[3] Calculation of any horoscope requires the establishment of 0° from which to construct a snapshot upon the heavens. This it seems was best achieved by the employment of convenient (if not irregular) stellar markers, that is, the stars.

Aries traditionally is taken to be the first sign of the zodiac and as such became the pivotal point about which the remainder of the signs were evenly sequenced. During a solar or tropical year[4] the Sun roughly traverses one zodiacal sign in a period of about 30 days, hence its apparent dominion over the zodiac.

Coexisting, yet completely separate from the solar zodiac, there resides an additional twenty-seventh division of the heavens named Nakshatras (see Chapter 25; sometimes called the lunar mansions[5]). One Nakshatra roughly equates to the daily passage of the Moon along its sidereal orbit. This passage is approximately twenty-seven lunar days,[6] hence its dominion over *Bhacakra* or the lunar zodiac.

The junctures (or portions) of Nakshatra are marked by certain stars called Yogatârâ,[7] which confusingly bear the same name as the Nakshatra within which they reside. For example, Ashwini Nakshatra extends from 0° to 13° 20' Aries and is marked by the Yogatârâ Ashwini, also known as β *Arietis* (Sheratan). This star resides close to 13° therein. As stars are randomly spaced and Nakshatra portions precise, it is virtually impossible to have all stars fall evenly within their allotted boundaries.

Ideally, the apportioning of junction stars should fall to a bright star/s well within the lunar orbit; in practice; however, this is not the case as a number of Yogatârâ stray far from the lunar orbit. Additionally, a number of these stars are of a magniītude[8] that is not easily discerned and call into question their suitability as Yogatârâ (see the Appendix).

The zodiacal belt comprises the twelve major constellations that find themselves close to the ecliptic (the Sun's apparent yearly course for Earthbound spectators). As *solar* ecliptic and *lunar* orbit are not so distant from one another (about +/−5°) a significant number of Yogatârâ used to identify Nakshatra divisions naturally find themselves attached to the familiar twelve zodiacal constellations. This is clearly reflected in ancient astronomical texts, which declare the start of Ashwini Nakshatra to correspond to 0° Aries.[9] The term *Rashi*, used to identify zodiacal signs, is commonly translated as 'tied' or 'heaped' together, confirming a reconciliation of solar signs and lunar Nakshatras.[10] Every zodiacal sign therefore comprises 2¼ Nakshatras.

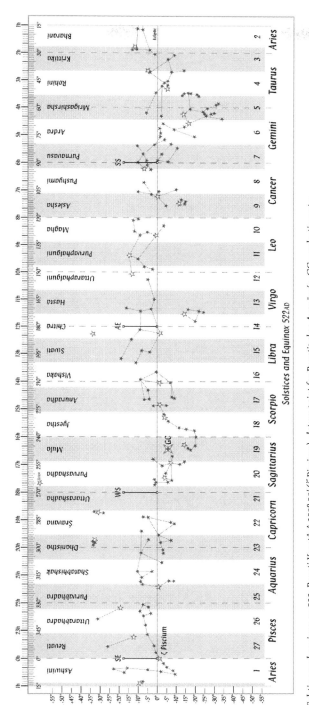

Solstices and equinox AD *522: Revati Yogatārā 359° 50' (ζ Piscium), datum point for Revatipakṣa Ayanāṃśa. GC = galactic centre.*

The three Yogatârâ of greatest concern to this narrative are Ashwini, Chitrā and Revati,[11] sequentially representing the first, middle and last of the Nakshatras and, latterly, the start, middle and end of the solar zodiac. Ashwini and Revati we'll consider briefly here; the importance of Chitrā will be outlined in Section 1.6.

The close of Revati[12] Nakshatra is marked by a Yogatârâ (of the same name), close to the ecliptic in the constellation of Pisces. Today this star is most commonly identified as ζ Piscium. Due to its 5.2 magnitude it is easily lost to the naked eye, making its choice questionable for such a significant Yogatârâ, that is, that which marks the commencement of the sidereal sphere – 0° Ashwini and subsequently 0° Aries.[13]

The importance attached to this part of the sky has led some researchers[14] to conclude that another star close to ζ Piscium may once have been preferred, but has subsequently been lost to us. Others have considered the possibility that ζ Piscium's radiance has diminished over the ensuing millennia. Needless to say, there is much conjecture over missing, muted and/or surrogate star theories.

From an astronomical point of view ζ Piscium is not a singular star but in fact a trinary, meaning what is apparently singular (to the naked eye) is in actuality three stars separated by great distance, these being: ζ A[15] (+5 magnitude), ζ B[16] (+6 magnitude) and ζ C[17] (a white dwarf companion to ζ B). White dwarfs are often interpreted as stars of failing longevity so there is a possibility that a more active ζ C had at some point in the past been more radiant.[18] Additionally, many stars exhibit degrees of variability[19] over time, their incandescence shifting substantially or subtly. During such periods, luminance may range from thousandths to several increments of difference in magnitude.[20]

According to recent findings; our own pole star α Ursae Minoris is currently 2.5 times brighter than it appeared in the first century AD to notable astrologer/astronomer Claudius Ptolemy. There is also the enigma of *irregularly variable stars*, such as η Carinae, surrounded by the Homunculus Nebula. Between the 1830s and 1850s η Carinae was gauged to be the second brightest star in the southern hemisphere.

Could ζ Piscium (trinary) have displayed similar irregularities over the millennia?

With something like five thousand stars visible to an unaided eye, making sense of the stellar clutter is a challenge to any observer. Admittedly, over time and with familiarisation, patterns slowly come into focus, but generally any foray out on a clear night requires good orientation skills and visual acuity. It soon becomes apparent that an equidistant distribution of stars along the ecliptic or lunar orbit is non-existent and that that all divisions are idealised.

Astrology therefore seeks to impose order upon apparent chaos. As zodiacal constellations remain greatly unequal in proportion, their man-made borders (according to various sources) divide the heavens into lots of 30°, 13° 20' and 3° 20',[21] and so on. The ancients called the zodiac 'Manomaya Chakra' or 'mind-wheel', reminding us that any segregation of the heavens ultimately resides within the minds-eye of the beholder.

1.4 THE PHENOMENON OF PRECESSION

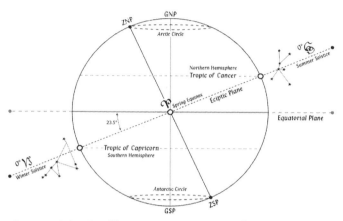

Ecliptic and equatorial plane key: ♈ *= 0° Aries (spring equinox),* ♋ *= 0° Cancer (summer solstice),* ♑ *= 0° Capricorn (winter solstice), GNP = Geographic North Pole, GSP = Geographic South Pole, ZNP = Zodiacal North Pole, ZSP = Zodiacal South Pole.*

Inclined to the Earth's equatorial plane at an angle of about 23.5°, the ecliptic was and is a very convenient reference point with which to measure the relative distances between various astronomical bodies. Following their varied orbits, the planets in our solar system appear to stray no more than 9°+/–[22] above or below this convenient reference plane.

Due to a phenomenon known as *equinoctial precession*, the point at which the ecliptic and equatorial plane meet, that is, the equinoxes, does not remain fixed. Instead these points slowly retrograde over time. Currently the spring equinox frames our Sun against the constellation of Pisces, but this was not always so. Fifteen hundred years ago it was the constellation of Aries that hosted the spring equinox. The rate of precession at this time is in the order of 1° every 72 years. This imperceptibly shifts our Sun backward through each zodiacal sign in a period of 2160 years. The Sun then circumnavigates the entirety of the zodiac every 25,920 years.

Note: When considering *precession* it should be kept in mind that this is a direct consequence of Earth's own orbital instabilities and has nothing to do with the position of the Sun, which remains at the centre of the solar system.

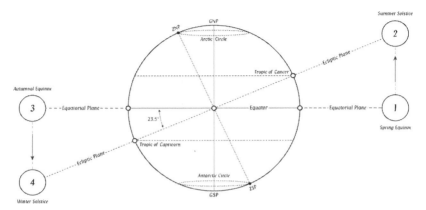

Equinox and solstices: 1 = spring equinox (days of equal length), 2 = summer solstice (longest day), 3 = autumnal equinox (days again of equal length), 4 = winter solstice (shortest day). Key: GNP/GSP = Geographic North and South Poles, ZNP/ZSP = Zodiacal North and South Poles.

Although the true mechanism behind precession is not understood (see Section 1.5) its measurement at the spring equinox allows its *variable* rate to be determined and averaged. Ayanāṃśa therefore is a *corrective value* applied to the Sun's current position at this equinoctial juncture – effectively reasserting a point from a former epoch – previously agreed to represent 0°, that is, the initial point of the zodiac.

Of course the exact date of this *reasserted point* is hotly debated, but for the sake of argument we'll assume the last time it occurred was AD 522. Taking this date as coincident, there is currently some 20°+ difference between the Sun's current position and its former position as of 1493 years ago.

Although the Sun's location (at the spring equinox) has some tradition of being used to identify 0°, it is not known how long observers were aware of this position's instability, due mostly to its imperceptible crawl. In truth, remote sky-watchers were probably more akin to seeing precession in terms of solstices[23] rather than equinoxes – the latter marking an highly important yearly juncture in their calendar such as the Sun's movement from south to north, that is, marking the longest and shortest day of the year. See the equinox and solstices diagram above.

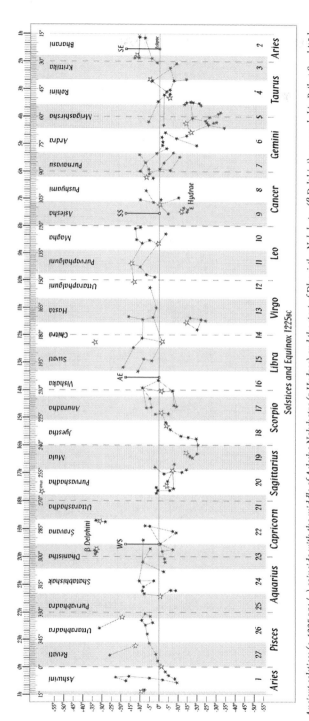

Ancient solstices (c. 1225 BC+/−) coincide with the middle of Dhanistha Nakshatra (ε Hydrae) and the start of Dhanistha Nakshatra (β Delphini) as recorded in Brihat Samhitā by Varāhamihira. Key: SE = Spring Equinox, SS = Summer Solstice, AE = Autumnal Equinox and WS = Winter Solstice.

This sentiment is clearly echoed in the opening quote of this chapter by Varāhamihira, taken from his *Brihat Saṃhitā*[24] in which the esteemed astrologer notes earlier classics identifying different Nakshatras occupying the solstice positions from those of his day. Although little is revealed about the source of his information, Mihira offers no explanation as to why these positions might have changed, indicating he remained unaware of precession.

1.5 MODELS OF PRECESSION

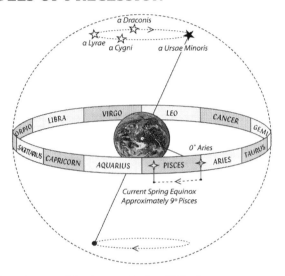

Precession of the equinoxes and the circumnavigation of Polar Stars

Nicolaus Copernicus proposed three planetary motions. First the Earth spins upon its own axis, second it completes an annual orbit about the Sun and third it inscribes a rotational axis upon the heavens at the celestial pole, completing a single revolution every 25,920 years. This third motion, now called nutation, was thus termed 'The Great Year' and featured heavily in the mystery schools[25] of the ancient world.

The phenomenon of precession plays a pivotal role in the history of astrology and astronomy yet, to date, its explanation still remains an unsolved mystery; and while its effect might be simulated in sophisticated computer models, mechanically they remain untenable.

Although there are some interesting theories that seek to account for precession, none really seem to put the issue to bed. Arguments for and against various mechanisms are basically 'big science' and well beyond the scope of this work; however, presented here for readers' interest are three interesting possibilities. Which explanation ultimately proves correct remains to be seen; but for now the jury is out.

Chandler's wobble (polar motion)

Seth Carlo Chandler Jr (1846–1913), an amateur astronomer and businessman, first proposed his 'wobble' theory in 1891, having the Earth akin to a spinning top whose lessening momentum develops a slight destabilisation of spin axis. This might be likened to a child's spinning top that develops similar properties prior to toppling or 'when gyroscopic forces can no longer resist the hand of gravity'. He reasoned that geographically the Earth has a greater land mass north of the equator and that this subtle pear-shaped[26] profile would cause its more 'pointed' end (or southern hemisphere) to subtly displace the Earth's centre of gravity, producing an incremental 'wobble' effect.

Chandler proposed that Earth's North Pole moved in an irregular circle of 4–16 metres in diameter over a period of about 1.2 years. This 'eigenmode'[27] was reckoned to have a six-year cycle, during which two spiralling extremes were attained – one small and one large with a 3.5-year break in between. Since its proposal, the amplitude of the effect appears to have remained inconsistent, performing a number of surprises (referred to as phase-jumps) in the last 100 years. One significant jump occurred in the 1920s followed by a similar episode in 2000.

This 'wobble' had been predicted to subside after a number of decades, unless some unseen force worked upon it to reinvigorate motion. This, JPL[28] believed, it had uncovered in July 2000 in the form of fluctuating oceanic pressures, coupled with changes in water temperature, ocean salinity and weather patterning. The totality of these influences were proposed to contribute to at least two-thirds of the observable phenomenon.

Although this new theory looked tenable, events in November 2005 cast doubts upon this line of enquiry as further monitoring of the smaller spiralling cycles saw Earth's spin-axis veer rather sharply at a right angle to its normal circular motion. This anomaly was completely unexpected and not predicted in any of the computer simulations.

To date, the 124-year-old free nutation model remains unexplained. The most current revision of *Polar Motion* was published in August 2009,[29] with its investigators concluding that the historical phase-jumps were not likely to be unique and that the accrued data (so far) should be revisited and reprocessed to attain clarity in predicting future cycles.

Binary Companion Theory

A more recent, 'extraterrestrial', proposal by Walter Cruttenden and Vince Dayes[30] draws largely upon a popular theory called *luni-solar causation*. This sees the Sun's gravitational force (along with the Moon) torqueing upon Earth's equatorial bulge, resulting in axial gyration.[31] Though the original luni-solar precession model dealt largely with near and visible objects, Binary Companion Theory is an upscaled hybridisation of the effect, working in tandem with distant *unseen* forces. Its protagonists claim that this alternative model of the solar system (and beyond) better accommodates the observable data whilst nicely trimming away a whole swathe of previously annoying loose ends.

One troublesome factor for the luni-solar causation camp had been the prolonged and unrelenting torque exerted upon the Earth's axial tilt. This, over longer periods, predicted a displacement of the seasons, that is, our seasonal routine eventually swapping hemispheres. To date, however, no noticeable switching has occurred as the equinoxes occur right on schedule – requiring only minor adjustments in the form of leap years to synchronise calendars.

Supporters of the original luni-solar causation had attempted to account for this annoying oversight with complex mathematics, concluding that equinoxes were attained *slightly* earlier each year – along Earth's orbit. This idea was eventually defeated by observable phenomena such as the lunar cycle, which showed Earth to complete the entirety of its equinoctial year. This again cast doubts on the accuracy of the luni-solar model.

All was not lost, however, as luni-solar causation was about to get a shot in the arm; this time in the form of a new dark stellar companion to our Sun some 2–4000 A.U.s[32] distant. This twinning effect was proposed to have a warping effect on our Sun's great orbit about the galactic centre, forcing it to accommodate the demands of its distant binary.

In this revised model of precession, the Earth is constrained to a near-perfect circular orbit whereas our Sun now takes on a vastly accentuated elliptical orbit about its twin. The outcome for Earth is the effect of precession, which according to the laws of celestial mechanics predicts that objects in elliptical orbits accelerate to *periapsis* and decelerate toward *apoapsis*.

This last prediction has proved to be the theory's most promising indicator of correctness, as the rate of precession is anything but constant and does indeed appear at this time to be accelerating. See Section 1.10.

Earth nodes

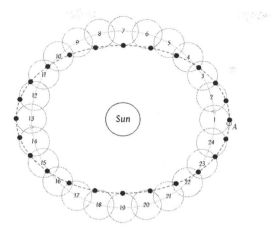

Earth nodes/precession as proposed by astrologer Carl Payne Tobey. Earth's 'great' solar orbit is here represented by 24 circles in increments of 15°. Individual circles represent Earth's 'lesser' orbit or epicycle, moving clockwise in 15° increments. The faint grey inner circle represents the deferent. Position (1) marks the commencement of great and lesser orbits; position (13) sees epicycle and great orbit re-conjoin. As Earth returns to position (1) and closes its great orbit, its lesser orbit/ epicycle completes imperceptibly quicker, making its great orbital plane precess; see position (A).

This explanation of precession was first proposed by American astrologer and mathematician Carl Payne Tobey. In his 1973 book *Astrology of Inner Space*, Tobey asks the question, 'Is the axis of the Earth's spin wobbling or is the whole orbit wobbling?' In other words he seems to be asking: if the other planets (or for that matter any orbiting body) have nodes, shouldn't the Earth have nodes[33] also? Tobey had never encountered an astronomer who had considered the possibility of Earth nodes, but makes the observation that all ellipses are essentially epicycles or small orbits and that by moving in two different circles simultaneously a planet (or satellite) will automatically describe an ellipse (see diagram).

Here the black dot (representing Earth) orbits the Sun in a counter-clockwise direction. In moving from position 1 to 2 it travels 15° about its great solar orbit whilst simultaneously moving 15° anticlockwise within its lesser orbit. At position (7), 90° of both orbits have been completed by Earth and here it drops maximally inside its great solar orbit. At position (13) Earth is again synchronous with its great solar orbit, having moved 180° in both orbits. At position (19) 240°, Earth again moves maximally inwards on its lesser orbit. In returning to position (1) Earth finalises its great orbit but imperceptibly completes its lesser orbit ahead of the former – making its now *elliptical* orbital plane appear to precess, that is, slip backward. If we accept this precessionary model, Earth would begin its next great orbit

50 arc seconds back (or clockwise) from position (1), meaning that its polar axis would continually precess in seconds of arc with each successive solar orbit, which is exactly what we see at the spring equinox each year.

Tobey notes that to be a perfect ellipse the revolution of both orbits must be identical; however, planets and satellites do not move in perfect ellipses, hence they move in regressive ellipses. He also makes the observation that the elliptical shape of Earth's orbit is being somehow mirrored by Earth's ellipsoid profile, having a polar diameter of 7901 miles with a girth of 7926 miles (a difference of 25 miles). Lastly, special note should be made of the influence exerted by our rather unique (and intimate) companion the Moon, which is proportionally far larger than any other satellite (to its primary) in our solar system.

1.6 CALENDAR REFORM COMMITTEE

Note: This section concludes the information previously outlined in Section 1.3.

> We are not aware how the Hindu savants determined Dhruvaka (polar longitude) and Vikṣepa (ecliptic latitude), it appears they had a kind of armillary sphere with an ecliptic circle which they used to set to the ecliptic with the aid of standard stars like Pushya (δ Cancri), Magha (α Leonis), Chitrā (α Virginis), Vishaka (ι Libræ), Shatabhishak (λ Aquarii) and Revati (ζ Piscium).

> *Saha and Lahiri (1992)*

In an effort to unify India's many regional calendars,[34] November 1952 saw an appointment of a Calendar Reform Committee or CRC whose principal task was 'to examine all existing calendars being followed by the country and after scientific study of the subject submit proposals for an accurate and uniform calendar for the whole of India.'

Any reformed dates were then hoped to be adopted for both civil and religious purposes, ratifying the country's numerous festivals, luni-solar calendars, Panchāng[35] and of course Ayanāṃśa. Though not directly incorporating Christian/Gregorian or Islamic considerations,[36] some indirect study of these calendars was also included.

The Calendar Reform Committee, chaired by Professor Meghanad Saha, comprised seven members[37] hailing from varied backgrounds in higher education and the sciences. Together they laboured over the task for about three years, finally submitting their 279-page report to the Council of Scientific and Industrial Research (CSIR) in 1955.[38]

N.C. Lahiri, whose surname ultimately hijacked Chitrāpakṣa[39] (now popularly referred as Lahiri Ayanāṃśa), was one Sri Nimal Chandra Lahiri, then acting secretary of the committee. As well as being a meteorologist, Lahiri was by all accounts something of an astrologer/astronomer as well as (and most interestingly) a publisher of ephemerides.

During the course of investigation into ancient Indian calendrical systems, the committee considered modern astronomical data as well as examining a large number of classical works including Siddhântic and Vedāṅga Jyotish.[40] Although concluding that 'no definite values on the initial point of the zodiac' were to be gleaned directly from the latter's pages, it was felt the location of 0° might be inferred from the positions of junction stars (Yogatârâ) as presented in Chapter VIII of the *Sûrya Siddhânta* (generally agreed to be an authoritative and accurate Siddhântic work). Indeed, this text was to become their principal guide during the investigation. In the words of the committee: 'Our modern *Sûrya Siddhânta* is a book of 500 verses divided into 14 chapters... A scrutiny of the text shows that it is, with the exception of a few elements, almost completely astronomical.'[41]

1.7 WHY CHITRĀ?

While attempting to uncover a true measure of ancient astronomical calendars, it soon became apparent that previous researchers had hit a similar impasse, concluding the *initial point* of the zodiac to be close to Revati's Yogatârâ (ζ Piscium), situated at 359° 50' Pisces, yet the absence of a 'prominent' star marking this critical juncture had also prompted the question, could another Yogatârâ have been used indirectly to *infer* this auspicious point?[42]

Directly opposite the Revati/Ashwini juncture lies Chitrā Nakshatra (23° 20' Virgo – 6° 40' Libra). Its Yogatârâ Chitrā/α Virginis is given a longitude of 180° (0° Libra) by *Sûrya Siddhânta*. Situated about 2° below the ecliptic with an impressive 0.9 Mv (magnitude), Chitrā is the 15th brightest in the northern hemisphere.[43]

Had Chitrā been considered fiducial, it only remained to calculate the coincidence of this Yogatârâ with the autumnal equinox and infer the initial point of the zodiac. This, you might think, neatly wraps up the matter on two counts: first, Chitrā's rather exacting degree of longitude; and second, having such data endorsed by an esteemed Siddhânta, adding legitimacy to the whole proposal. However, the referral star idea is not without controversy!

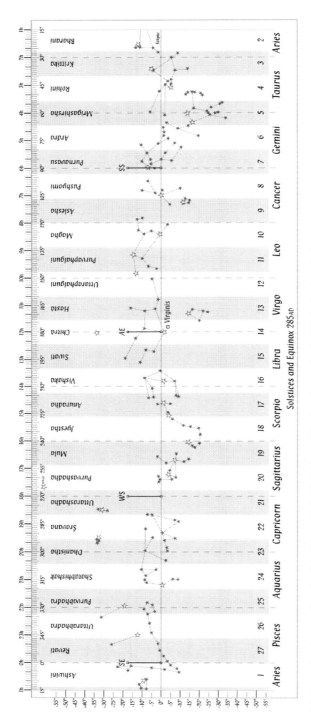

Solstices and equinox as of AD 285, Chitrā Yogatārā (α Virginis) providing the referral point for Chitrāpakṣa Ayanāṃśa.

1.8 CONTROVERSIES

The astronomical classics use a number of techniques to determine the positions of stars and the one favoured in our surviving[44] version of *Sūrya Siddhânta* is known as *Dhruvaka*. This system of measurement we now interpret as polar longitude. Converting this measurement into something akin to a modern reckoning adjusts the longitude of Chitrā/α Virginis to 180° 48' 48" (a difference of almost 1°), a discrepancy noted by the CRC[45] yet curiously put aside in their final deliberations.

Added to this there is a lack of corroborative evidence within the Indian astronomical tradition of Chitrā serving as referral star for the initial point. There are also the contemporary Siddhântic works such as *Brāhma Sputa*,[46] *Śiromani*[47] and *Vaṭeśvara*[48] to be considered, which vary in their longitudinal measurement of Chitrā/α Virginis. These give positions ranging from 179° to 184° 20',[49] yet, unperturbed by all this, on 21 March 1956 following CRC's recommendations, the Indian government adopted Chitrāpakṣa (an Ayanāṃśa value based upon Chitrā being the referral star for the initial point of the zodiac) on whose positioning as of 22 September AD 285 at 11.18am IST[50] inferred the coincidence of the sidereal and tropical zodiacs, that is, 0° Aries.

In defence of this conclusion it may be said that the absolute identity of ζ Piscium as the initial point of the zodiac is not without some doubt but overall there is good historical as well as astronomical reasoning behind its use. First, ζ Piscium rests almost exactly upon the ecliptic and resides at the juncture of Pisces and Aries. Second, *Sūrya Siddhânta* itself informs us that the initial point is to be found 10' east of Revati's Yogatârâ, with no mention of any referral point. Revatipakṣa is not without some traditional astrological credence, having been favoured by south India astrologers prior to the 19th and into the 20th century. Before the emergence of Chitrāpakṣa, Revatipakṣa was one of the more widely accepted Ayanāṃśa in recent Indian history.

One of the main criticisms levelled at Chitrāpakṣa is its lack of Siddhântic support as well as the CRC's negation of Revatipakṣa, already nominated for just such a purpose in their primary Siddhântic reference. Additionally, use of an Ayanāṃśa based upon Chitrāpakṣa raises the question as to why *Sūrya Siddhânta* assigns a longitude to Chitrā's Yogatârâ that contradicts supportive texts. A question mark also hangs over the influence of N.C. Lahiri within the CRC[51] and their final decision to adopt Chitrāpakṣa – a decision that to this day is rejected by a number of influential Indian astrologers and researchers.

1.9 AYANĀMŚA CORRECTION

Forewarning: Adjustment of Ayanāmśa requires a sense of adventure and experimentation, but mostly an open-mindedness on the part of the astrologer. Armed with these, all corners of the Jyotish toolbox become accessible, even its darkest, dustiest draws!

I imagine readers making it this far without skipping pages are hitting their heads against a wall or starting to appreciate why this subject seldom gets an airing. Some well-meaning astrologers have made it their personal mission to prove one Ayanāmśa over another; however, such claims become difficult to substantiate or turn out to harbour vested self-interest.

In his 1939 book *Hindu Astrology*, Shil Ponde offers the following value for Ayanāmśa: 19° 27′ 00″ as of 12 noon, 9 October 1920 with an annual precession rate of 50.1″. Ponde's suggested value is actually Revatipakṣa with a slight discrepancy on a date of coincidence,[52] but for those wishing to experiment I've given its full calculation method below. I should also mention here that Ponde himself did not appear to claim ownership of the value, just endorsed its use.

In Chapter 2, 'General Theory of Astrology', of the same book, Ponde suggests an epoch value of AD 522, yet in one Ayanāmśa calculation mistakenly cites AD 239 as being the most recent epoch of coincidence. He also suggests an annual precessional rate of 50.1″ in his primary calculation yet later amends the value to 50″. These anomalies, though slightly frustrating, should not detract from the overall validity of the calculation. It is highly likely the inconsistencies relate to a historical confusion on the part of the author, or were just publishing oversights.

Ponde's value was first introduced to me by an astrologer I consider to be a particularly accurate astrologer and after a good number of years of comparison (between it and other popular rivals), I eventually opted for the former.

To date I've found this value to be the most reliable, specifically with regard to Varga charts.[53] As always, the best course of action appears to be personal trial and error with familiar (intimate) horoscopes where major life events can be cross referenced against the dasha periods, Vargas and transits. Character analysis can be more open to interpretation and so ultimately unreliable. Predictive astrology and the detailed examination of divisional charts is where most gratification of this value is likely to be found.

The following Ayanāmśa correction is given by Shil Ponde for an epoch of 9 October 1920 at 12.00pm GMT:

1920

−522 (AD 522 – date of sidereal/tropical coincidence)

= 1398

×50.1" (annual precession value)

= 70039.8 (precession value at birth)

/3600 (converts seconds of arc to degrees of arc)

= 19.4555

(4555)×60 = 273,300

19° 27' 00"

Note: Software permitting, an easier method of applying Shil Ponde's calculation (or any alternative value) would be to enter:

Epoch Value: AD 522

Value at Epoch: 0° 0' 0"

Annual Precession Value: 50.1"

Note: Applying this Ayanāṃśa value (as of J-2000[54]) we arrive at a value of 20° 32' or 9° 28' Pisces. Using the comparative Ayanāṃśa value proposed by the CRC we arrive at a value of 23° 57' or 6° 3' Pisces. The difference between the two values is a constant 3° 25' – or one Navamsha (see Section 21.1). This in effect guarantees that the Navamsha ascendant will be displaced by one sign when converting from the latter to the former.

1.10 A NOTE ON NUTATION

The following table lists a number of popular nutation values along with their epoch and Ayanāṃśa correction values. As can be seen, annual arc seconds remain in dispute with best-guess estimates ranging between 50"/50.34". Recent measurements of the phenomenon suggest a rate of 50.28" annually, equating to 1° every 72 years. Providing this current measurement does not fluctuate too wildly, each zodiacal revolution should be completed over a period of 26,000+/− years. Of course there is no way to be sure the recorded data is accurate in making long-term predictions. For now it appears that precession is following the lead of Binary Companion Theory and accelerating slightly.

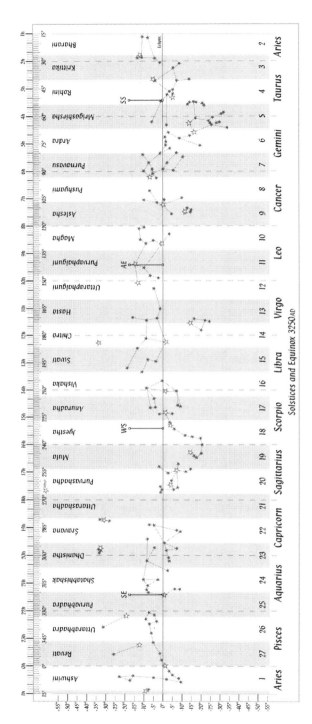

Solstices and equinox: AD 3250 *should see the spring equinox (SE) closely conjunct Shatabhishak's yogatārā (λ Aquarii).*

Popular Ayanāṃśa values

Name	Coincidence Date	Date of Epoch	Value at Epoch	Annual Precession (in arc seconds)
Usha Shashi	AD 559	1950	19° 25'	50.26"
Shil Ponde*	AD 522	"	19° 52'	50.10"
B.V. Raman	AD 397	"	21° 43'	50.34"
Sri Yukeswar	AD 499	"	21° 45'	54.00"
Swaminarayan	AD 320	"	22° 47'	50.30"
J.N. Bhasin	AD 364	"	22° 10'	50.33"
Krishnamurti (KP)	AD 291	"	23° 09'	50.23"
N.C. Lahiri	AD 285	"	23° 15'	50.28"
Fagan/Bradley	AD 221	"	24° 09'	50.25"

* All Ayanāṃśa calculations in this book are based upon the value suggested by Shil Ponde.

With a lack of concise data, astrologers sometimes opt for the *mean rate* of precession. Having already imposed a number of abstract divisions upon the heavens it seems totally in keeping to round-up annual nutation to 50"; indeed, all recorded values to date would not be in opposition to this value.

Numerologically speaking, 50 routes to number five (5+0 = 5). This number is already rich in occult symbolism and so more than qualifies for the task at hand.[55] The use of 50 arc seconds neatly rounds up the numerical symbolism for the entire zodiac, so for example: 50×72 = 3600 (3+6+0+0) and (7+2) both routing to the all important astrological 9 (see Chapter 29). Precession through each 30° sign would be 2160 years (2+1+6+0) = 9 and of course the Great Year itself: 2160×12 = 25,920 (2+5+9+2+0) = 18, 1+8 = 9.

1.11 CONCLUSION

Simplified Pythagorean model of the universe; with each of the planets attached to crystal spheres, nested within the circle of fixed stars. At its epicentre resides Earth, prominent, protected and basking in the harmonic symphony of the planets; imagined to correspond to a divine musical scale.

When considering any aspect of precession it is important to remember this is an Earth-born phenomenon. Ayanāṃśa therefore should be more appropriately termed *the wobble value of Earth's orbit* and should not be confused with the issue of where 0° resides in the zodiac, although the former is intrinsically linked to the latter.

For many it is almost natural to assume the Earth is somehow suspended or nested in space, with everything else kicking-off about us. Watching sunrise and sunset each day it is easy to forget that we are the ones doing most the moving while the Sun is at the hub of events (in our solar system anyway). This idea of a somewhat removed and passive Earth is a hangover from the Pythagorean notion that all heavenly bodies were interconnected and immersed in a kind of mathematical musical harmony.

Pythagoras termed this unity *Musica Universalis* or *music of the spheres*, and resting at the heart of this symphony was Earth, safe, secure and, most importantly – special. Indeed, Earth's safety begged such urgency as to require guardian angels to be thrown in for good measure, lest some unruly extraterrestrial force threaten it. The idea of instability or vulnerability appears to have been a terrifying concept for the ancient Greeks. And so the idea of a fixed Earth arose, permeating into modern culture and thought with terms such as *sunrise* and *sunset*. Perhaps this is another reason why Ayanāṃśa (subconsciously) remains partly veiled in astrological consciousness and why many remain fixated on a *Firma Terra*.

After reviewing the arguments set forth you'll have hopefully gleaned a clearer understanding of Ayanāṃśa and its implications. Additionally, when considering the amount of general astrological material available, how little weight is given to this subject. How to a greater or lesser extent this subject is just railroaded, often consigned to an appendix or mentioned only in passing while still (of course) endorsing the CRC's recommendation.

In general, this reception to Ayanāṃśa may be a way of placating boat-rocking energetics; after all, who wants to be told a particular value may be questionable or inaccurate and that all analyses given during the interim years require a rethink. I'd imagine (for the most part) that this kind of proposition would be unwelcome.

Some astrologers argue Chitrāpakṣa's validity and that corrective values are unnecessary, having (in their eyes) achieved consistent results and excellent rapport with clients. To this retort, little then can be said except that there are (and remain) major unanswered questions in the field of Ayanāṃśa – which on the whole appears to have been given a fairly thick coat of whitewash.

NOTES

1. Also known as Ayanacalana – a shifting of the solstitial points.
2. Sidereal = pertaining to the stars.
3. The zodiac generally constitutes 9° (+/–) above and below the ecliptic.
4. A year of seasons = 365 days 5 hours 48 minutes 46 seconds.
5. Known also as *Manázil al-Kamar* – meaning lunar stations.
6. Sidereal transition = 27 days 7 hours 43 minutes. Synodic transition = 29 days 12 hours 44 minutes.
7. Yoga = position and Târâ = star.
8. Measurements of magnitude are: *apparent (mv)* and *absolute (Mv)*. Apparent magnitude is measured by appearance to the human eye. Absolute magnitude is the measurement of a star at a standard distance, such as a light-year or parsec.
9. This particular assumption is based upon the Aśvinyādi system and although there remains some uneasiness over their true relationship of 0° Aries and the Nakshatra Ashwini, the two positions are taken to be mutual. Antagonists of Aśvinyādi (as the original point of coincidence) argue that its use cannot be found prior to 300 BCE.
10. Nakshatras may precede zodiacal signs, but at some point Indian astrologers began to incorporate both elements into their system.
11. For more information about Nakshatra positions and stellar designations see the Appendix.
12. Revati Nakshatra is held to be the initial point of all planetary motion. At the start of Kali Yuga all planets were set into motion at the point marked by Revati yogatârâ. All planets then complete a set number of sidereal revolutions before conjoining every 1,080,000 years or ¼ of a Great Age or Yuga. Something close to this appears to have occurred at midnight 17/02/3101 BC.
13. Sûrya Siddhânta identifies the spring equinox (c. AD 560) as coinciding with a point 10' eastward along the ecliptic from the star Revati (longitude 359° 50').
14. See Lesson 3 in Shashi (2009[1978]).
15. Category: sub-giant, approximately 150 light years distant.
16. Category: white (main sequence star), approximately 200 light years distant.

17. Category: pale yellow/white dwarf, approximately 250 light years distant.
18. White dwarf = stellar remnants in their final stage of evolution. Final stages include swelling of mass (a red giant), then the shedding of outer layers to an emission nebula (ionised gas) leaving only its heated core to cool over time.
19. There are five categories of variability: cataclysmic (explosive/nova), pulsating (contraction and expansion), eruptive (solar flaring), rotating (high sunspot activity) or eclipsing (close proximity of binary twin).
20. χ Cygni is known to vary from +3.3 mv to +14.2 mv over a 400-day period. These observations may explain the phenomenon of *guest stars* (the accounts of new stars) appearing and disappearing in the past two millennia.
21. 30° = Rashi, 13° 20' = Nakshatra and 3° 20' = Nakshatra Pada.
22. Not including the recently de-planetised Pluto with its whopping 17°+ inclination to the ecliptic.
23. The word Solstice means 'motionless Sun' indicating the ancients' obsession with solar declination.
24. *Brihat Saṃhitā*, Vol. 1, Chapter III – 'On the Sun'.
25. The Great Year has been discussed at some length in *Hamlet's Mill* by Giorgio de Santillana and Hertha von Dechend (2014[1969]) and *The Seven Ages of Man* by Andrew Kirk (2013).
26. Also known as non-spherical or subject to free nutation.
27. Vibrations expected to be produced by a system of oscillation.
28. JPL = Jet Propulsion Laboratory, California Institute of Technology.
29. Chandler wobble: two larger phase jumps revealed by Zinovy Malkin and Natalia Miller, Central Astronomical Observatory, Pulkovskoe, Ch. 65, St. Petersburg 196140, Russia, 23 August 2009.
30. See Binary Research Institute: http://binaryresearchinstitute.org.
31. In simpler terms, luni-solar causation sees the combined gravitational force of the Sun and Moon acting upon the Earth to produce its third eccentricity of orbit, precession of the equinoxes.
32. A.U. (astronomical unit) = 92,928,090 miles or 149,597,870,700 metres.
33. As Earth's orbit effectively defines the ecliptic, establishment of Earth nodes requires another plane of reference, such as the Sun's equatorial plane. Assuming Revatipaksha identifies 0° Aries, the longitude of Earth's ascending node is currently close to 54°.
34. Prior to the CRC, thirty different calendar systems were used in India, including: Hindu, Buddhist, Jain, Muslim and Gregorian.
35. Hindu astrological calendar and almanac.
36. Islamic Hegira Calendar, inception date 15 July AD 622, is purely lunar.
37. Committee members consisted of: Professor M.N.Saha, D.Sc., F.R.S., M.P. (Chairman); Professor A.C. Banerji, Vice-Chancellor, Allahabad University; Dr K.L. Daftari, Nagpur; Sri J.S. Karandikar, Ex-Editor (*The Kesari*), Poona; Dr Gorakh Prasad, D.Sc., Allahabad University; Professor R.V. Vaidya, Madhav College, Ujjain; and Sri. N.C. Lahiri, Calcutta (Secretary).
38. The CRC's report was eventually circulated in a book format titled *History of the Calendar in Different Countries Through the Ages* by M.N. Saha and N.C. Lahiri (1992). This investigation still makes interesting reading some sixty years on and should, regardless of any shortcomings, be included in the list of essential reads for those wishing to gain greater insight into this fractious issue.
39. Chitrā = α Virginis, Pakṣa = relating to half.
40. Collectively given the acronym S.J. or Siddhânta-Jyotish, that is, covering the calendrical switch between the earlier Vedânga Jotish (lunar) to the later Siddhantic period (solar).
41. Varāhahimira in his *Pañca Siddhântika* regarded it as his most authoritative and reliable reference source.
42. See Ketkar (1921).
43. Spica/α Virginis is actually a double-variable, appearing to fluctuate between +0.9 and +1.05 mv.
44. The *Sûrya Siddhânta* referenced by Varāhamihira (in *Pañca Siddhântika*) does not include the use of polar longitude.
45. See Saha and Lahiri (1992, p.265).
46. *Brāhma Sphuṭa Siddhânta* by Brāhma-Gupta (c. AD 580).
47. *Siddhânta Śiromani* (Crown of Knowledge) by Bhāskarācārya II (c. AD 1100).
48. *Vaṭeśvara Siddhânta* by Vaṭeśvara (c. AD 880).
49. Al-Bīrūnī concluded the longitude of Chitrā to be 183° or 3° Libra.
50. IST = Indian Standard Time, 5h 30 minutes ahead of Greenwich Mean Time.

51. It has been suggested N.C. Lahiri's own astrological practice had personally convinced him of Chitrāpakṣa's validity. For more information read *Ayanāṃśa Controversy* (Chandra Hari 1985).
52. Sûrya Siddhânta commentaries estimate a date to be closer to AD 570, with an annual precession of 54'.
53. Varga = divisional; for more information see Chapter 21.
54. J-2000 = Julian epoch 2000 (AD).
55. Number 5 recurs throughout Vedic literature, largely in connection to calendrical cycles or ritual. Thus, the 5 worlds: air, fire, Sun, Moon and stars; 5 devatās: atman, æther, trees, planets and water; or the 5 forms of prāṇa: prāṇa, udāna, vyāna, samāna and apāna.

2

– CELESTIAL 'ROYAL' COURT –

To the Kālapurusha, the Sun is the soul, the Moon is the mind, Mercury is speech, Mars is strength, Jupiter is knowledge and health, Venus is desire and Saturn sorrow. Of the planets the Sun and Moon are kings, Mercury is first prince, Mars is general, Jupiter and Venus are counsellors and Saturn – servants.

Brihat Jataka by Varāhamihira

Planets (in the ancient world) were categorised in a number of ways, most commonly by appearances or qualities. As the Sun and Moon were primary illuminators they were termed *prakāśagrahas*. Mercury, Mars, Jupiter, Saturn and especially Venus were named *tārāgraha* (or brightest stars) as this was how they appeared to observers. The lunar nodes (Rāhu and Ketu) were delineated *tamograha* or dark/concealed planets.

One popular way to visualise complex planetary interactions was to imagine their ranks to mimic an archetypal royal court, or in this case celestial court. Their characteristics were best exemplified by analysis of their daily duties and routines. As dispensers of Earthly karma the above-mentioned planetary lords were seen to direct their influence down upon Earth – their energies carried on subtle planetary rays, permeating each and every facet of human daily life.

The following planetary summaries outline the position of each within their heavenly hierarchy, followed by individual portraits of each.

2.1 SUN – THE KING

The Sun (Sûrya), who is king of all planets, full of infinite radiance, the image of the good soul, the eye of this world; I adore the primeval Lord Govinda in pursuance of whose order the Sun performs his journey, mounting the wheel of time.

Brahmā Saṃhitā

Sûrya is a strong yet wise, benevolent ruler. He commands the respect of the people. Acknowledging that even his light must one day diminish, he plans to relinquish power to his son, Budha (Mercury). He has charged the instruction of his son to Brihaspati (Jupiter), his chief minister, and Kuja (Mars), his commander-in-chief. Preparation of the fanciful youth has proved to be more troublesome than expected, as other forces at court seek to ingratiate themselves with the impressionable youth. Keeping his court advisor and tactician close, Sûrya fears the occult power and allures of his secondary minister Shukra (Venus). His servants (represented by Shani/Saturn) fear him but wait patiently in the wings awaiting a change in court politics. His militia Rāhu and Ketu are not to be trusted and may be subverted if price or justification were sufficient. Behind all court intrigue his consort Chandra (Moon) remains trustworthy and loyal.

2.2 MOON – THE QUEEN

> The Moon (Chandra), whose strength lies to the north, whose nature is like that of a mother cow (Kamadhenu); dresses in fine white silk and snow-white ornaments, exudes soma (nectar) that falls and spreads upon the Earth, seeding all divine herbs. The Moon's chariot is crafted from rajata (silver) and pulled by ten white horses.
>
> *Forty Vedic Hymns*

Consort to Sûrya, Chandra brings stability to the court and royal family. Though inwardly sensitive and easily troubled, Moon seeks cordial relations with all, determined to keep the status quo. Moon seeks to support and honour all stately roles performed by her subjects – but also has her favourites (see the table in Section 2.8). Although a great luminary in her own right, Moon cannot shine without the light from her husband. If caught sharing the sky together, her own radiance is greatly diminished. Being a highly gregarious planet, Moon hates to be unaccompanied and is greatly relieved to share any of the twelve Rashis/Bhavās with other grahas, whatever their social status within the celestial court.

2.3 MERCURY – REGENT

> Budha: who rules Mithuna (Gemini) and Kanya (Virgo) is green of body and ornament. Seated upon the lion, his four limbs encircle Mount Meru. His strength lies in the east, his symbol is an arrow and his metal is pārada (quicksilver).
>
> *Forty Vedic Hymns*

Mercury is fast-talking, fast-acting and quick-witted.[1] He views the Queen (his mother) with enmity, suspicious of her emotions and sensitivities. These cloud his judgement and intellect. Counselled and tutored by Venus (his father's lesser-favoured advisor), self-worth and strength have been kindled. In his own right he has become a magician of some note. Well-skilled in matters of the healing arts, herbalism, alchemy and commerce, Mercury is also master of word-play, delighting in all manner of practical jokes and humour. When focused on the task at hand, he is a perfectionist and skilled artisan; when disinterested or frustrated, his inventive mind quickly turns to counterproductive pursuits and quarrelsome banter.

2.4 MARS – COMMANDER-IN-CHIEF

Kuja, who rules Mesha (Aries) and Vrishchika (Scorpio), is red of body and ornament. Powerful like lord Yama, he is four-limbed; his symbol is trikona (having three angles). Born of Bharadwaja Rishi clan he fares well in a southern direction, facing Yamaraj and the infernal regions, his metal is loha (iron).

Forty Vedic Hymns

Loyal to the king and his consort, Mars takes counsel from Jupiter, but in the young regent (Mercury) senses instability and impending difficulties for the kingdom. His ascendancy to ruler is a sure precursor to the removal of Mars and his martial skills. Harsh in action and speech, Mars is also a fighter, necessary to enforce law and triumph over the kingdom's enemies. He is honorific and courageous; he does not suffer fools gladly. The presence of Mars in the celestial court maintains its hierarchal construct – keeping all subordinate grahas in line with the fear of punishment for wrongdoers.

2.5 JUPITER – MINISTER

Brihaspati: whose strength lies in the east, his body and ornaments are of a yellow colouration. He is four-limbed, calm and mighty and holds a rectangular water bowl. Lord of Sindhu Dweepa (India's peninsula), he is lord of Dhanus (Sagittarius) and Meena (Pisces), his metal is vanga (tin).

Forty Vedic Hymns

Closest advisor to Sûrya, Brihaspati (like Kuja) feels his position in jeopardy, the role of state advisor being slowly usurped by the charismatic wiles of Venus, who now counsels the regent. Venus has already threatened the delicate balance of power by granting the worldly demons access to saṃjivani (the mantra of resurrection) and, conversely, access to immortality.[2] Jupiter preserves diplomacy and prosperity at court, serving the greater spiritual needs of the kingdom. Master of ceremonies, Jupiter leads the planets and other celestial deities in the performance of ritual and sacrifice.

2.6 VENUS – MINISTER

> Shukra: whose strength lies in the north, is four-limbed and peaceful, he stands upon the lotus bearing flowers and divine herbs and his symbol is a pentagram. White of body and ornament he is Shukracārya (instructor to demons), Lord of Vrishabha (Taurus) and Tula (Libra), his metal is tamra (copper).
>
> *Forty Vedic Hymns*

Shukra delights in breaking tradition and social etiquette; as a secondary guru-figure in court his revolutionary ideas and colourful demeanour earn him looks of disdain yet he manages still to gain favour and standing within the royal court. Viewed with suspicion by Sûrya, this potent planet has long understood that his future is assured with the regent and with the support of the palace servants (Saturn). Like all of his enemies, Sûrya keeps Shukra close at hand, but declines to act against him unless he oversteps his authority.

2.7 SATURN – SERVANT

> Shani: is blue of body and ornament, his strength lies in the west; his symbol is an archway, his eyes are black. Riding upon a crow, his caste is Sourastraka (Gujarat), his star is Bharani, his metal is nāgā (lead). Shani is lord of Makara (Capricorn) and Kumbha (Aquarius).
>
> *Forty Vedic Hymns*

Moving unbeknownst in the background of the court, Shani bides his time. His presence and patience ensure all daily tasks are fulfilled. Like a well-oiled machine, Saturn is unrelenting. He waits for the king to pass rulership to his son. Only then does Saturn feel that his status within the royal household will improve. Moving slowly about the kingdom, Shani conserves strength by metering energy; he knows everything must come to he who waits.

2.8 RĀHU AND KETU – MILITIA

Rāhu: is blue of body and of ornament, he rules the south-westerly direction; four-limbed, his teeth are fanged and irregular, his nature similar to that of the lion. His symbol is a winnowing basket, his metal is pittala (brass). Ketu: is variegated (multicoloured) of body and of ornament, his direction is similarly south-west, his symbol a flag. Riding upon a lion his temperament is likened to Kuja, his presence associated with Dhumraketu (comets) and smoke, his gaze is terrifying, his metal is kansya (bronze).

Forty Vedic Hymns

Both nodes are considered outcast or undesirable – far removed from events within the palace walls. Collectively they form the King's militia. Begrudgingly they perform the bidding of the King, yet secretly await the downfall of their monarch. Rāhu is outwardly reckless and covets all manner of excitement and danger. Ketu broods inwardly on self-destructive thoughts and revenge. Both nodes maintain cordial relations with Saturn, Venus and Mercury. Rāhu is likened to Saturn (with somewhat less self-control), Ketu is likened to Mars; both having extremely wild and unpredictable temperaments.

The table below outlines Parasara's views on the friendships, enmities and neutrality of planets.

Friendships, enmities and neutrality of planets

Mercury (Regent)	*Friendship:* Sun, Venus	Venus (Minister)	*Friendship:* Mercury, Saturn	Moon (Queen)	*Friendship:* Sun, Mercury
	Enmity: Moon		*Enmity:* Sun, Moon		*Enmity:* None
	Neutral: Mars, Jupiter, Saturn		*Neutral:* Mars, Jupiter		*Neutral:* Mars, Jupiter, Venus, Saturn
Jupiter (Minister)	*Friendship:* Sun, Moon, Mars	Sun (King)	*Friendship:* Moon, Mars, Jupiter	Mars (Comm-in-Chief)	*Friendship:* Sun, Moon, Jupiter
	Enmity: Mercury, Venus		*Enmity:* Venus, Saturn		*Enmity:* Mercury
	Neutral: Saturn		*Neutral:* Mercury		*Neutral:* Venus, Saturn
Ketu (Militia)	*Friendship:* Mars, Venus, Saturn	Saturn (Servants)	*Friendship:* Mercury, Venus	Rāhu (Militia)	*Friendship:* Jupiter, Venus, Saturn
	Enmity: Sun, Moon		*Enmity:* Sun, Moon, Mars		*Enmity:* Sun, Moon, Mars
	Neutral: Mercury, Jupiter		*Neutral:* Jupiter		*Neutral:* Mercury

NOTES

1. As Kāraka for the intellect (and scholarship), Mercury's disposition in the horoscope decidedly affects an individual's power to discriminate.
2. The offspring of Brihaspati and Târâ (Kaca), apprenticed himself to Shukra in an effort to sequester the saṃjivani mantra. Kaca (a name meaning radiance) eventually succeeds in his mission, giving demons the chance of immortality.

Sûrya (Sun): I pay respects to Sûrya, whose flaming disc dispels all darkness. Born to Kaśyapa and Āditi, he is the king of planets, his solar orb blazes like Hiṅgula, his power destroys all the world's sins.

3

──── SÛRYA (Sun) ────

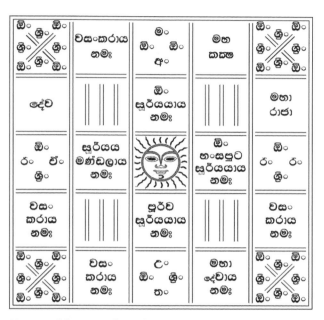

Śrī Laṅkān Sûrya Mandala Yantra effective for the propitiation of Sûrya, warding off enemies, enmity and legal disputes. This yantra appeases the Sun god, bringing prosperity, health and wisdom; it protects one's heart, home and happiness. Sûrya Mandala Yantra helps elevate one to a position of authority and respect.

> Possessed of energy and of square build, black-red in mien and eyes bright as wine, bilious in nature with a limited quantity of hair, the Sun consists chiefly of the quality of goodness.

Jātaka Pārijāta by Vaidyanātha Dīkṣita [1]

Sûrya is the lord of planets (or grahapati);[2] he is Kṣatriya (warrior),[3] masculine in stature and sattwika[4] in guna. His complexion is blood-red, His taste is bitter. Dressed in fine red silks he gains directional strength in the south, is Pitta by nature and rules the element of fire. The effects of Sun mature in the 22nd year of life.

Sûrya lords the sign Leo, gaining strength in fire signs and exaltation (neecha) in the sign of Aries (specifically 10°). He is in a state of uchcha (debilitation) at the same degree in the sign Libra. Sun is considered representative of Atma[5] (the soul). He rules Ayana (solstices), his metal is gold. He is also considered a mildly malefic force,[6] mostly through the severity of dehydrating actions.

Sun indicates our allotment of life-giving prāṇa (vital energy). Well-positioned in the horoscope he promotes strong healthy bones, teeth, a radiant complexion and sharp vision. He also shows our ability to assimilate and utilise nutrients, representing Agnī (digestive power) located primarily in the small intestine. Positioning and strength of the Sun reflect our stamina, the physical strength of the heart and courage. If well disposed, Sûrya supports the immune system and gives strength to organs of assimilation (by enkindling Agnī/digestive fire). Strong Agnī facilitates absorption and assimilation of nutrients. Agnī also burns up and expels toxins/waste from the body.

Sûrya's chariot is pulled by seven horses, each representing one of seven spectral rays/colours. These in turn empower the remaining six planets. In return, each planet (imbued with his emissions) transmits its own rays Earthward. *Linga Purāṇa* identifies Sûrya as radiating one thousand subtle rays[7] (likened to a wind), which radiate outward, warming and penetrating the void.

Favourable Sûrya: Increases life-force, sattva and strengthens the father's position or those who preside over the mundane affairs of the people – kings, governments, ministers and so on. Sûrya increases personal wealth, grants success in business and overseas trade through commodities such as gold, copper, hardwood, wheat, leather, herbs, heating spices, medicines and coarse fabrics (including wool). If well-positioned and powerful, the horoscope incurs favours from Lord Śiva and Agnī. Sûrya prospers in the 1st house of self, 9th house of dharma and 10th house of career.

Unfavourable Sûrya: The person may be forced to suffer at the hands of a cruel father, king,[8] government or minister. The person risks injury from fire, burns, scalding and diseases of the blood, heart, bones, eyes and small intestine (provocation of Pitta dosha). The person may lack lustre and vitality, incur losses through investment or receive poor financial advice, experience restrictions in business or suffer loss or social influence through slander, incarceration or wrongful arrest.

Bala (strength): Sûrya is considered well-disposed if the following are applicable: falling on his own day (Sunday) or in the 1st or 10th house, occupying Leo in Hora, Drekkana, Navamsha Vargas or exalted in Aries. The Sun gains power during Uttarāyana, at midday or during Rashi Sankránti (transition into a new sign).

Undertakings on Sunday: Sacrificial offerings, the lighting of sacrificial fires, burning wood, making charcoal, journeying through forests or across mountains, marching, fighting/battles, meetings with famous or skilled personages, giving service or attending to monarchs. Working with stone (masonry), copper (casting), manufacture of jewellery from gold, training of horses, manufacture of medicines, extraction of poisons (serpents), trading in shells, bones, woollen clothing, fine silks, perfume or weapons, undertaking cruel acts or administering punishment to wrongdoers, dealing with thieves (theft).

Alternative names for Sûrya

Sûri	Staying true to one's course
Arka	Likened to Arka/Calotropis procera (gigantea species), its energetics are hot and pungent. Secretions from this plant are well-known for their healing properties. Arka also means 'distillation' (retrieval of essence); its heating/cooking process purifies and cleanses
Bháskara	Radiates light and heat; also Calotropis procera
Ravi	Rasa-vis, one who evaporates moisture
Vivasvant	Father of Manu, he who creates, sustains and protects mankind
Bhánu	One who illuminates (a ray of light)

Heli/Helius	Likened to a sunflower; a variety of ligulae flora (Hēlianthus species)
Loka-chakshuh	Eye of the world
Graha-rāja	King of Planets

3.1 ASTRONOMICAL

Our Sun is described as a 'field star', that is, having little association with other stars and seemingly free to wander throughout the galaxy.[9] This leviathan of light and heat is the epicentre of our planetary system, largely comprising hydrogen and helium with additional trace elements: nitrogen, oxygen, neon, carbon, silicon, magnesium and iron. The presence of our Sun in the solar system constitutes 98 per cent of its total mass.

Governing the motions of all that fall under its warming and encompassing rays, the Sun boasts an enormous diameter of 860,000+ miles (roughly 12,000 times the diameter of our planet). At a local distance of 93,000,000 miles from Earth, our Sun takes around 25 days to rotate once upon its own axis, an axis that is not perpendicular to the ecliptic. The tilt of this stellar giant is approximately 7°; this in effect tips the Sun's polar regions closer toward the Earth during our equinoctial intervals, to be neutrally disposed or midway during our solstices. The position of the Sun's axis is determined by sunspot transition across the solar disc – these move parallel to its equator, close to our solstices.

From antiquity this fiery sphere was regarded as 'patriarch of vegetation', its matriarchal consort (Moon) its balancing and cooling counter-force. As 'lord of the seasons' and 'that which brings colour to the landscape', his rays were divined the agent by which all atmospheric phenomena were driven – the rains, wind, seas and rivers.[10] When first imaged by telescope, astronomers described its surface features as 'delightful'. As its light was deemed eternal, so too were imagined its seasons and inhabitants, the latter believed to be perfectly adapted to the peculiarities of their fiery orb!

3.2 KĀRAKA

Throughout this book there are multiple references to *Kāraka*, a word often translated as 'he who signifies' or 'initiates'. The concept of Kāraka therefore is a large part of integrating and understanding Jyotish, particularly with regard to recognising and interpreting its signals – which are (after all) ultimately relayed to us through nine planets, twelve signs and twelve houses.

There are an infinite number of Kārakas attached to the planets, signs and houses (see Chapters 11 and 13), far more than could ever be mentally retained; however, from this vast reservoir it is advisable to keep at least a generous handful of primary significations committed to memory. Over time and with patience the true import of each Kāraka will grow ever more meaningful as you begin to feel the presence of the planets in everything about you.

Note: For the purposes of this planetary introduction, we shall consider only those types of Kāraka relevant to planets. These, as we shall see, may be active, stable or natural:

- *Chara/Active:* temporarily designated (corporeal) status due to their current degree of advancement through Rashis.

- *Sthira/Stable:* holding specific (corporeal) status regardless of degree.

- *Naisargika/Natural:* connected with a particular object/action (corporeal and non-corporeal).

The three energetic states in greater detail are as follows.

Chara

Chara (active) = current degree of planetary advancement through Rashis (relative to one another). From highest to lowest degree planets are assigned a particular signification; for example, if Sun is found to occupy the highest degree, let's say 28° 41', with the next highest degree of a planet, let's say Mercury, occupying 28° 40' (in the same Rashi or otherwise), the former is then to be considered significator of *Atman* or spirit. The latter (Mercury) becomes *Amatya*, minister or advisor to Atman, and so on.

Note: This example also illustrates some aspect of Sthira (or stable) Kāraka as Sun is also considered the unchanging significator for Atman; so in this case, should Sun prove to be Atman by highest degree, it would represent the soul on two counts, as both Chara and Sthira Kārakas, adding extra weight to this signification.

If two planets are found to occupy identical degrees (in the same or different Rashi), hierarchies of Kāraka then fall to minutes of degree. If their minutes are also found to be identical, then seconds of degree would be implemented. In the unlikely event that seconds of degree are identical, both planets are to be designated the same signification. In this way, all planets (except Ketu[11]) become significators for causative factors and influences surrounding our birth, such as Father and Mother, as well as indicators of *primary desires* that hold us in the cycle of death and rebirth.

The following diagram and table outline Chara Kārakas in their descending order of planetary degrees. This sample also demonstrates how Rāhu's retrograde activity is dealt with – as here the north node is Atma Kāraka (AK). In this horoscope Rāhu[12] is situated at 6° 18' Virgo and so its current retrograde degree is to be subtracted from the 30° span of the Rashi: 30° – 6° 18' = 23° 42'.

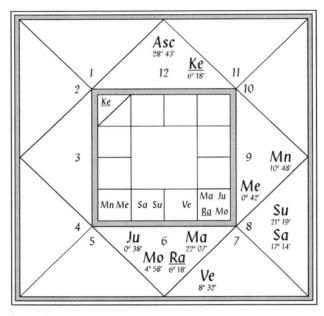

Chara Kāraka sample image.

Planet and Degree	Acronym	Kāraka
Rāhu 23° 42'	AK (Atma Kāraka)	Atma (soul) – might also be interpreted as an individual's core nature or true-self, indicative of higher goals, inspiration or the willingness to be of service to others
Mars 22° 07'	AM (Amatya Kāraka)	Minister (advisor) – indicates those we put our trust in or take counsel from. This Kāraka is studied to gain better insights into how to receive advice from others and how successfully we are able to use that advice. AM also speaks about the loyalty and morals of those we keep close to us and depend upon for guidance and support in difficult times

Sun 21° 19'	BK (Bhratri Kāraka)	Siblings – or support through show of arms, camaraderie and bodily reserves; it also shows our capacity to work and ability to endure under pressure
Saturn 17° 14'	MK (Matri Kāraka)	Mother – that which births and nurtures, MK can represent mother and home as well as sanctuaries, a keep or place of rest. It also indicates our inner reserves, ability to sustain and feed others
Venus 8° 32'	PIK (Pitris Kāraka)	Father (Pitris) – traditionally represents those that watch over us, instruct and educate, providing role models for conduct, sense of honour/duty and willingness to fulfil our obligations (contracts, etc.)
Moon 4° 54'	PUK (Putra Kāraka)	Children – as well as progeny might also be interpreted as one's creativity, prosperity, good fortune and intelligence, that is, our capacity and willingness to learn and develop
Mercury 0° 41'	GK (Gnaati Kāraka)	Competitors – commonly representing those things we choose to fight or fall foul of. This Kāraka also includes health matters as both environment and mental stability rail against our physiology and immune systems. Gnaati Kāraka also gives some insight into the nature of our protagonists and their favoured methods of attack
Jupiter 0° 38'	DK (Dara Kāraka)	Partner (spouse) – taken to represent those closest to us, or those fulfilling a supportive role in our lives. Conversely; this Kāraka also shows an individual's ability to return affection or share in a relationship
Ketu	–	Moksha (Liberation)

Sthira

Sthira (stable) = regardless of degree, situation or position each of the planets (Rāhu and Ketu excluded) become significators for primary individuals featured in the life of the person; these Kārakas have been given as:

Father, Teacher/Instructor/Supervisor	Sun or Venus (whichever is stronger)
Mother, Carer, Healer	Moon
Younger Sibling/s, Spouse of Siblings	Mars
Maternal Relatives (aunts and uncles)	Mercury
Husband, Children (sons), Paternal Relatives (aunts and uncles)	Jupiter
Wife/Partner, Mother-in-law/Father-in-law	Venus
Elder Siblings, Mature Associates, Business Partners	Saturn

Naisargika

Naisargika (natural) = a mixture (and multiplicity) of all worldly matters both corporeal (of the body) and non-corporeal (inanimate objects). These have been represented in the following Kāraka tables occupying each planetary portrait.

Note: Kāraka tables (in this whole section) contain only a selection of popular significations appropriate to their featured graha. These should in no way be considered exhaustive.

3.3 PRIMARY KĀRAKAS OF THE SUN

Primary Kārakas
Father, Atma (soul), prāṇa (life-force), kings, fame, favours, fortune, governments, dealings with officials, powerful people, authority figures, gold, goldsmiths, copper, brass, yellow colouration, power, heat, fires, strength, vigour, courage, blind ambition, career, appearances, personality, optimism, domineering attitude, self-reliance, public opposition, political power, regal stature, easterly direction, anger, jealousy, clarity, purity, sattvic disposition, bitter taste, self-knowledge, enlightenment, generosity, good fortune, quadrupeds, wool, travel, social affairs, noon time, saffron, Lord Śiva, worship of Lord Śiva, Rudra, the Nakshatras Krittika, Uttaraphalguni and Uttarashadha, Sunday, thorny trees, fruiting trees, banks of a river, grass, a circle, ayana (six months), Leo (sign), blood red gemstones, rubies, long-standing anger, direct gaze, penetrating stare, capture of enemies, law and order, punishment, incarceration, prisons, poisons,[13] serpents, pungent substances, strong coarse fabrics, earrings, the wilderness, woods, strong trees, red lotus, long pepper, black pepper, cardamom, honey, seeds and husks, yams, wheat, medicines, a hero, herdsmen, warriors, elders, reliable people, physicians, aristocrats, captains, leaders, evil doers, cruel disposition, clean habits, palaces, temples, sacred sites, grand buildings, paying respect to the gods or one's guru, fortresses, armed forces, currency exchange, solstices, six-year dasha period

Physical and Medical Kārakas
Digestive power, indigestion, small intestine, bones, physical heart, Pitta dosha, inflammatory complaints, cholera, fevers, sun stroke, headaches, bile, blood, arteries, veins, bilious conditions, high blood pressure, freedom from disease, blood, bones, thinning hair, right eye, visual acuity, burning sensations, broad shoulders

NOTES

1. *Jātaka Pārijāta*, authored by Vaidyanātha Dīkṣita c. AD 1500.
2. Brahmā Prajāpati crowned the Sun as Lord of Planets.
3. Kṣatriya = those who defend or are capable of punishing wrongdoers.
4. Sattwika: one of three gunas (or states of matter). Sattwika is thought to be pure and without defect, promoting non-attachment to worldly desires.
5. Atma is 'soul' or sustainer of consciousness; it is considered eternal.
6. Within the hierarchy of planets, Sûrya is noted to harbour malefic tendencies yet still ministers to the Devas in some capacity.
7. Of this multitude seven are of prime importance; these are Susumna, Harikeśa, Viśvakarman, Viśvavyacas, Sannaddha, Sarvāvasu and Svarāt. Of these, Susumna brightens horizons and flourishes in southern regions. Harikeśa is the source and substance of Nakshatras, brightening their appearance in the east. To the south, Viśvakarman is seen as the origination of Budha (Mercury), to the west Viśvavyacas is the origination of Shukra (Venus). From Sannaddha comes Kuja (Mars), while Sarvāvasu brightens and promotes Brihaspati (Jupiter). Lastly, the ray of Svarāt nourishes and sustains Shani (Saturn).
8. One might also consider the wealthy, landed gentry, corporations and large businesses interests.
9. See Binary Companion Theory in Section 1.5, which challenges the field star designation, postulating our Sun to be influenced by a distant dark stellar companion.
10. Early astro-meteorology observations appear to have been proved correct, inasmuch as the Sun (principally) and planets (secondarily) drive Earth's weather patterning.
11. As Ketu is the primary Kāraka for moksha (liberation), it is considered beyond worldly desires and so presence as Chara Kāraka has been excluded.
12. Some astrologers prefer to exclude both nodes as Chara Kāraka, instead opting for the degree of Lagna as substitute.
13. Visha in a curative capacity.

Chandra (Moon): I pay respects to Chandra, whose complexion is likened to pearls, conch and curds. Born to Atri and Anasuyā, he is the king of stars (Nakshatras) and medicine, granting wealth and prosperity to those who make offerings to him.

4

—— CHANDRA (Moon) ——

ඕං සෙහෙරවාය නමඃ			
9 නවග්‍රහාය නමඃ ඕං සෙහෙරවාය නමඃ	16 ඕං ආරම්ලුබාය නමඃ	5 ඕං රාජ්වරාය නමඃ	4 ඕං හුර්මාය නමඃ
7 ඕං එලෙසුදාය නමඃ	2 ඕං රූපාය නමඃ	11 ඕං රාමාය නමඃ	14 ඕං ලුභාය නමඃ
12 ඕං සත් හිරු රාජ්කාය නමඃ	13 ඕං මුලමන්ත්‍ර රාජ්ය නමඃ	8 ඕං අෂ්ඨ රූපාය නමඃ	1 ඕං උල්කාය නමඃ
6 ඕං ලුබ පෙරුමාය නමඃ	3 ඕං රූධාය නමඃ	0 ඕං පතිවාය නමඃ	15 ඕං අරාමාය නමඃ
ඕං සෙහෙරවාය නමඃ			

Śrī Laṅkān Sadu Chandra Navagraha Yantra deemed effective for the propitiation of Moon, warding off negative graha aspects, removing fear from the mind and grief from the heart. This yantra appeases the Moon god, granting longevity, health and wisdom. Its use protects one's home, happiness and heart. Sadu Chandra Navagraha Yantra brings fame, beauty and wisdom to its wearer.

The Moon is phlegmatic and windy in constitution and is given to rambling, his speech is soft. He has fine eyes and limbs that are firm and exceedingly lovely. He is always sensible, discriminating and of slim (yet rounded) of figure.

Jātaka Pārijāta by Vaidyanātha Dīkṣita

Chandra is considered the queen of the grahas, beautiful and feminine. Sattwika in guna, her taste is salty, her caste Vaiśya.[1] The complexion of the Moon is tawny, her dosha Kapha. Her element is water. Chandra is often depicted dressed in finely embroidered white silk. She has a magisterial manner, but one softened by emotive caring tendencies. The effects of the Moon mature in the 24th year of life, when strong Moon indicates clear thinking and emotional maturity, abundant blood, clear complexion and untrammelled vision. The Moon is representative of mind, that is, the apprehender of the senses. It is said that Brahmā Prajāpati crowned the Moon both lord of the lunar constellations and master of all medicinal (herbal) arts.

A powerful Moon lifts one toward poignant social interaction, perhaps bringing fame or at the very least a deep respect for their level of expertise. The Moon is considered representative of Chitta[2] (consciousness); she reveals our ability to digest impressions, emotions and thoughts. Moon is also representative of the digestive system, primarily the stomach, mucosa and gastric juices. The Moon gains strength in Earth signs and is exalted in Taurus (specifically 3°); she is equally debilitated at the same degree in Scorpio. Moon is comforted by the gemstones pearl and moonstone, her metal is silver. Moon is said to prosper in the fourth house of the home; she also rules *Muhūrta* (increments of forty-eight minutes).

Chandra rides in a three-wheeled chariot, each wheel born of one hundred red spokes. Ten white horses bear her across the heavens, racing with the speed of the mind. When transiting the heavens she emits a whitish ray that falls upon the Earth and ocean[3] as a light dew. Both Deva and Pitris alike were known to accompany the Moon. In her masculine personification, Moon fell nightly into the embraces of 'his' twenty-seven lunar brides or Nakshatras (see Chapter 25).

Jyotish regards the Moon as 'special'; its relatively swift motion not only marks the passage of time and season, but was deeply interconnected to Vedic rituals and the performance of magic. As Sūrya is lord of the (solar) zodiac, so Moon reins supreme over the lunar zodiac, better known as Nakshatras.

Somewhat overpowered by Sūrya's intensity, she receives nourishment from the great luminary via *sushumna*, the name of the Sun's rays emitted during her opposition. During her subsequent waning period both Deva and Pitris feed hungrily upon her transmuted nectar called soma, accumulated during her waxing.

Note: When viewed from a locale close to the Earth's equator our Moon seems to ride upon its back, passing almost directly overhead. From this vantage point its 'seas' or 'maria' appear akin to that of a hare,[4] birthing a host of legends tying the exploits of such an animal to the god of the Moon. Shifting geographically northward, observers tend to envision apophenic markings upon the same lunar surface, birthing a host of 'Man in the Moon' legends.

Favourable Chandra: Rejuvenates the body and nourishes the vital organs and tissues. Moon helps in retaining moisture/integrity through aqueous/synovial fluids, salts and secretions. One may see an increase in personal wealth through the trading of fine silks, silver, pearls, ghee, milk, cattle, rice, herbs and cooling spices. A comfortably placed Moon in the horoscope incurs favour from the goddess Pārvatī (Śiva's consort), Durga and Apas (see Section 27.2).

Unfavourable Chandra: One may be forced to suffer at the hands of a cruel mother, or seek to project sickness upon one's mother. One may incur the anger of powerful feminine figures (such as queens), enmities from relatives or immediate family. One may undergo mental anguish, emotional turmoil, excess blood toxins or reduced longevity by association with women of ill repute.

Bala (strength): Chandra is considered well disposed if the following are applicable: falling on his own day (Monday) or in the 4th house, occupying Cancer in Hora, Drekkana or Navamsha Vargas or exalted in Taurus. Moon gains strength during Dakshinayana, periods of darkness (night time), toward the close of Rashis, when aspected/conjunct by a benefic graha.

Undertakings on Monday: Sacrificial offerings on Mondays were considered fruitful/auspicious for those wishing to receive benefit from Chandra. These acts or undertakings include: the attainment of pearls, mother of pearl, conch, moonstone, ornaments, lotus flowers, moon-water, milk to aid in the manufacture of soothing (rejuvenating) medicines or those which reduce phlegm (Kapha), wearing of new clothes, perfumes, the arrangement of flowers, bathing, fertility of lands, horned cattle and excellence in all manner of agricultural pursuits.

Alternative names for Chandra

Soma	Rasāyana drug/elixir of youth and immortality
Indu	Changing reflection and cooling effects
Vidhu	Strong, intelligent and wise
Himanshu	One who is filled with or reflects cooling white energy
Anushnagu	Absence of heat, that which transforms hot into cold
Nakshatra-nâtha	Lord of Nakshatras
Niśeśa	Lord of the night
Śītāṁśu	Of cooling rays
Oshadhi-pati	Lord of herbs and healing
Śiva-sekhara	Adorning the forehead of Lord Śiva
Sasī	Marked like a hare

4.1 ASTRONOMICAL

Second only to the Sun, our Moon is the nearest and brightest object in the sky. Moody and enigmatic, it slowly rotates and librates[5] through its various phases over the lunar month, showing but one face to Earth's inhabitants. The length (or period) of a lunar cycle may be determined both sidereally (fixed star to fixed star) = 27.32 days or synodically (full Moon to full Moon) = 29.53 days. Moving about us in an elliptical orbit, less than 238,000 miles distant, its daily momentum is some fourteen times greater than that of Earth. For every twelve months spent by Earth orbiting the Sun, our Moon makes an additional thirteenth revolution about us – travelling at speeds in excess of 2200 miles per hour. Being almost one-third of the Earth's mass, its relationship to its primary is unique.

As with the Sun, the ancients witnessed the Moon's power over vegetation, fertility and agriculture. Its cooling rays were deemed equal to those of its fiery consort. When first imaged via telescope, astronomers likened its highlands to the Alpine regions. Its plains were thought to be littered with great rivers and lakes. In truth the Moon is largely a rocky body (not unlike Mercury) with radically different hemispheres. Earth-side, the Moon is awash with large basalt basins, undulating hills and pockmarked craters. Its so-called dark-side consists largely of heavily cratered highlands broken only by a few small maria (seas). Being our nearest and dearest celestial overseer, it has been gazed upon intently for millennia. The celebrated astronomer Johann Hieronymus Schröter (1745–1816) once conjectured the existence of a great city on her east side, just north of the equator, with fields of vegetation and extensive canal networks!

4.2 PRIMARY KĀRAKAS OF THE MOON

Primary Kārakas
Mother, women, mind, femininity, fertility, longevity, intelligence, infancy, nursing, convalescence, herbal medicines, eating, memory retention, fickle-mindedness, the colour white, silver, bronze, crystals, beads, glass, moonstone, pearls, contentment, salt, honey, curd, milk, ghee, sweet fruits, sticky substances, plants residing in water, oily plants, creepers and vines, sense of humour, personality, sattvic temperament, fame, beauty, romance, strength during the night, north-west direction, fair-faced, softness, radiance, immoral pleasures, inventive minds, lethargy, laziness, the senses, rain, oceans, new clothes, fine clothes, Mondays, wealth, affluence, sleep, happiness, midnight, liquids, fish, fermented foods, Cancer (sign), the Nakshatras Rohinī, Hastā and Śravana, Buddhism, popularity, general public, advertising, comforts, moodiness, fear of death, hypochondria, maternal instincts, healing sanctuaries, welfare, meritorious deeds, looking squarely ahead, a protective canopy, patronage and favours, pale complexion, white umbrellas, scents and fragrances, jasmine, rice, sandalwood, gardenia, lotus and lily, house boats, fair seas, rotting wood, beaches, aquariums, salty foods, monsoon (rainy season), inns, public houses, opium dens, breweries, hospitals, aquatic creatures, born of water, tourism, photography, Durga (goddess), occult studies, pilgrimages, over-expenditure, faith, journeys to distant lands, ten-year dasha period

Physical and Medical Kārakas
Breasts, blood, lungs, chest and respiratory conditions, asthma, lymph, glands, kidneys, uterus, ovaries, bladder, hernia, loss of taste, water retention, diabetes, enlargement of the spleen, jaundice, appendicitis, mouth ulcers, neurological disorders, cancer, memory loss, child-birth, phlegmatic conditions, consumption, stomach, ulcers, left eye,[6] lubrication of eyes (tears), lunacy, mental instability, over-acidity, stout build, facial lustre, circulation, injury to shoulders, anaemia

NOTES

1. Merchant caste.
2. Moon legends describe Chandra as being born from the mind of the cosmic Puruṣa.
3. The Moon's action upon the tide and oceans was noted from great antiquity; the ocean (like the Moon) was considered both feminine and capricious, often referred to as 'she'.
4. Sasa-Jātaka relates the tale of the selfless hare (in reality an incarnation of the bodhisattva) whose residence at the foot of the mountain was shared by three other friends: an otter, a monkey and a jackal. Noting the current lunar phase, a hare realised that feast-day was almost upon them and reminded his friends to prepare food lest some beggar should come their way. The four set out to find food. The otter, monkey and jackal all procured food with ease; the hare, however, found nothing and resolved to offer up his body if someone should be in need of food. Sakka (lord of heaven) was watching the hare and decided to test him by incarnating as a beggar asking for food. True to his word, the hare leapt into the cooking flames so that the stranger might eat. To his amazement he did not burn but was instead honoured by Sakka, who embracing the mountain squeezed forth its essence and daubed the Moon with an image of the hare.
5. Minor but periodic variations in the Moon's spin axis.
6. See Sarvarth Chintamani of Vyankatesh Sharma.

Budha (Mercury): I pay respects to Budha, offspring of Chandra and Tārā, born of intelligence and unrivalled in form. Dark like phalapriya and adorned in akṣamālā, he is quiet of nature and charming.

BUDHA (Mercury)

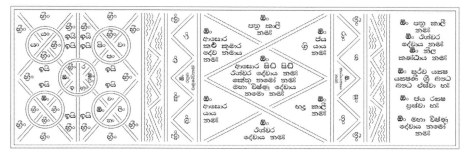

Śrī Laṅkān Budha Vishnu Mandala Yantra deemed effective for the propitiation of Mercury warding off childhood illness, skin disease, speech and learning difficulties. This yantra appeases Lord Budha, granting wisdom, health, youthfulness and longevity, granting one success in scriptural study, education, business and public speaking.

Mercury's colour is like that of Durva or panic grass. He has a distinct articulation, is spare and thin. He is both sovereign and sage of those that are endowed with the quality of Rajas (passion). He delights in damage and fun, having a wealth of energy; he is of mixed constitution having equal amounts of bile, wind and phlegm.

Jātaka Pārijāta by Vaidyanātha Dīkṣita

Mercury[1] is *yuvaraja*, 'of royal blood'. He rides a chariot fashioned from fire and air, pulled by eight horses, deep yellow in colour. Vaiśya[2] by caste and neuter in sex, his complexion is likened to the colour of panic grass. His dosha is an equal apportionment of dosha,[3] his taste *shad-rasa* (six tastes). Mercury's element is earth. Mercury dresses in fine black silks and gains strength in air signs. Exalted in the sign of Virgo (specifically 15°), he is in his fall at the same degree of Pisces. Mercury is representative of Buddhi (intellect). His guna is Rajasic.[4] The effects of Mercury mature in the 32nd year of life. Mercury also rules Ritu (seasons) for a period of two solar months. Having a youthful appearance and mannerism, he is fond of word play and witticism. If well-positioned, he indicates a strong intellect and analytical disposition.

Healthy of skin with quick dexterous movements, Mercury prospers in the 1st, 4th and 10th houses. His metal is pārada (quicksilver).

Mercury represents the learned student, apprenticing himself to any would-be instructor.[5] As an artful negotiator, investigator and magician, Mercury is equally skilled in the theft of knowledge (espionage, etc.). Specifically he relates to speech patterns and timing. Mercury is said to rule Atharva Veda.

A powerful Mercury will lift the chart toward quick thinking, sharp talking (in sales or trading), global communication and profiteering. Mercury may enter all places – holding the key to every room in the palace!

Mercury's strength is reflexed by the body's ability to irrigate and connect bodily systems, from the electrical activity of its neurons and synapses to the plasma content of blood, constantly readjusting the suspension of materials carried in the many fluidic mediums. Other significations of Mercury include: reflexes (agility/speed) of the nervous system and the body's ability to recover from injury. Mercury is symbolically the planet of healing; its relatively small planetary body was thought to emit a powerful green healing ray.

In the ancient world his metallic namesake and element Hg[6] was considered of paramount importance in the quest for life-extension. Even today, Mercury is the foundation of many Rasa medicines used in Rasa Shāstra (Vedic Alchemy).

Favourable Budha: If well disposed, Budha maintains a youthful appearance and keen intellect as well as an inquisitive and questioning mind. Those benefiting from Mercury are aided by Brahmins and trustworthy advisors, legal representatives and righteous persons. Wealth may be accumulated via the trading of horses, real estate or precious metals. One may acquire fame through the written or spoken word, through feats of magic (illusion), humour or mass media. Featured in a prominent position, Mercury incurs the favours of Lord Vishnu.

Unfavourable Budha: One may endure the wrath of Lord Vishnu or the heir-apparent/regent. One may be co-opted into crime (theft) and other nefarious acts or be themselves the subject of hoaxes, in receipt of counterfeit goods, legal deception, character defamation (through the written word), suffer from slurred speech or stuttering, coordination impediments, tremors or slow or poor performance throughout educational life, diseases of the skin, respiratory ailments and vertigo.

Bala (strength): Budha is considered well-disposed if the following are applicable: falling on his own day (Wednesday), in his own signs or exalted in Virgo. Budha favours the middle portion of Rashis; he prospers when distanced from the Sun's rays, in either period of ayana, acquiring vigour during the day or night.

Undertakings on Wednesday: Sacrificial offerings on Wednesdays are considered fruitful/auspicious for those wishing to receive benefit from Budha. Acts or undertakings include: study of shāstra, fine art and poetry, scientific study including mantra, astrology, alchemy and the manufacture of medicines, compounds, mixtures, attainment and cultivation of fertile land, green produce and grasses, mining of gemstones (taksya/emerald), apprehension of languages, observance of vows, meritorious deeds, delivering of messages and holding of secrets or untruths (lies).

Alternative names for Budha

Sâumya	Mild, tender, polite in manners and speech
Bodhana	Teacher and instructor of great wisdom
Induputra	Child, hence child of the Moon
Jña	Wise and learned
Bud	To perceive, gain enlightenment
Syāmānga	Black-bodied

5.1 ASTRONOMICAL

Mercury is the smallest and swiftest of the grahas; just larger than our Moon, its sidereal year is approximately 88 days. Its axial rotation is 58+ days, almost two-thirds the length of its mercurial year. With a mean distance of only 28,000,000 miles from the Sun, this planet remained an enigma for a great many years, dazzling astronomers with its swift motion, brilliance and Moon-like phases.[7] Mercury seldom presents itself long enough to view this world in any detail. Rising two hours before sunrise or glimpsed briefly before sunset, Mercury is never observable against a fully darkened sky.

Bathed in a solar brilliance six times that of the Earth, its surface temperature boasts a sizzling 400°C+, its twilight face an equally staggering −180°C. During its passage across the orb of the Sun, astronomers noted that its disc remained opaque, allowing the early deduction that its mass was a rocky composition[8] with little or no atmosphere. It was later confirmed to have a disproportionally large and extremely dense metallic core, with a somewhat reduced surface crust.[9]

Mercury's presence appears to have been documented as early as 3000 BC. It was also an important deity for both Greek and Roman temples. Ancient observations of Mercury believed him twinned,[10] as one pin-point of light receded from the Sun at dawn, while another later approached the Sun in the evening. As one was never seen until the other had vanished, it was eventually concluded to be the same world. Notoriously swift in its flight about the girth of the Sun, the best opportunity to gain a glimpse of this fleeting world is between the months of March/April and August/September.

5.2 PRIMARY KĀRAKAS OF MERCURY

Primary Kārakas

Youthfulness, intellect, education, mathematics, astrology, astronomy, alchemy, liquid mercury (Hg), speeches, lectures, script writing, grammar, scholarly, wearing of new clothes, medicines (taking and making), healers, doctors, princes, regents, the colour green, sculpture, pilgrimage, commerce, magic, magicians, childhood, devotion, wordplay, anagrams, vitality, shrewdness, self-control, worship of Lord Vishnu, benefic nature, one skilled in mantra, tantric powers, reporters, authors, printers, publishers, accountants, insurance brokers, messengers, comedians, critics, emeralds, yantras, trade, horses, treasury, infantry, dvija (twice-born[11]), construction of palaces and temples, ornaments, soft speech, eunuchs, bad dreams, northerly direction, bell metal, bitter fruits, fears, dancing, humour and pranks, strong in the morning time, autumn, all seasons, compound substances, agile animals, birds, younger siblings, Atharva Veda, dust, religious rites, exploration of villages, delights from the northerly direction, the Nakshatras Aslesha, Jyestha and Revati, well-versed in shāstras, purāṇās, gemmology, sideways glances, 17-year dasha, rajasic temperament, verbal diarrhoea, performance of sacred rituals, mischievous children, playgrounds, short-distance travel, translation of texts, mental arithmetic, vantage points, success in undertakings, magical charms, alloys, betel leaves, attention to detail, currency, commerce, imports and exports, counterfeit money, hidden secrets, racecourses, gambling, book dealers, science, software writers, computer viruses, mimicry, confusion, speak impediments, courage, comprehension, enemy of Mars, green gram, adherence to superstition

Physical and Medical Kārakas

Skin and skin lustre, blood plasma, the navel, brain, nervous system, the neck, hearing, larynx, thyroid problems, the tongue, bronchial tube, the hands, nerve centres, gastric juices, oleation and lubrication, vertigo, sexual organs, dyspepsia, memory loss, impotency, lingering bouts of depression

NOTES

1. See Mason (2014).
2. Assignment of Vaiśya caste may have been earned by this planet's obsession with mercantile activity and perpetual travel – acting more like a tradesperson than royalty.
3. Vāta, Pitta and Kapha in equal measure.
4. Rajas = one of three gunas (states of matter). Rajas is considered to be outwardly seeking, reactive, turbulent and restless.
5. Close conjunctions by Budha allow it to mimic its neighbours' attributes.
6. Hg = hydrargyrum.
7. Mercury is considered Moon's progeny; superficially their façades (surfaces) resemble one another while Mercury boasts three times Moon's gravity and twice its surface area.
8. Mercury presides over the earth element.
9. It is believed that the planet actually shrank sometime during its traumatic past. Perhaps this is why Mercury is considered youthful in form (small) yet intelligent in years?
10. This observation may have contributed to its dual nature and rulership of Gemini (twins).
11. Dvija = male member of the first three varṇas (paths) in Hindu society, that is, Brahmin, Kṣatriya or Vaiśya.

Kuja (Mars): I pay respects to Kuja (devagraha), born to Mahāviṣṇu and Bhūmi. Lustrous as lightning and burning coals – he bears multiple arms and is adorned with akṣamālā (rudrākṣa garlands).

6
KUJA (Mars)

Śrī Lankān Abisambidana Yantra deemed effective for the propitiation of Mars, warding off accidents, injury, infections and fevers. This yantra appeases Lord Kuja, grants strength, endurance and the will to defeat of one's enemies. This yantra promotes technical skills and respect from one's subordinates, elevating its wearer to a position of authority.

Mars has fierce eyes, a youthful appearance (thin waist) and is generous in disposition. His constitution is predominately bile; he is extremely fickle by nature. His limbs are fine and of a reddish hue, he is energetic and lustful, his tendencies are toward the quality of Tamas (darkness).

Jātaka Pārijāta by Vaidyanātha Dīkṣita

Kuja pre-eminently holds the position of commander-in-chief. He rides in a golden chariot born of fire. He is masculine, of reddish complexion and Kṣatriya by caste. Pitta in dosha, his taste is pungent, his element fire. Mars dresses in coarse red fabrics gaining strength in Earth signs. Mars is exalted in the sign of Capricorn (specifically 28°), and is similarly debilitated at the same degree in Cancer. Mars is said to be representative of Sāmaveda. The effects of Mars mature in the 28th year of life.

Mars is martial in his manner and represents *shakti* (power/energy). His guna is tamasic; his build is muscular (without height), his waist is narrow. If strongly placed in a horoscope, Mars promotes tactical skill and a combative temperament. He is fierce and able to endure prolonged physical hardship. Mars is a fighter and survivor. He floods the body with freshly oxygenated blood, creating heat, drive and passion helping to burn up āma (toxins) with the fire element. Sometimes he can push the body to its utmost limits, ultimately bringing fatigue and burnout.

Mars can be a lifesaver, but prefers fight to flight. If he withdraws it is only to regroup before continuing the onslaught. Ironically, Mars may be the most philanthropic of planets, always craving a just cause!

Kuja is cruel of nature, but was also thought to be less so to those who afford him propitiation. Mars is deemed to prosper in the 3rd, 4th, 6th and 10th houses of the horoscope. His metal is iron. Kuja rules Dina, the day.

Favourable Kuja: Kuja maintains youthful vigour, passion and competitive edge (literally 'a will to win'). Kuja excels in stratagem, decisive acts and technical skill. One may benefit or profit from a younger sibling, acquire land (real estate) or receive patronage from a king. Kuja easily sequesters military force or wins the kinship of military personnel. Mars incurs the favour of both Karttikeya (god of war) and Bhumi (goddess of earth).

Unfavourable Kuja: One may be forced to suffer at the hands of siblings, endure difficult relations with a younger brother or sister, face losses through inheritance issues, lose properties to fire, or undergo periods of theft, accident or injury. One may feel restraint at the hands of military personnel, policemen or the law, manifest blood imbalances through toxins, contract muscular ailments, eye disorders, fever and injury through edged weapons or sharp objects. Kuja Dosha[1] is a notorious disturbance of married life, initiated by a challenging Mars residing in houses that relate to marital harmony.[2]

Bala (strength): Kuja is considered well-disposed if the following are applicable: if highlighted on his own day (Tuesday) or in the signs Aries and Scorpio (own), Capricorn (exalted), Aquarius or Pisces. Mars gains in stature during the night or when journeying toward the southern regions (Dakshināyana). Mars favours the earlier degrees of Rashis and brings prosperity when 10th from Lagna. Kuja is said to gain in potency when retrograde.

Undertakings on Tuesday: Sacrificial offerings on Tuesdays are considered fruitful/auspicious for those wishing to receive benefit from Kuja. Acts or undertakings include: the art of warfare and military tactics, surgeries, construction of forts, combat and the procurement of weapons, competitions, exercise, taking command of subordinates, philanthropic endeavours, mining ores, working with metals (forging), the manufacture of weapons, harvesting of coral (red), redwoods and red flowers, heating spices, pungent foods, crudeness, roguery and ostentatious behaviour.

Alternative names for Kuja

Angáraka	Glowing like a heated coal
Mangala	Auspiciousness or auspicious actions
Bhūmiputra	Child of the Earth
Śiva-gharma-ja	Born from the sweat of Lord Śiva
Vakra	Curved or crooked (orbit)
Janma	Birthed
Navārchi	Nine-rayed
Rināntaka	Ender of debts

6.1 ASTRONOMICAL

First of the exterior planets, Mars is well noted to resemble (in apparent magnitude and colour) the stars Antares (α Scorpii) and Aldebaran (α Tauri), over which it frequently passes. Easily visible to the naked eye and discerned as having a reddish hue, its radiance is best witnessed when rising, just after sunset, or when setting before sunrise (both indicating its greater proximity to Earth). Although twice as distant from the Sun as Venus, during opposition (see Chapter 18) Mars can at times be less than

35,000,000 miles from Earth. During conjunction it can be as far distant as 230,000,000 miles.

Wariness of the red planet appears to have been documented as early as 1000 BC, the Babylonians referring to this martial wanderer as *Nergal* (god of death and pestilence). Later discoveries of its twin satellites bestowed the names *Phobos* (meaning fear) and *Deimos* (terror) upon the two small rocky bodies. Both names are Greek in origin and previously awarded to the sons of Ares and Aphrodite (Mars and Venus).

Martian terrain is breathtakingly unique and largely asymmetrical, making its hemispheres a forged-welded affair, with smooth northern plains or lowlands sharply contrasted against the cratered, mountainous southern highlands.[3] Generally the borders between hemispheres differ significantly with some areas exceeding 1.5 miles in elevation. This gives Mars the appearance of an orange stripped of skin toward its northern axis. Martian soil has been shown to contain high concentrations of iron oxide (essentially rust), giving the planet its characteristic red colour – yet ironically this planet emits an extremely weak magnetic field, perhaps one thousand times less than of the Earth.

A Martian sidereal day is 24 hours 37 minutes and 22 seconds in length; its axial inclination to its orbital plane is approximately 25°, strikingly similar to the Earth and matching our own seasonal cycles.[4] Were humans to colonise the red planet,[5] inhabitants would enjoy the spectacle of Earth as both morning and evening star, with Moon-like phases and periodic retrograde activity. On occasion Earth could also be seen to transit the face of the solar disc, appearing as a distant dark orb, accompanied by its rather disproportionate satellite – the Moon.

6.2 PRIMARY KĀRAKAS OF MARS

Primary Kārakas

Fighting, competition, competitive nature, vitality, physical strength, short stature, thin waist, firmness of limbs, leanness, warring, battles, carrying weapons, masculinity, anger, arguments, violence, injuries, fire, firearms, iron, ironware, steel, copper, metals, alloys, strength, honour, courage in the face of adversity, armies, military personnel, the colour red, philanthropy, abuse and criticism, resilience, accidents, minerals, gemstones, red ochre, carnelian, red agate, a wicked person, southerly direction, property, buildings, bloodshed, dictatorship, lust, youthful figure, edged weapons, mechanisms, contraptions, thieves, opposition, controversies, heat, forges, metalcraft, alchemy, chemistry, pungent taste, the Nakshatras Mrigashirsha, Chitrā and Dhanistha, foul language, consumption of meat, alcohol, gains strength in the late evening and early morning, skill in archery, mismatched clothes, scandalous persons, fierce gaze, persistence, fickleness, imbalanced judgement, seven-year dasha, extremes, invincibility, invigorates the body, follower of Hanumān,[6] irritation, quick-tempered, thievish nature, ruthless, full of self-praise, upward glances, wolves, ferocious quadrupeds, traps, worship of Kārttikēya,[7] favours from kings, earthenware, roaming in forests, village chiefs, butchers, sexual perversions, place lit by fires, slaughter house, burning sulphur, burning buildings, gases, explosive gases, arid lands, destruction, concealed power, unhappy domestic life

Physical and Medical Kārakas

Fevers, inflammation, reddish complexion, sores, wounds, ulcers, blood circulation, bleeding, dried blood, surgery, painful urination, bladder, muscle tissue, bone marrow, ligaments, sinews, fistula, haemorrhoids, boils, carbuncles, typhoid, cholera, sprains, aches, torn muscles, abortion, menstrual flow, haemoglobin, bile, digestive fire, smallpox, chickenpox, miscarriages, sunstroke

NOTES

1. Also known as Maṇgalik Dosha.
2. Recognised to be a disruptive force in long-term relationships, Kuja Dosha is formed when Mars tenants the 1st, 2nd, 7th, 8th or 12th house from ascendant, Moon or Venus. If Mars is found to tenant more than one of these positions its acrimony intensifies during married life.
3. In actuality the Martian northern plains comprise far less of the planet's total surface area.
4. Due to Mars's extreme elliptical orbit and axial tilt, summers in its southern hemisphere are warmer and shorter (approximately 154 Martian days). Its cooler northern hemisphere has a summer season closer to 178 days. It has been speculated that this cycle is itself fluctuating, as Martian obliquity is unstable, meaning its axial tilt wanders over time. These fluctuations could see a reversal in seasonal cycles within 25,000 years.
5. In his popular 1961 sci-fi novel *Stranger in a Strange Land*, Robert A. Heinlein presents the novel's hero Valentine Michael Smith as a human born on Mars who later returns to Earth. During his adventures he meets a famous astrologer who tries to read his horoscope, only to realise Mars must be absent from the horoscope as this is his birthplace. The astrologer is then forced to consider the implications of having Earth in a particular sign or house.
6. An ardent devotee of Rama, Hanumān was one of the central figures in the Hindu epic poem Rāmāyaṇa.
7. More commonly worshipped as Kataragama in Śrī Laṇkā.

Brihaspati (Jupiter): I pay respects to Brihaspati, lord of the three worlds and teacher to Deva and Rishi. Born of Aṅgiras and Vasudā, he is wise beyond compare, large in stature with eyes the colour of honey.

7

—— BRIHASPATI (Jupiter) ——

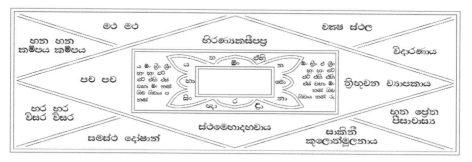

Śrī Laṅkān Narasiha Yantra deemed effective for the propitiation of Jupiter, removing ignorance negativity and darkness (tamas). This yantra appeases Lord Brihaspati, granting health, wisdom, fame and wealth. Narasiha Yantra makes one a respected minister, elevates career and social standing, bringing happiness and material comforts.

Brihaspati is large-bellied, yellow in colouration and is of a phlegmatic constitution. He possesses all virtues; is endowed with an aptitude for all sciences. His eyes and hair are brownish in colour; he possesses the qualities of goodness and purity, he is exceedingly intelligent. His person is graced with the marks of royalty, not to be despised.

Jātaka Pārijāta by Vaidyanātha Dīkṣita

Brihaspati is the King's closest advisor. Brahmin[1] by caste, he rides in a chariot of gold, pulled by eight yellow horses. Masculine, his complexion is tawny, his stature large. Jupiter's taste is sweet, his element is æther. He dresses in fine saffron-coloured fabrics and gains strength in water signs. Jupiter is exalted in the sign of Cancer (specifically 5°); similarly he is debilitated at the same degree in Capricorn. His dosha is Kapha. Considered primary Kāraka for progeny (children), he grants knowledge, happiness and corpulence; his guna is Sattwika. Jupiter is learned in all shāstra including Jyotish; he is deemed representative of Rig-Veda. The effects of Jupiter mature in one's 16th year of life.

If strongly positioned in the horoscope he indicates one with a large or firm frame. He is the great benefic, both generous and philosophical.

His gaze is considered to promote wealth and happiness, whilst protecting the individual against misfortune or ill-health. Jupiter prospers in the 2nd, 5th, 9th, 10th and 11th houses; his metal is Vanga (tin). He presides over Masa, a period of one solar month.

Jupiter protects and cushions from life's external knocks and scrapes. King of corpulence, this graha acts as the body's store-house of fatty tissue. Jupiter aids in the absorption and assimilation of nutrients (enzymes), removing toxins through the liver and assimilating healthy oils via bile secretions from the gallbladder. Although Jupiter does partly contribute to pancreatic health, Venus is generally regarded as having the greater impact on its functionality.[2] Jupiter's association with *akasha* (æther element) permits his passage into the most subtle of tissues, bringing fortification, lubrication and cohesion via essential lipids (including cholesterol). Jupiter is unctuous (slippery) by nature. His presence adds smoothness, resistance, flexibility and elasticity.

Favourable Brihaspati: Empowers the ability to study or retain knowledge, granting mastery in our chosen profession. Jupiter grants blessings from Brahmins and instruction from a guru. Jupiter is very people-friendly, quickly putting others at ease and gaining their trust. One's wealth may be accumulated through the trading of horses, elephants and/or precious metals, their notoriety through the recitation of *Vedas*, mantra, piety, service to others or invocations to gods. In good standing, Brihaspati incurs the favour of Lords Brahmā (creator) and Indrā (king of the gods).

Unfavourable Brihaspati: One's child may suffer a protracted childhood illness or incur enmity from teachers/instructors. One may befriend wicked people, be cursed by Brahmins or scolded by priests. An ill-placed Jupiter can manifest through obesity, liver disorders, excess Kapha (phlegm), excess sweating, water retention, diabetes, loss of hearing or episodes of prolonged vertigo.

Bala (strength): Brihaspati is considered well-disposed if the following are applicable: falling on his own day (Thursday) or in the signs Cancer (exalted), Scorpio, Sagittarius and Pisces (own). Jupiter gains in stature while journeying northward (Uttarāyana), at midday or in the middle portion of Rashi. He bestows much prosperity when occupying Lagna, the 2nd, 4th or 10th house from Lagna.

Undertakings on Thursday: Sacrificial offerings to Jupiter on Thursdays were considered fruitful/auspicious for those wishing to receive benefit from Brihaspati. These acts or undertakings included: construction of sacred sites (temples, etc.), honouring of deities, ceremonies/sacrifices, performance of

Dharmic acts, study of shāstras, recitation of mantra, speeches, propitiation of Brahmins, the trading of excellent goods such as precious metals (gold and silver), horses, elephants, umbrellas, cowrie and conch shells as well as yellow sapphires.

Alternative names for Brihaspati

Ganapati	Grand leader of willing followers/assembled troops
Angira	A reference to the son of Brahmā, famed for great intelligence, often called the lord of Gurus
Amarejya	Superior or elder teacher to the gods
Suraguru	Divine teacher, an instructor of gods
Brihaspati	Great teacher who leads the way
Guru	Large teacher who burns away ignorance and darkness
Gish-pati	Eloquent and learned guide

7.1 ASTRONOMICAL

The solar system's giant contains about 2.5 times the mass of all the other planets combined. Imaged from Earth its oblate spheroid (slightly flattened orb) reveals a banded structure of vibrant interlaced clouds swirling speedily about its interior (Jupiter's axial rotation being fastest of all planets – it performs a full rotation in less than 10 hours). Having an equatorial diameter of nearly 89,000 miles, Jupiter's rotation period has been noted to vary at different latitudes, each of the three 'rotational zones' displaying slight variances in speed when completing each circumrotation.

Jupiter itself is thought to be composed largely of hydrogen and helium, enveloping a core of iron and metallic hydrogen. Amidst its turbulent weather system this planet's infamous eye or 'great red spot' (21,000 by 9300 miles) rotates once every sixty days; this has remained unchanged for at least 300 years of observation. Jupiter emits an intense magnetic field stretching as far as Saturn's orbit. This extraordinary emission is believed to be made possible by its rotating liquid metallic core, which acts like a gigantic dynamo.

If this magnetosphere were made visible to the naked eye, Jupiter would be surrounded by a discharge whose diameter would exceed the circumference of our Moon (relatively speaking). It has been speculated that Jupiter's influence on our solar system acts as a protective figure, scooping up rogue comets and asteroids that stray toward the inner system and inhabitable worlds. Jupiter may literally have enacted its astrological portrait as 'great benefic', ensuring the survival of life on Earth, protecting us from catastrophic collisions, etc.

Viewed from Earth, Jupiter (during opposition) is almost as resplendent as Venus, making it perhaps one of the easiest planets to track across the skies. Holding a steadfast course through the heavens (Jupiter's orbital plane is almost perpendicular to the ecliptic plane), its advance at a mean rate of one zodiacal sign every 361+/– days became a popular means by which to reckon time.[3] Indeed, so reliable was this planet's motion that Indian astrologers began favouring its sixty-year cycle, known as Saṃvatsara, as an adjunct to other calendrical systems.

At a mean distance of some 483,000,000 miles from solar centre, Jupiter experiences only one-thirtieth of the light and heat received on Earth. As well as shepherding a host of dependants (sixty-seven satellites at last count),[4] Jupiter also boasts a lesser-known Jovian ring system (albeit extremely faint). In many ways Jupiter's dependants (or 'children') are often likened to a miniature solar system, its nearer bodies passing regularly into the broad shadow of its parent, or caught transiting its sunlit side. Many of these transits cast a shadow across the face of the leviathan planet.

7.2 PRIMARY KĀRAKAS OF JUPITER

Primary Kārakas
Teacher, guru, dharma, sattvic-natured, rituals, fame, mantra, Jyotish, astronomy, critical reflection, knowledge, knowledge of sacred texts, Rigveda, pilgrimages, benefic, sacred sites, alter stones, progeny, sons, the colour yellow, saffron, honey, golden hair, honey-coloured eyes, sesame oil, ghee, turmeric, sweet taste, elephants, horses, buffalo, clarity of mind, orators, judges, scholars, attorneys and intellectuals, fame, recognition, merit, investments, over-extending oneself financially, religious duties, devotion, respect, justice, wise elders, grandfather, elder brothers, ministers, advisors, affluence, legacies, treasures, misfortune, gold, tin, sulphur, Indrā (king of the gods), grand places, offerings to the gods, acts of piety, fire ceremonies, penance, clarity, abundance, refinement in old age, great proficiency, scriptures, holy works, near-death experiences, poems, yellow sapphire, yellow topaz, yellow quartz, banks, finance, safes, secure premises, polished woods, trees, the Nakshatras Punarvasu, Vishaka and Purvabhadra, Thursdays, long journeys, pilgrimages, residence in foreign lands, publishing, bookshops, spouse (for women), sense of justice, fair play, truthfulness, promotion, Brahmins, spiritual transformation, cows, wealth connected to elephants, precious stones, pre-winter (Hemant), holy water, palaces, throne rooms, churches, shrines, standing circles, archers, educational institutions, installations of idols, coconuts, decorations, candlelight, technical subjects, extravagance, over-eating, benedictions, broadminded, diplomacy, sympathetic, greed, lawsuits, politicians, political power, occult sciences, reading of scriptures

Physical and Medical Kārakas
Corpulence (large-bodied), broad-chested, fats, childhood development, digestive disorders, the liver, bile and gallbladder, arteries, gallstones, Kapha (phlegm), healing, hearing, loss of hearing, ears, earlobes, colds, asthma, diarrhoea, water retention, abscesses, carbuncles, lipoma, diabetes, pale complexion, weight gain in old age, tumours, vertigo

NOTES

1. Brahmin = he who serves the gods.
2. Pancreatic functionality is considered a part of the body's water metabolism system or channel known as Ambhuvaha Srota; this primarily connects the hard and soft palates in the mouth to the pancreas and bladder. These srotas are deranged by the intake of excessively sweet, oily, salty or dry food and liquids such as alcohol.
3. Brihaspatya Varsha became a popular method of time reckoning in Southern India around the 10th century AD and continues to this day. At present each Luni-solar year is also named after one of sixty corresponding Jovian years called Saṃvatsara.
4. The most famous of these include its four famed Galilean moons: Io, Europa, Ganymede and Callisto.

Shukra (Venus): I pay respects to Shukra, born to Bhṛgu and Pulomā, preceptor of the Asuras and favoured by Indrā. Adorned with garlands of flowers, fragrant and pale as snow, he is the keeper of gemstones, bestower of comfort and pleasure.

8

SHUKRA (Venus)

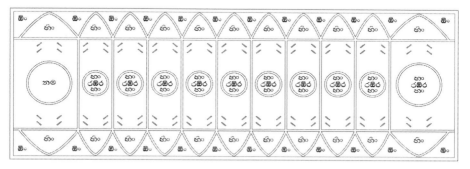

Śrī Laṅkān Sanjeewani Yantra deemed effective for the propitiation of Venus, elevating one through eloquent speech, manners and refinement. This yantra appeases Lord Shukra bestowing wealth, fame and physical beauty. Sanjeewani Yantra makes one respected in the arts, adored by the opposite sex, brings material comforts and enjoyment from wine and fine foods.

The hair of Venus is black and curled; his complexion is brown and handsome. His limbs are symmetrical and very lovely, his eyes are soft and his disposition is amorous. His constitution is both phlegmatic and windy; his tendencies are toward Rajas (passion). He has amplitude of grace, ease, vigour and all kinds of excellence.

Jātaka Pārijāta by Vaidyanātha Dīkṣita

Shukra is the king's second advisor. Brahmin by caste, he rides in a chariot of extreme elegance, adorned by multiple flags. Feminine in stature and complexion, his colour is variegated. His dosha is a mixture of Kapha and Vāta. The taste of Venus is sour and acidic; his element is water. Also learned in shāstra (Venus rules Yajurveda). Dressing in fine silks, he gains strength in signs ruled by water. The effects of Venus mature in the 25th year of life. Exalted in the sign Pisces (specifically 27°), he is likewise debilitated at the same degree in Virgo. Prospering in the 4th and 7th houses, he rules paksha (a fifteen-day period). His metal is tamra (copper), his guna is rajasic.

If well-positioned in a horoscope, Venus indicates smoothness of skin and fullness of figure. One may be artistic/creative, well versed in the musical arts and those of the occult. Personalities strongly influenced by Venus are noted to be charming, emotive and tactile, displaying a love of all things refined and beautiful; particularly drawn to fine clothes, exotic scents, foods and wine.

In matters of health, Venus aids in digestion (and removal) of toxins through the water element (kidneys and bladder) and the ultimate refinement of foods through Sapta Dhatu[1] (seven tissues). Venus fortifies the tissues by supporting *ojas* (immune system). Both Venus and Moon preside over the metabolism of the water element, helping to further reduce (or delay) the loss of vital moisturising secretions and elasticity/suppleness of tissue. Venus is also considered Kāraka of shukra (semen/reproductive fluids) and physical potency (procreation).

Favourable Shukra: Heightens vitality, social refinements and sexual charm. One dines on fine food, is adored by females and displays refinement in clothes and jewellery. Venus promotes artistic/musical inclinations as well as an interest in scriptural studies. One's wealth may be accumulated through the trading of fine foods, oils (paints), diamonds or inheritance through marriage. Acquisition of precious metals or sources of hidden wealth (within the Earth) is also indicated. In good standing, Venus incurs the favours of nāgā folk (see Section 27.9), *Indrā* and *Indrāni* (King and Queen of the gods).

Unfavourable Shukra: Female relatives or wife may suffer ill-health, one derives only sorrow from intimate (loving) relationships, feels enmity toward servants (lower caste) or envy of those who find happiness in love. If Venus suffers, one will lose social standing and/or a loss of reputation, lack fine garments or have items of value stolen from them. When dissatisfied, Venus may manifest through reproductive/fertility issues, pancreatic imbalances (diabetes), lymph stagnation, under-functioning of the kidneys, cataracts (blurred vision) and water retention.

Bala (strength): Shukra is considered well-disposed if the following are applicable: falling on his own day (Friday) in the afternoon period or in his own signs (Taurus and Libra). Exalted in Pisces, Venus gains strength when distanced from Sûrya's rays or when seen in advance of the Sun. Prospering in the 4th, 7th and 12th houses from Lagna, his qualities are pronounced during lunar conjunction, retrograde periods or Uttarāyana motion.

Undertakings on Friday: Sacrificial offerings on Fridays are considered fruitful/auspicious for those wishing to receive benefit from Shukra. These acts or undertakings include: indulging in amorous activities, leisurely pursuits, enjoying beautiful places, being in the company of courtesans, artistic endeavours, musical recitations, trading in commodities such as sugar cane, fine clothes (silks), perfumes, lotus seeds, sour products (preserves), vehicles, rejuvenating medicines, autumnal crops and agriculture of luxury crops.

Alternative names for Shukra

Bhṛgu[2]	Bhri = waves; gu = illumination of creation
Bhṛiguja	Similar interpretation to Bhṛgu; ja = next generation
Sita	Refined, pure
Swetha	White
Aaspujit	Completion of cycles
Kāvya	Poet
Shodasānsu	Sixteen-rayed
Shukracārya	Instructor of demons

8.1 ASTRONOMICAL

At times our nearest companion and unquestionably the brightest object in our nightly skies (excluding Sun and Moon), the incandescence of Venus is undisputed amongst the planets and certainly worthy of the name *Shukra* (meaning 'to shine').[3] Venus was of particular interest to the ancients; unmistakable and marked for keen observation by many cultures including Egyptian, Chinese and Indian. To the Babylonians she was the goddess *Ishtar*, to the Greeks the bearer of two names: *Phosphorus* 'morning star' and *Hesperus* 'star of evening'.

Early optical observations of this world proved disappointing, its whitish-yellow orb permanently veiled with impenetrable cloud. Almost equal to the Earth in size and mass, she was initially labelled 'Earth's twin',[4] although later physical encounters revealed her beautiful exterior to hide a heated, acrid and inhospitable terrain, far removed from anything Earth-like.

Of all the worlds, Venus is truly spherical, lacking the equatorial bulge seen in other planets. She also rotates extremely slowly, her sidereal day lasting 240+ Earth days. Like our Moon, the rotational and orbital period of Venus are closely synchronised to Earth's orbit in such a way as to present us with the same face at inferior conjunction. During such encounters what we are actually gazing upon is her shadowed hemisphere. If we were able to view her fully illuminated face, Venus would appear twenty-five times brighter, resembling something closer to a lesser Moon.

The almost true circular orbit of Venus takes it to within 67,000,000 miles of the Sun – where it receives roughly twice as much light and heat as Earth; the intensity of which by its solar proximity, according to the inverse-square law, raising her surface temperature to 450°C+, with atmospheric pressures one hundred times greater than on Earth. In addition, 'showy'[5] Venus displays an extreme axial tilt of 177.3° to its orbital plane; this in effect makes its rotational direction clockwise and unique amongst the planets, which otherwise rotate anticlockwise when viewed from their northern pole.

8.2 PRIMARY KĀRAKAS OF VENUS

Primary Kārakas
Beauty, marriage, female partner, shy damsels, women, attractive women, fine arts, music, dancing, average in stature, youthful in limb, graceful movement, silks, perfumes, sour taste, conveyances, secret pleasures, rounded faces, small chins, worship of Lakṣmī, priestly caste, mother (as indicated by daytime birth), fortunes, fame, guru of the demons, income, diamonds, pearls, gemstones, precious metals (silver and gold), copper and zinc, hidden wealth, pentagrams, white and pink colours, Yajurveda, eminence in chosen career, oils (sesame and castor), Fridays, comfortable furniture, craftsmanship, black hair, buying and selling quality goods, excesses, indulgence, enjoyment, flowers, south-easterly direction, fashion, clothes, white cloth, performing arts, happiness from partner, husband, dancing, flattery, eloquent in speech, sex, Pātāloka (serpent underworld), middle age, honour, respect, gentleness, benefic qualities, pride, love of humor, speaking the truth, worship of Gauri,[6] the Nakshatras Bharani, Purvaphalguni and Purvashada, cows, dairy products, botanists, beauty salons, body-care products, death of wife, occult powers, foresight, bipeds, horses, commands, seal of authority, governmental seals, watery places, bedrooms, cinemas, nightclubs, decline of physical beauty, ornaments, rajasic nature, self-indulgence, adultery, downward glances, swimming, peculiar poetry, stringed and wind instruments (such as violin, clarinet, flute), pleasure, happiness

Physical and Medical Kārakas
Eyes, irises and eyesight, diabetes, ojakshya (emaciation from excess sexual activity), reproductive organs, loss of vitality, bodily fluids, ovum, semen, asthma, anaemia, cough, colds, urinary tract, bladder, pancreas, Kapha/Vāta dosha, phlegm, well-proportioned (symmetrical) frame

NOTES

1. The concept sapta-dhatu (meaning seven tissues) is related to a series of subtle channels, each with interlocking dependencies, supporting and being supported by a collective whole. The seven tissues in order are: rasa (plasma), rakta (blood), māṃsa (muscle), medas (fat), asthi (bone), majjā (nervous system) and shukra (semen/ovum), culminating in the formation of ojas or vital essence.
2. Maharishi Bhṛgu, famed for the composition of *Bhṛgu Saṃhitā*, an enlightened work on Jyotish that not only interpreted the horoscopes of those who have already existed but also of those who are yet to be.
3. Legend notes that Shukra shone out in the assembly of Indrā; he was also considered 'custodian of all gemstones.'
4. The mean radius of Venus is about 95 per cent that of the Earth.
5. Astrologically, Venus likes to 'stand out'.
6. Consort to Lord Śiva.

Shani (Saturn): I pay respects to Śanaiścara, born to Surya and Chhāyā, brother to Yamaraj (lord of death). Intense and restrictive in form, he is dark of skin and emaciated in statue. Feared by all, he is lord of Karma.

9

SHANI (Saturn)

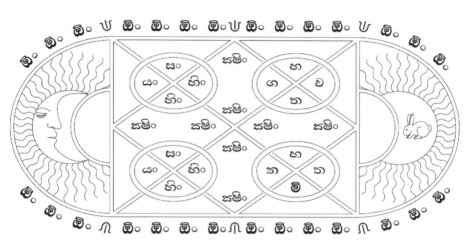

Śrī Laṅkān Maha Vishnu Mandala Yantra deemed effective for the propitiation of Saturn, protecting one from hardship, sorrow and injury. This yantra appeases Lord Shani (most feared of all grahas), granting longevity, health and strength in old age. Maha Vishnu Mandala Yantra promotes good vision, strong teeth and bones. It also gives relief from pain and respect from one's servants.

Saturn has stiff hair and limbs, he is emaciated, his body as dark as Durva grass. His constitution is that of vāyu (windy), his teeth are large, his eyes a fine reddish brown. He is intent upon dark designs and disposed toward inactivity.

Jātaka Pārijāta by Vaidyanātha Dīkṣita

Shani represents servants; he is Śūdra[1] by caste. Riding in an iron chariot, he is borne across the skies by horses of indescribable colour. Saturn is neuter in sex; his complexion is dark, his stature emaciated. His taste is astringent; his element is air, his dosha Vāta. Dressed in multicoloured robes, he gains strength in air signs. Exalted in Libra (specifically 20°), Saturn finds debilitation at the same degree in Aries. The effects of this planet mature in the 36th year of life. Saturn prospers in the 6th, 8th, 10th and 12th houses; his metal is lead (nāgā). Saturn rules Samā, a period of one year.

Saturn is Kāraka for ill-health, sadness and grief; his guna is Tamsika. Called *Pangu* (meaning lame), Saturn was observed to be the slowest of planets, completing one revolution of the zodiac in just under thirty years. Furthest from the Sun's warming illumination, Saturn is considered a cold and wanting planet. He is uneducated, lean and hungry, his stare terrifying to behold. His countenance is dark and oppressive.

As 'Lord of Karma', he is often the most feared of planets. Saturn presides over material gains and longevity; when strong in a birth-chart he indicates a person of few words, a narrowing yet tall frame, hunched posture, obsessive, methodical and detail-oriented. Any individual incurring his close consideration is considered highly inauspicious, bringing trial and tribulation. Saturn's presence is desiccating, weakening the body and subjecting its tissues to rapid ageing. His counteractive gemstones are primarily blue sapphire, blue amethyst and lapis lazuli.

Considered an anchoring force, Saturn stays the wheel of the solar system, keeping all planets in check; he is extremely people-unfriendly, preferring solitude and abstinence from social interaction. Saturn assists in the erosion of bodily tissues via the accumulation of Vāta dosha. He resides mainly in the muscular/skeletal system (bones and joints), aiding in the reabsorbing of liquids and the final elimination of solid wastes from the colon. When Saturn concentrates Vāta in the body, he creates dryness and brittleness of tissue, often manifesting as emaciation or atrophy of muscle. Saturn is also signified by falling teeth, greying hair, haemorrhoids, fistula and loss of strength in the hand/fingers.

Within the sapta dhatu (vital tissues), Saturn rules Majjā – his presence here is often witnessed through a dulling or dryness of the sclera (whites of the eyes). A pronounced darkness rimmed about the eye socket is also symbolic of a saturnine influence.

Favourable Shani: If well-disposed, Shani grants long life, material gain through hard work, endurance and an ability to overcome hardship. Saturn is the great teacher (usually through discipline, fortitude and accountability) throughout life and beyond all caste. One may accumulate wealth through the trading of iron/ironware and coal, care of the elderly, and law (particularly if connected to fixed assets, inheritance or taxes). Shani in good standing incurs the favour of Lord Yamaraj (god of the underworld and death) and Prajapati (the force of creativity).

Unfavourable Shani: One may be forced to suffer Vāta ailments, and be exposed to harsh environments and/or rancid food. The native may incur falls (injury to limbs) or accidents which incapacitate or require long periods of recuperation. Typically one may experience joint problems, lameness, paralysis, general debility or darkened vision. When falling foul of Saturn, one may be forced to steal, cheat or become enmeshed in cycles of ongoing poverty.

Bala (strength): Shani is considered well-disposed if the following are applicable: falling on his own day (Saturday) or in the sign of Libra (exalted), Capricorn and Aquarius (own). Saturn gains strength whilst retrograde, during planetary war, in the concluding portion of Rashi, during his dasha period, the dark half of the month or the motion of Dakshināyana.

Undertakings on Saturday: Sacrificial offerings on Saturdays are considered fruitful/auspicious for those wishing to receive benefit from Shani. These acts or undertakings include: performance of harsh duties, working with the elderly, austerity and fasting, agricultural works, foundry work, sewing, pest control, long tiring journeys, settling of old debts, trading in such commodities as root vegetables, preserved (dry) foods and rancid foods (fermented), second-hand clothes and leatherwear, dark metals (ironmongery), broken goods, slaves, stolen goods, she-goats, birds, camels, traps, poisons and hunting equipment.

Alternative names for Shani

Arkaja	Arka = Sûrya/Sun, ja = born of
Sûryatanaya	Sûrya = Sun, tanaya means 'progeny (child) of the Sun'
Sanaiścara	Sanai = slowly, ścara = at great distance (orbit) about the Sun
Manda	Coming to fruition, steadfastness and determination
Pangu	Lame
Krûra-dris	Evil-eyed
Asita	The dark one
Saptârchî	Seven-rayed (emits seven distinct rays)

9.1 ASTRONOMICAL

To the ancients, Saturn's orbit marked the boundaries of the solar system prior to the discovery of trans-Saturnians (Uranus, Neptune and Pluto). He was known to the Greeks as Krónos (god of harvest/reaping and time). The Romans similarly venerated him as an agricultural deity. At a mean distance of around 887,000,000 miles from our Sun, Saturn is probably the most distant world visible to the unaided eye.[2] With an axial tilt of 27° to its orbital plane, Saturn also displays similar seasons to that of Earth and Mars (albeit seasons of extreme length[3]) as it completes its protracted sojourn around the Sun every 29.5 years. Likened to the star Fomalhaut[4] (α Piscis Austrini),[5] Saturn was identified by its emission of a pale yet steady light, its course the most ponderous about the zodiac.

Perhaps the most iconic of planets, Saturn is braced with resplendent rings that play host to a multitude of satellites (sixty-two at the latest count). Its rings proved to be of enormous interest to early astronomers[6] who struggled to identify two close stars and flattened band, parallel to the planet's equator. It was not until 1659 that the enigma was finally unravelled by Christian Huygens in his *Systema Saturnium*. He correctly interpreted this phenomenon as an orbital ring (later becoming rings). Eagerly glimpsed by both amateur and expert astronomers alike, these rings are never seen perpendicularly but instead present themselves edge-on or obliquely to the eyes of any Earthbound observer.

Although this gas giant is the second largest planet in our solar system, its density is less than half that of its near companion Jupiter. Its strange lack of mass accompanied by its rapid rotation (around ten hours+) account for its extreme oblateness, easily determined through the eyepiece of any telescope.

Like Jupiter, Saturn's atmosphere appears to be composed largely of hydrogen and helium, interposed with lesser amounts of methane, ammonia, oxygen and nitrogen. Saturn's cloud cover displays dramatic weather patterning, awash with high winds and violent electrical storms. Strangely, this gas giant emits something like twice the amount of heat it receives from the Sun, suggesting an active and heated internal core. Saturn also hosts the solar system's second largest moon, Titan – complete with a dense primitive atmosphere, water and a rocky surface, promising to be the most Earth-like body found in our solar system.

9.2 PRIMARY KĀRAKAS OF SATURN

Primary Kārakas
Karma, longevity, old age, death, health, ill-health, employment, discipline, endurance, established position, poverty, ownership of land, machines, agriculture/farming, vegetables, blackness, dark blue, dirty clothes, old clothes, traditional duties, enmity from friends, westerly direction, long-standing fears, sorrow, sadness, servants, slaves, life-restoring remedies, herbal remedies, astringent taste, cold and damp places, basements, inaccessible places, abandoned houses, ancient ruins, graveyards, crematoriums, undertakers, long journeys, worship of Lord Yamaraj, lead, iron, steel, dark wood, coal, minerals, metals, salts, glassware, oils, gem-mining, blue sapphires, lapis lazuli, ashes, things hidden below ground, hidden treasure, archaeology, black birds, crows, scavenging animals, dogs, beggars, coverings (sheets blankets), low caste, cruel dispositions, hunters, hardships, unclean, unwashed, shoes, fasting, sewage, drains, blockages, obstructions, keys, locks, jails, prisons, outcasts, suffering, sins, one's father (if born during the hours of darkness), theft, the Nakshatras Pushyami, Anuradha and Uttarabhadra, Shishir (winter season), uncooked food, preserved foods, downward glances, austerity, melancholy, disappointments, dangers and accidents, birds, buffalos, elephants, horses, camels, charities, adultery, eunuchs, the handicapped, roaming hilltops, howling winds, torn clothes, holes in clothes, wanderings, toxic environments, petroleum, petrochemicals, wicked valour, one hundred years (in age), misfortune, misadventure, physical hardship, wandering on battlefields, one year, subordinates, low-caste women, concubines
Physical and Medical Kārakas
Vāta dosha, Vāta diseases, joints and bones, knees, muscles, tendons and nerves, thighs, falling of hair, falling of teeth, constipation, bowels, gallbladder, gout, rheumatism, skin conditions, fasting, insanity, physical height (tallness), sore feet, lameness, emaciation, stiffness, difficulties in digesting, unkempt hair, ugly hair, perfuse body hair; typically, the house and/or sign where Saturn resides in a horoscope indicates vulnerability in the corresponding body part/s

NOTES

1. Śūdra = he who serves.
2. Uranus may be visible (+5.5 mv) during opposition. As of 2015 it is situated in late Pisces.
3. Each Saturnine season lasts approximately 7.5 years.
4. α Piscis Austrini may originally have been considered part of the Aquarian constellation and so have given rise to Saturn's strong association with this Rashi.
5. Situated at the foot of Aquarius, Saturn's moolatrikona sign.
6. Discovery of Saturn's rings is largely attributed to the astronomer, physicist, engineer and philosopher Galileo Galilei (1564–1642).

Rāhu (North Node): I pay respects to Rāhu, offspring of Kaśyapa-prajāpati and Siṁhikā, whose valour obscures the Sun and Moon. Fearsome to behold, he is without body, his skin the colour of ash, his eyes burn like charcoals.

Ketu (South Node): I pay respects to Ketu, whose valour obscures the Moon and Sun. Fearsome to behold, he is without a head, his skin is the colour of ash, his scales variegated.

10

RĀHU AND KETU
(Lunar Nodes) AND
——— MĀNDI (Upagraha) ———

Nodal glyphs, thought to be inspired by the ocelli (eyes), seen at the rear of the Asian Cobra's hood.

By this point, readers should be somewhat familiar with the seven planets; however, the lunar nodes (collectively known as *Rāhu* and *Ketu*) may require some additional introduction. In essence both are considered *tamograha* (dark/invisible planets), that is, points of sensitivity along the lunar orbit – or more specifically where the Moon cuts the plane of the ecliptic.[1] These points of transition have no physical existence, yet are noted to produce powerful astrological effects.

When the Moon occupies a point close to either of its nodes and is either *new* or *full*, the outcome may be a solar or lunar eclipse. This phenomenon gave rise to the obscuration myths associated with Sun, Moon, Rāhu and Ketu. Both nodes were imagined to be the ghastly remnants of an enormous serpent that once partook of Amrita (an immortality elixir), and gained planetary status.[2] Their mission henceforth was to terrorise, taunt and obscure (literally 'devour') all planets when caught crossing their axis. Though birthed from a single entity, the portraits of each node are unique, yet at the same time inseparable. Wherever one goes, the other is sure to follow. This is also the case for their *nodal axis* which sweeps around the zodiac with its metaphorical head and tail always separated by 180°.

The nodes tend to augment and warp planetary energetics, the closer the conjunction the greater their ability to transfigure the planet concerned. Planetary rays are then filtered through the nodes and skewed onward tainted by their own particular energetics. As a rule, Rāhu tends to amplify planetary rays whilst Ketu scrambles them like a prism or rarefies their emission. Varāhamihira and his later commentator Bhaṭṭa-utpala both express the view that Rāhu emits darkened rays that mute and distort all colourful emissions whereas Ketu produces the opposite effect.

In truth, both nodes are to be considered wild-cards in the deck of life – you'll never be completely sure how they will show up. Both Rāhu and Ketu create attachment and suffering through addictions and compulsions. Rāhu feeds on physical pleasure, fame, greed, power and illusion; Ketu craves calamity, disorder and vengeful acts.

Collectively their dispositions are of great interest to an astrologer, offering a tantalising glimpse into the past (Ketu) or future (Rāhu). Both nodes help to break saṃsāra (our repetitious life-patterns) that lead to cyclical rebirth. Every nodal axis helps highlight the houses, signs or planetary lords that will play a critical role in our evolution. This can be toward greater ignorance and greater suffering or toward enlightenment and self-discovery, ultimately moksha (liberation from rebirth).

Note: Vedic Astrology's Rāhu/Ketu interpretation takes on a far more malefic tone than anything ascribed to them in Western Astrology; in which Caput Draconis (north node), termed Dragon's Head, is considered masculine, of good fortune and (largely benefic), combining the qualities of Jupiter and Venus. Cauda Draconis (south node) or Dragon's Tail is feminine and largely sorrowful, acting more like Saturn to bring misfortune or calamity wherever it falls in contradiction to its counterpart.

10.1 RĀHU

ඕං වං බුධ මණ්ඩලං	ඕං වං වෙසමුනි මණ්ඩලං	ඕං වං රජ මණ්ඩලං	ඕං වං දේව මණ්ඩලං
ඕං වං විෂ්ණු මණ්ඩලං	ඕං ශ්‍රී ඕං වං දේවතා මණ්ඩලං	ඕං ශ්‍රී ඕං වං ෂඩු මණ්ඩලං	ඕං වං දුත මණ්ඩලං
ඕං වං ඉසුරු මණ්ඩලං	ඕං වං රාක්ෂ මණ්ඩලං	ඕං වං මණ්ඩලං	ඕං වං යක්ෂ මණ්ඩලං
ඕං වං වරුණ මණ්ඩලං	ඕං වං ඉට කැම් පිට කැම් යක්ෂ යක්ෂ නි ඉටු කබ්වා මු පුතුල් ස්වා හා	ඕං වං රාජ්ශ්වර මණ්ඩලං	ඕං වං කහ කහ එටි එටි ඒස් චහ්‍

Śrī Laṅkān Nāgārjuna Yantra deemed effective for the propitiation of Rāhu, warding off snake and animal bites, poisons, blood impurities, malevolent spirits, alcoholism, injuries and addictions. This yantra appeases Nāgā folk, wins jewels, brings fame and protects one whilst travelling.

This son of Kaśyapa-prajāpati and Siṁhikā is powerful, even his sight is death-inflicting, he who makes the Moon lustreless resides in the heart of Neelakantha.[3]

Prayer to Rāhu, Skanda Purāṇa

The name *Ra-hu* is composed of *Ra*, meaning solar or creative, and *hu*, meaning veiling or shocking. As one of the eclipsing agents, the north node does just that. Called *abhra-pisācha* (sky-demon), Rāhu is wholly preoccupied with antagonistic ventures that seek to undermine or oppose the deva (gods).

Rāhu represents the king's militia; his caste is Śūdra (sometimes Mleccha[4]), his sex neuter. Rāhu rides a brown-coloured chariot pulled by eight black horses. He is Vāta in nature, dressing in multicoloured robes. His effect is likened to an angry form of Saturn. Rāhu gains strength in air signs, yet particularly enjoys Mercury-ruled Gemini and Virgo. Rāhu is said to hold joint lordship of Aquarius.

Rāhu experiences moolatrikona[5] in airy Libra, his effects maturing in the 48th year of life. There remains some speculation over Rāhu's exaltation point; however, the most compelling idea seems to be that both nodes find themselves exalted in Scorpio and similarly debilitated in Taurus.[6]

Rāhu rules psychotic episodes, desires, cravings, deranged thinking and a hunger for power. He revels in conspiratorial activity, running wild spreading warped perceptions. Frequently this graha is drawn to the darker 'addictive' aspects of life. He rules intoxicating substances, hallucination and poison, the latter usually instigated by biting animals and fanged reptiles (symbolically Rāhu represents the head and fangs of the snake). Once the head of a large demonic serpent, he now signifies insatiable appetites and dark desires. Now separated from his tail these attributes became intensified; for while still able to bite and consume, the absence of a body precludes digestion and assimilation. Like a starving man he thinks only of satiating his hunger.

In health matters, Rāhu creates all manner of imbalances, causing deficiency in one channel and excess in another. Rāhu is seen to leap between tissues – a typical hallmark of his presence. Rāhu is more often than not a causative factor in diseases that spread out of control, requiring the use of strong toxins to stem their advance. The influence of this node may confound a remedy or treatment by unhealthy preoccupation, unclear thinking or cravings.

Close conjunction with other graha is a factor that should be considered with some care; if its associate planet is well-placed and contented it may well be able to resist the influence of Rāhu; if ill-disposed and under stressful circumstances, Rāhu's handiwork can be all the more disruptive. The north node holds no dominion over any particular bodily tissue per se; as mentioned previously, by virtue of its subtlety it easily penetrates sapta-dhatu, allowing it to move with relative ease throughout all bodily systems.[7]

Viruses and other nano-pathogens may be partly attributable to Rāhu's influence; his hallmark seems to fit their shadowy masquerade of micro-visitor who quickly goes to work replicating itself and subverting the organism's bio-functions. Modern research into the complexities of viruses highlights the adaptability of their structure, allowing them to lie dormant (as a shadow virus) or embed themselves deep into the DNA – becoming trans-generational (future-orientated) in nature.

On a positive note, a well-placed Rāhu can be particularly useful in predictive astrology (tending to be future-orientated and visionary). Rāhu can also be technologically driven and innovative, pioneering many of the cutting-edge sciences. A strong Rāhu may be particularly active and helpful in chemistry, bio-chemistry, advanced medical research, laser surgery or behavioural psychology. Rāhu's influence on modern pharmaceuticals shows their tendency to be highly toxic and quite pervasive – though they are able to expel pathogens, the process also aggravates dosha. Where Rāhu's subtleties are successfully applied to medications they tend to produce beneficial effects by the principle of stimulation; that is, toxic materials are administered in minute quantities to provoke an immune system response and ultimate neutralisation of pathogens, so transmuting poison into nectar.

With regard to *favourable* and *unfavourable* nodal positions, there are no absolutes given in authoritative astrological texts. In truth, both are likely to bring instability and unexpected events, wherever their axis falls. As mentioned previously, they may fare well in some Rashis, and less so in others. Generally their placement is damaging to the Kārakas of the house concerned.

Unfavourable Rāhu qualities may be largely equated to those of an unfriendly or angry Saturn. Favourable placements of Rāhu might indicate insights into mass trends (such as future-orientated investments), predictive psychology or social/behavioural patterning. Rāhu can be a tireless and cutting-edge researcher, scientist, pharmacist, adept in alchemical arts or a language specialist. He also shows his prowess in electrical engineering, the medium of film, media/broadcasting or recording technologies.

Bala (strength): Rāhu is considered well-disposed if the following is applicable: falling in the signs Aries, Gemini, Cancer, Virgo and Scorpio. He gains strength in the 10th house from Lagna. Ketu becomes similarly well-disposed when falling in Gemini, Virgo, Scorpio or Sagittarius; both are strong in the night-time or for one whose birth occurs during a striking phenomenon – such as an eclipse.

Alternative names for Rāhu

Abhra-pisācha	Sky demon
Saimhikeya	Descended from Simhikā
Māyāvi	Magician
Kabandha	Headless
Graha	Primary seizer
Hastā-bhū	Born of Hastā Nakshatra

Primary Kārakas of Rāhu

Primary Kārakas

Foreign-born, exotic, heretic, revolutionary tendencies, social outcasts, harsh in speech, sharp intellect, irreligious, a longing to travel, foreign lands, immigrants, lost in unfamiliar places, escapee, labyrinths, toxins, serpents, biting animals, strong medicines, accidental ingestion of poison, reptiles, astrology, psychic prediction, divination, occult practices, wild-eyed, wrestlers, narcotics, addiction, alcohol, maternal grandfather, conspiratorial acts, cursing god, cases of insanity, neurosis, eccentrics, electricity, shocks, sparks, ultraviolet spectrum, phobias, epilepsy, cancer, incurable diseases, demonic forces, ghosts, poltergeist, advertising industry, outside of any caste, unclean, deceit, falsehood, mistrust, south-west facing, emeralds, hessonite, quartz, agate, strange dreams, clairvoyance, bright regalia, Pātāloka (subterranean serpent abode), animalistic qualities, wickedness, writing, Urdu language, a winnowing basket, downward glance, physical height (tall and slender, but can also be small and slender), the Nakshatras Ardra, Swati and Shatabhishak, foreign languages, originality, illusion, fantasy, putrid foods, indigestible foods, heavily preserved foods, sins of the father, mortuaries, bone mills, hides, corpses, slaughterhouses, politics, mass hypnosis, popular trends, dark forests, barren land, gravel, stone, cement, guerrilla warfare, explosions, stabbing, knives, piercing objects, tattoos, black coarse hair, jugglers and wrestlers, wolves, camels, ass, mosquitoes, ant hills, light-headedness, flight, airplanes, aviation, trapped animals, instant results, smoke, course fabrics, sex with low-caste women, tantric practices, murder, foul play, smuggling, speculation, unserviceable goods

Physical and Medical Kārakas

Vāta disorders, blood impurities, bone deformity, indigestion, accumulated gas in digestive tract, skin diseases, leprosy, swellings, oedema, falling of teeth, tooth decay, cases of insanity, neurosis, phobias, epilepsy, cancer, incurable disease, elimination-excretory system, piles, legs, varicose veins, ulcers, sores, necroses of tissue, small sharp teeth, parasites, intestinal worms, tremors, sleeplessness, blackish discolouration of skin

10.2 KETU

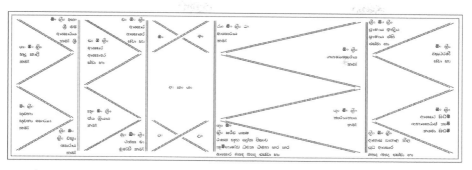

Śrī Laṅkān Aghora Yantra deemed effective for the propitiation of Ketu, warding off insect bites, fevers, psychic disturbances, malevolent spirits, accidents, injuries and insomnia. This yantra appeases Naga folk, protects one's health and promotes meditative practice (attainment of moksha).

Ketu's eyes are of a reddish hue, his looks are brutal and fierce, he has a venomous tongue, his body is lean and elevated, he wears arms and is an outcast. The colour of his body is of smoke, he is always inhaling smoke and his skin is marked with bruises.

Phaladeepika by Mantreswara

It is often said, 'As Rāhu, so is Ketu', and while true to some extent, both parts of his once whole have their own peculiarities. Like Rāhu, Ketu also represents the King's militia. Neuter in sex, Ketu is *varṇa-sankara* (of mixed caste); he is also symbolic of moksha.[8] Riding in a brown-coloured chariot pulled by eight red coloured horses, Ketu matures in the 48th year of life. Gaining power in signs dominated by the fire element (Sagittarius is his moolatrikona sign), the southern node enjoys air signs (especially those signs lorded by Mercury); Ketu is Vāta in nature. As previously mentioned, both nodes seemingly attain exaltation in Scorpio and are both similarly debilitated in Taurus.

Ketu is symbolised by a flag, a summit or crest; his alternative name *Shikhi* describes his situation after decapitation, relating in gruesome detail the loss of his head by Vishnu's chakrika. After severing the head of Rāhu some small part of the skull (below the occipital region) remained attached to his tail-end, giving him the name Shikhi.

Ketu is sharp, impulsive and aggressive in nature; he carries something of a Martian temperament – laying low in the shadows or suddenly lashing out unpredictably. His attire is unassuming (preferring to dress in rags) yet suddenly shocks his onlookers with a dizzying display of colour. As *Bhikshu* Kāraka, Ketu symbolises those without material wealth: beggars or aesthetics of those who have renounced the world, capable of soaring to the greatest of heights or sinking to the depths of depravity. Symbolically Ketu rules over creatures that crawl, fly or deliver poisons via a sting. Ketu signifies discord, global calamity and mass destruction;[9] he is frequently assessed to judge the likelihood of an individual being affected in such catastrophes.[10] Ketu is also associated with mass psychosis, psychic attacks, metaphysical pursuits or paranormal apparitions such as ghosts, phantoms and other disincarnate spirits.

In health, Ketu rarefies bodily tissues, creating a loss of structural integrity or malabsorption. These deficiencies often accrue over longer time periods, avoiding detection through stealth. Stealing small amounts of energy here and there, Ketu-type diseases manifest slowly with a noted decline in physical strength. Ketu favours residence in subtle tissue, causing imperceptible damage over extended periods. His handiwork often confuses any attempt to render a diagnosis. Ketu-related health issues are more than likely to abate quickly yet reoccur in longer cycles, spreading (relocating) from their initial site of injury and exhibiting colourful bruising (often a mustard/yellow hue), subsiding to a greyish pallor.

Ketu inclines toward bacterial infection and/or inflammation; his hallmarks are deferred location, heat, swelling, suppuration and general pain. Ketu is typically associated with infected bites such as those incurred by animals (particularly dogs). Ketu also rules over the bites of lizards, scorpions, leeches and arachnids.

On a positive note, Ketu proves highly useful in those undertaking historical research, archaeology, forensics or esoteric studies. Ketu also facilitates an exploration of the microcosm (subatomic structures, etc.). If well-positioned, a strong Ketu can penetrate deeply into 'hidden' organisations (for journalistic or crime fighting purposes). Ketu types readily assume a variety of identities, seemingly able to blend into any environment. Ketu on the ascendant either hides the person from common view or elevates them to the summit of success!

As previously mentioned, there are no absolutes given on *favourable* or *unfavourable* nodal positions, both points likely to manifest instabilities along their axis. Some of the more unfavourable qualities displayed by Ketu might be equated to those of a particularly violent or deranged Mars. Favourable placements of Ketu might indicate psychic abilities, foreknowledge of events (i.e. premonitions of disasters) and the ability to avoid such catastrophes. There may be artistic/graphic inclinations such as the rendering of monochromatic fine art (pen and ink); or display of subtle healing abilities in such disciplines as homeopathy, acupuncture, colour therapy and aromatherapy. Ketu delivers great results when tasked in the pursuit of ancient knowledge; such as might lead to enlightenment, extended longevity or moksha.[11]

Alternative names for Ketu

A-kacha	Without hair
Asleshā-bhāva	Part (segregation) of a serpent
Munda	Bald, smooth
Dwaja	Flag (marker) or summit
Dānava	Implacable enemy of the gods

Primary Kārakas of Ketu

Primary Kārakas
Catastrophes, calamities, fires, accidents, moksha (final liberation), esoteric studies, penance, worship of Lord Ganesha, servant of Lord Śiva, worship of Lord Śiva, suffering at the hands of one's foes, serpents, snake bite, insect bites, religious retreats, yogic practice, psychic ability, occult interests, witchcraft, talismans, charms, Jyotish, toxic chemicals, chemical fires, paternal grandfather, infrared spectrum, computers, internet, unconsciousness and disturbed dreams, cuts from thorns, lack of self-confidence, loss of faith, foreign languages, one's own ethnic group or race, falsehood, venomous speech, medicines, practitioners of medicine, those who acquire prosperity through generosity, loss of wealth, Mantra Shāstra, study of Vedanta, self-analysis, shaved skin, science, electronics, chrysoberyl, turquoise, eccentricity, compulsions, prisoners, self-doubt, self-esteem, spirituality, subtlety, unconventionality, philanthropic gestures, Pātāloka (subterranean serpent abode), historians, archaeologists, a discerning eye, varṇa-sankara (mixed caste), chores unbecoming of one's caste, vows of silence, the Nakshatras Ashwini, Magha and Mula, the tail-end of living things, bathing in the Ganges, renunciation, sharp thorns, zoology (knowledge of animals), horned animals, injury from horned animals, vultures, dogs, cockerels, insects with stingers, flying insects, hunger, sacrifices, back-biting, religious doctrines, fanaticism, violence, murder, suicide, trauma, idealism, traps, espionage, invisibility, flags, refuse, sewage, foul smells, decay, association with lower caste women, an end to bondage, imbalanced attitudes, scandals, scare-mongering
Physical and Medical Kārakas
Wounds, plagues, fevers, bruises, ulcers, kidney/urethra stones, surgery, diseases of the eyes, stomach disorders, Vāta diseases, ulcers, leucoderma (loss of skin pigmentation), poisoning, incurable disease, weakness of the spine, diseases of the stomach, tuberculosis, cataracts, smallpox, consumption, boils, blood disorders

10.3 MĀNDI

Shanair shanair eva Shani putra janmam gamyam
mruta aatma pretadhika masahaja mrityu:
Gati kaala bhramayet dhruvam chalam tam
yateeshwara aaraadhana yatna kaaryam.

Kālidāsa

The non-luminous planets (Aprakash and Upagraha) remain relatively unsampled by the majority of Vedic astrologers (although there is always the odd exception). For my own part, I did find a number of Śrī Laṅkān and Indian astrologers working with interesting interpretations of these shadowy planets. Having no physical manifestation there are naturally some parallels drawn between Upagraha and the lunar nodes but in truth their origination and calculation are something quite different.

In addition, *Brihat Parāśara Hora Shāstra* (hereafter *BPHS*) introduces its readers to non-luminous grahas in its third chapter (at the tail end of *Navagraha* introductions). This would appear to indicate that Parāśara[12] considered Chhaya-graha (shadow planets) important enough to flag up at the start of his treatises, instead of consigning them to a footnote at the close of volume II.

Of the non-luminous grahas, Māndi is generally considered the most potent, having an active reach of 7.5° either side of his position, making his sphere of influence greater than most.

According to the poet Kavi (Kālidāsa), the nature of Māndi is both slow and steady; he alone rotates in a clockwise fashion while the other shadow grahas rotate anticlockwise. Based on these descriptions of the arch malefic, Māndi is most symbolic of Pitruja (one's ancestral origins), holding sway over spirits and those who have perished by unnatural means. He is most placated by the blessings of Lord Śiva and pleased by the actions of yati.[13]

The effect of Māndi is most likely to be felt around health issues and longevity where his handiwork shines with particular brilliance. Affliction to the ascendant degree or via conjunction, this health-controlling graha will almost certainly manifest as a disturbance to wellbeing. Māndi is particularly adept at usurping and/or corrupting any conjoining grahas. His ailments often have a particular saturnine quality – chronic, debilitating or mentally disturbing. Māndi manifests as vitiated Vāta, that is, dryness, coldness, aching, stabbing pains and irritability. His positioning relative to Saturn should also be studied for additional insights on heath-related issues. Both grahas share familial connections to Lord Yamaraj (god of death): Māndi is usually credited as his progeny, Saturn his elder brother.

On a positive note, Māndi (being future-orientated) may give an individual a type of precognitive ability or an ability to avert potential health disasters by early detection (self-diagnosis).

Detailed descriptions of Māndi's appearance/attributes, doshic inclinations[14] remain sketchy; however, exposure to his presence is generally concluded to be a destructive influence and overwhelmingly malefic in content. Grahas conjoining this Upagraha in the 1st, 2nd, 4th, 5th, 7th, 8th, 9th or 12th feel his icy grip. Māndi, by close association, often imbues grahas with exacerbated unfriendly characteristics, personal hygiene issues and/or a physical weakness. Astrologers have noted Māndi to be raised (exalted) in Aquarius and debilitated in Leo, both situations adding to his mixed results in a birth chart.

Alternative names for Māndi

Pranhara	Destroyer of prāṇa
Atipapi	Most malefic
Shanisuta	Child of Saturn
Yamaatmaj	Child of Yamaraj
Gulik	Rounded and compact, fast-acting[15]

NOTES

1. See the lunar nodes image in Section 24.1, where I have provided a detailed diagram to help explain their motion.
2. Rāhu and Ketu seemed to have achieved full planetary status during the Tantric period (5th–9th century AD).
3. A synonym for Lord Śiva, meaning 'blue-throated' one.
4. Typically representative of barbarians/non-Aryan or Greeks. The science of astrology was known to be well established (and honoured) among the latter; hence Râhu becomes strongly affiliated with Jyotish.
5. Moolatrikona = the sign where best results are attained (barring exaltation).
6. Scorpio is a Rashi of scorpionic venom and fire, thus exhilarating Rāhu and Ketu. Following the basic 180° rule of graha debilitation it would follow that both nodes would subsequently find debilitation in Taurus (Moon's exaltation Rashi). *Pañca Siddhântikâ* applies an amendment to the stanza for nodal calculation, advising a deduction of 25' from any previously obtained position. This is on account of vrishchika-bhāgāḥ (vrishchika = scorpion and bhāgāḥ = division/organ), suggesting some connecting nodal calculation to the sign of the scorpion.
7. Rāhu particularly favours majja-dhatu (nervous system); its drying, cold and erratic influence can quickly impair nervous system functionality.
8. Ketu in his most evolved form is likely to seek moksha.
9. Ketu is frequently associated with unexplained aerial phenomena such as meteors, comets, strange clouds, swarming insects (particularly locusts), coloured haze or pollution, all of which were considered portents of impending disaster.
10. Including plagues, epidemics, fires, war, floods and famine.
11. Ketu is also Moksha Kāraka.
12. More recent research into the authenticity of this work have raised some concerns over content. Conclusion: our current version of BPHS (with unequal houses and Jaimini techniques) may have incorporated later adaptations to the original text, perhaps within the last 500 years.
13. Performance of Sannyasa (a life of renunciation).
14. Due to his smoky nature, any disturbance of dosha is mainly through the vitiation of Vāta.
15. Gulik is likened to a swallowed pill that acts with great speed, or a lethal projectile.

PART II

RASHIS, THE ZODIAC AND THE SYMBOLISM OF THE TWELVE SIGNS

11

— RASHIS (Zodiacal Signs) —

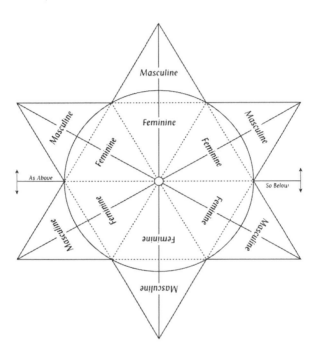

The twelve signs beginning from Aries are respectively (Aries) red, (Taurus) white, (Gemini) the colour of the parrot, (Cancer) the colour of Patali/dattura, (Leo) black and white, (Virgo) variegated in colour, (Libra) black, (Scorpio) of a golden colour, (Sagittarius) the colour of paddy husk, (Capricorn) white and red, (Aquarius) the colour of the mongoose and (Pisces) the colour of fish.

Brihat Jataka by Varāhamihira

Within the visual chaos of the heavens there resides a coherent mythos, one firmly rooted in a twelve-fold division. This mathematical/geometrical division is not something haphazard, but reflects the inherent or rather the unique twelveness associated with circles.

It is a mathematical fact that circles are geometrically entwined about the number six. A hexagram whose sides are of equal length (see diagram) will nest its six points perfectly and equidistantly within that circle. When the opposing points are then joined, they become the circle's diameter and form six equilateral triangles. When each triangle is reflected 180° outward and its points connected, the radius of the circle can be divided equally into twelve. This relationship between circles, 6s and 12s had been explored by Archimedes in his quest for π (the ratio of a circle's circumference to its diameter). Noting the relationship of hexagons to circles, he was able to compute the lower and upper bounds of π by continuing to double its sides until reaching 96, eventually yielding the well-known formula $\pi = 3.142$ with the reductional numerology of $96 = (9+6 = 15, 1+5) = 6$.

11.1 ZODIACAL SYMBOLISM

The word *zodiac* is based on the Greek *zōidion*, meaning animal signs, and *kuklos*, meaning circle. The Latin word for 'circle of animal signs' is therefore *zodiacus*.

Animals were fervently worshipped by a great many ancient civilisations, featuring heavily in the myths and symbolism of magical arts. The zodiac in this regard is no exception, having seven of its twelvefold divisions dominated by animals: the ram, bull, crab, lion, scorpion, crocodile and fish. Its three humanistic elements are characterised by the twins, a virgin and water-bearer, with an eleventh and liminal being the Sagittarian centaur. The final division is given over to a man-made contrivance, that of the merchant scales.

The zodiacal sequence is:

1. Ram	2. Bull	3. Twins	4. Crab	5. Lion	6. Virgin
7. Merchant's Scales	8. Scorpion	9. Centaur	10. Crocodile	11. Water-Bearer	12. Fishes

Iconography of the zodiacal signs clearly mirrors seasonal cycles in the northern hemisphere, their sequence locked to that yearly changing landscape. Fifteen hundred years ago +/–, when sidereal and tropical zodiac coincided, these descriptions held good for both models. Due to precession of the equinoxes, sidereal and tropical zodiacs continue to become more disparate with the passage of time. Jyotish is firmly sidereal (based upon stars) and so no longer bound to earth's seasons; however, it's still worth taking some note of their seasonal echo. The following is a short précis of a tropical transition through the twelve zodiacal signs.

- Aries signifies the start of the yearly cycle (spring equinox), youth and the next generation.

- Taurus sees a return of cattle to pasture and a heightening of fertility.

- Summer and early monsoon constellations signify Sûrya's dualistic Geminian motion, first moving northward toward the summer solstice followed by its retrogressive southern retreat.

- This latterly 'backward' motion was thought indicative of a crab's movement (Cancer).

- Late monsoon and early autumn constellations signify the escalation of heat, initially humid then drying; portrayed by a fearsome lion (Leo).[1]

- Early autumn and the harvest are aptly portrayed by a virgin (Virgo) reaper with an ear of corn in her hand.

- Late autumn marks the equilibrium of days (autumnal equinox), symbolised by the balancing scales of Libra.

- Pre-winter sees fruits begin to sour and ferment, signifying suppuration, sickness and poison, represented by the venomous stinger of the scorpion (Scorpio).

- With the falling of leaves comes the season of hunting and the bow of the archer (Sagittarius), ensuring survival through the harsh winter months ahead.

- Capricorn marks both an end to the shortening of days at the winter solstice and the Sun's re-birth; rising slowly in the skies, appearing metaphorically 'to climb the mountain'. Capricorn's iconography is a fusion of goat (agile and tenacious), fish (streamlined and unbounded) and crocodile (long-lived and amphibious).

- The winter constellation of Aquarius (water-bearer) symbolises a time of conservation, metering one's resources through the season of hardship.

- The zodiacal sequence is completed by the appearance of the sign Pisces, ending winter's deadlock with the return of warmth and sustenance – afforded by the rivers and seas (seafood/fishes, etc.).

Each zodiacal sign is ruled by a planet and dominated by one of four elements. Each sign also presides over a particular caste and stature, sex[2] and temperament – akin to its symbology.

Although many of the signs' common traits are in basic agreement with one another, there remain multiple levels of sign interpretation. The table represents a general overview of each Rashi and some of its more commonly agreed attributes.

Signs	Characteristics
Sign: Aries *Ruler:* Mars *Symbol:* Ram *Element:* Fire	Masculine and of reddish complexion, its element is fire; its lord is Kuja (Mars). Residing in the deep forest, Mesha is Kṣatriya by caste, its guna is rajas, its symbol a ram. Mesha individuals often display a lean, muscular frame with a thin waist, their head may be broad or bear a prominent scar (usually upon the forehead, temple or cheek). Teeth are often strong and well-set, eyes may be widely set but prone to redness/itchiness. Their temperament is dynamic, excitable, quick acting and decisive, they are often adventurous and enjoying taking (calculated) risks. Prone to feats of martial prowess they excel in sports that require both aggression and strategy. Easily roused to anger or irritation they do not suffer fools gladly. In matters of health they may be prone to diseases involving Pitta dosha, that is, blood, bile, liver and skin. They are also likely to suffer from bouts of neuralgia (temporary paralyses), migraines and skin eruptions such as rashes, boils and acne. Mesha types have a marked tendency to suffer febrile conditions, inflammation (tendonitis), itchiness and muscular strain. *Note:* Later iconographical forms of Mesha[3] portray this deity as human (masculine), ram-headed and seated upon a lotus. Clothed in red garments and adorned with gold, his hands gesture the knowledge mudra.
Sign: Taurus *Ruler:* Venus *Symbol:* Bull *Element:* Earth	Feminine, sensual and of pale complexion, its element is earth, its lord is Shukra (Venus). Residing on grassy land, Vrishabha is Vaiśya in caste; its guna is rajas, its symbol a bull. Those of this Rashi are middling to large in stature, their frames broad and fleshy. Stout of neck and beautiful of eye they are often broad shouldered with well developed musculature. In temperament they are slow and methodical, often tenacious and practical; they have excellent stamina (both physically and mentally). Vrishabha often excels in matters of business, having a sharp memory and cheerful disposition; they are known to have an eye for bargains and a love of acquisition (especially luxurious items). In matters of health they may be prone to diseases that involve Kapha dosha, that is, phlegm and lymph; there may also be a propensity toward respiratory weakness, excess mucus and/or heart conditions. Those born under this sign may also have a marked tendency toward hyper- or hypo-thyroidism, tonsillitis, periodontitis, hearing loss, gout, constipation or injury/accidents to the neck, jaw-bone or teeth. *Note:* Later iconographical forms of Vrishabha portray this deity as human (masculine). Clothed in white and pale of face, his vāhan[4] that of a large white bull. This deity holds a pot of nectar in one hand and mala (rosary) in the other.

Signs	Characteristics
Sign: Gemini *Ruler:* Mercury *Symbol:* Twins *Element:* Air	Neuter in gender, youthful and fickle in nature, with a hue of grass green; its element is air, its lord is Budha (Mercury). Residing in towns and villages, Mithuna's caste is Śūdra; its guna rajas, its symbol twins (one holding a mace, the other a lute). Those of this Rashi are often lighter of frame and slender of hand. Clear in speech with attentive eyes, their temperament is both erratic and animated; their mood highly changeable. Original in thinking, they are highly adaptable and intellectually driven. They may be great conversationalists, talented musicians, writers, orators or poets whilst retaining both cunning and guile. Those of this Rashi are given to notoriety and providence in two distinct areas of life. They are prone to falling foul of fraudsters or deceit (usually over matters of inheritance, investments or tax). Those born under this sign prosper well in the sciences (both theoretical and practical) making excellent engineers, statisticians and inventors. In matters of health they may be prone to diseases of a dryness (Vāta) creating ache and 'moving' pain that lodges deep in the joints and muscles. Chest and lungs (respiratory conditions) may also be an issue; instances of bronchitis or childhood asthma are not uncommon. Other areas of the body likely to accumulate Vāta dosha include: the colon (constipation), shoulders and arms (muscle fatigue), ears (tinnitus), nervous system and the hands (tremors or numbness in the extremities) as well as chapped, itchy or dry skin. *Note:* Later iconographical forms of Mithuna are portrayed as a young couple, the man holding a mace, the female carrying a veena (stringed instrument). Both are clad in green garments.
Sign: Cancer *Ruler:* Moon *Symbol:* Crab *Element:* Water	Feminine, shy and possessive, its hue is a pale red; its element water, its lord is Chandra (the Moon), its residence is in ponds and deep wells. Bulky in frame and many-footed,[5] Karkata is Brahmin caste, its guna is sattva, its symbol a crab. Those born under this sign may appear shorter in stature or larger in the chest area (often with squared shoulders). Their faces are somewhat rounded, the eyes bright with an awkward shyness. Tenacious, reliable and highly communicative, those born under the auspices of this sign are renowned for their great memories, hospitality, fairness and intellect; however, these traits may be equally balanced against bouts of self-obsession, hypochondria and frequent mood swings. Karkata prospers in commerce and social enterprises, frequently found in the catering industry, health, social or caring industries, journalistic or advisory roles. In matters of health they may be prone to Kapha type diseases (phlegmatic) – bronchial congestion, high cholesterol, abdominal bloating, nausea and digestive disorders such as stomach ulcers and hyperacidity. There is a strong lunar component affecting the functionality of the heart; imbalances here often manifest through powerful 'undigested' emotion which may place excess strain upon the circulatory system and additional pressure upon the heart. *Note:* Later iconographical forms of Karkata portray this deity as human (masculine). Red of skin (complexion), he carries a golden ring upon which is displayed a turtle; his vāhan is that of a turtle.

Sign: Leo *Ruler:* Sun *Symbol:* Lion *Element:* Fire	Masculine, regal, proud and of pale complexion, its element is fire, its lord Sûrya (the Sun), its guna is sattva. Four-footed and of warrior caste (Kṣatriya), it resides in mountainous or cavernous areas; its symbol is a lion (bulky, muscular with its head held high). Simha individuals may appear more weighted in the upper frame (broad shouldered), ovular in face with a posture that commands respect. Their eyes (though often reddish) are penetrating yet thoughtful. Those born under this sign are often dynamic, ambitious and warm-hearted but are also given to arrogance or excessive periods of procrastination. Simha Rashi inspires self-confidence and loyalty, finding favour with kings, that is, those individuals who occupy some position of authority/power. They prosper best when pursuing an independent (yet respected) career, often charming their way into people's hearts and minds without needing to say very much. In matters of health, Simha may be prone to conditions of excess Pitta – inflammation, congestive heart conditions, blood/bleeding disorders, hyperacidity (and other digestive weaknesses), recurring rheumatic fever, weakness of vision (cataracts, myopia, macular degeneration, etc.) and/or periods of lowered or weakened immunity largely brought about by stressful intimate or familial relationships. *Note*: Later iconographical forms of Simha portray this deity as human (masculine). His face is that of a lion, his complexion is golden. In one hand he carries a nectar pot; with the other hand he makes the mudra of fearlessness.
Sign: Virgo *Ruler:* Mercury *Symbol:* Young Maiden *Element:* Earth	Feminine, child-like and of fair complexion, its element is earth, its lord is Budha (Mercury). Residing near cultivated lands, its guna is tamas, its caste Vaishya; its symbol is parvatiya (a youthful maiden) holding a sheaf of wheat in one hand, whilst cupping fire in the other. Kanya individuals are inclined toward a taller or leaner frame, often with a slight stoop or drooping shoulders. Their appearance is often athletic, their limbs supple and dexterous but often lacking the aggression and ambition needed to become powerful sportsmen. In their youth they are often painfully shy, over-analytical and over-sensitive with a meticulous sense of inner-order they feel compelled to place upon the outside world. They show a marked ability with languages, literature or mimicry and have a particular love of word-play and humorous stories. This Rashi appears to favour the acting profession; perhaps trying on different personae for size might help it discover its own true identity, or perhaps because Kanya has no strong identity to move out of the way. Other preferred careers may include researcher, scientist, mathematician, physician or diplomat. In matters of health, Kanya may be prone to various nervous disorders or skin conditions; they may also be likely suffer periodic digestive complaints and/or constipation. There is also a marked tendency toward respiratory weakness such asthma, bronchitis, wheezing and other congestive conditions. Overall they have a marked interest in matters of health and wellbeing and, although not the most constitutionally strong of signs, may be able to live a relatively long and healthy life due to their ability to exercise moderation in all their daily living habits. *Note*: Later iconographical forms of Kanya portray this deity as human (feminine). Pale in complexion and clad in autumn colours, she is seated upon a lotus holding the bud of a lily.

Signs	Characteristics
Sign: Libra *Ruler:* Venus *Symbol:* Merchant's Scales *Element:* Air	Masculine, idealistic, changeable and sensual, its element is air, its lord Shukra (Venus). Tula resides in the marketplace of towns and cities; its guna is rajas, its caste Śūdra, its complexion black, its symbol the scales of a merchant. Those of this Rashi are of medium yet well proportioned frames, their eyes small and their forehead broad. Handsome of feature, the nose is often prominent, the skin fair. Connoisseurs of all things luxurious, they naturally gravitate toward beauty, art and music; loved by opposite sex, they often encounter their greatest challenges in relationships, giving their all (energies) to the other and expecting undivided attention, recognition and tacit adulation in repayment. Classical texts sometimes ascribe a judgemental and violent nature to this sign, lurking just below its veneer, sharply contrasted against a sympathetic and sensitive exterior. Like the merchant's scales their persona shifts somewhere between the two extremes. Tula individuals fare well in travel and in the trading of goods and services, taking a special interest in land (property) and conveyancing, furniture and fine clothing. In matters of health, Tula may have a tendency to suffer problems of the lower back, skin, kidneys, bladder, urinary tract and spine, as well as pancreatic (diabetic) conditions, renal calculi, nephritis and diseases involving the body's water/sugar metabolism. *Note:* Later iconographical forms of Tula portray this deity as human (masculine). Youthful, red-eyed and pale in complexion, he carries a pair of scales in his arms.
Sign: Scorpio *Ruler:* Mars *Symbol:* Scorpion *Element:* Water	Feminine, reclusive and defensive; its forepart is sharp, its body slender. Vrishchika's element is water, its lord Kuja (Mars), its residence (on land and in the water) is holes or cavities. Its guna is tamas, its caste Brahmin. Multi-footed, its symbol is that of a scorpion, its hue a reddish-brown. Those of this Rashi are of a medium to tall build, broad of face and dark of complexion. Strong jointed, muscular and fearless of eye – Vrishchika is the eighth sign, the form of the character 8 revealing a circulatory process from low to high levels; the eighth house also resonates with some weighty significations such as: death, occult/magical arts, legacies, poisons, seduction and sex, rebirth and transformation. Somewhat renowned for their inexhaustible thoroughness, those of this Rashi are well noted for their tenacity, single-mindedness and acridity. These traits are matched only by their ability to accrue an impressive list of enemies. Their dictatorial mannerisms and romantic escapades have earned them a reputation of becoming the sign most ready to engage in 'secret crimes'. Periodically they vanish from sight, only to reappear in the most unexpected places looking none the worse for wear or forthcoming with an explanation. In matters of health, those of this Rashi may be inclined to incur ailments of the urino-generative organs, such as: renal calculi, bladder infections, fistula, haemorrhoidal conditions, cystitis and venereal disease. In addition there may be a likelihood of lower back pain (sciatica), menstrual problems and autointoxication (alcohol or other chemical stimulants). *Note:* Later iconographical forms of Vrishchika portray this deity as human (masculine). Tawny in complex, his eyes are dark. In his hands he carries mala and a jar of wine, his vāhan is that of a scorpion.

Sign: Sagittarius *Ruler:* Jupiter *Symbol:* Centaur/ Bow *Element:* Fire	Considered favourite of Brahmā, it is masculine and fiery, its lord is Brihaspati (Jupiter). Resident in cities and/or military posts, its guna is sattvá, its caste Kṣatriya. Its form is that of a centaur bearing a bow. Its hue is pale; it resides in the east and is said to 'wander the Earth'. Those of this Rashi often display a well-developed physique, are long of nose, and fair of face with pronounced 'bushy' eyebrows. Generous and reliable, Dhanus is considered free-spirited, honest and god-fearing, desiring nothing more than straightforwardness in their dealings. Diligent and methodical in temperament they are often noted to rise quickly in any chosen profession. They may be adaptive, cheerful and philosophical in outlook, pushing themselves to far-flung places to experience a wide variety of social situations in a quest for greater truth. Physically they often show great prowess in sports or excel in the arts (including music), yet at the same time abhor external showiness or hypocrisy. The negative face of Dhanus often manifests as a kind of impatience or recklessness; surfacing if forced to endure sustained prosaic environments, goading them to adopt an argumentative or preachy persona. In health matters, they may be inclined toward conditions of vitiated Pitta, that is, circulatory/blood-related diseases such as tetanus (blood poisoning), arteriolosclerosis, gout, thrombosis, strokes (internal haemorrhaging), rheumatic fevers and varicose veins. Other areas of susceptibility include injuries to the hip area (usually from a fall), sciatica, temporary paralysis (usually in the extremities), liver and gallbladder disturbances as well as pancreatic imbalances. *Note:* Later iconographical forms of Dhanus portray this deity as human (masculine) and horse-headed, armed with a bow. Clothed in yellow fabrics, his posturing indicates a readiness to fight.
Sign: Capricorn *Ruler:* Saturn *Symbol:* Sea Monster *Element:* Earth	Feminine, variegated of colour, strong-willed, ambitious and seemingly invincible, its front part is quadruped (crocodile) walking upon the Earth, its tail (a fish) glides effortlessly through water – a symbology that hints at extremes. Its element is earth, its lord is Shani (Saturn), it resides in dark forests and watery places, its guna is tamas, its caste Vaishya. Classic descriptions of this Rashi often portray it as large and unwieldy, though in truth it tends toward the slender or taller-framed individual. The constitution of Makara becomes more robust with age, having a distinct Saturnine quality of looking much older than its actual years (in youth) yet appearing more graceful with the advance of years. Those of this Rashi are often coarse-haired and dark of eye, pale of hue; their foreheads and teeth are somewhat pronounced. These may be highly self-reliant and motivated people, often intellectual and having some distinct acumen (or sparkle) for business, economics and politics; particularly masterful for their quick appraising of workflow, current trends and statistics. Craving financial security they work tirelessly and efficiently to build their nest/empire; always wary of their prize being snatched away from them at any time, they aggressively guard their stockpile. In matters of health they often fall prey to airy (Vāta) diseases such as constipation, arthritis, paralysis, rheumatism, dental decay, sciatica, osteoporosis and abdominal distension. Other nagging complaints include knee injury, inflammation of the small joints, carpal-tunnel syndrome, eczema, psoriasis (dry skin conditions) and cataracts. *Note:* Later iconographical forms of Makara portray this deity as human (masculine). His face is that of a deer, his garments dark green. Seated upon a crocodile, he carries a pot of nectar and mala.

Signs	Characteristics
Sign: Aquarius *Ruler:* Saturn *Symbol:* Water-Bearer *Element:* Air	Masculine, future-orientated and progressive, its element is air, its ruler Shani (Saturn). Kumbha resides in villages; its guna is tamas, its caste Śūdra, its symbolism often represented by a masculine figure cradling a pitcher of water. Those of this Rashi tend toward a taller and leaner frame, yet are of strong constitution being strong-jointed with prominent arteries. Their faces may favour a distinctly rounded or broad appearance, their eyes fixed (staring) yet mild; hair may be dark, coarse and thick. Renowned for idealism and humanitarianism (selfless service), those of Kumbha strive to be loyal, rational and inventive, preferring the 'alternative route' or at least an unconventional viewpoint. Often outspoken and of good education, their minds are sharp, focused and practical, drawn to scientific/electro-mechanic careers that aim to unburden mankind from their drudgery and/or social inequalities. Kumbha individuals seem to display a predilection toward the eccentric[6] or unpredictable, sometimes appearing quite confrontational, aggressive and/or rebellious. These traits often culture a reputation of their being tactless, non-conformist or self-interested when in truth they perceive their inner mission is to free mankind from his bonds, even if his release might be painful. In matters of health, Kumbha are prone to circulatory conditions such as arterial hardening, numb extremities, water retention, itchy skin and impeded recovery from infections or complications arising from injuries/ wounds. Other prominent conditions include: damage to cartilage, tendons and muscular tearing, severe cramping, dental infections, gum disease and prolapsed gums. Tooth decay and/or throat infections such as tonsillitis, adenoids and thyroid instabilities are other conditions that tend to plague their wellbeing. *Note:* Later iconographical forms of Kumbha portray this deity as human (masculine), reptilian in features, his garments are dark. His vāhan is a sea monster and in his hands he busily empties a large pot of water.
Sign: Pisces *Ruler:* Jupiter *Symbol:* Fishes *Element:* Water	Feminine, reserved, orthodox, intuitive and dualistic; its element is water, its ruler Brihaspati. Meena resides in watery places. Its guna is sattva, its caste Brahmin, its symbol is a two-headed fish (that share a single tail).[7] They are often fair of complexion, wider or rounded in frame, average in height with a slight protruding belly. Faces may be lustrous, their eyes mild and caring. Noted for a sympathetic and compassionate nature, Meena are often amenable, artistic, musical, kind-natured and receptive people; impelled 'to do good' for the world but also suffering extended periods of stagnation, indecision or inner malaise. Often prone to 'losing the thread' or being led astray, they naturally gravitate toward 'enigmatic' dominant characters or they themselves become entrenched in religious escapism and/or superstition. Troublesome 'romantic' interludes or (bouts of) obsessive greed/jealousy are classic traits experienced by those born under this Rashi. Inclined to travel, they revel in cultural history, are skilled diplomats and most adept at integrating the customs and religions of other cultures. If driven to a trade they may gravitate toward liquid commodities such as oils, scents, medicines or spirits. In matters of health, the constitution of Meena may be prone to ailments of a Kapha nature – congestion, catarrh, stomach mucosa (nausea), high cholesterol, lipoma and an encumbered lymph system. Other conditions may include: oedema, gout, chilblains, itchiness/urticaria, watery swellings, weak ankles, poor circulation (especially the feet) and tendencies toward addiction, particularly alcohol or sugars. *Note:* Later iconographical forms of Meena portray this deity as human (masculine), large-bellied and emerald-coloured. His face is that of a fish, his vāhan are two great fishes (possibly sea monsters).

11.2 ATTRIBUTES OF RASHIS

Attributes / Rashis	Energetic	Guna	Stature	Orientation and Direction	Partiality and Colouration	Disposition
Mesha	Movable	Rajas	Quadruped	Back East	Nocturnal Red	Krūra Mobile
Vrishabha	Fixed	Rajas	Quadruped	Back South	Nocturnal White	Sâumya Stable
Mithuna	Dual	Rajas	Biped	Dual West	Nocturnal Green	Krūra Spacious
Karkata	Movable	Sattva	Crawling	Back North	Nocturnal Pale Red	Sâumya Aqueous
Simha	Fixed	Sattva	Quadruped	Head East	Diurnal White	Krūra Ferocious
Kanya	Dual	Tamas	Biped	Head South	Diurnal Variegated	Sâumya Nourishing
Tula	Movable	Rajas	Biped	Head West	Diurnal Black	Krūra Harmonising
Vrishchika	Fixed	Tamas	Crawling	Head North	Diurnal Terracotta	Sâumya Vitiating
Dhanus	Dual	Sattva	Quadruped	Back East	Nocturnal Tawny	Krūra Vitalising
Makara	Movable	Tamas	Quadruped/ Aquatic	Back South	Nocturnal Variegated	Sâumya Endurance
Kumbha	Fixed	Rajas	Biped	Head West	Diurnal Dark Brown	Krūra Accelerating
Meena	Dual	Sattva	Aquatic	Dual North	Diurnal Blue-silver	Sâumya Emolliating

Energetic: Each sign displays one of three qualities: *Chara* (movable), *Sthira* (fixed) or *Dvisvabhāva/Misra* (dual or mixed). Chara represents dynamic, forward motion and restless energy, overflowing with the impetus to re-shape and change. Sthira represents the power and will to resist change, preserving and protecting traditions and the status quo. Dvisvabhāva falls somewhere between the two previous states, having more of an oscillatory quality.

Guna: One of three primal states of matter; these are *Sattva*, *Rajas* and *Tamas*. Each performs a vital function and supports the creative process. Sattva encourages development and intelligence; it facilitates clarity, harmony and growth toward self-awareness. Rajas is both a dispersive and distractive force, driven by the need to satiate desires; although direct and motivated, it is also aggressive, forceful and turbulent in nature. Tamas represents inertia, degeneration and darkness; its presence creates weight, dullness and obstruction. Ultimately Tamas paves the way for new growth, providing decay from which new life may emerge.

Stature: Tentatively offered here as bipedal (human), quadruped (animal), aquatic (fish/shellfish) or crawling (insect). These categories are often used to identify/interpret the manner or means of agents. These distinctions are more relevant to such branches of astrology as *Prasna* (questioning) and *Mhurta* (timing).

Orientation: This particular criterion may have partly contributed to the misnomer that the constellations (star patterning) and Rashis iconography are analogous to one another. Sign orientation is therefore not to be considered an accurate account of star configuration (as these seldom resemble one another); instead, orientation is best considered as the momentum displayed by Rashis, that is, *śirodaya* (head-rising) = single minded, progressive future orientated and driven, *pṛṣṭodaya* (feet-rising) = cautious, conservative, broody and introspective. Mithuna (Gemini) and Meena (Pisces) fall into the category of *Ubhayodaya* (dual-natured), the iconography of the former already aligned to twins and the latter traditionally depicted as the single body of a fish bearing two heads. Astrological seers of old appear to have concluded that either energetic (head or back rising) was likely to befall those born under the auspices of these Rashis. *Note:* Some astrologers consider Mithuna to belong to the head-rising category.

Direction: Confers each of the cardinal directions upon the movable signs: Aries = East, Capricorn = South, Libra = West and Cancer = North. Remaining signs *of the same element* follow in sequence: East = Leo/Sagittarius (fire), South = Taurus/Virgo (earth), West = Gemini/Aquarius (air) and North = Scorpio/Pisces (water). Again, these distinctions were and are more relevant to such branches of astrology as Prasna (questioning) and Mhurta (timing).

Partiality: Rashis may favour nocturnal hours (ruled by the Moon) or diurnal hours (ruled by the Sun). Nocturnal Rashis are: Aries, Taurus, Gemini, Cancer, Sagittarius and Capricorn. The remainder (Leo, Virgo, Libra, Scorpio, Aquarius and Pisces) favour the daytime.[8] If the opposite situation is encountered, the 'strength' of each Rashi is to be accordingly adjusted. For example, Mesha – known to be *Krura* ('cruel', that is, bearing more hardship and propagating confrontation) – will have his cruelty exacerbated if found to occupy the hours of daylight. Conversely Pisces – known to be *Subhadra* (auspicious in nature, preserving peaceful relations and promoting health) – will become less so if found to occupy nocturnal hours.

Colouration: Another important distinction of Rashi, most relevant to forms of astrology such as Mhurta and/or Prasna. Determination of colours was often used to discover the hidden location of lost property, identify physical complexion, propitiate deity or help select balancing colours for imbalanced dosha.

Disposition: Rashis are said to be Sâumya (mild/tender/auspicious) or Krūra (cruel/harsh).

The following are also to be considered:

- Aries: restless and invigorating, adventurous and pioneering.

- Taurus: promotes stability, a strong foundation, determination or long-term support.

- Gemini: openness, inspiration, growth/expansion and the desire for change.

- Cancer: that which is connected to water, that is, rain, lakes, rivers, irrigation and so on.

- Leo: courage, victory and honour, reigning unchallenged.

- Virgo: replenish and recuperate, heal all wounds.

- Libra: mediation and consolidation, the pooling of resources and profits.

- Scorpio: imbalances, fomentation, suppuration, evacuation of toxins.

- Sagittarius: renewed strength, innovation and journeying (free-spirited).

- Capricorn: lamentation and solace, the conservation of resources, longevity.

- Aquarius: future orientated and socially progressive, ushering in new eras.

- Pisces: softening and ease of transition, in anticipation of vicissitude.

11.3 HOROSCOPE STYLES

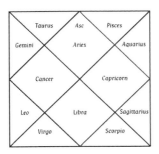 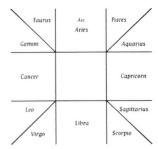

Popular horoscope styles: North (left), South (middle) and East Indian (right).

- *North Indian style:* Displays houses (see Chapter 12) but no fixed position of signs. Each Rashi occupies the ascendant marked by *Asc* for a period of two hours, moving in a clockwise fashion. In the example pictured, Aries (Mesha) occupies the ascendant, the next sign to occupy in sequence will be Taurus (Vrishabha), and so on. The North Indian style is *house-orientated*, placing great emphasis upon the positions of Kendra (central diamond shape). This represents the all-important 1st, 4th, 7th and 10th houses. Kendras are then hemmed at their periphery by eight additional (and supportive) astrological houses, here represented by smaller triangles.[9]

- *South Indian style:* Displays signs but no fixed position of house. Each of the 12 squares (or boxes) permanently retains its zodiacal sign, whilst the ascendant, marked this time by a diagonal line, moves clockwise; here again the ascendant sign is Aries. The South Indian format also affords greater ease in rectifying charts. When rectifying, zodiacal signs are permanently placed in the chart. Most planets are likely to remain in the same sign for 24 hours (except the Moon), thus the ascendant sign can be moved rapidly around the chart to gain alternate perspectives in determining the correct ascendant.

- *East Indian style:* Graphically similar to the North Indian style, this design also favours fixed houses and prominent Kendra. Again, each Rashi occupies the ascendant marked by Asc for a period of two hours, moving in a clockwise fashion.

While all styles have merit and are encouraged to be committed to memory, it is not an absolute requirement. In truth, most astrologers show preference for one particular style of horoscope. It has been the author's observation that many Western astrologers migrating to Jyotish often favour the South Indian style.

NOTES

1. Denebola (β Leonis) or the tail of the royal lion is described by Al Bīrūnī as 'turning the heat of summer away with its rising and forewarning of the cold's return with its disappearance.'
2. Puruṣa Rashi = masculine signs, Strī Rashi = feminine signs.
3. Iconography of Rashis as given by Caturvarga-chintāmani by Himādri (13th century AD).
4. Vāhan = vehicle (mode of transportation).
5. Crabs are decapods (literally 'having ten appendages'). Those born under this Rashi (Karkata) are noted to display a slight rolling gait which disposes them to side-stepping a little, not unlike a crab.
6. In some instances Rāhu is said to co-rule this sign; hence its reputation to be eccentric and unpredictable.
7. Also described as tethered fishes swimming in separate directions.
8. Sequence taken from *Phaladeepika* by Mantresvara 1st Adhyaya.
9. The use of North and East Indian styles of horoscope gained some prominence during the medieval Islamic period in Europe.

12

BHĀVAS
—— (Astrological Houses) ——

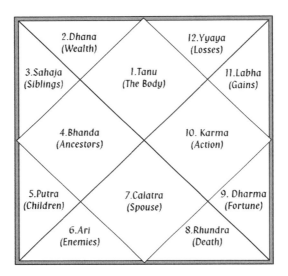

Construction of astrological houses, also known as *domification*, can be a complex affair, with differing thoughts on how best to apportion their twelve-fold division. Bhāvas (Sanskrit for 'house'[1]) are after all the critical framework within which all events and activities are set to unfold. Though the interpretation of Bhāvas remains fairly consistent in Jyotish, their calculation and apportionment do not, so it is worth investing a little time to review the various options.

It should also be kept in mind that horoscopes (like any map) are two-dimensional representations of three-dimensional spaces, seeking only to convey a 'sense' of something vast and highly detailed.[2] To this end the following hopefully simplifies the process of *bhāva madhya* (house apportionment).

The three most popular house systems in Jyotish are: *Rashi Chakra*, *Bhāva Chakra* and Śrīpati Bhāva.

Note: Somewhat akin to the Ayanāṃśa quandary outlined in Part I, Bhāva calculation can be another area of astrology that receives a broad brush-stroke, largely because both topics at their core share some points of commonality.[3]

12.1 RASHI CHAKRA

Rashi Chakra sample: Wheel style overlaid on North Indian horoscope[4] clearly showing Rashi and house to be synonymous.

The most traditional and common method of house apportionment is called *Rashi Chakra* (or whole sign chart). This approach simply determines the sign (currently intersecting the eastern horizon) to be the first house. This sign is then referred to as *Lagna*; its lord becoming the all important Lagna lord (or the planet most indicative to the person's fortunes). Whatever the degree of the sign rising or planets within its 30° span, be it 1° or 29°, all are considered to be occupying the 1st house.

In our Rashi Chakra sample the sign Gemini is rising at 9° 16'; its Lagna lord *Mercury/Me* occupies the sign Virgo at 4° 15' (in the 4th house). The middle portion of Gemini is marked (as are all signs) to indicate the *cuspal point*; a cusp here being defined as 'the high point of a jaw, a tip of a canine tooth or the apex point of a leaf.' The cusp therefore is the degree of maximum 'bite' or discharge of house energy. When constructing charts using this method, all house cusps are located at 15° of the occupying sign.

This common, and in some respects simplistic, method of division ties Rashi to house, making them synonymous in terms of their 30° allotment. Rashi Chakra may be erected at any latitude or location and is employed by all Jyotishi in some capacity. *Note:* House cusps are interpreted differently in Western Astrology.[5]

12.2 BHĀVA CHAKRA

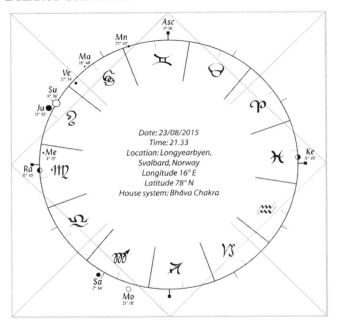

Bhāva Chakra sample: Here the rising degree becomes the cuspal point of the 1st house; successive houses commence 15° either side of this point (note the disparity between the centre of Rashi and house cusp).

Bhāva Chakra is an alternative method of house calculation, one which gives precedence to the degree of the rising sign, making it the cuspal point; that is, 15° either side of this degree becomes the 1st house. Any planet/s falling beyond 15° of the ascendant/cuspal point are deemed to occupy adjacent houses.

In our Bhāva Chakra sample, Gemini is still rising at 9° 16' but now the cusp of each house relocates to 9° 16' of all signs. *Note:* Venus (positioned at 27° 14' Cancer) now relocates from the 2nd house (as seen in the previous Rashi Chakra) to the 3rd house, as does Māndi 27° 20' Gemini, moving from the 1st to the 2nd house. Planets falling close to 15° of the cuspal point are considered especially potent and likely to perform with some notoriety during their dasha or sub-dasha periods (see Chapter 22). In this horoscope both Sun and Saturn reside extremely close to cuspal points, therefore their effects become pronounced in the overall horoscope analysis.

12.3 ŚRĪPATI BHĀVA

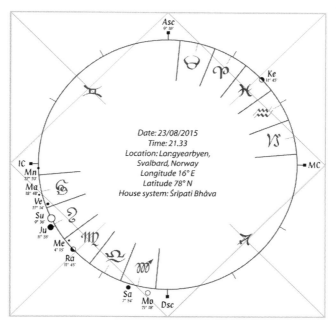

Śrīpati Bhāva sample: Illustrates geocentric (or unequal) houses, highlighting the distortion of Rashi at greater latitude (case in point – Svalbard, Norway). Key: Udaya Lagna/ascendant (Asc), Madhya Lagna/mid-heaven (MC), Asta Lagna/descendant (Dsc) and Pātāla Lagna/nadir (IC).

Like Bhāva Chakra, Śrīpati[6] Bhāva defines the ascendant degree as first house cusp but also introduces a mid-heaven or *MC* (medium coeli). This is then used to determine the cusp of the 10th house.

The mid-heaven is reckoned from a north/south meridian[7] passing through one's zenith and intersecting the ecliptic, a point known as *Madhya Lagna* or middle horoscope. This effectively becomes the cusp of the 10th house. The space between Lagna (ascendant degree) and 10th house cusp is then trisected to create the 11th and 12th house cusps. The descendant or 7th house cusp[8] (marked *Dsc*) naturally falls 180° opposite the ascendant. The 4th house cusp or *nadir* marked by IC (imum coeli) falls 180° opposite the MC. The resulting quarters are again trisected to create the remaining six house cusps. This methodology of house division is aptly referred to as a quadrant system.

The failing of quadrant systems (and those of a similar ilk) is that in a vast majority of cases the 'subject in question' is unlikely to have been born exactly upon the equator and so Ascendant and MC will seldom be perpendicular to one another. While Rashi Chakra confines itself to the ecliptic plane, Śrīpati attempts to unite ecliptic and equatorial planes, the end result of which is the distortion of Rashi and the apparent distribution of house cusps therein. The closer one moves toward either pole the more pronounced this effect becomes; in our Śrīpati Bhāva sample this ascendant degree shows three house cusps falling into a disproportionate Gemini, while the signs Taurus, Cancer, Virgo, Scorpio, Capricorn and Pisces are devoid of house cusps altogether.

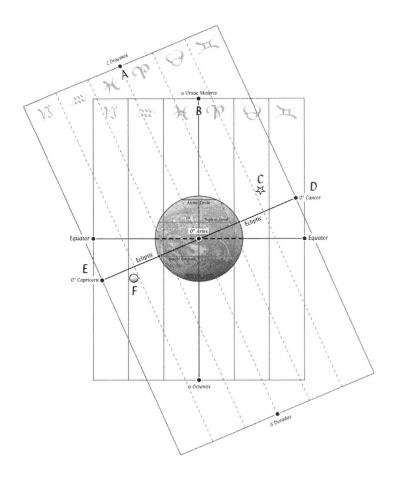

The diagram helps illustrate how the ecliptic plane (A) and equatorial plane (B) are at variance with one another; except at their points of common reference: 0° Aries/0° Libra (tropical).

Here (C) = Yogatârâ, (D) = 0° Cancer, (E) = 0° Capricorn and (F) a planet. Is the Yogatârâ early Gemini or late Taurus? Is the planet late Capricorn or early Aquarius? This conflict arises from a meshing of the ecliptic and equatorial plane. The reader may now start to imagine themselves at varying latitudes, witnessing the ensuing astrological chaos as they climb steadily toward either pole. Note that the stars ζ Draconis and δ Doradus are the brightest and closest candidates for Ecliptic Pole Stars.

Note: Quadrant systems automatically give precedence to mid-heaven, descendant and nadir yet, interestingly, descendant and nadir are seldom considered in any astrological portrait, raising the question: Why is the mid-heaven awarded such high status? Additionally (and in fairness to quadrant systems) the distortion of Rashis lessens at latitudes of less than 40° north or south of the equator or in those horoscopes of greater latitude where the ascendant degree is close to 0° Aries/Libra (tropical).

12.4 CONCLUSION

Rashi Chakra is the most traditional method of house analysis and favoured by most (if not all) Vedic astrologers. On occasion this method may be preferred to the exclusion of all others. Horoscopes erected using this system of house apportionment are noted to give reliable results, *regardless of locale or latitude*, as the plane of one's birthplace is in perfect synchronisation with the plane of the ecliptic.

Use of Bhāva Chakra has become increasingly popular of late, yet is still primarily viewed as a *mathematical variant* of Rashi Chakra. Some astrologers place great emphasis upon its inclusion in any astrological analysis, proclaiming the former to be incomplete without the benefits of Bhāva Chakra's fine-tuning.

Use of unequal house systems (such as Śrīpati) appears to be a later addition to Bhāva techniques,[9] becoming popular with south India astrologers.[10] For the most part, geographical houses form the bulk of preferred domification techniques in Western Astrology and branches of neo-eastern astrology,[11] seeking to unite the traditions. In the final analysis it is proposed here that all techniques founded upon the meshing of ecliptic and celestial equator are both philosophically and *astr*-ologically unsound as Jyotish is founded upon fixed stars, signs and planets. It is therefore hard to fathom why zodiacal signs or houses are so readily distorted to conform to celestial considerations after so much effort had been made to detail the courses and positions of tārāgraha relative to the zodiac and asterisms (see Chapter 25). The use of unequal houses does seem to abandon the ancients' maxim: 'As above, so below.'

Note: For those wishing to further explore the topics sketched out in this section, readers are encouraged to obtain a copy of *The Elements of House Division* (Holden 1977), which is perhaps one of the few critical astrological works that focuses its attention solely on the diversity of house systems, exploring their techniques, merits and shortcomings.

NOTES

1. One literal translation might also be a 'state of being'.
2. One of the great criticisms levelled at astrology by astronomers is its interpretation of data perceived in the heavens. They ask why planets are represented as being strung out along the ecliptic when in reality most planetary orbits cross the ecliptic. Zodiacal signs are similar, being shrunk back to 9° above and below the ecliptic. Vedic Astrology partly addresses positional astronomy when considering Graha Yuddha, whereby planetary declination becomes paramount.
3. Both Ayanāṃśa and Bhāva calculations highlight Earth's axial tilt relative to the ecliptic plane. As the Earth provides the vantage point for stellar observations our position appears eternally fixed, yet early astrologers/astronomers had noted Earth's instability via its wandering pole star and slipping solstices.
4. As far as I am aware, only Sri Jyoti Star software (see Resources) offers this highly useful graphic facility, clearly delineating house, sign and cusp therein.
5. The commencement of the house is taken to be its cusp, so the end of the preceding house signifies the cuspal point of the following.
6. Śrīpati is generally recognised as a prominent Indian mathematician and astrologer (c. 11th century AD). His treatises include *Śrīpatipaddhati*, *Śrīpatiya* and *Siddhānta Śekhara*.
7. Celestial Meridian or geographic arc of longitude that passes through the celestial poles, zenith and nadir – relative to the viewer's location upon the Earth.
8. Also known as *Asta-lagna*.
9. Although descriptions of a quadrant house system is given in *BPHS* Vol. 5, it is thought to be a later addition into what remains of the ancient classical work. Mention of Madhya Lagna and its calculation are also made in *Siddhānta Śiromani*, a 12th century astronomical classic reportedly written by Bhāskara (II).
10. Śrīpati himself is believed to have been resident in southern India.
11. See Krishnamurti Paddhati, also known as KP Astrology, etc.

13

BHĀVAKĀRAKA
—— (House Significations) ——

Note: This chapter is a continuation of the information presented in Chapter 3 on Kāraka.

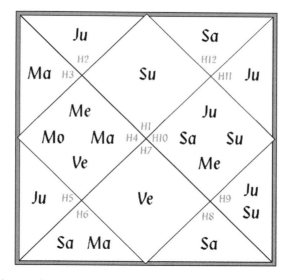

Bhāvakāraka key: Sun (Su), Moon (Mo), Mars (Ma), Mercury (Me), Jupiter (Ju), Venus (Ve) and Saturn (Sa), Houses (H) 1–12. With the exception of Moon (4th house), all planets hold Bhāvakāraka status for at least two houses, and in some cases five; any assessment of houses should reflect their strengths and weaknesses.

Here we explore *Bhāvakāraka* or house significations and their myriad of meanings. Analysis of any *house* represents an exploration into their fields of activity, or, more simply put, that area of life most likely to be influenced by their activation. Regardless of houses being tenanted by planets (or not), the sign and its lord therein similarly act as a dispenser of that house's energetics – for the two hours of their transition in any 24-hour period. This temporary status is referred to as *anitya* and simply confers the significations of that particular house upon its tenanting sign and lord, so for example if a horoscope happens to be ascendant Pisces, Jupiter would be considered Kāraka for the 1st (Pisces) and 10th house (Sagittarius).

When assessing ascendant lord strength, astrologers look primarily to the current state of its lord (in this case Jupiter), but would additionally consider the Sun's condition – in a supportive role to the 1st house/ascendant. Sûrya assumes importance here as it is *nitya* or permanent Kāraka for the 1st house. So both planets (Jupiter and Sun) are evaluated in tandem to establish the overall stability of the ascendant/1st house. Likewise, Mars's position as temporary 2nd house ruler (Aries, for a Pisces ascendant) would also be studied to assess the merits of the 2nd house in unison with Jupiter (the latter being permanent Kāraka for the 2nd house), and so on. Please refer to the diagram at the start of this section showing all permanent Bhāvakāraka positioned in their relevant houses.

13.1 NITYA KĀRAKA

Although temporary signs and their lords are nearly always taken to be the more important of the two factors, any detriment projected upon a permanent Kāraka would inevitably weaken their house significations. Additionally, by the law of averages you will often find a permanent Kāraka occupying one of its significating houses. For example, if the ascendant happened to be Leo and Sun was also found to tenant the 1st house, it would signify the 1st house on both counts, that is, as temporary and permanent Kāraka planet. When this happens to be the case, the planet in question can be expected to 'shine' in some way, becoming outstanding in its chosen sphere of influence. Conversely, under heavy affliction or being poorly positioned, a permanent Kāraka is doubly diminished, severely weakening its status in both fields of influence.

Overall, Bhāvakāraka planets bring support and nourishment to their respective houses if well placed and content. Overwhelmed, weakened or agitated, they obscure, starve or subdue the radiance of their signifying house/s. All planets are fully capable of imbuing their Kāraka house/s with potency, boosting delivery of significations. When assessing any house, care should be taken to study the current states and strengths of Nitya Kāraka. For more information of permanent Kāraka see the Bhāvakāraka table.

Table of Bhāvakāraka

Sun	1st	As Kāraka for atman (soul), Sûrya supports the 1st house, showing stamina, individuality, self-determination, self-esteem, pride and the ability to achieve.
	9th	Sun is significator for the house of dharma (right action). When strongly positioned, he delivers faith, endurance and ability to stay on track. Sûrya naturally commands respect, elevates one's social standing and delivers strong-willed or opinionated instructors, helping to propagate an interest in dharma.
	10th	Kāraka for the house of career, Sûrya's state and strength naturally enhance (or limit) one's elevation to their zenith (or tenth house cusp). The Sun widens one's sphere of influence, naturally commanding respect from subordinates and/or co-workers.
Moon	4th	As Kāraka for manas (mind), Moon aptly assumes 4th house signification, indicating mental health and inner contentment. Chandra also signifies home comforts, health and constitution, mental stability, personality, popularity and wealth (all additional and important 4th house significations). In Vedic Astrology, Moon attains the appellation 'special', therefore any affliction to Moon severely compromises the status of the 4th house.
Mercury	4th	As Kāraka for buddhi (intelligence), the state and strength of Mercury is another important factor to the stability of the 4th house. Budha promotes logic, precision, communication skills, travel, ideas, inventiveness, charm and wittiness. Well-placed, he gives health and healing skills, creativity, fame, respect – helping to finding balance between logic (Mercury) and emotion (Moon).
	10th	In forming a 180° axis between 4th and 10th houses, Budha shows his ability to project the mind into the workplace (the 10th house of action). Mercury (if well-positioned) shows academic achievement, professionalism, business acumen and long-term business ventures. Less than favourable or afflicted, Mercury may manifest itself through procrastination, instability, timidity, restless mental activity, immature behaviour or confused speech/ideas.
Mars	3rd	As Kāraka for vikrānta (courage), Mars supports the status of the 3rd house. Well-positioned, he brings physical prowess, competitiveness, victory over obstacles (enemies), energy/vigour and the passion to succeed. The overall state and strength of Kuja will likewise determine these same traits in one's younger siblings.
	4th	Mars as Kāraka of 4th house matters specifically relates to property, that is, investments, landed property/inheritance relating to the mother. Kuja is also noted for his stratagem, technical skill, strength and problem-solving abilities, all of which may be affected by his 4th house signification.
	6th	As Kāraka for ari (hostilities), that is, things in life that force us to fight, the state and strength of Mars is also important for the following: health, ability to overcome disease, avoidance of accidents, injury by weapons, fight or flight, cunning, defeat of enemies, legal aid and avoidance of litigation. If weakened, Kuja may promote the opposite effects. As Mars is a relatively fast-moving planet, his effects on the 6th house bring heat (febrile) and are unexpected and short-lived (e.g. short-term debilitation from health issues).

Jupiter	2nd	As Kāraka for sampatti (good fortune), Jupiter is sole significator for the 2nd house. His state and strength help promote attributes such as happy formative years, familial support, earnings, credibility, integrity and overall prosperity.
	5th	As putra Kāraka, Jupiter is again sole significator of the 5th house, his state and strength presiding over a number of important considerations such as children, creativity and good merit. The 5th house is considered to promote intuition, intelligence and a strong sense of duty; it also aids in spiritual development, successes through ritual as well as foreknowledge of previous lives. If Jupiter state is found to be favourable, all of these significations become fortified.
	9th	Jupiter is also a significator of dharma. If favourably positioned in the 9th he brings luck and good fortune, respect and discrimination. Jupiter commands respect, elevating one's social status and delivering wise and knowledgeable teachers who propagate an interest in the pursuit of dharma.
	10th	As Kāraka for ādhāra (patronage), Jupiter exerts much influence over the 10th house, helping to promote an individual's successes and furtherance in life. Well-placed and content Brihaspati ensures encouragement, promotion and in some cases financial backing (sponsorship). When his position is found to be troubled or lacking, many of these comforts remain veiled or removed from life.
	11th	As Kāraka for lābha (advantage), Jupiter holds sole dominion over our material gains (11th house = 2nd from the 10th). The state and strength of Brihaspati promotes wealth, conveyances, comfort in accommodation, good fortune, influential friends, success of older sibling/s, prominent social circles, involvement in grand schemes and a trusted advisor to kings and others. If Brihaspati is well-suited in a birth chart, the aforementioned are more easily attained.
Venus	4th	As a Kāraka for saukhya (comfort), the state and strength of Venus also helps support the 4th house and its significations. Venus (like Jupiter) is a powerful benefic as well as a great instructor and so naturally flourishes in the 4th house of the mind. Venus also represents shukra dhatu and so supports the immune system and other creative pursuits. Note: Venus is not always used as a Kāraka for the 4th house, but as the 4th signifies vehicles, health, wisdom, the underworld and mineral wealth, Venus as 4th house Kāraka seems worthy.
	7th	As the sole Kāraka of calatra (spouse/partnerships), Venus becomes the most significant graha in determining overall health and longevity of relationships. A well-placed Venus supports partnerships (both personal and business related) as well as marriage. Venus may also be consulted to determine the quality of one's partners that is, physique, mannerisms, fertility, passion and creativity.

Saturn	6th	Saturn is the primary Kāraka of kṣaya (decay/astringency) and as such is also a powerful significator for the 6th house of disease. Unlike Mars (joint Kāraka), Shani represents long-term debility, taking his toll over the years, sometimes a lifetime. Shani represents the body's resistance to wear and tear as well as overall longevity. As Venus meters our 'shukra', that is, shine/lustre, emollition, fullness of tissue, resistance and youthfulness, so is Shani his antithesis, metering our kṣaya (decay), emaciation, discord, dryness and old age.
	8th	As sole Kāraka for rhundra (death) and the 8th house, Saturn is often the most feared of graha. His overall strength and positioning provide insight into a number of his 8th house significations that is, longevity, karma, chronic disease, unearned income (such as inheritance), partner's income, hidden illnesses, loss of vitality, general constitution and ability to retain and assimilate minerals.
	10th	As one of four Kāraka planets, Saturn's signification in 10th house matters reflects an individual's effort and hard work. Well-positioned Shani brings reward through genuine effort, bestowing slower (yet sustained) promotion in the workplace. If ill-disposed, Shani may add drudgery and repetition to any career options, delaying our rise to a position of authority or a situation where lesser tasks may be delegated to younger or less experienced co-workers.
	12th	As sole Kāraka for vyaya (loss) and the 12th house, Shani's signification of all Dussthana (see Chapter 14) houses is complete, these being: 6th (sickness), 8th (death) and 12th (loss). The 12th house has many diverse connotations, ranging from losses to hidden enemies to personal sacrifice, rest, recuperation and worldly renunciation. The 12th similarly has strong agricultural significance, representing the conclusion of growing cycles, seasons and planting. Favourably positioned Shani may assist in bringing long-term life successes and feelings of achievement, or may require you to atone for past wrong-doings. Any conclusions on the benefits and weaknesses of the 12th house should also include a detailed consideration of planet Saturn.

Note: BPHS[1] assigns one planet to each of the houses, these being: Sun (1), Jupiter (2), Mars (3), Moon (4), Jupiter (5), Mars (6), Venus (7), Saturn (8), Jupiter (9), Mercury (10), Jupiter (11) and Saturn (12). Later astrological works from the medieval period such as *Phaladeepika* and *Jātaka Pārijāta* apply the aforementioned Kāraka, with the exception of Venus as Kāraka to the 4th house.

13.2 NAISARGIKA (INNATE KĀRAKA)

Note: The following tables contain a *selection* of popular innate significations for the twelve houses; however, these should in no way be considered exhaustive.

First house significations

Primary	Secondary
Atma, allocation of prāṇa (vitality), appearance, attractiveness, strength, physical body, proportion of limbs, height, stature, head (brain and forehead), self-esteem, confidence, self-expression, imagination, skin and complexion, digestive strength (agnī/fire), longevity, freedom from disease, wisdom, general respect, livelihood, childhood, fame and infamy, honour, personal wealth, character, willpower, temperament, successes and failures, happiness and sorrow, defeat of one's enemies, ability to study, protection from accidents and injury	Deafness and bilious diseases, the stomach, constipation, sleep and insomnia, headache, mental tension, stammering, old age, rate of ageing, quality of hair, ability to work, taking the initiative, place of birth, dreams, dignity, political life, early-life, potential, mode of expression, defamation by others, capacity to enjoy, new ventures, asking questions (querent), Varṇa (caste), gambling and debt, storehouses and gold reserves, accidents, pain tolerance, personal struggles, epic voyages, immediate environment, masculinity, study in temporary accommodation

Second house significations

Primary	Secondary
Wealth (prosperity), daily earnings, family, liquid assets, speech and vocal cords, learning ability, teaching, writing skills, general knowledge, enjoyment, pleasures, appetite, food intake, quality of foods, addictions, truthfulness, lineage, boyhood, the face, mouth and tongue, teeth and eyes (visual acuity right eye), observational power, preference for taste, sense of smell (nose), strength of jaw and neck, determination, self-control, resilience, strength of character, business enemies, winnings/gains through self-effort, misunderstandings, unkind words, profanity and language abilities, second marriage, family life and home security	Adherence to sacred texts, support and being supporting by others, toenails, fingernails, falsehood, reading habits, the written word, writing skills, ability to conceive (female barrenness), strength of progeny, fertility, vigour, semen production (male), copper, gold and silver (metals), precious stones, diamonds and pearls, counsellors, lawyers, bankers, bonds, stocks and shares, loans, mortgages, inheritance, generosity, splendour, clothes, perfumes, one's ardent followers, liberality of mind, horses and trading with friends, fathers associated and business partners, loss of younger siblings, children's professions and worldly attainment

Third house significations

Primary	Secondary
Physical strength (fitness) and temperament, musculature, right ear, arms, shoulders, hands, wrists and palms, younger siblings, vitality, willpower, longevity, courage, fighting, conflict, contests, stratagem, comrades, technical ability, fulfilment of desires, ears (hearing in right ear), hand–eye coordination, dance, movement, acting talent, public performance, pastimes, hobbies, art, musical ability, craftsmanship by one's hand, publications, physical movements/dexterity, daily challenges, obstructions to advancement, rumours, pleasures, freedom of speech, self-presentation, assistance from friends, agreements, signing of contracts, physical health of siblings, transitions, walking, short journeys (by land, air or sea)	Adventures, roads, pathways and wanderings, navigation, diseases of the respiratory tract, throat, feet, nervous system, accidents involving the shoulders, collar bone, arms, hands or wrists, mental instability, evil inclinations, confusion, neighbours and local neighbourhood, a soldier, dreams, casual friends, division of inheritance, the apportionment of wealth, material advancement, profits, godly abode, change of residence, one's personal shrines, servants, vehicles of carriage, buses, trains, carriages, messengers, libraries, post offices, general media, writing, correspondences and publishing, successful short journeys, indecision and technical errors

Fourth house significations

Primary	Secondary
Mother and mother's ancestors, nephews, the mind and self-reflection, education, physical heart, emotional heart, stomach, breast/chest and lungs, one's home environment, general happiness (peace of mind), accumulated savings, secret reserves, home security, wealth, protection of investments, vehicles (conveyances) and travel, mental contentment, one's character, popularity, affluence, private affairs, secret dealings, personal faith, places of public ritual, victories, quality of water, farming, agriculture, crop fertility, land/estates, fixed assets, title deeds, letting of property, tenants, antiques, gardens (ornamental and agricultural), fruitful crops, weather, livestock (especially cows/buffalo), birthplace, inclination to study	Varṇa, quality of clothes, purity of drinking water, milk, spices, perfumes, effective medicines, ambrosia/nectar, divine herbs, blood impurities, heart disease, feeling cold, false allegations, works that promote suffering and sorrow, intellect, sculpture, architecture, promotion of Vedas, abundance, quality of life, psychology and dreams, relaxation and peace of mind, beds (cots), quality and freshness of foods to be ingested, nourishment and transformation of foods and private thoughts, storage of stolen goods, curiosities, temporary accommodation (that is, tents, pavilions, garages, etc.), digging, ground works, construction and subsidence of homes, treasures, digging of wells, mineral wealth and underworld

Fifth house significations

Primary	Secondary
Progeny, intelligence, weakness of mind, mental illness, creativity, fame, higher education, purvapunya (previous good deeds), high morals, artistic endeavours, drama, dance, musical ability, character, pregnancy, undertaking of good work, memory, power of discrimination, physical heart, abdomen, stomach, small intestine, liver and gallbladder, spleen and kidneys, indigestion, means to earn one's living, literature and scholarship, condition of the mind, religious teachings, recitation of mantra (mantra siddhi), ability to give wise counsel, increase of consciousness, good fortune, celebrated actions	Health of children, discretion, storytellers, kings or kings ministers, death of kings, auspicious documents, mantra, yantra, tantra, hymns, ritualistic success, occult powers, foresightedness, wealth accrued through one's spouse, mother's wealth, affairs, seriousness, anger, wrathful actions, greed and over-indulgence, secrets and the reporting of events, deeper learning, romances, foreknowledge of future lives, authorship, love of books, charity and welfare, lotteries, gambling and speculation, distribution of food, contracts with foreigners, social intercourse

Sixth house significations

Primary	Secondary
Health, healing, disease, doctors, surgeons, hospitals, nursing, obstacles, fighting, war and disputes, competitors, accidents, foes, thieves, enmity, enemies, cruelty, ferocity, miserly deeds, debts, slander, wounds, defeat of enemies, worries and mental anguish, poisons, ulcers, six tastes (Āyurveda), digestive capacity, indigestion, strength of Agnī, quarrels with siblings, adopted children, students, sorrows from those that serve (employees), kama (lust), krodha (anger), lobha (greed), moha (infatuation), ahankara (arrogance) and errkha (jealousy), animals/pets, purchase or selling of vehicles, a semi-fruitful house	Injury from weapons/projectiles, calamities, accumulation of phlegm, tumours, boils, smallpox, madness and insanity, falling, lawsuits, pets, boiled rice, respiratory conditions, diseases of the eyes, despised by others, receiving alms (welfare), profits through litigation, duodenal ulcer, physical restraints, urinary ailments, hips, back and waist, pain in the lower back, woods, timber, stone and stone working, favourable results in competitions, punishment, prisons, loss of investment, vices and irregular eating habits, fear of theft, superstitions, death of friends, the loss of spouse or partner

Seventh house significations

Primary	Secondary
Marriage, purity of spouse, victory in love and passion, marital happiness, sexual desires, cohabitation, sangama,[2] business partner/s, business competitors, general relationships, commerce/trade, foreign travel, distant lands and residence in such lands, income from distant lands, memory loss, one's taste in clothing, production of semen and ovum (female), multiple partners, valour, charities, adopted child, sexual union, relationship to the public, diplomacy, honour in foreign lands, travellers, pride, beds (cots), birthplace of spouse, family relationships, social interactions, official status, mixing in society, longevity, loss or dangers to life	Lifelong partners, sateetvama,[3] auspicious pathway, deviation from pathways, music, perfumes, delicious foods, enjoyment of food, royal patronage, pan (betel leaves), eating curd, consumption of milk, cereals and ghee, theft, a description of thieves, desires, the end of disease (cure), social and official interaction, wanderings and the loss of wealth, legal bondage, dowries, cooking with ghee, marital affairs, nuptials, abdomen, urinary tract, kidneys and bladder, large intestine, abdominal bloating, diabetes, uterus, private parts, death, lost or hidden goods, death of enemies, westerly direction, encounters with thieves

Eighth house significations

Primary	Secondary
Death, dying and longevity, chronic conditions, misery, ruin and woes, disgrace and defeat, sexual diseases, sexual attractiveness, worry, partners relatives, mental disturbances (anxiety), death by poisoning, mode of death, overdose, suicide, degradation, one's mortician or undertaker, funerary rites, chronic disease, diagnosis of disease, incurable diseases, legacies, gratuity, unearned income, other people's wealth, partner's finances, dowries, tax evasion, hidden wealth, ill-repute, inheritance tax, occult powers, magic, psychic abilities, haunting, spirits, witchcraft and black magic, genitalia (male and female), debts, oversensitivity, restlessness, killing of living beings, science, unsolved mysteries, occult sciences, astrology, palmistry, psychic abilities, chakras, life-changing experiences	Afflictions to the face, deformed limbs, worries from death, cause of death, place of death, siblings and enemies, urinary diseases, an enemy's strong hold, fear of punishment, loss of money, long-awaited monies, wicked people, narcotics, prostitution, murder, loss of limbs, capital punishment, poisons, outhouses, servants, conspiratorial acts, assignation, armed robbery, terrifying stories, bodily eliminations, anus and rectum, constipation, piles, fistula, obstructions, things that shorten or increase one's lifespan, gifts and foreign travel, travel over water, difficult journeys, accidents, delays to travel, crossing of water, drowning, fruitless journeys, corruption, injury by weapons or projectiles, partner's wealth, partner's family, partner's dowry

Ninth house significations

Primary	Secondary
Dharma, fortune, truth, righteousness, religion, philosophy, higher knowledge, luck, acts of kindness, spirituality, intuition, meditation, virtuous acts, faith, pilgrimages and short journeys, higher education, conveyances, father (South India), grandchildren, charities, spiritual questing, culture and good conduct, teachers, guru, devotion, fortunes, luck and prosperity, spiritual nourishment, temples, churches, religious rites, blessings by a priest (benedictions), Vedic sacrifices, fire rituals, giving of alms, distribution of money, stiffness in the thighs, circulatory problems, arterial obstructions, thrombosis, arthritic conditions, health complaints involving toxic blood or circulatory stagnation	Purity of mind, worship of lord Śiva, honouring of deities, good conduct, libations with milk and ghee, gifts to and from the gods, visions, prophecies, efforts to learn, colleges, problems with instructors and teachers, learning institutions, teaching, ability to listen, initiation and enlightenment, spreading good tales, listening to moral stories, contact with virtuous people, inspired words, paternal legacies, acquirement of elephants, cows and buffalo, greed, restlessness, urges to travel, drastic changes to weather, explorations and discoveries, sea voyages, natural forces, nature, water reservoirs, absolution of past actions, fruits from one's successes, books and sacred texts, publishing and editing

Tenth house significations

Primary	Secondary
Karma/action, career/livelihood, ambition, commerce, social status, material world achievement, honour from a ruler/prince, patronage, governmental works, service industry, agriculture, medical practitioners, pre-eminence, mercantilist, prosperity, influential persons, an expert teacher, father (North India), self-respect, able to support oneself, weakness of joints, damage to the knees (joints), worn cartilage, asthi dhatu/skeleton (bone formation), conditions aggravated by damp and coolness, diseases of the skin and hypertension	Elder brother, losses to elder brother, service under others, places of worship, council offices, elections, conveyance in a grand vehicle, yantra, use of symbolic diagrams (seal of authority), qualities of leadership, wearing of talismans/ornaments, morality, the chanting of mantra, acquisition through the use of mantra, retirement, worship, mother, adopted children, Maraka for father (2nd from 9th), last rites for the father, externalisation of the 4th house, capital held by religions, gains, profits and worldly activity

Eleventh house significations

Primary	Secondary
Financial gains, fulfilment of desires, major goals, success and attainments, side ventures, self-indulgence, quest and attainment of knowledge, evil desires, friends of influence, groups, elder brothers and sisters, uncles, monetary gain, trade, dependence on others, skills in earning, long-term investments, large sums of money, acquisition of gold, precious stones, speculation, ancestral property, occult studies, ministerial positions, skill in the art of painting, dancing, malice and fraud, secret mental anguish, secret sorrows, debts of spouse, sickness of spouse, recovery of spouse, discharge of debts	Left ear, hearing in the left ear, shanks (ankles and calves), legs, impaired circulation, lymph stagnation, rheumatism, heart problems, mental disturbances, low or loss of immunity, recovery from illness, injuries, accidents, wounds, worship of gods, sattvic deities, moksha, education, loss of wealth, longevity of mother, father's fixed assets, money of friends, entrapment by Earthly desires, confinements in gilded cages, falling from high places, bearing of fruits, foreign residence, overseas vacation

Twelfth house significations

Primary	Secondary
Moksha (liberation), losses and expenditure, loss of position/profession, despised by a crowd, incarceration, relief from debts, freedom from suffering, paternal property, disputes, loss of spouse, finances of elder siblings, living abroad, clandestine affairs, sexual pleasures, death of the individual, convalescence, an end to journeys, psychic phenomena, metaphysics, secret mental toils, overseas voyages, crossing great expanses of water, undoing of self, successes in foreign lands	Injury to left eye, visual acuity in left eye, the feet, broken bones, falling (Vāta), pain in the joints, dysentery, physical discomfort, long-term ailments, lymph stagnation, enlarged lymph nodes, lipoma, an end of power and influence, kept in chains, sedation, an asylum, homes for the elderly, impediments, prisons, bondage, drudgery, suicide, conditions of extreme misery, successes through occult practice, deliberate wastage of wealth, entry into heaven

NOTES

1. Brihat Parasara Hora Shāstra.
2. To unite with one's partner.
3. Closeness/intimate contact with one's partner.

IMPORTANT HOUSE
COMBINATIONS

Jyotish considers certain houses to be grouped or like-natured, that is, noted to produce similar auspicious or inauspicious effects. In this chapter we take a look at popular configurations that form the bedrock of house analysis: *Kendra*, *Trikona*, *Dussthana*, *Upachaya* and *Maraka* houses.

14.1 KENDRA

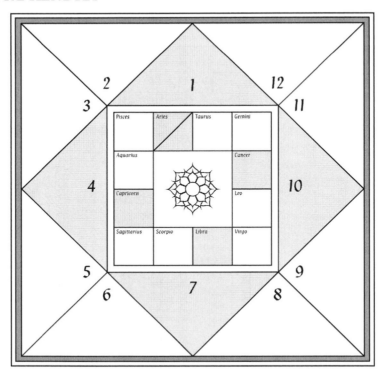

Kendra houses (1-4-7-10) are clearly delineated in the (outer) North Indian format. The (inner) South Indian format favours Rashis; here houses are read from the ascendant sign (bearing a diagonal line).

Kendra[1] (also known as quadrants) are usually given extra weight in Jyotish for their ability to sustain and nourish. Sacred to Lord Vishnu, they grant power and facilitate action. Each Kendra and its lord determine the energy we are prepared to spend (or sacrifice) in a particular area of life. The 1st house represents the body and our physical condition, that is, resistance to disease and ageing, our personal resolve, conscience or self-esteem. The 4th house represents our inner-personal space, that is, thoughts and emotions, home life, happiness/contentment and sense of inner security. The 7th house indicates the spouse/partner, personal relationship to others or our business/career partners and 10th house, indicating career, our need to be seen and those who would aid us in our effort to achieve recognition. Numerologically, numbers 1-4-7-10 are considered angular, resolute and productive, that is, those which produce palpable, initiatory effects.

The North Indian style of horoscope makes Kendra identification extremely simple, instantly recognisable at the horoscope's core, providing its underlying structure. Note also that Kendra constitute the greater part of the chart's total area. In effect they are four essential pillars: self, home, partner and career. Kendra houses uphold the integrity of all houses, but are themselves contained or nested within the remainder, supported at their base by two Trikona houses and surrounded by the remaining 2nd, 3rd, 6th, 8th, 11th and 12th (for the most part considered troublesome areas of life). When strong, Kendras remain unscathed by extraneous forces; when compromised (weakened), the risk of collapse from pressures exerted by external influence becomes greater.

Planets in Kendras may become pushy, extrovert and self-serving, often carrying weighty agendas. Multiple planets in Kendra positions 'lift' an individual, making them appear charismatic, supercharged and compelling – able to motivate those about them with ease. Much like the movable signs Aries, Cancer, Libra and Capricorn (signs naturally associated with these houses), the 1-4-7-10 positions are highly energetic – assuredly amplifying the dynamic attributes of occupying planets.

Kendras also accentuate planetary traits; for instance, Mercury in the 10th might ignite one's desires for a successful career, bringing multiple business opportunities. However, that same person having Saturn positioned in their 10th house may modify those same career opportunities to slowly manifest or mature at the cost of physical detriment (injury or sickness), both representative of a Saturnine energetic.

14.2 TRIKONA

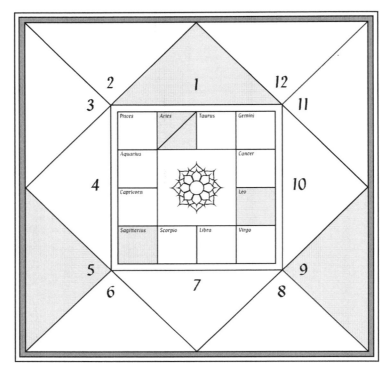

Trikona houses, represented by the 1st, 5th and 9th.

Trikona[2] or trinal houses are second only to Kendra and in some cases considered to supersede them. Trinals are supported by the goddess Lakshmi (she who supports all manner of wealth, luxury and prosperity). The prominence and strength of Trikona disclose personal successes and failures in all undertakings; they also indicate unconscious or preordained acts directed toward 1st self/body, 5th previous good merits/creativity and 9th dharma/right action. Numerologically, numbers 1-5-9 are connected to dharma and truth; they are considered fire numbers, that is, able to penetrate and clarify, assimilate and digest.

The 1st house doubles as both Trikona and Kendra as the self/body interacts and connects with everything; this then becomes the focal point for the manifestation of all karma. The 5th house is considered highly auspicious, helping to manifest previously accrued actions (both auspicious and inauspicious). The 9th house indicates one's pathway toward enlightenment and ultimate liberation (moksha[3]).

All Trikonas ultimately guide one toward salvation, trying hard to keep one on the pathway of dharma. Interactions between Trikona and Kendra houses (via planetary placements) are deemed especially favourable, indicating helping-hands in life or speedy attainment of ladder runs. Planet/s in such favourable circumstances are considered pre-aligned with dharmic considerations – readily activated by events or actions that facilitate forward momentum along the path of right action.

Note: The descending trinal houses (in opposition to Trikona), that is, 3rd, 7th and 11th, are often portrayed as the antithesis of Trikona, aligning themselves to factors that reject moksha, that is, embracing the physical world and its various attachments. Their energetics include: physical prowess and personal power (3rd house), partnerships and agreements (7th house) and, finally, reward through material benefit (as expressed by the 11th house).

14.3 DUSSTHANA (TRIKASTHANAS) HOUSES

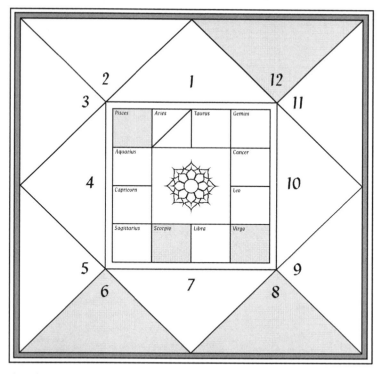

Dussthana houses, represented by the 6th, 8th and 12th.

Dussthana houses are generally indicative of suffering in the form of illness (6th), death (8th) and loss (12th). There are many rules regarding the manifestation and severity of their force; however, these are also balanced by a number of mitigating circumstances where their detrimental forces may be lessened, and sometimes even improved.

Dealings with 6th house energy may open the door to *dis*-ease (that is, sickness and frailties) or even physical attack from external sources – yet also endow one with excellent self-healing skills (well able to administer to their own health issues) or shortcomings. The 8th house is known to deplete longevity through wrongful or unwholesome action yet may also promote longevity (depending upon the nature of its lord and its disposition). The 8th house is also noted to give occult/clairvoyant faculties. The 12th house is considered a house of hidden enemies, things which creep up on us unawares, yet also promote states of illumination and awareness through moksha; 12th house energy can equally bring recognition or status in lands beyond the country of one's birth.

Numerologically, numbers 6-8-12 are generally considered inauspicious (evil) numbers, that is, less likely to promote stability and harmony. Dussthana *push* an individual onward in life, driving one to succeed (sometimes dominate) in their chosen undertakings. Dussthana are assuredly houses that relish confrontation and/or attract difficulties, yet are also great tutors, doling out real life-challenges where much may be learnt and benefited from.

Note: Collectively, Dussthana houses (and their lords) need to be carefully assessed, their situations indicating problematic areas and/or life challenges.

14.4 UPACHAYA

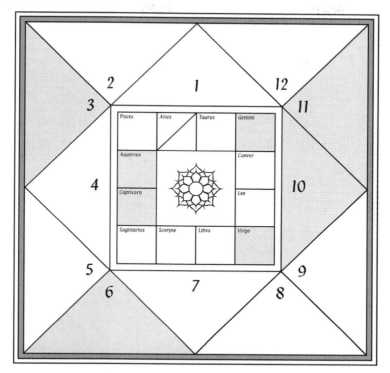

Upachaya houses, represented by the 3rd, 6th, 10th and 11th.

In contrast to the potentially destructive power of Dussthana, *Upachaya* are duly considered for their long-term growth and improvements over time. These appear in the form of: 3rd, physical prowess; 6th, health and healing; 10th, social status/vocation; and 11th, material gains and comfort. An interaction between Upachaya and Dussthana occurs with the (6th) house. Its interplay of energetics continues to promote disruptive wares, while simultaneously delivering merits of an Upachaya.

Upachaya are thought to sit patiently in the background, amassing strength through periods of suffering, taxation or mental anguish. These experiences appear to be 'cached' during youth (taken to be the years prior to age thirty). Passing this period of life we often experience an 'awakening' as Upachaya slowly shift their emphasis from passive to active, gaining in intensity, their storehouse of energy now assisting in overcoming life's more difficult or troublesome circumstances.

It should be mentioned here that the 6th house (Dussthana) does not simply switch off in later life – its capacity to inflict harm or undesirable effects never ceases. What can be said is that the passing of years somewhat diminishes its capacity to hurt us with such intensity as we begin to see the potential benefits of its earlier blows, now slightly softened and in some cases even propitious.

14.5 MARAKA

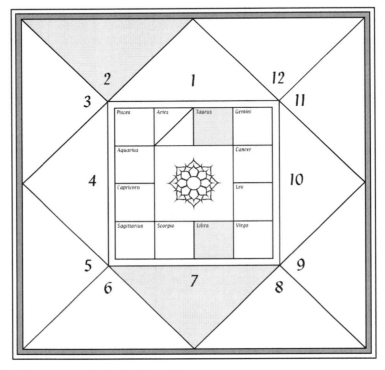

Maraka houses, represented by the 2nd and 7th.

Rather unfortunately referred to as *killer houses*, Maraka are represented by the 2nd and 7th houses in the horoscope. The *houses of life* are considered to be the 3rd and 8th, with the latter (as already noted) 'a house of longevity'. As the 3rd house falls eight houses from the 8th,[4] it too is considered to augment the power of the 8th house and its ability to sustain life. The 12th (or loss) of these houses is to be read from the 2nd and 7th houses, hence Marakas are to be considered numbers that deal in death. Typically any account of Marakas (and their lords) appears in weighty discussions of ultimate longevity.

Of the two houses, the 7th and its lord are considered to have the greater potential to end life during their dasha and antardasha periods (all things being considered; see Chapter 22). The ability of Maraka to inflict death is usually considered in conjunction with Maraka lords or additional malefics situated in the 2nd and 7th houses. Atop all of these considerations, as the 8th lord rules longevity it was also often considered to present the nearer or greater danger. As always, each case must be considered individually, as it is seldom that one factor determines all outcomes.

NOTES

1. Greek for 'centre of the circle'.
2. Meaning 'three angles' – also known as *Tryasra* ('triangle' in Sanskrit).
3. Moksha = enlightenment or ultimate liberation.
4. Also known as Bhavat Bhavam, meaning 'to the house from a house'.

15

DIK BALA
—— (Directional Strength) ——

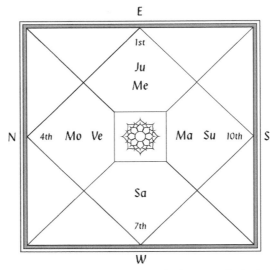

Dik Bala (planetary strengths). Key: Sun (Sun), Moon (Mo), Mercury (Me), Mars (Ma), Jupiter (Ju), Venus (Ve) and Saturn (Sa).

One advantage of the diagrammatic style of northern Indian horoscopes is its usefulness in identifying planets displaying *Dik Bala*[1] or 'best cardinal direction'. This quite literally is the occupation of Kendra by certain planet/s noted to perform well in one of the four angular houses. All told, Jyotish recognises seven grahas (excluding the lunar nodes) that attain directional strength.

Dik Bala is wholly determined by house rather than sign placement, although the two impact upon on one another; that is, a planet receiving directional strength may become weakened due to poor sign placement. One example of this would be Saturn receiving directional strength when tenanting the 7th house yet occupying Aries, the sign of its fall. In this example Saturn gains directionally yet loses via sign placement. Conversely,

Saturn positioned in Libra (exalted) and found to occupy the 7th house intensifies its strength due to the benefits of both Dik Bala and sign placement. Planets found tenanting Kendra directly in opposition to their favourable courses are equally weakened or subject to inactivity.

The designation of planets to cardinal points appears to incorporate both territorial concerns[2] as well as qualitative observation; for example, Sun and Mars gaining strength in the 10th house (south). The two hot planets were noted to promote respect and leadership qualities, climbing to their highest and fiercest positions in southerly skies. The *Vedas* also considered the southern hemisphere to be infernal/demonic regions, associated with fire and malefic intent. By example, hearth-stones were always laid in southerly quarters, paying tribute to Agnī (god of fire), promoting quality heat and strengthening digestive power.

The northerly direction was deemed auspicious, representative of cooling breezes, furtive rains and divine herbs from the Himalayas (source of the great rivers and life-giving waters). Here the two feminine planets (Moon and Venus) gained in strength; renowned for their nightly radiance, youthfulness and luxury, both planets promote stability and home comforts – as signified by the north and 4th house.

Jupiter (wisdom) and Mercury (intelligence) were noted to gain strength in the easterly direction, benefiting from the refreshment of the dawn and rising Sun (the clean page of a new day). The easterly direction (1st house) is representative of atma, prāṇa and wisdom, symbolising one's 'potential' spiritual growth. The morning hours represent heightened alertness and mental acuity, a period when the mind and senses are most open to instruction and learning.

The westerly direction finds planet Saturn strong with the loss of sunlight and the lengthening of shadows. Associated with diminishing longevity, this juncture between day and night (dusk) was noted to be a period of cooling, lethargy and disorientation. The west was often associated with Mleccha (barbarians/migrants), the seventh house indicative of travel, trade and remote foreign lands.

Note: The fusion of cardinal direction with destiny is nothing new or unique to astrology; their significance formed an integral part of many esoteric earth sciences, which incorporated forms of geomantia (earth divination), such as Vāstu and Feng Shui.

NOTES

1. Also known as Drig Bala or Kāṣṭhabala.
2. Possible correlations between territories or provinces include: Sûrya – Orissa (south/east); Shani – Gujarat (west); and Chandra – Uttarakhand (north).

16

──── KARMA ────

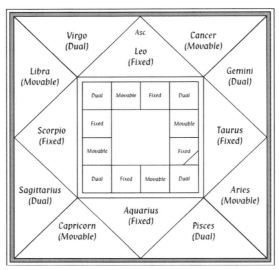

Sample horoscope: Prarabdha Karma (fixed signs), Aagama Karma (movable signs) and Kriyamana Karma (dual signs).

Planets are always favourable to one who is harmless (who does not injure others), who possesses self-control, who has earned wealth through virtuous means and who is always observant in religious discipline.

Phaladeepika by Mantreswara

The term *karma* first appears in *Atharva Veda*, then *Brāhmaṇas*[1] and *Upanishads* referred to as a life-ritual. The word itself simply denotes action/s, and by ancient accounts appears to be a natural or inherent law, displaying indifference toward the moral concepts of good versus evil. Indeed, *Vedas* ascribe the highest state of being (which we might term good) to contentment, peace and self-awareness; evil per se was seen simply as our fall from this state toward ignorance and darkness. In today's world we mostly associate the term 'karma' with the idiom 'what goes around comes around', ascribed to either positive and negative events or outcomes.

In the Vedic tradition, accrued karmas become attached (or meshed) with an individual, becoming a kind of 'mobile' ledger of past action/s, seeking to manifest at a preordained moment in the near or distant future. As individuals were believed to be subject to metempsychosis (multiple births), karmas were noted to follow their host into future incarnations. In some cases the metaphor of a wheel is used to describe this action, turning *in perpetuum* until its course is fully run. Therefore, Jyotish presents us with a unique opportunity to review (and in some cases placate) the karmic ledger, taking stock or taking action to deal with its manifestation. The skill of the Jyotishi is to identify (through analysis of a birth chart, dasha periods and transits) when such karma/s may be likely to confront us and to gauge their impact. Jyotish has long recognised that the behaviours and mannerisms of the individual, be it their speech, actions or thoughts, may be nothing more than the result of past karmas.

16.1 TYPES OF KARMA

During my travels in Śrī Laṅkā, I was able to spend time studying with local Naimittika.[2] These local wise men, sometimes referred to as Kapurala, employ a mixture of Jyotish, Hastā Rekha Shāstra[3] (palmistry) and omenology. These methods they use to great effect, considering the energetics of Rashis inseparable from various types of karma, as given below:

- *Sanchita Karma:* A kind of sum total/cosmic inventory that an individual carries across multiple lifetimes. Jyotish might interpret this as the entirety of a Rashi chart with its multiplicity of signals from past, present and into the future. Like a hologram the Rashi chart holds multiple harmonic values within itself, facilitating the generation of many subdivisional charts known collectively as Vargas (see Chapter 21).

- *Prarabdha Karma:* Denotes karmas of a fixed nature; these may be interpreted by studying the quality of the fixed zodiacal signs, that is, Taurus, Leo, Scorpio and Aquarius. Prarabdha indicates karma that has ripened and is ready to manifest (for better or for worse). Prarabdha Karma can often feel oppressive and unrelenting, appearing to heap an invisible weight upon an individual regardless of age, physical resistance or personal circumstances.

- *Kriyamana Karma:* Denotes karmas of an instantaneous nature; these may be read from the dual zodiacal signs, that is, Gemini, Virgo, Sagittarius and Pisces, mirroring the nature of these signs. Kriyamana may be dualistic in nature, that is, some slighting and easily accommodated whilst others may carry more ominous undertones. This type of karma arises and dissipates quickly within the current lifetime. Karmas of this nature may be experienced and cancelled out without need for any future propagation of debt.

- *Aagama Karma:* Highly potent and energetic karmas, which push relentlessly forward, breaking through the constraints of the current lifetime and depositing themselves into the cache or sum total (Sanchita). Aagama Karma can be read from the movable signs of the zodiac, that is, Aries, Cancer, Libra and Capricorn.

16.2 JYOTISH AND KARMA

Ascendant signs set the precedent of the horoscope, their elevation upon the eastern horizon automatically distributing the different manifestations of karma to their allotted partitions (houses). For example, Gemini ascendants automatically place the remaining three dual signs (Virgo, Sagittarius and Pisces) in Kendras. Ascendant Aries distributes the remaining three movable signs (Cancer, Libra and Capricorn) into Kendras, and so on.

The energetics of the Rashis play a significant part in the way a planet manifests itself in the horoscope. For example, planets in movable signs tend to be revved-up with drive, enthusiasm and charisma, sometimes brutally unaware of their single-mindedness and quashing effect on those around them.

Planets in fixed signs may tend to appear unyielding, obstinate or stubborn in nature, resisting innovation and change. The *modus operandi* behind signs of a fixed nature is to try and 'hold things in check' and above all protect the status quo.

Planets in dual signs display a combination of the aforementioned states, though somewhat reduced in both tenacity and drive. Planets in dual signs appear to manifest in a much more *fluidic* and *flexible* manner.

Looking at our sample horoscope (planets temporarily removed), the ascendant is Leo (fixed), thus placing the remaining three fixed signs in Kendra. For Taurus, Leo, Scorpio and Aquarius, Prarabdha Karma will tend to dominate in those areas of life ruled by Kendra houses. Ascendant Gemini, Virgo, Sagittarius and Pisces (dual signs) represent Kriyamana, this type of karma tending to manifest in those areas of life ruled by Kendra, but still experiencing Prarabdha Karma in houses 3-6-9-12; as would our Leo ascendant experience Kriyamana in 2nd, 5th, 8th and 11th houses, and so on.

16.3 RELIEF FROM PLANETARY KARMA

Fire sacrifice (Ahuti) offered at the close of Śrī Rudram.

> A frightened mouse runs to its hole; a scared serpent to a well; a terrified
> elephant to its stake – but where can a man fly from his karma?
>
> *Garuda Purāṇa*

Typically, grahas are ceremonially propitiated in an effort to relieve their
malefic glances (which fructify negative karma/s), this being punctiliously
performed through acts of pooja, devotional acts[4] or the recitation of
mantra. One of the most effective remedies for the affliction of deleterious
planets is the chanting of the Vedic Hymns.

Śrī Rudram (also known as *Rudraprasna*) is found in *Krishna Yajurveda*
and is particularly suited (and auspicious) for just such an occasion. This
early and important Vedic deity was renowned to be 'satiated with ease'
through praise and recitation of Śrī Rudram (*Namakam* and *Chamakam*)[5]
and then willingly granted requests made of him. The hymn itself is
composed of eleven *anuvaka* (passages), each in propitiation of varied
aspects of this frightening storm god.

Śrī Rudram is primarily chanted by those seeking divine benevolence
to avert an untimely death or to shield one from danger. Its power is also
evoked for the relief of virulent fevers, fatal diseases, attacks by wild animals
or supernatural forces. Its recitation is said to avert *asādhu* (evils/cruelty) of
malefic tārāgraha while promoting *sādhu* (their benefic properties), whilst
protecting one's home and family and livestock.

Rudra is also renowned as a great healer (as well as a promoter of all
Earthly healing agents), empowering medicinal compounds whether
they be herbal, metallic or mineral in origin. Rudra may be implored to
remove all ills and enemies (be they internal or external), that is, diseases

that ravage the body from within or wounds inflicted upon us by those seeking to harm. Śrī Rudram also grants intelligence and loosens the grip of Māyā, as its verses urge this powerful stormy deity to steal away our 'tamas' (darkness and ignorance).

NOTES

1. See *Śatapatha Brāhmaṇa*.
2. Nimitta (omens). See the Introduction.
3. See the author's additional work, *Vedic Palmistry* (Mason 2017).
4. Devotional acts are said to release one from the grip of Māyā (illusory force), leading one away from external attachments and material desires.
5. Śrī Rudram comprises eleven *Anuvaka* and recited in two parts: *Namakam* and *Chamakam*.

17

—RETROGRADE PLANETS—

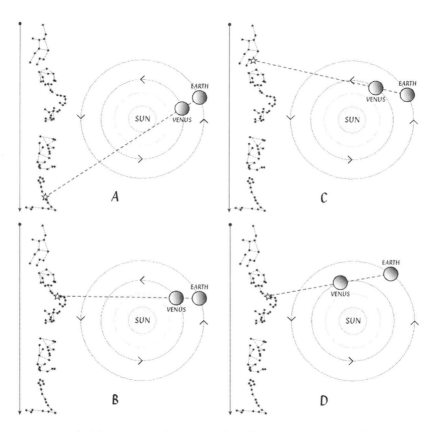

Venus retrograde: (A) Venus approaches Earth, its forward momentum appearing to slow. (B) Venus passes Earth, now appearing retrograde in motion. (C) Venus appears stationary against the starry backdrop. (D) Venus regains forward momentum. Note: The elongated arrow to the left of the zodiac indicates west-to-east motion; the inner dotted line represents Mercury's orbit.

In our solar system, Sun takes centre stage keeping planets locked into heliocentric motion, that is to say, all rotate roughly about its equator following their own highly varied orbits. As the ecliptic is in reality Earth's orbit, the Sun's motion remains uni-directional. From the Sun's perspective all planets remain uni-directional, completing their various orbits about its girth in accordance with their orbital speeds and distances. This in effect means that whatever constellation is currently framed against the Sun (let's say Capricorn), from the Sun's perspective Earth will be framed against the opposite stars, that is, Cancer.

As terrestrial spectators, our view of the other planets is quite different as we ourselves are participants in the mass revolution of worlds. Much like a racing car speeding about a circuit, we are viewing the other participants inside and outside of our lane. At certain points along our yearly orbit some planets are said to be *vakragati*,[1] that is, retrograde in motion, appearing first to lose momentum against their starry backdrop until at last becoming stationary. When motion again returns to these worlds, they appear to us to be retrograde – that is, journeying backward against the same stars they had only recently traversed. It is at such junctures in our orbit that we experience the effects of *gaining* and *slipping* as others pass us or are passed by us. This gives the illusion of backward movement. This phenomenon might be likened to a passenger's sensation of sliding backward (in a moving train) when overtaken by a faster-moving train.

As the Sun is central to all planets in the solar system, it cannot appear retrograde in motion (from the perspective of any planet). Likewise the Moon, swept along in unison with Earth, negates retrograde motion for spectators of either body. Retrograde activity therefore falls to the five remaining planets, which are then divided into two camps: *interior* planets, Mercury and Venus; and *exterior* planets, Mars, Jupiter and Saturn. These allocations are in no way derogatory; merely descriptive of their relative distances from the Sun. That is, the former mark orbits close to the solar centre, within the orbit of Earth; the latter mark distant orbits that lie beyond Earth's orbit. As the nodes of the Moon (Rāhu and Ketu) are permanently engaged in retrograde activity[2] and lack any 'illuminated' physical mass, they are precluded from consideration here (for more information on the lunar nodes see Section 24.1).

Note: Within the ancient hierarchy of the planets,[3] Moon and the inferior planets (Mercury and Venus) were correctly determined (or intuited) to be positioned *below* the Sun; that is, closer to us. The superior planets (Mars, Jupiter and Saturn) and finally the stars were determined to reside above (*beyond*) the Sun. Trans-Saturnians are similarly subject to retrogressive motion (from Earth's perspective), but are not considered here.

17.1 INTERPRETATION

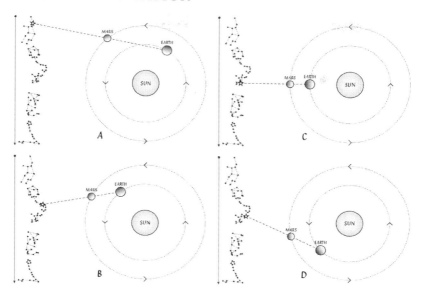

Mars retrograde: (A) Earth approaches the red planet. (B) Earth gains on Mars as its forward motion appears to slow. (C) Mars appears stationary against the zodiac. (D) Earth passes Mars, which now appears to retrograde. Note: The elongated arrow to the left of the zodiac indicates west-to-east motion.

Retrograde planets are a hot topic with most astrologers and their correctness of interpretation greatly speculated upon. That being said, retrograde planets appear to have attracted far less attention in classical texts, whose observations are sporadic at best – if described at all. Quite often the subject of retrograde motion appears only in planetary states and strengths,[4] and is seldom explored to any great depth.

On the whole, classical authors seem fairly united in their opinion of the five planets periodically undergoing retrogressive activity, seeing their reversal of direction to 'empower status to a greater degree'. Though not entirely free of contradictions, most also seem content to accept a planet's tendency to deliver (positive) results, saying:

> Planets that are victorious in war are retrograde in motion and free from combustion become strong.

Saravali of Kalyana Varmas[5]

A planet can be said to be strong when associated with, aspected by or hemmed in-between benefic planets, or is exalted, occupies its own house/s, the house of a friend or is retrograde.

Prasna Marga[6]

When a planet is retrograde its strength is equal to of exaltation. A planet exalted in its Rashi while retrograde is similar to a debilitated one, it has no power.

Uttara Kalamrita by Kalidasa[7]

All planets are strong when posited in their sign of exaltation. Moon is strong and auspicious when she has her full Paksha Bala. The Sun receives Dik Bala when he is in the 10th house. The remaining five grahas are strong when retrograde.

If a planet happens to be retrograde in motion, it will produce the same effect as if posited in its sign of exaltation, even if he may be in an enemy's sign or the sign of its debilitation.

Phaladeepika by Sri Mantresvara[8]

Malefics cause good by having retrograde motion. In this way should be ascertained planetary movements, by the learned.

Bhāvārtha Ratnākara[9]

17.2 CONCLUSION

What can be said *for certain* is that any of the five planets found in a state of retrogradation will noticeably impact a horoscope, primarily due to the fact that they are that much closer to the Earth and – more importantly – luminous, that is, showing more brilliancy. Any considerations above and beyond this fact relate to a planet's overall comfort in terms of individual state and strength at the time of the observation. When ascertaining the performance of a retrograde planet, it is necessary (as always) to consider sign placement, aspects (benefic and malefic), lordship of houses, temporary and fixed Kāraka, and so on. Given the added quota of strength availed to them by retrograde motion, planets are more than likely to radiate their traits above and beyond the norm!

How the 'specifics' of each planet might be experienced (or predicted) during retrograde activity is of much greater complexity, due to the many variables unique to each horoscope. As always, the true nature of the planet concerned has to be considered; that is, malefic grahas appear more likely to damage health and vitality or manifest detrimental effects during their period of retrograde motion, as is a benefic to produce supportive, people-friendly attributes including health and vitality during their period of retrograde activity.

One of the best interpretations of retrograde motion through the twelve zodiacal houses is given in *The Art and Practice of Ancient Hindu Astrology* (Braha 2001). Here the author (through a series of teacher/instructor transcripts) gives a great house-by-house analysis of retrograde planetary lords. His overall conclusions agree that the effect of retrograde motion gives strength to each planet, but also internalises it, placing emphasis upon the bearer's willingness to developing its latent potential. Or, as he puts it, 'makes the planet strong, but also quite *passive* and less likely to produce on its own'.

The following excerpts from the book have been reproduced with the kind permission of the author:

> The statement that a retrograde planet is more powerful is misleading, however, if you expect that planet to readily and powerfully manifest its results in the outer world. A retrograde planet is never strong and active. It is neutral or passive.

> If the 1st house ruler is retrograde, the person's outgoing tendencies are curtailed. The person is introspective or introverted, and has a harder time gaining recognition or fame. I (James Braha) actually consider a retrograde ruler of either the 1st or 10th house to be not very helpful, because the person is slower in actualising his or her abilities and worldly power.

> If the 2nd house ruler is retrograde, money comes in slower. If the person has literary or teaching talent, he or she probably won't want to write or teach until a later age.

> If the 3rd house ruler is retrograde, the person won't be overly ambitious. Desires will be less. There is less chance of having younger siblings, and less chance of pursuing music, dance or drama.

If the 4th house ruler is retrograde, there is less desire to own land or engage in real estate. Also, the person might have less desire to gain higher educational degrees.

If the 5th house ruler is retrograde, the person will not feel *compelled* to have children. Sports, politics, spiritual techniques, and other 5th house matters would probably remain hobbies until the age of thirty. One thing I don't like about the 5th house ruler being retrograde is that it generally weakens the poovapunya (past life credit) connected to that planet. In other words, if the ruler of the 5th house occupies the 10th house without affliction, it means there is past life credit connected to the career. But if that 5th house ruler is retrograde, the poovapunya factor is weakened or even non-existent.

If the 6th house ruler is retrograde, the person may hold back from a medical or healing career, even if talents exist in that area.

If the 7th house ruler is retrograde, the person simply doesn't feel compelled to get married. It also holds back his desire to become a merchant or to do business.

If the 8th house ruler is retrograde, it could slow down the ability to get money from wills, legacies, insurance companies, and one's spouse. It could stop the person from becoming an astrologer or any career involving research or secretive activities, like the CIA or KGB.

If the 9th house ruler is retrograde, it could lessen a person's desire for travel. The person might also consider religion and philosophy a hobby rather than a profession.

If the 10th house ruler is retrograde, the person is slower to *choose* a career and slower to actualise a career. This is one of the least favourite retrograde placements because it slows a person's career and status.

If the 11th house ruler is retrograde, there is less likelihood of having an older sibling. Friends and groups are not a high priority, and it may take longer than usual for a person to realise his or her major goals and ambitions.

If the 12th house ruler is retrograde, is slows a person's sexual desires as well as desires to visit remote foreign countries.

17.3 RETROGRADE MOTION OF PLANETS

Table of planetary motions

Graha/Planet	Bhagaṇa/Orbit*	Rashi Parikrama/Sign Transit*	Gati/Daily Motion**
Sun	365.265 days	30 days	1°
Moon	29.53 days	2.5 days	12°–14°
Rāhu/Ketu	18.7 years	1.6 years	3'
Mercury	358 days	15–30 days	1° 20'
Venus	290 days	25–60 days	1° 14'
Mars	1.9 years	1.4 months	40'
Jupiter	11.86 years	1 year	12'
Saturn	29.46 Years	2.5 years	6'

* all values based on mean geocentric measurement
** approximate values

Mercury

Of all grahas, planet Mercury enjoys the most frequent spells of retrograde activity (around three times in any twelve-month period), never straying more than 28° from its symbolic paternal guardian (Sun). Mercury's true sidereal year is close to 88 days but from our geocentric perspective it is closer to 358 days; however, this figure (not unlike Mercury's nature) is highly variable. With frequent sojourns this small planet may adjust the length of its geocentric year from 358 to 400+ days. Similarly, this nigh-solar companion may choose to traverse each zodiacal sign in as little as 15 days or take more than 30 days. During periods of retrograde activity, Mercury can take 60+ days to traverse a single zodiacal sign. Earthbound observations of this tiny world witness its path to adhere to a maximum distance of about 5°+/- above or below the plane of the ecliptic.[10] The Mercurial arc of retrogradation varies between 16° at perihelion[11] and 9° at aphelion.[12]

Venus

Never straying more than 48° from the Sun, Venus completes its sidereal orbit in 225 days. From our geocentric perspective Venus completes its full zodiacal revolution every 290+/- days and enters into a state of retrograde motion every 590+/- days, for a period of 40+/- days. Venus traverses each zodiacal sign over a period of 24+/- days. Due to orbital proximity (during retrograde intervals), Earthbound observations of this planet may witness it soaring and plummeting as much as 8°+/- above or below the plane of the ecliptic,[13] perhaps giving rise to the notion of Shukracārya (instructor of demons), as Venus was noted to stray so far from Ravi-marga/Sun's pathway (ecliptic). The Venusian arc of retrogradation varying between 16° at perihelion and 14° at aphelion.

Mars

Planet Mars completes its sidereal orbit in approximately 1.9 years; from our geocentric perspective it is a little longer, performing a single retrograde motion during this time for a period of 70+/– days. On occasion this may even extend to 200+/– days, hence its name in Sanskrit, *Vakri* (irregular or unpredictable). Mars traverses each zodiacal sign over a period of about 40+/– days. Due to the orbital proximity of the red planet and Earth at certain points along their trajectories, Mars's latitude may appear to stray 6°+/– above or below the ecliptic plane during periods of retrograde activity, the Martian arc of retrogradation varying between 10° at perihelion and 19° at aphelion.

Jupiter

Jupiter's orbital plane is virtually identical to that of the ecliptic, completing its sidereal orbit in approximately 11.86 years; from our geocentric perspective it is virtually identical. During this period Jupiter performs about 9+/– retrograde motions, in each case lasting around 4+/– months. On average, Jupiter traverses one Rashi per year, depending upon its cycle of retrograde activity. The Jovian arc of retrogradation is approximately 10° at both perihelion and aphelion, perhaps interpreted by the ancients as a sign of its fastidious and devotional nature.

Saturn

Considered the most ponderous of graha, this distant world completes its sidereal orbit in approximately 29.46 years; again, from our geocentric perspective Saturn's orbital plane is virtually identical to that of the ecliptic. Saturn performs about 27+/– retrograde intervals during its far distant voyage about our Sun, with retrogressive activity lasting 4.5+/– months. Saturn traverses one Rashi every 2.5+ years during which time it may retrograde 2–3 times. The Saturnian arc of retrogradation varies between 6.5° at perihelion and 7° at aphelion (approximately). *Note:* Saturn traditionally marks the outer boundary of the grahas in Jyotish and although trans-Saturnians exhibit retrograde activity, their invisibility to the ancients precludes analysis here.

Rāhu and Ketu

For more on the retrogradation of the lunar nodes see Section 24.1.

NOTES

1. Vakragati = to pursue a winding or crooked course.
2. Exacting modern calculation of the lunar nodes reveals perturbations in their orbit which add stationary as well as direct states to their motion. Classical texts note only their retrograde activity.
3. References to the hierarchy of planets are found in most Siddhântic materials, including *Pañca Siddhântika*.
4. Retrograde motion is but one factor included within Shadbala, a complex six-fold assessment of planetary strengths.
5. Excerpt from Chapter 4, 'Planetary Characteristics' – authorship dated to the 10th century AD.
6. Excerpt from Chapter 9, 'Determination of Long Life' – authorship dated to the mid-17th century AD.
7. True authorship remains undetermined; however, its contents reveal it to contain many similarities to *BPHS*, *Brihat Jataka* and *Phaladeepika*, making 16th–17th century AD seem a likely date for compilation.
8. Excerpt from taken from Chapter 4, 'Strength of Planets and Houses' and Chapter 9, 'Effects on Different Ascendants'. This work is believed to have been composed between the 13th and 14th century AD.
9. Excerpt taken from Chapter 14, 'Grahamalika Yogas', authorship attributed to Ramanuja and dated to the 11th century AD.
10. As symbolic 'Moon Child' (lunar offspring), this small rocky world appears bound by similar constraints to that of its parent (Moon), never exceeding ecliptic latitudes of 5°+/−.
11. Perihelion = an orbiting body's closest proximity to the Sun.
12. Aphelion = an orbiting body's most distant point from the Sun.
13. Venus appears to exercise the most extreme levels of declination relative to the ecliptic plane. As the zodiacal belt is frequently described as being 18°, it is possible that this designation had been assigned to accommodate Venus retrograde.

18

── DAGDHA (Combustion) ──

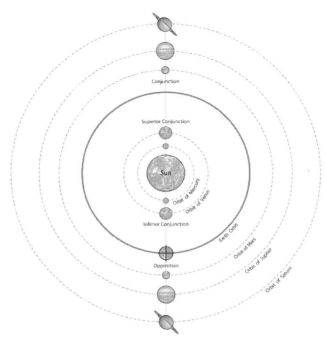

Opposition and conjunction of planets from an Earthbound perspective: Planets are considered conjunct when passing behind the Sun, opposition infers (Earth) to be in-between a planet and the Sun. As the orbits of Mercury and Venus lie closer to the Sun their combustion may occur behind (superior conjunction) or in front of (inferior conjunction) the Sun. Note: Orbits represented here are idealised (circular) and do not portray their true orbits or the distances between planets.

Dagdha means to 'ignite' or to be 'set alight'; from an astrological (and Earthbound) perspective it simply implies that a planet currently occupies a portion of the sky close to the Sun, either obscured by the Sun's mass or lost (in plain sight) to the glare of this luminary. That is, through solar obscuration the Sun temporarily hides superior planets (Mars, Jupiter and Saturn) at conjunction and the inferior planets (Mercury and Venus) at both superior and inferior conjunction, the latter backlighting inferior planets with such intensity that they become invisible (see Chapter 17).

Jyotish recognises an observable disempowerment of any planet encroaching upon Sûrya's position (or vice-versa) with periods of greater proximity noted to weaken positivity from a benefic planet whilst simultaneously charging a malefic with increased hostility. From observations of their repeated interaction with the great luminary, rules pertaining to individual degrees of combustion or dagdha[1] were formulated as shown in the table.

Table of degrees of combustion[2]

Graha/Planet	Combustion (Direct)	Combustion (Retrograde)	Combustion (Prasna)
Chandra/Moon	12°	–	8°
Kuja/Mars	17°	17°	12°
Budha/Mercury	14°	12°	7°
Guru/Jupiter	11°	8°	9°
Shukra/Venus[3]	10°	8°	7°
Shani/Saturn	15°	"	9°
Rāhu/North Node	–	–	–
Ketu/South Node	–	–	–

Generally, all planets are deemed safe 15° either side of the Sun (a coverall distance noted to relax and stabilise their functionality). Placements of 10° (or less) induce partial combustion, with planets becoming fully combust at 5° or less – all typically delivering worsening results, not only for their sign/s of rulership and Kārakas but also for the house/s under their stewardship. Combust planets are said to become *kopa* (angry) with ever tighter degrees of combustion, eliciting compounded intensity and frustration until finally lost, that is, eclipsing or being eclipsed by the solar disc.

Mercury (notably) and Venus (somewhat) enjoy a closer solar relationship, both attaining some added resilience to Sûrya's brilliance. This intransigence becomes apparent not only during periods of direct motion, but is noted to increase during periods of retrograde activity (see table); that is, Mercury may even display heightened activity and influence as it nears its limits of combustion. Additionally, Venus (also known as the *morning star*) had long been recognised to challenge the dawn, earning itself the highest degree of solar resistance. In regard to the remainder of the planets – Moon, Jupiter and Saturn – all fare a little better than Mars, who as a *heating* planet quickly succumbs to the blistering radiance of Sûrya. As the lunar nodes are without visibility and mass they are not inclined to suffer combustion;

in fact quite the reverse, as they relish the chance to distort (Rāhu) or taint (Ketu) either luminary, projecting their presence with renewed intensity.

NOTES

1.   Also known as Astangata.
2.   *Jātaka Pārijāta* advises that *asubha* (inauspiciousness) of Venus occurs within 5° of the Sun.

19

GRAHA YUDDHA
——— (Planetary War) ———

If (in their conjunction) planets both be very near to one another and bright, then their fight is called saṃágama. If both the planets be small or overpowered, then the fight is called kūṭa or vigraha (respectively).

Sûrya Siddhânta

Through years of extensive and patient observation, astrologers were able to confidently map vikśepa (planetary orbits), noting how (on occasion) their courses would lead to head-on encounters. While normal journeying about the firmament often brought planets into close proximity, periodically they appeared to collide as if entangled upon their astral tethers. Such instances were termed *Graha Yuddha*[1] and at distances of 1° or less were interpreted as open hostility between grahas.

Witnessed from Earth's perspective, these engagements were duly categorised according to the severity of their interaction: *occultation, grazing, clashing of rays* or *heading south*:

- *Bheda (occultation):* The brighter (or nearer) graha cleaves its neighbour; at such times one planetary body may appear divided. This event was noted to defeat or disempower the vanquished. During such observances rains were noted to fail, along with discord amongst influential families.

- *Ullekha (grazing):* Literally 'pairing'; the discs of planets appear to touch but not obstruct one another. During such observances famine was likely, along with war and dissent.

- *Aṁśu mardhana (clashing of rays[2]):* Planetary rays (colour), albeit subtle, are detectable by the unaided eye; here some mixing (or disturbance) of their rays becomes apparent. During such observances disagreements between kings and the likelihood of war loomed close.

- *Apasavya (heading south):* Conjunct grahas (at distances of less than 1°) are said to be warring; *Vijita* (defeated or vanquished) planets are symbolically struck down, that is, found *standing to the south* (lesser ecliptic latitude) of the victor. During such observances, hostilities between monarchs came to the forefront of daily life.

The following relate some engagement rules and pronouncements on a planet's warring status:[3]

1. The great luminaries are considered invulnerable and therefore beyond any matters of yuddha; their brilliance outshines all planets.

2. Aprākāshaka (lunar nodes) are also ineligible, having no weight (mass/physical body) with which to collide.[4]

3. Eligible tārāgraha (star planets) for a warring status include: Mercury, Venus, Mars, Jupiter and Saturn.

4. Any planet found to be in a warring state that lacks brilliance is to be considered vanquished.

5. Planets appearing small, rough, quivering, lacking in colour or unnaturally coloured are to be considered vanquished.

6. Retrograde planets in a warring state are to be considered vanquished, although their defeat is sometimes less considerable.

7. Planets standing south (lesser ecliptic latitude) of their opponent are to be considered vanquished.

8. A planet is considered *jayin* (victorious) when displaying lustre, brilliance or largeness; these qualities redeem a planet, even when left *standing south.*

Note: Due to the qualitative attributes of Venus, its shukra (literally 'shine and lustre') outclasses all competitors, making defeat by Mercury, Mars, Jupiter or Saturn highly unlikely.[5] *Sûrya Siddhânta* states: 'In the fight of Venus with any of the minor planets (tārāgraha), Venus is usually the conqueror, whether she be north or south (of the other).'

19.1 EFFECTS OF A PLANETARY WAR

Vanquished planets are considered *nipiditha* (afflicted), unable to project benefit or strength. Benefic planets lose much of their active positivity while malefics create greater strife, conflict or suffering, inflicting injuries or presenting other forms of physical danger. This situation may become especially troublesome (or pronounced) if the vanquished/fallen planet happens to be the ascendant lord.

Planetary war (alternate viewpoint)

Modern Vedic astrologers tend to minimise or even bypass the complex issues presented by Graha Yuddha, in part because the classical texts present so many conflicting views on the subject. One contemporary Jyotishi who has researched and written extensively on this subject is Edith Hathaway.[6] She uses principles originating from master practitioner Chakrapani Ullal and his family of astrologers in Kerala, India. These principles in turn are based on the Vedic classics, Varāhamihira's *Brihat Saṃhitā* and Kalidasa's *Uttara Kalamrita*, and her 15 years of comprehensive research into these phenomena. See her 2010 article on this topic, *Graha Yuddha: Testing the Parameters of Astrology and Astronomy* (Hathaway 2010a). Precedence is given to planets in this descending order: 1) size (Saturn's giant ring system gives it dominance over Jupiter); 2) effulgence, or brightness; and 3) speed of orbital motion. See also her book *In Search of Destiny* (see Hathaway 2012), which covers in depth the importance of Graha Yuddha as it impacts the great Jupiter-Saturn conjunctions.[7]

As an example of bypassing the complex issues of Graha Yuddha, some modern Jyotishis may tend to focus solely on the inherent nature of the warring planets and how they influence one another. For example, is the losing planet battling with a benefic or malefic (the latter damaging the former on two counts)? If both planets are benefic in nature then even the fallen planet reaps some positive benefit. Alternatively, a close conjunction of benefic Venus with malefic Mars automatically corrupts some of the former's positivity, regardless of the latter's defeat (which to all intents and purposes will actually render it a greater malefic force). In such cases (argue some), how important is the effect of Graha Yuddha when the overall situation of a planet is foreshadowed by the closeness of a powerful malefic?

NOTES

1. Also known as grahayuti.
2. Also referred to as obliteration of rays.
3. See planetary conjunction/conflicts, *Brihat Saṃhitā* and *Sûrya Siddhânta*.
4. Even if excluded a warring status with other planets, the nodes wreak considerable damage upon the Sun and Moon during saṃágama (conjunction).
5. One possible contender may be Jupiter's transition through Cancer. In this Rashi, Jupiter was noted to be particularly radiant.

6.   A brief summary of Edith Hathaway's working methods: Graha Yuddha occurs when two planets are within one degree of each other in the same sign or in adjacent signs, and this applies only to Mercury, Venus, Mars, Jupiter and Saturn. The winner takes on the energy of the losing planet, while overpowering it with its own energy and agenda. Unless other factors soften the outcome, the affairs of the loser, as Kāraka (significator) and house lord are diminished considerably, especially during its major or minor dasha (planetary period). The victorious planet is chosen in this descending order:

- Size and influence of the planet (Saturn and its rings over Jupiter).
- Effulgence, or brightness.
- Speed of orbital motion.
- If the victorious planet (as determined by factors #1 through 3 above) is also situated north of the defeated planet, by either celestial longitude, declination or latitudes – but especially by declination – then it is also usually the decisive winner. However, the winner may also be to the south.
- Mars is a special exception, being generally the loser in Graha Yuddha, even when situated further north, or within one degree of Mercury – the one exception in which the losing planet is also the larger planet. But in general, the other four planets are all bigger, brighter, or faster than Mars, which as loser creates particular havoc.

7.   For more on Edith Hathaway's work on Graha Yuddha, please see her articles at www.edithhathaway.com (particularly Hathaway 2010b) and her lecture (http://edithhathaway.com/shop).

PART III

MEDICAL ASTROLOGY AND ĀYURVEDA

20

MEDICAL ASTROLOGY

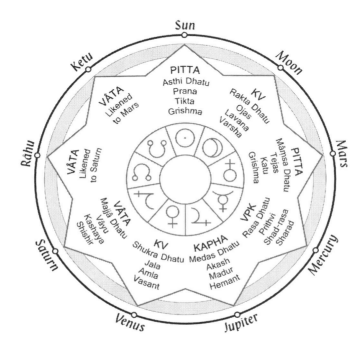

The Sun and Moon are respectively of the nature of fire and water, and the five (minor planets) Mars, Mercury, Jupiter, Venus and Saturn sprung severally from fire, earth, æther, water and air.

Sûrya Siddhânta

According to Vedic cosmology the visible universe was divided into three realms of existence: Bhū (Earth), Bhūvaḥ (atmosphere) and Svaḥ (heavenly abodes). The Sun, Moon and stars distantly shone in heaven, devas and demi-gods resided in the middle kingdom or atmosphere, while mankind dwelt upon the surface of the Earth.

To be *seized* by planets (casting impressions upon Earth's inhabitants) was deemed partly if not wholly responsible for afflictions/ailments.

Propitiation of these same planets therefore became an important means by which to arrest disease and return the body to a state of health.

Interactions between medicine and astrology appear in most of the world's ancient cultures, as starlight and planetary motion were deemed an inseparable yet essential part of the healing sciences. The attributes of many medicinal ingredients (be they animal, vegetable or mineral) were often likened to planetary attributes or considered to fall under the auspices of a particular planet. This mutuality could be based upon certain physical appearances or be the result of observed curative actions. Needless to say, such ingredients were often included in formulae seeking to *counteract* or *placate* the effects of an inauspicious grahas.

Medical astrology is a tradition that remains wholly intact into our present age, awash with ritual, yantra, mantra, figurines, amulets and of course medicines, all aiming to relieve or remove affliction (see Chapter 29).

Observation of planetary courses (transits) or the reappearance of certain fixed stars (at their helical rising) still continues to determine some forms of medical *muhūrta*, under whose auspices the preparation of certain medicines is undertaken or becomes ill-advised. This appended 'astr-potentiating' can at times be used to great effect.

In consulting a horoscope the astrologer attempts to *access* information that may aid in the negation of arisen medical conditions or, better still, dispel those that are yet to manifest. To each of the grahas, Rashis or Nakshatras, the ancients assigned a particular constitutional quality, which – when read in totality – helped relate the potential for optimal health or provide probable health trends set to manifest throughout life.

Much like the precepts of Āyurveda (discussed next), one of the principal aims behind medical astrology is to advise such 'life-regimes' that sought to avert potential health risks prior to their manifestation. If such conditions seemed emphasised (beyond the point of avoidance), an astrologer might still be able to intercede with a host of techniques designed to placate such malefic planets or wrathful deities that seek to undermine health.

20.1 ĀYURVEDA

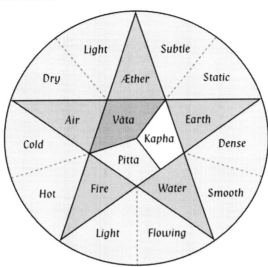

Pañca Mahābhūtas (five element theory in Āyurveda).

Perhaps one of Vedic Astrology's greatest assets is its allied and interwoven relationship with *Āyurveda*, the indigenous healing system of India. Both are best considered complementary studies in a series of deeply interconnected *sister-sciences* that unite upon the pathway toward holistic health and vitality. Associated branches of wisdom include: internal medicine, surgery, psychology, astronomy, astrology, alchemy, geomancy (sacred spaces), asana (yogic postures) and mantra (sacred utterances) – to name but a few.

The true origins of Āyurveda remain unknown; however, many believe it to be a concise healthcare system with a written history of some three thousand years. If its oral traditions are also considered, this date might be pushed back to 5000 BC, and beyond. As India was and is a culture famed for its oral rather than written traditions, discernment of an absolute date for the emergence of Āyurveda may never be possible or agreed upon.

Learning Āyurvedic philosophy is not such a complex undertaking; however, applying that knowledge as an effective diagnostic and treatment tool can take a lifetime. Āyurveda is truly 'the science of life' and so the best way to understand it is to become 'a student of life'. To this end Āyurveda recognises every constitution to be unique – yet composed of three coexisting and universal principles, constantly subject to variance. These imbalances are given rise to in the mind through inappropriate thoughts or physically through impaired digestion, poor assimilation of nutrients or ingested toxins. Imbalances may also be brought about through external agents such as repetitive physical action, over-exhaustion, bad posture, lack of sleep or prolonged exposure to harsh environmental factors, such as excessive coldness or high temperature.

Āyurveda uses the term *dosha* (meaning to taint or spoil) in describing these three universal principles, which – if held in balance – regulate and maintain vitality. When imbalanced, disturbed or vitiated, dosha quickly leads to diminished health, lowered immunity and loss of vitality. Left un-remedied and sufficiently imbalanced, the body starts to manifest various types of *dis-ease*. If an individual's ability to repel and reverse this disease process is severely compromised, the eventual outcome may be the loss of life.

20.2 DOSHA AND ELEMENTS

> The three doshas, Vāta, Pitta and Kapha, are the cause of all pathology in the physical body. The Gunas, Rajas and Tamas are the cause of all pathology in the mind.

> *Caraka Saṃhitā*

Āyurveda recognises the three dosha named Vāta,[1] Pitta and Kapha, each composed of *Pañca Mahābhūta* or primal elements: *Vāta dosha (æther/air), Pitta dosha (fire)* and *Kapha dosha (water/earth)*. Vāta-Pitta-Kapha (hereafter V-P-K) was believed to relate to the three primordial deities and forces witnessed in nature, these being:

Indrā (wind/vitality) = Vāta

Agnī (fire/heat) = Pitta

Soma (rain/moisture) = Kapha

Pañca Mahābhūta defines the five states of matter:

Space (æther)

Movement (wind)

Heat/Transformation (fire)

Liquid (water)

Stability/Density (earth)

Genesis and interaction of Pañca Mahābhūta are often described as having arisen from the eternal void (æther), stimulated by subtle consciousness. From these primordial stirrings gaseous substances (air) and movement (wind) came into being, expanding the void. As the pressure and friction of these gases intensified, they became heated (fire), forming humidity and eventually condensation (water), which began to settle and condense, forming solid and cohesive substances (earth). The qualities of each primary element help also to define the characteristics of their corresponding dosha, as shown in the table.[2]

Element and Ruling Planet	Element Qualities and Associations
Akash (Æther) Jupiter	Pervasive, expansive, light, subtle and diffuse. Æther provides the space within which all elements interact. Æther relates to the mind, nervous system and cavities (spaces) within the body. Æther is directly related to the sense of hearing (ears) and to the voice (sound).
Vāyu (Wind) Saturn Rāhu Ketu	Dryness, coldness, roughness and restlessness, Air pushes (moves) all other elements. Any form of movement within the body relates to the air element, that is, respiration, circulation, elimination of waste, physical posture. Air is directly related to the tactile sense (skin) as well as to holding (hands).
Tejas (Fire) Mars Sun	Heating, radiant, vibrant, subtle, colourful and transformative. Fire aids in the process of conversion and assimilation. Within the body, fire resides in the small intestine, heart, eyes and blood. Fire is directly related to hunger, thirst, digestive capacity and the regulation of bodily temperature. Fire is directly related to vision (eyes) and to motion (feet).
Jala (Water) Venus Moon	Coldness, sliminess, moistness and taste; its concentration brings fluidity and viscosity; it provides softness and lubricates the body. Water is directly associated to plasma, sweat, mucus and urine; it also accumulates in the urino-genital system. Water is directly related to the sense of taste (tongue) and the elimination of excess liquid (urino-genital system).
Prithvi[2] (Earth) Mercury	Heaviness, dullness, density and fragrance, its concentration governs stability, resilience, mass and overall endurance. Earth relates to the physical structure such as skeletal frame, solid tissue (muscle), the skin, hair, teeth and nails. Earth directly relates to the sense of smell (nose) and the elimination of solids (anus).

20.3 V-P-K

Āyurveda asserts that all living things possess unique combinations (or ratios) of dosha that help define the myriads of individual constitutions and variations of life forms. Your own allocation and ratio of dosha determines your digestive capability, metabolic rate (including excretion), immune system, senses, nervous system and overall longevity.

As guardians of health and wellbeing, the qualities of each dosha are described below.

Vāta

Vāta means 'that which moves' or 'motivates' the remaining doshas; that is, Pitta and Kapha are both regarded as lame dosha. Vāta was intuited and observed to reside within the hollow organs and bone cavities within the body, filling the subtle channels (nervous system) of the body. Vāta controls the tactile sense, balance (including physical coordination) as well as our mental inclinations. Vāta is the prominent force behind adaptability, changing emotions and the capacity to think clearly (or not), often acting without thinking. When balanced, Vāta readily provides energy through the steady movement of breath and the control of bodily urges. Vāta sharpens the senses and enables the body to react to external stimuli in a timely fashion.

Vāta predominates in the autumn and pre-winter, its propensity to confuse or diffuse rising as the days grow steadily shorter and colder. Autumn sees the accumulation of Vāta in the body; its effects are both drying and cold, creating exhaustion, fear and nervous energy. Vāta is associated with the senses, particularly those of touch and hearing; imbalances to Vāta dosha quickly impact the body through physical tremors/spasm or muscular cramping. Vāta firstly accumulates in the colon (its primary location and associated organ) or manifests itself through the auditory channels of the body – creating sensitivity to loud noise or manifesting itself as a faint high-pitched whistle or ringing in the ears. Imbalances of Vāta dosha often show an inclination/craving for dry, pungent or astringent foods, all of which ultimately increase Vāta dosha (see the table 'Planets in association with the 2nd house' in Section 20.7 for more information). Common characteristics of Vāta include: coldness, dryness, lightness, subtlety, motion, sharpness, hardness, roughness and clarity. Hard, cold, changeable environments aggravate Vāta whereas warm, comfortable, safe environments pacify Vāta.

As Vāyu is a highly mobile element its pathways are numerous; therefore excesses of Vāta (within the body) move freely, accumulating wherever they may, in often quite disassociated parts of the body. Mentally, Vāta is a quick study, absorbing information in a timely matter but unable to retain that knowledge for prolonged periods. A mind dominated by stimulated Vāta constantly reaches out for external stimuli, thrills or instant gratification, only to drop suddenly into extended periods of exhaustion or depression. Vāta is highly mobile dosha yet normally resides in the hollow organs of the body or within the porous structure of the bones, especially the joints. Arthritis, tooth decay/falling teeth, dry skin and constipation are classic signs of Vāta accumulation. Any diseases that involve the senses/nervous system show strong indications of an imbalance of Vāta. In the ancient Greek humeral system (the preferred diagnosis system employed by western physicians until the 18th century), the attributes and disease patterns of Vāta dosha were mostly attributable to their equivalent *Melancholic* or *black-bile* temperament.

Pitta

Pitta, meaning 'that which digests' or 'cooks', is the dosha most responsible for metabolic and chemical/transformative processes in the body. Pitta also regulates and maintains our capacity to mentally digest thoughts, emotions or impressions received via the senses, particularly vision (a Pitta-dominated sense). Within the digestive system Pitta may be likened to fire suspended in a liquid form such as acid, bile salts and other important digestive enzymes which assimilate nutrients. Good assimilation helps build tissue, maintain bodily heat and destroy rogue pathogens.

Pitta helps maintain suppleness by lubricating the tissues with vital oils, such as those found upon the skin or in the hair. Pitta also imparts colour, blushing our skin in health or discolouring it during periods of disease – such as inflammation or bruising incurred through blood pathogens or external injury (such as insect bites). When balanced, Pitta provides hunger (appetite), thirst and a balanced digestion; it supports the blood, heart, eyes, liver, spleen and small intestine. Pitta promotes the intellect and the power of discrimination.

Pitta predominates during the summer season, as the lengthening days increase in dryness and heat. Those in whom Pitta dosha predominates tend toward heightened states of dynamic activity and passion during this period. With increased accumulation this dosha quickly spreads outward and upward from its centralised location, creating heat (fevers) inflammation, itchiness or allergic reactions (such as hay fever). Emotional states are also prone to flare up (like fire) during periods of Pitta accumulation, tempers often becoming frayed as their own unattainable perfectionist goals start to eat into their reserve of patience, fuelling greater irritation and frustration. An imbalance of Pitta dosha often creates the craving for pungent, salty or sour foods – all of which increase heat (see the table 'Planets in association with the 2nd house' in Section 20.7 for more information). The balancing tastes of sweet, bitter and astringent all help cool and regulate Pitta, dispersing heat and oiliness, sedating appetite and digestive juices.

Common characteristics of Pitta include: hot, oily, light, subtle, flowing, mobile, sharp, soft, smooth and clear. Competitive or aggressive environments aggravate Pitta, whereas cool, relaxed and quiet environments displace its intensity. Those in whom Pitta predominates are fast, intensive or obsessive students of knowledge; Pitta types enjoy the accumulation of knowledge on a large range of subjects but mostly tailor their library to maximise information which gives them a competitive edge or helps accelerate their ascent through the ranks. Pitta likes to attain some position of authority or respect.

Pitta is primarily concentrated in the small intestine; any disease involving heat, bleeding, itchiness, inflammation or skin eruptions (boils, etc.) indicate the presence of vitiated Pitta. Typically, imbalanced Pitta may be seen as a yellowish discolouration of the eyes or skin; it may also be detected via the olfactory senses (in the form of pungent smells emanating from the body). In the ancient Greek humeral system the attributes and disease patterns of Pitta dosha were mostly attributable to their equivalent *Choleric* or *yellow-bile* temperament.

Kapha

Kapha, meaning 'that which binds' or 'sticks' is the dosha most responsible for bodily cohesion. Kapha supports the mucous membranes, flexibility and lubrication of joints, muscles, ligaments, and so on. Kapha is related to the element of earth and has many similar (metaphorical) attributes, particularly its susceptibility to cracking or erosion if it is allowed to become overly dry (much as the soil becomes parched and dusty when deprived of rain). As the body is comprised mostly of water, adequate (and good quality) hydration is essential to maintain healthy tissues; that is, a body can survive a reasonable amount of time without nutrition, but perishes quickly once deprived of water. When balanced, Kapha provides steadfastness (resistance), cohesion, lubrication, assuredness and patience.

Kapha predominates during the late winter and early spring, with its damp, dark and cold nights slowly giving way to the thaw and flow of the spring waters. This latter period sees an end to winter's deadlock and with it the evacuation of bodily toxins accumulated throughout the sedentary winter months – toxins which now find themselves mobilised and flowing outward from the body. True Kapha types naturally seek to conserve energy and this becomes greatly exacerbated during the winter months; however, the arrival of warmer weather again returns mobility, pliability, softness and the need to shake off the winter blues. An imbalance of Kapha dosha often creates a craving for sweet, sour or salty foods – all of which increase heaviness and stickiness (see the table 'Planets in association with the 2nd house' in Section 20.7 for more information). The balancing tastes of pungent, bitter and astringent all help dry excess secretions, dispersing dampness and cold.

Common characteristics of Kapha include: cold, wet, heavy, gross, dense, static, dull, soft, smooth and cloudy, as well as lethargy (sluggishness), introversion, attachment and greed. Those in whom Kapha predominates tend to be compassionate, caring, nurturing and sensitive, have excellent memory recall, are cautious, steady, dependable and reliable. Kapha types are not normally obsessive but may drift into periods of worry or doubt during which their need to accumulate or 'make safe' is fuelled. It is during such periods that Kapha may indulge in such unhealthy practices as greed, meanness and ignorance. Kapha generally enjoys assimilating knowledge, but may be highly selective about subject matter, tending to focus on sentimental or purely practical information that might help prepare them for those proverbial 'rainy days'.

Kapha dosha is concentrated in the chest (primarily lungs), stomach, lymph, synovial joints, fat tissues, aqueous fluid and mucous membranes. Diseases involving coldness, dampness, itchiness, circulation, nausea or oedema often indicate the presence of excess Kapha. Typically, imbalanced Kapha may be seen in the frame or face; that is, weight gain, puffiness, paleness, or excess mucosa of the eyes or palate. Kapha may also be detected via the olfactory senses (in the form of sweet smells emanating from the body). In the ancient Greek humeral system the attributes and disease patterns of Kapha dosha were mostly attributable to their equivalent *Phlegmatic* or *white-bile* temperament.

Note: An extensive and highly practical explanation of Āyurvedic principles has been presented by Vaidya Ātreya Smith (2009) in his *Ayurvedic Medicine for Westerners*, Volumes 1–5. Readers are referred to these works for more comprehensive information on Āyurveda.

20.4 ĀYURVEDA, PLANETS AND HEALTH

Vāyu (Vāta), Pitta and Kapha are the three doshas; in brief they destroy or support the body when they are abnormal or normal respectively.

Aṣṭāṅga Hṛdayam

More than any single component (in Jyotish), the impact of planets upon health are paramount; their positioning and inter-relationships are noted to ward off or instigate various ailments during a lifetime's course. Each of the planets display doshic tendencies, which taken into consideration alongside Rashis and Nakshatras help determine *prakriti*, that is, one's constitutional apportionment of dosha. The 6th house of disease, its lord and fixed Kāraka (in this case Mars and Saturn) also prove useful in the determination (or likelihood) of various infirmities.

As a rule, all malefics – Mars, Saturn, Rāhu, Ketu and Sun (in that order) – tend to weaken the constitution by providing the means by which dosha are encouraged to accumulate and proliferate. Conversely, the benefic planets – Jupiter, Venus, Moon and Mercury (in that order) – seek to preserve (and protect) bodily health/longevity.

The following tables detail both general planetary health effects, positive and negative (Part 1) and specific effects such as dosha, taste and Kāraka (Part 2).

Table of planets in health (Part 1)

Malefic	
Mars	*Positive:* Well-positioned or favourably aspected, Mars promotes vitality, discipline and potent Agnī (balanced metabolism, etc.). Mars helps the body resist attacks (externally and internally).
	Negative: Mars promotes accidents, injury, surgeries, infections, inflammation, fevers, sudden illness, acute conditions, blood poisoning, burns (including chemical burns), radiation and other toxic measures applied in a medicinal fashion (petro-chemical-based medicines).
Saturn	*Positive:* Well-positioned or favourably aspected, Saturn gives physical endurance (strong constitution) and longevity. Saturn can delay the onset of disease or consign illness to later periods in life. Saturn is favourable for fasting (austerity), which may help alleviate certain conditions.
	Negative: Saturn promotes long-term/chronic conditions that dry and emaciate tissues; it seeds diseases that thrive in cold, damp environments, causing degeneration that prematurely ages the body. Saturn also promotes fatigue, loss of mobility, numbness and necrosis.
Rāhu	*Positive:* Rāhu may promote health through inquiry; its thirst for knowledge may be useful in discovering the underlying cause of a disease. Rāhu rules Visha (toxins), which may also be used to great effect if given in correct dosage and frequency.
	Negative: Rāhu generally acts unfavourably in health, promoting addictions to intoxicants that undermine longevity; Rāhu also indicates long-term conditions such as genetic disorders or those conditions that spread out of control. Viral conditions that seek to undermine the immune system are one of Rāhu's hallmarks.

Ketu	Positive: Ketu may promote health through abstinence, intelligence or spiritual development, particularly if associated with a strong benefic.
	Negative: Ketu generally acts unfavourably in health, promoting addiction to intoxicants, intake of poor-quality food, loss of intelligence and poor concentration. Ketu indicates long-term conditions such as recurrent fever, blood disorders or bacterial infections.
Sun	Positive: Well-positioned or favourably aspected, the Sun promotes allocation of prāṇa (life-force), vitality and strong Agnī (digestion). It affords protection through good circulation (healthy heart) and vigilant immune system.
	Negative: Sun is a weak malefic, but if encumbered by additional malefic aspects or poorly positioned it can undermine health through lowered immunity and a loss of vitality.
Benefic	
Jupiter	Positive: Often termed 'Great Benefic', Jupiter promotes long-term health and vitality. It can under certain circumstances counteract or strongly alleviate the effects of other malefic grahas.
	Negative: If poorly positioned or unfavourably aspected, Jupiter may promote lethargy, overindulgence and obesity; Jupiter may also show some involvement in the retention of water (swellings) or arterial blockage.
Venus	Positive: Overall, Venus promotes long-term health and supports the immune system.
	Negative: If poorly positioned or unfavourably aspected, Venus may be implicated in ongoing infections, water retention, lowered immunity and urino-genital infections.
Moon	Positive: Moon generally gives better results if waxing or at full Moon. Whatever its condition, Moon promotes some positive health results; it cannot do otherwise as it is considered a caring mother.
	Negative: If poorly positioned or unfavourably aspected, Moon may promote negativity, mental anguish or lowered immunity. Moon may be implicated in fevers, infections, blood impurities or water retention. As Moon is also a Kāraka for longevity, its state and strength are paramount in Jyotish.
Mercury	Positive: Mercury is potentially a weak benefic, but able to give excellent results if well-positioned or aspected by other benefics. Association with malefic planets renders its health potential neutral, even slightly malefic.
	Negative: When afflicted, Mercury may be implicated in nervous conditions, respiratory ailments or partial paralysis. Mercury is the planet of health and healing; it also governs intelligence (and mental health). The ancients considered afflictions to Mercury to be extremely troublesome as damaging one's intelligence leads to unwise life decisions.

Table of planets in health (Part 2)

Planet	Dosha	Taste	Body Parts	Kāraka
Sun	Pitta	Bitter	Heart, eyes, bones and pituitary gland	Health and Vitality
Ailments	Heart disease, bone porosity, fractures, falling of teeth and tooth decay, cataracts, blurred vision, injury to eyes, fevers and inflammation, circulatory problems, strokes, skin diseases and stomach disorders, injury to the head, dysentery, burns and poisoning			
Moon	Kapha	Salty	Blood, lymph, spleen, reproductive fluids, digestion, aqueous fluid and pineal gland	Mind and Emotions
Ailments	Diseases of the breast (mammary glands), uterus, menstrual disorders, heart, stomach, chest and lungs (TB, etc.), blood poisoning, fevers, jaundice, oedema, weakness of the kidneys, diabetes, appendicitis, diarrhoea, cough, colds and flu			
Mercury	Tri-dosha	Shad-rasa	Plasma, skin and nervous system and thyroid and parathyroid gland	Intellect
Ailments	Kustha (all skin diseases), paralysis, facial ticks, epilepsy, vertigo, tinnitus, sores and ulcers, nervous indigestion, mental imbalances (madness), mercury poisoning, viral infections, diseases involving all three dosha, diseases of the mouth and tongue			
Mars	Pitta	Pungent	Muscle, ligaments, blood and adrenal glands	Strength and Courage
Ailments	Infections and inflammation due to accidents, injury to the head, conjunctivitis, bleeding disorders/blood poisoning, anaemia, blood loss (internal haemorrhaging), hypertension, boils and ulcers, bleeding haemorrhoids, fistula, itching, rashes, bruises, blood cancers, excessive or heavy menstruation			
Venus	Kapha-Vāta[3]	Sour	Kidneys, the eyes, reproductive fluids, immune system, pancreas and thymus gland	Passions and Physical Proportion
Ailments	Diseases of the eye, reproductive organs (venereal diseases), urinary infections, painful bladder syndrome, functionality of endocrine (secreting) glands – specifically pancreatic imbalances (diabetes), metabolism of water – oedema, vitiligo, sexual impotency, gonorrhoea, syphilis, goitre, gout, cysts and hernia			
Jupiter	Kapha	Sweet	Liver, gallbladder, spleen, fat tissue and pancreas	Wisdom and Happiness
Ailments	Diseases of the liver, gallbladder and spleen, ear infections, oedema, excess fatty tissue (lipoma), benign tumours, high cholesterol, swelling of limbs, swelling of tongue, memory loss, Alzheimer's and dementia, heartburn, blood poisoning and slow-healing abscesses			
Saturn	Vāta	Astringent	Joints, marrow, teeth, nervous system, sinew and gonadal glands	Death, Disease and Longevity
Ailments	Arthritis, rheumatism, rheumatic fevers, rickets, bone spurs, torn ligaments, neuralgia, paralysis, kidney stones, urinary calculi, diseases of the colon, abdominal bloating, dry skin, leprosy, leucoderma, osteoporosis, tumours, tooth decay and the premature falling of teeth, gum disease, greying of hair, loss of hearing, mental anguish, ailments of the feet, all chronic conditions or infections, diseases common to old age or those that affect the movement of hips, thighs, knees and ankles			

Rāhu	Vāta	As Saturn	As Saturn	Addictions, Intoxicants
Ailments	Generally any conditions attributed to Saturn are similarly displayed by an ill-placed north node. Diseases specific to Rāhu include: snake bite, poisoning from chemical toxins, infections of the chest, cancers, cataracts, viral infections, food poisoning, genetic disorders, blood cancers, long-term mental disorders including psychosis and schizophrenia			
Ketu	Vāta[4]	As Mars	As Mars	Parasites and Confounding Diseases
Ailments	Generally health conditions attributed to Mars are similarly displayed by an ill-placed south node. Diseases specific to Ketu include: worms (all parasites), poisoning from chemical toxins (side effects of other medicines), blood poisoning, bacterial infections from animal or insect bites, rashes, strange bruises or skin discolorations, low blood pressure, stomach pains and those diseases that defy explanation or are notoriously difficult to cure			

Although planets are categorised by dosha, it should also be noted their ability to derange may not be evenly distributed. For instance, vitiated Vāta as produced by an ill-disposed Saturn may surpass that produced by an equally ill-disposed Rāhu, and so on. The following table shows a sliding scale of doshic potential.

Vāta - Pitta - Kapha

Vāta	Saturn, Rāhu, Ketu, Mandi, Mercury (afflicted) and Moon (waning or afflicted)
Pitta	Mars, Sun
Kapha	Jupiter, Venus and Moon (waxing and afflicted)

20.5 DHATU AND SROTA (METABOLISM AND TRANSPORTATION)

One of the most important concepts behind Āyurveda is its insights on tissue functionality and interdependence – and nowhere is this more highlighted than in the assimilation of food taken into the body. *Sapta dhatu*[5] (seven tissues) is best visualised as a series of continually rarefied tissues that individually reduce, assimilate, rebuild and replenish failing structure. They also form deep interlocking dependencies with each other, every level of their processing supporting and being supported by the collective. Srota (very simplistically) are the channels of communication that connect these vital tissues; their pathways are innumerable, their network feeding every part of the organism. Srota and dhatu are to be considered inseparable.[6]

The seven tissues in sequence are:

- *Rasa:* Its chief function is to nourish; its name means 'to go'. This nutritive fluid immerses and bathes the bodily tissues; it represents the largest portion of the dhatus. When weakened or diminished there is tiredness, dryness, pains in the chest and heart, despondency and an intolerance of loud noises.

  Mercury is considered to be the lord of Rasa Dhatu; its state and strength in a horoscope indicate the functionality and performance of this tissue.

- *Rakta:* Its chief function is to enliven; it gives courage, brings warmth and colour to the tissues. When weakened or diminished one takes pleasure in fermented foods, the tissues become lean, there is flaccidness of skin.

  The Moon is considered to be the lord of Rakta Dhatu; its state and strength in a horoscope indicate the functionality and performance of this tissue.

- *Māṃsa:* Its chief function is to surround and protect; it gives strength, the will to fight and move. When weakened or diminished the eyes become dull, the joints become painful, the cheeks and buttocks reduce.

  Mars is considered to be the lord of Māṃsa Dhatu; its state and strength in a horoscope indicate the functionality and performance of this tissue.

- *Medas:* Its chief function is to lubricate and insulate; it provides a cushioning effect for the skeletal framework, allowing free movement. Medas helps protects the physical structure from the harshness of the environment. When weakened or diminished the buttocks shrivel and become numbed, the limbs become thin and the joints appear to creak.

  Jupiter is considered to be the lord of Medas Dhatu; its state and strength in a horoscope indicate the functionality and performance of this tissue.

- *Asthi:* Its chief function is to support; it gives strength and stature to the body. When weakened or diminished, the joints become painful, the bones feel brittle, teeth and hair will fall prematurely.

  The Sun is considered to be the lord of Asthi Dhatu; its state and strength in a horoscope indicate the functionality and performance of this tissue.

- *Majjā:* Its chief function is to fill the empty spaces; it nourishes the vital organs, gives strength to the eyes and keeps the senses sharp. When weakened or diminished the bones feel weightless and hollow, giddiness and darkness of vision may be experienced.

  Saturn is considered to be the lord of Majjā Dhatu; its state and strength in a horoscope indicate the functionality and performance of this tissue.

- *Shukra:* Its chief function is to give rise to offspring; it promotes creativity and resistance, it gives lustre to the skin. When weakened or diminished procreation may be difficult, the mind and body become listless or subject to lowered immunity.

  Venus is considered to be the lord of Shukra Dhatu; its state and strength in a horoscope indicate the functionality and performance of this tissue.

20.6 INTERPRETATION OF DHATU

Although these seven tissues have no real comparisons in allopathic medicine, there are some modern correspondences to the popular biochemical appraisals of the body; however, the functionality and assimilation models accredited to sapta dhatu remain tenuous. Generally these seven tissues might be interpreted as:

Rasa = plasma/lymph (clear part of blood)

Rakta = haemoglobin (red part of blood)

Māṃsa = muscle tissue/ligaments

Medas = fat tissue (adipose) loose connective tissue

Asthi = bones and joints

Majjā = brain tissue/marrow and nerve tissue

Shukra = semen/ovum (all reproductive fluids)

The culmination of sapta dhatu supports and sequesters the vital essence known simply as *ojas*, a life-giving substance that imbues the body with power, resilience and immunity from disease. The full process of food conversion and assimilation, that is, from *Rasa Dhatu* to *Shukra Dhatu*, was believed to correspond to a period of 708 hours or 29.5 days (roughly a synodic lunar month), hence the Moon is considered an important Kāraka for longevity, youthfulness and fertility.

20.7 THE SCIENCE OF TASTE AND THE 2ND HOUSE

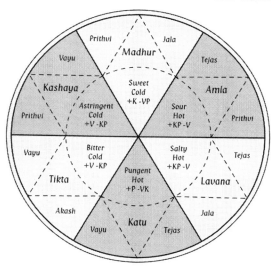

The six tastes, dosha and elements.

The science of taste is a large and complex study in its own right, but here we content ourselves with the qualities of taste and the 2nd house in Astrology. Food has perhaps one of greatest impacts on health and forms a large part of our daily routine, therefore what we choose to consume on a daily basis, that is, healthily vibrant foods or processed de-mineralised/synthetic foods, we naturally reflect in our bodies. Literally, 'we are what we eat'.

Āyurveda uses a system of six tastes (see illustration) to help categorise their actions, the basic premise being that during a normal dietary regime a balanced mixture of the tastes should be sought. It had been noted that over-consumption of foods which predominated in a particular taste ultimately lead to similar types of disease. Likewise certain foods or herbs prescribed in terms of predominant taste/s help to correct imbalances seen in the bodily tissues. The six tastes have been given as:

- *Sweet:* Promotes growth, strength, moisture and longevity. It helps build and maintain all seven tissues. Sweet improves lustre/texture of skin, is soothing to mucous membranes and gives lubrication to the tissues and supports the immune system. In excess, the sweet taste increases Kapha dosha and āma, causing obesity, lethargy, reduced digestive capacity (low Agnī), parasites, excess mucus/catarrh and vomiting. Foods that typically predominate in the sweet taste include: milk, honey, fruit sugars, grains, nuts, herbs (cinnamon) and vegetable starches.

- *Sour:* Stimulates the palate and appetite, promotes strength, reduces Vāta, refreshes the sense organs, nourishes the heart, increases bodily secretions and expedites digestion by its moistening effect. In excess it aggravates Pitta and blood, causing oedema/swellings, itching, burning sensations in the chest, vertigo, ulcerations and the suppuration of wounds, turbid urine and the weakening of muscle tissue. Foods that typically predominate in the sour taste include: cheese, yoghurt, sour fruits, fermented wines, pickled vegetables and tomatoes.

- *Salty:* Promotes digestion through its agglutinative effects, reduces Vāta, reduces accumulation and obstruction (mild laxative), hydrates and brings softness to the tissues, liquefies Kapha, neutralises all other tastes, improves circulation and reduces stiffness of the limbs. In excess it aggravates Pitta and blood, aggravates skin diseases, and causes greying of hair, inflammation and stiffness of joints, morbid thirst, falling teeth, wrinkles, patchy balding (alopecia) and general ageing. The salty taste increases the desire to eat more and consume (physically as well as materially). Foods and minerals that predominate in the salty taste include: rock, sea and table salts, processed foods (monosodium glutamate), sea foods and sea vegetables (seaweeds).

- *Pungent:* Promotes digestion and keeps the palate clean. It aids in the elimination of waste and the burning up of toxins; it reduces obesity and it removes agglutinative substances. It reduces Kapha, kills pathogens/bacteria and removes clotted blood. In excess it aggravates Pitta and blood, causing dryness, emaciation, burning sensations, pain in the extremities, bodily tremors, reduction of muscle mass, light-headedness and morbid thirst. Foods that typically predominate in pungency include: garlic, chilli, ginger, cayenne pepper and cardamom. Milder pungent tastes include coffee and tea.

- *Bitter:* Promotes the tastes of other foods, digestion and tautness of the skin, dries excess moisture, reduces Kapha/Pitta and increases the removal of mala (bodily wastes). The bitter taste reduces itching of the skin, fevers and burning sensations, its action being both germicidal and antibacterial. Used in excess it depletes dhatu (emaciation), especially rasa, rakta, māṃsa, medas and shukra. The bitter taste creates coldness, lightness and dryness of the palate and aggravates diseases of a Vāta nature. Foods that typically predominate in bitterness include: barley, dark leafy vegetables, bitter gourd, and spices such as sage and turmeric. Herbal bitters include: gentian root, neem, coptis, goldenseal and malabar tamarind.

- *Astringent:* Promotes the reduction of bodily fluids. Its action is drying, binding, cold, heavy and stiffening. The astringent taste reduces Kapha and helps to relieve Pitta-type ailments such as bleeding disorders. If astringency is used in excess it causes dryness of the tissues, constipation, distension of the abdomen, reduction of blood circulation, pain in the sides of the chest, weakness of the heart and a darkness of countenance. The astringent taste causes spasms, stiffness of joints and vitiation of Vāta dosha. Foods that typically predominate in astringency include: dried pulses, beans, tofu, sprouts, lettuce and alfalfa. Fruits such as apple, pomegranate and plantain are a good source of the astringent taste.

Once sensed upon the tongue, taste (requiring jala mahābhūta for rasa to be apparent) stimulates the metabolism accordingly, allowing foods to be broken down into their constituent elements.

The following table is a general guide to interpreting planets strongly influencing the 2nd house (in the horoscope). This should be judged first from sign rulership and the situation of its lord, second by direct occupation of planets and third by planetary aspects (although the latter is given slightly less importance). The ancients interpreted the 2nd house as indicative of appetite, sustenance (food intake), quality of foods and bodily support (being 2nd from the 1st house, the house most determining the structure of the physical body). This awareness and appreciation of 'daily intake' as underpinning health illustrates the importance of the 2nd house in all matters of constitutional analysis.

Planets in association with the 2nd house

Sun/Bitter	A liking for flavoursome 'heating' foods – mildly spiced with such herbs as cardamom, long pepper and black pepper. As Sûrya is a royal planet, one may have expensive (or exclusive) tastes in food and drink; that is, costly brands or officially endorsed products. As Sun is the Kāraka for Agnī (digestive capability), its placement in the 2nd house indicates that food is likely to be well-assimilated. Sun in a fire sign may show a tendency to over-consume overcooked, caramelised foods, heated upon an open flame/charcoal (often containing larger amounts of carbonised material). There may also be a fondness for wheat. Sun in the 2nd indicates a strong appetite.
Moon/Salty	May show a preference for sour food such as curds, cheeses or certain fruits. Moon generally indicates highly 'nutritive' foods but is also inclined to over-consume if waxing. When combust there may be some digestive instabilities due to over- or under-eating. Like the lunar phases, appetite may be variable. As Chandra is a royal planet, one often enjoys expensive (or exclusive) foods or drink (especially the latter). Moon in a water sign indicates a liking for cool foods or chilled drinks with over-consumption often giving rise to bloating or nausea.
Mars/Pungent	Indicates a liking for pungent 'spicy' foods, particularly spiced meats, favouring wild game. Mars in the 2nd indicates undercooked (rare), barbequed (cooked upon an open flame) or hastily prepared foods. There is a tendency to eat on the hoof, or to eat with heightened speed (often biting one's own lip – drawing blood) or choosing foods that aggravate the palate, causing mouth ulcers. This insufficiency of mastication invariably leads to acid reflux. There is generally a liking of strong beverages, such as coffee, wine and spirits – although all derange Pitta dosha. Mars in the 2nd might also show a tendency toward heightened aggression (in words or manners) when hunger pangs begin to arise. All of these traits become emphasised if Mars is located in a sign ruled by the fire element. Mars generally indicates foods of a lesser or lower quality.
Mercury/ Shad-rasa	Considered positive if Mercury is optimally positioned or aspected, shad-rasa (six tastes) shows a balanced consumption of the various food groups. As Budha is a royal planet, one may have expensive (but fickle) tastes in food and drink. As Mercury is a natural mimic, the ruler of the 2nd house should also be carefully appraised as well as malefic aspects that fall upon this most impressionable of planets. Mercury indicates food of better quality but may also indicate over-commerciality (mass-produced foods) or as Kāraka for mimicry might also indicate ersatz (substitute) materials being used to imitate the real thing; inverted sugars being used instead of jaggery, honey or cane sugar, for example.
Jupiter/Sweet	Jupiter in the 2nd indicates a liking for madhu 'sweet' (indulgent foods). Its presence here may give a relaxed approach to food, eating a little more than required, or continually sampling foods throughout the day. The sweet taste comprises water and earth and so most likely to build tissue; its cooling characteristic suppresses Agnī and may even dampen the digestive fires when over-consumed. Jupiter indicates the most extravagant and exotic of tastes; it's also a Kāraka for overindulgence and weight gain. Jupiter (alongside Venus) has some part to play in the body's metabolisation of water and so should be studied carefully for difficult conjunctions or aspects increasing the likelihood of water retention.

Venus/Sour	A liking for sour or fermented foods, mildly heating but generally nutritive. Venus shows an inclination to 'showy' foods, perhaps better 'presented' than actual nutrition content. As both Jupiter and Venus are teachers/instructors they both indicate an awareness of the links between food and health, hence either generally make sensible decisions as to what may be nutritious. Like the Moon, Venus in the 2nd may also gravitate to heavy, mucus-forming foods causing disturbances in the body's metabolisation of water and sugars. Venus generally indicates high quality (and relatively expensive) foods, unless combust or under difficult aspect.
Saturn/ Astringent	May show a liking for preserved 'old' out-of-season foods; that is, pickled, salted or freeze-dried. Saturn in association with the 2nd house may also feel comfortable with eating out-of-date food, rancid or overly fermented foods; his influence here may also a show a tendency to seek out 'reduced' items – sold cheaply to clear the shelves. One may consume foods not necessarily appealing to them but satisfied to get a bargain. Saturn in the 2nd may also indicate fasting on a regular basis, or able to stick to a monotonous diet for long periods. Saturn can also indicate a liking for root vegetables or highly simplistic foods, such as broths, soups and salads. Saturn generally indicates foods of lesser quality or, at the least, eating foods that are out of season.
Rāhu/ Astringent	Although similar to Saturn, Rāhu does boast a few independent attributes. These include: a taste for the exotic (foreign foods), heavily processed, mildly toxic or banned (restricted) substances. Rāhu in the 2nd almost always indicates some type of craving (addiction), be it for coffee, tea, sugar, alcohol or cigarettes. It is almost a given that there is some disturbance in the initial part of the digestive process, not to mention ailments of the teeth, gums and palate that disturb normal eating habits. Rāhu in the 2nd also indicates a proclivity to try new or unknown substances – whether this be 'new takes' on old recipes or chemically synthesised/genetically modified produce that attempts to mimic natural foods. Rāhu generally indicates foods of an unnatural 'enhanced' quality.
Ketu/Pungent	Although similar to Mars, Ketu also boasts a few independent attributes. These include: a love of exotic, foreign foods, spicy (pungent) or brightly coloured foods – particularly yellows and reds. As Ketu is Bhikshu Kāraka it might also indicate one who is fed by strangers or is often given food by friends and others. As Moksha Kāraka, Ketu might indicate a neutrality toward food, favouring little intake of sustenance (eating only to satiate hunger). Generally Ketu in the second is not favourable for quality foods; like Rāhu it also indicates some type of craving (addiction), particularly for alcohol, cigarettes or highly pungent spices.

20.8 GRAHAS, RASHIS AND NAKSHATRA PURUṢA – PLANETS, STARS AND BODILY DIVISIONS

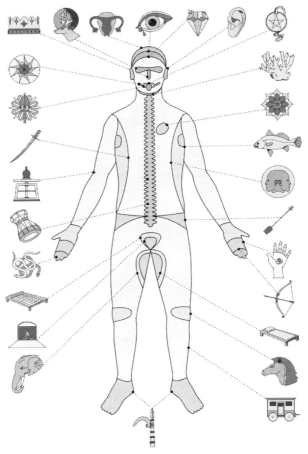

Nakshatra Puruṣa or Cosmic Man.

He who observes the Nakshatra Puruṣa Vrita[7] will after his death become a star and, along with the innumerable stars of brilliant lustre, live until the end of Brahmā's day (432,000,000 years), after which the dissolution of the universe occurs.

Brihat Saṁhitā by Varāhimira

Astrological folklore recounts how Lord Śiva once demonstrated to his consort Pārvatī the connections between grahas, Rashis and the human form, temporarily filling the heavens with his body as he flowed across the zodiac, matching his proportions with those of the *Rāshi Puruṣa* (personified zodiac). To this his head and face fell in Aries and Taurus, his neck and shoulders in Gemini, his breast and heart in Cancer and Leo, his abdomen in Virgo and Libra, his genitalia in Scorpio, his thighs in Sagittarius, his knees and calves in Capricorn and Aquarius and his feet in Pisces (see table for a more detailed account of Rāshi Puruṣa).

Rashis	Element	Planetary Lord	Corresponding Body Parts
Aries	Fire	Mars	Crown, bones of the head and face, brain
Taurus	Earth	Venus	Facial tissue, eyes, nose, tongue, throat, ears and neck bone
Gemini	Air	Mercury	Collar bone, shoulders, lungs, arms, hands and fingers
Cancer	Water	Moon	Breast/chest, ribs, stomach, lungs and elbows
Leo	Fire	Sun	Heart, small intestine, liver, spleen, gallbladder and spine
Virgo	Earth	Mercury	Colon, abdomen and intestines, lower back
Libra	Air	Venus	Pancreas, bladder, kidneys, uterus, ovaries and internal reproductive organs
Scorpio	Water	Mars	External genitalia, prostate gland and organs of elimination
Sagittarius	Fire	Jupiter	Pelvis/hips, thighs and thigh bone, arteries and veins
Capricorn	Earth	Saturn	Joints, specifically the knee and knee cap, and hamstrings
Aquarius	Air	Saturn	Calves, ankles, small joints, tendons and ligaments
Pisces	Water	Jupiter	Foot bone, feet and toes, lymph system

The planets too become aligned (during this demonstration), displaying their dominion over bodily parts. Within this *Graha Puruṣa*, Mars signified the head and forehead, Venus the eyes and face, Mercury the neck and shoulders, Moon the heart, breast and chest, Sun the abdomen, Jupiter the thighs and genitals, Saturn the knees and upper leg, Rāhu the shins and, finally, Ketu the feet.

Added to these associations Sun was noted to preside over Atma (soul) and prāṇa (life-force), Moon (the mind), Mercury (the intellect and speech), Mars (strength and courage), Venus (potency and sensuality), Jupiter (happiness and knowledge), Saturn (suffering and grief), Rāhu (desires and addiction) and Ketu (rebellion and moksha).

Additionally, some reference to *Nakshatra Puruṣa* is to be found in the Purāṇas, specifically *Vāmana* and *Matsya Purāṇa*, although little explanation of their origination or medical use is expounded upon. Whilst most Purāṇa make *some* mention of Nakshatras, it is more with reference to their seasonal arrival or sacrificial acts. Many rituals coincide with the seasonal appearance of important stars that herald a renewal of oblations to one's ancestors/progenitors or the pacification of the luminaries during eclipses. The appearance of Nakshatras also signals auspicious times to bathe in sacred rivers or perform abhisheka (a consecration of sacred idols) and other rituals.

Generally, planetary and (solar) zodiacal anatomical associations are considered to take precedence over their (lunar) counterparts. The reasoning behind this hierarchy is Chandra's appropriated light from Sûrya, which then animates Nakshatras. Because of this their radiance is accordingly subtle or diffused. That being said, Nakshatras are still worthy medical indicators, when exploring *subtle* health risks. The lunar-zodiac often pinpoints hidden strengths or potential weaknesses inherent to their respective body part/s.

Health conditions specific to Nakshatras have been included in the table.

Nakshatras	Dosha	Body Part/s	Specific Conditions
Ashwini	Vāta	Knees	Higher instances of febrile conditions
Bharani	Pitta	Crown of head	Intestinal infections; loss of beneficial intestinal flora
Krittika	Kapha	Waist	Prone to irregular elimination (constipation) or bouts of diarrhoea
Rohini	Kapha	Shins	Poor elimination habits/disturbed apana Vayū, haemorrhoids, etc.
Mrigashirsha	Pitta	Eyes	Acid reflux and abdominal bloating
Ardra	Vāta	Forelock and hair	Low Agnī, insufficient or irregular digestive capability
Punarvasu	Vāta	Fingers	Recurring instances of digestive parasites, malabsorption of minerals
Pushya	Pitta	Mouth	Nausea, bloating and heaviness in the digestive tract
Aslesha	Kapha	Fingertips and nails	Poor circulation, fatigue and anaemia
Magha	Kapha	Nose	Respiratory weakness and/or cardio arrhythmia
Purvaphalguni	Pitta	Genitalia	Prone to chest infections, asthma or shortness of breath
Uttaraphalguni	Vāta	Genitalia	Skin irritation including rosaceae, blisters, sores and itchiness

Hastā	Vāta	Palm, hand	Hypoglycaemia, metabolisation of water and sugars, prameha (diabetes), etc.
Chitrā	Pitta	Forehead	Vertigo, inner ear infections and tinnitus
Swati	Kapha	Jaw and chin	Weakness of vision, cataracts and muscae volitantes (floaters)
Vishaka	Kapha	Arm and forearm	Damage to ears including reduced levels of hearing and/or inner ear inflammation
Anuradha	Pitta	Heart	Prone to sinusitis, rhinitis, nose bleeds, etc.
Jyestha	Vāta	Tongue, mouth	Diseases of mouth, gums and palate, including teeth, jaw and throat
Mula	Vāta	Feet	Respiratory weakness, shortness of breath and pronounced chest infections
Purvashadha	Pitta	Thighs	Weakness of kidney, water retention, urinary calculi
Uttarashadha	Kapha	Thighs	Sensitive stomach, over-production of mucus, nausea
Śravana	Kapha	Ears	Loss of appetite, sensitive gums (mouth ulcers)
Dhanistha	Pitta	Spine	Damage to tendons/ligaments, rheumatic conditions
Shatabhishak	Vāta	Teeth	Falling of teeth and hyperacid
Purvabhadra	Vāta	Sides of torso	Vitiated Kapha, over-production of mucus (chest)
Uttarabhadra	Pitta	Sides of torso	Vitiated Vāta; cramps, muscular fatigue in the chest area
Revati	Kapha	Armpits, lymph	Prone to skin inflammation such as rashes, sores and boils

20.9 ALTERNATIVE NAKSHATRA PURUṢA

A simplified version of Nakshatra Puruṣa is sometimes adopted in regard to general bodily divisions. This alternative arrangement effectively 'groups' Nakshatras into three primary zones, beginning with Krittika, segmenting the body into:

Head and neck

Torso and arms

Waist and legs

Head and Neck		Torso and Arms		Waist and Legs	
Krittika	Top of head	Uttaraphalguni	Shoulders	Uttarashadha	Reproductive organs
Rohini	Forehead	Hastā	Arms/hands	Śravana	Anus
Mrigashirsha	Eyebrows	Chitrā	Fingers	Dhanistha	Thighs
Ardra	Eyes	Swati	Upper chest	Shatabhishak	Knees
Punarvasu	Ears	Vishaka	Breasts	Purvabhadra	Calves
Pushya	Nose	Anuradha	Stomach	Uttarabhadra	Shins
Aslesha	Lips	Jyestha	Navel	Revati	Ankles
Magha	Chin	Mula	Waist	Ashwini	Feet
Purvaphalguni	Neck	Purvashadha	Hips/pelvis	Bharani	Toes

NOTES

1. Also Vāyu.
2. Coming from Pṛthu, meaning to nourish.
3. It should be noted that the doshic inclinations of Venus are complex, its rulership of Taurus and Libra incline it toward a Kapha (primary) and Vāta (secondary) disposition.
4. Parasara assigns Rāhu and Ketu a windy/Vāta temperament; however, some Ayurvedic practitioners judge Ketu to be predominantly Pitta in dosha. Ketu may often appear Martian-esque, yet deeper investigation inevitably reveals Vāta to be its driving dosha.
5. So called because they support Dhāraṇa (the body); see *The Roots of Āyurveda* (Wujastyk 2003).
6. For advanced information on the interaction between Dhatu and Srota, see *Āyurvedic Medicine for Westerners, Vol. 1* by Vaidya Ātreya Smith (Smith 2009a).
7. A devotee who worships Lord Vishnu (possessor of all constellations) in accordance with prescribed rituals attains liberation. Worshipping his varying body parts (and organs) associated with Nakshatras, one attains good health and freedom from all diseases. For more information see *Vāmana Purāṇa* (6.22.3).

21

–VARGAS (Divisional Charts)–

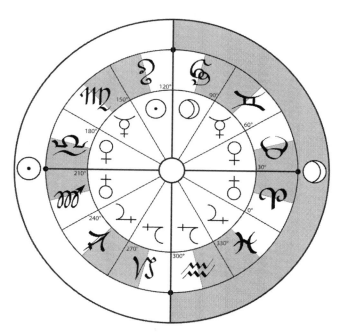

Leo to Capricorn indicates the solar division of the zodiac, Cancer to Aquarius its lunar division.
To determine a planet's Hora, odd signs (0°–15°) fall under the Sun's rulership and 16°–30° the
Moon. Even signs (0°–15°) fall under the Moon's rulership and 16°–30° the Sun.

Any foray into divisional charts, or Vargas, opens a doorway into one of the
most intriguing aspects of Jyotish, as well as one of its greatest predictive
assets. No other subject matter (it seems) preoccupies astrologers more
than its Vargas – and how best to harness their predictive powers.

Divisional charts are exactly what their name implies: subdivisions
of the D-1 or Rashi chart into ever-decreasing increments of degree.
Shodash-vargas (the sixteen most common divisions) represents subtle
projections that aim to provide additional insight into specific areas of the
horoscope. The energetic of each Varga is denoted by its numerical suffix,
its calculation centred upon the number 12.

To arrive at the core harmonic value of each Varga (larger than D-12) simply divide its suffix by twelve: the remaining value reveals its harmonic essence. For example, *Vimshamsha* or D-20 = 12 ÷ 20 = 1 remainder 8, therefore this Varga may be said to resonate with 8th house significations (see Chapter 13). *Note:* Vargas wholly divisible by 12 resonate with 12th house significations, that is, D-24, D-60, etc.

The ascendant (of each harmonic) and its lord represent you or the querent and your/its relationship to that divisional. Other noteworthy situations include the state and strength of each Varga's associative house, for example the 9th house in Navamsha, or the 3rd house in the Drekkana; as well as the planetary Kāraka most significant to such houses, for example Sun/Jupiter for the 9th house in Navamsha or Mars for the 3rd house in the Drekkana.

Note: Most Jyotish software provides instant access to Varga information (quickly and painlessly), making their inclusion in any astrological analysis a priority. It should also be noted here that Varga charts derived from a D-1 chart are abstractual and do not reflect the true astronomical placements of planets and signs (or houses). The table lists the qualities of Shodash-vargas.

D (1-60)	Name	Degree	Effects and Duration*
D-1	Rashi	30°	Main birth-chart. *Ascendant changes every 2 hours.*
D-2	Hora	15°	Wealth/poverty (financial status), confidence, receptivity and empathy. *Ascendant changes every 1 hour.*
D-3	Drekkana	10°	Physical strength, courage, relations with siblings, short-term accomplishments, alliances, accidents and injury. *Ascendant changes every 40 minutes.*
D-4	Chaturtamsha	7° 30'	Comforts, home-life, landed property, assets, liabilities and general contentment. *Ascendant changes every 30 minutes.*
D-7	Saptamsha	4° 17' 09"	Children, grandchildren, dynasties and their properties. Creativity, art and musical ability. Short-term relationships may also be considered from this Varga. *Ascendant changes every 17 minutes.*

D-9	Navamsha	3° 20'	Traditionally refers to marriage and long-term partnerships; this divisional chart is sometimes given greater weight with the passing of years, becoming 'pro-active' in adult life. In practice, however, D-9 represents the hidden strength of the grahas (as revealed in D-1). It also indicates one's dharma (fortune), luck, spiritual inclinations and constitutional strengths (health, etc.). Navamsha may also be used to describe possible future incarnations. *Ascendant changes every 13 minutes.*
D-10	Dashamsha	3°	Achievements, recognition, fame, career and vocational skills and social status. D-10 indicates overall ability to realise goals. *Ascendant changes every 12 minutes.*
D-12	Dwadashamsha	2° 30'	Ancestors, family lineage, hereditary traits, status and wealth/support of parents. D-12 indicates hidden or subconscious desires, dreams and the likelihood of distant journeys to be made. As much as D-9 affords glimpses into future lives, D-12 offers a flavour of previous incarnations. *Ascendant changes every 10 minutes.*
D-16	Shodashamsha	1° 52' 30"	D-16 projects a 4th house energetic, being studied for qualities of residence (property), modes of transportation (conveyances), domestic harmony and general happiness. D-16 is also useful in determining mental stability, rationale, consistency, reliability and inner contentment. *Ascendant changes every 8 minutes.*
D-20	Vimshamsha	1° 30'	D-20 projects an 8th house energetic, being studied to reveal spiritual inclinations, higher aspirations, devotional acts and benefits obtained through ritual. *Ascendant changes every 6 minutes.*
D-24	Siddhamsha	1° 15'	Siddha = one who is enlightened or accomplished in learning, likewise this Varga indicates breadth of wisdom, memory retention, academic achievement, general perception, skills and awareness. *Ascendant changes every 5 minutes.*
D-27	Nakshatramsha	1° 06' 40"	Also known as Bhamsa Varga, this divisional details inherent strengths and weaknesses of planets by virtue of Nakshatra lords shown to be highlighted in the D-1. It is also studied to assess one's mental, physical and spiritual prowess. The numerology of this Varga also indicates its use in determining the combined auspiciousness of one's Nakshatra placements. *Ascendant changes every 4+ minutes.*

D (1-60)	Name	Degree	Effects and Duration*
D-30	Trimshamsha	1°	Also known as the Karma chart. It is useful in determining adversities or general misfortune; its thirty-fold division harbours a '6' energetic. Traditionally trimshamsha Varga was thought to reflect evils likely to afflict one. *Ascendant changes every 4 minutes.*
D-40	Chaturvimshamsha	45'	Also known as Khavedamsa. This Varga ascertains general auspiciousness and inherited karma (through one's maternal lineage). *Ascendant changes every 3+ minutes.*
D-45	Akshavedamsha	40'	Akshavedamsha again ascertains general auspiciousness and inherited karma (through one's paternal lineage). *Ascendant changes in just under 3 minutes.*
D-60	Shashtiamsha	30'	Describes previous incarnations and karmas most likely to fructify in a current incarnation. Shashtiamsha describes happiness and reward attained in the present life. *Ascendant changes every 2 minutes.*

* Durations of Ascendant are approximate; that is, based on 1° = 4 minutes.
Note: Additional works on Jyotish consider higher values of Varga such as D-72, D-81, D-108, D-144, D-150 and D-300; however, all require incredibly accurate birth data.

21.1 D-9 (NAVAMSHA VARGA)

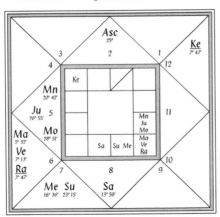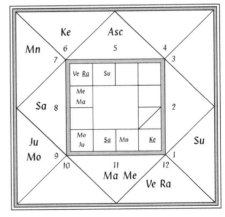

Rashi chart (left) and its corresponding Navamsha (right).

For relative completeness, we shall briefly discuss the most important of the divisional charts, that is, D-9 – better known as Navamsha – and outline its calculation method and implications.

The inclusion of Navamsha calculation in any astrological portrait cannot be overstated, many times being afforded *almost* equal status to that of its originating Rashi chart. To calculate this Varga each Rashi is divided into nine equal parts of 3° 20' each. Grahas falling into one of these nine subdivisions of Rashi are reapportioned to a new sequence of Rashi – beginning from the movable Rashi, that is, Aries, Cancer, Libra or Capricorn – dependent upon the sign's element shown in the horoscope, so fire starts with Aries, water/Cancer, air/Libra and earth/Capricorn.

The more perceptive reader may wonder why Navamsha is consulted to ascertain the quality of one's spouse/marriage partner while D-7 (Saptamsha) is not. The reasoning behind this is that D-9 (Navamsha) is greatly associated with spiritual development and that the 7th house happens to be the 11th house (gain) from it. As Venus is a prime significator for relationships or spouse, it should also be closely marked for analysis in Navamsha, together with the condition of the 7th house and the seventh house from Venus.

It is sometimes said that if the Rashi D-1 is the tree, then Navamsha D-9 is the fruit of that tree; and indeed there seems to be a great deal of truth to this as well-featured planets in Rashis often fail to materialise their full potential when ill-disposed in Navamsha. Additionally, all sign lords in the Rashi chart should be carefully assessed to see whether they occupy favourable signs in Navamsha.[1] This same method extends to any planetary ruler whose Nakshatra hosts planets in the D-1 as some consider the auspiciousness of the D-9 to be representative of *Nakshatra Kuṇḍalī*, that is, the combined 'hidden wealth' behind all the horoscope's asterisms.

The Navamsha is sometimes thought also to reveal future incarnations, hidden talents or abilities developed in later life. When and if this method is adopted, the D-9 gains in significance with the passing of years. Exactly how many years is debatable, but two possible junctures seem likely: the age at which one marries or if the native remains single, the D-9 may become more influential after the first Saturn return, that is, about 29+ years of age.

21.2 VARGOTTAMA

Planets gaining *Vargottama* status usually perform with added vitality and heightened activity. These usually come to the fore during a corresponding dasha period (see Chapter 22) or transit. Vargottama planets are those recurring in the same sign in both D-1 and D-9. *Note:* In the above sample charts, planet Saturn is positioned in the 8th sign (Scorpio) in both D-1 Rashi and D-9 Navamsha.

Planet/s found to be in a state of Vargottama have been highly praised in the classical texts, often awarded a lesser kind of exaltation status. This in practice may be a trifle optimistic, yet it also seems true to say that grahas lucky enough to find themselves in this position do indeed display some ability to 'stand out' or 'rise above the competition'. As always, careful examination of the planet in question and its Kārakas (active, stable or natural) may provide vital clues as to where its talents will most likely manifest.

Note: Connections between D-1 and D-9 are generally auspicious, or indicate the means by which personal distinction arises. However, planet/s debilitated in both D-1 and D-9 may doubly confirm a 'challenged status', this coming to the fore during any dasha of the respective planet.

NOTE

1. Some Vedic astrologers also consider house positions.

22

─────── DASHAS ───────

Dasha is one of the principal mechanisms of *Phalita Jyotish*[1] (predictive astrology) developed by the ancient seers to chart life's progression. The word *dasha* might be translated as 'stage' or 'current period' and aims through a series of divisions and subdivisions to attune itself to all aspects of daily life. With a good number of dashas to choose from, finding the most appropriate one can be a task in itself. That being said, many astrologers opt for the most recommended dasha system; or one with a track record of reliability that best serves the needs of the general populace. One such calculation, known as *Viṃśottarī*[2] (meaning 120 years) has risen to pre-eminence in India and is afforded great weight in many astrological analyses, often to the exclusion of all competitors.

During the *Age of Kali*,[3] an optimal 120 years was thought attainable by those with an intractable adherence to daily worship, who partake of wholesome diets, take residence in mountainous abodes, exercise and practise estrangement from life's daily distractions (see Wilson 1896). It is unlikely that most will ever live to see all nine planetary periods included in a Viṃśottarī cycle – but what can be said is that those chosen to become prominent during the allotted lifespan will each (in turn) make their presence felt.

22.1 CALCULATION OF VIṂŚOTTARĪ

Ruling Planet	Corresponding Nakshatras
Ketu	Ashwini, Magha and Mula
Venus	Bharani, Purvaphalguni, Purvashada
Sun	Krittika, Uttaraphalguni and Uttarashadha
Moon	Rohini, Hastā and Śravana
Mars	Mrigashirsha, Chitrā and Dhanistha
Rāhu	Ardra, Swati and Shatabhishak
Jupiter	Punarvasu, Vishaka and Purvabhadra
Saturn	Pushyami, Anuradha and Uttarabhadra
Mercury	Aslesha, Jyestha and Revati

As previously discussed, the zodiac, so divided into twelve equal parts, contains an equal twenty-seventh division of 13⅓ degrees or 800 minutes of the ecliptic: that is, 800×27 = 21,600 and 21,600/60 = 360. The numerological significance of 27 is tied to Moon's sidereal orbit – that is to say, its conjunction with a particular star along its lunar orbit until again returning to that same star. This happens over a period of approximately 27⅓ days (the latter ⅓ being disregarded for ease of calculation). These lunar portions called *Nakshatras* (see Chapter 26) became highly significant and highly ritualised in the Vedic calendrical system as the Moon was witnessed to (roughly) traverse 13⅓ degrees each day. These daily increments of lunar travel came eventually to signify the boundaries of Nakshatras.

Calculation of Vimśottari relies on knowing Moon's longitude at birth, commencement of its cycle being taken from this degree. The degree of the natal moon also denotes *Janma Nakshatra* or birth asterism. The planetary ruler of one's Janma Nakshatra presides over the initial dasha period. To calculate exact start/end dates for the full Vimśottari dasha cycle requires the degree and arc minutes remaining to the Moon as it transits this Janma Nakshatra.

Note: All Maha dasha periods indicate the overall 'long-term' trend; however, each major dasha period may be subdivided into lesser increments, helping to refine its predictive results. As manual calculation of dasha is more likely to be of academic interest only, I refer the reader to *Ancient Hindu Astrology for the Modern Western Astrologer* (Braha 1986, pp.217–224). Here the author has clearly and painstakingly reproduced the calculation tables necessary. Most modern astrological software already caters for a large assortment of dasha systems, including the ever-popular Vimśottari, and here tedious calculation has been catered for.

22.2 CYCLES OF VIMŚOTTARĪ

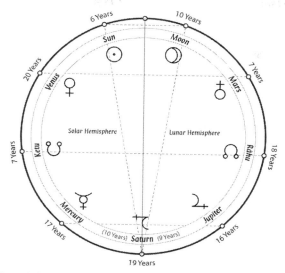

Viṃśottarī dasha cycle from Solar (left) to Lunar (right). If Saturn's 19-year dasha is split into 9 and 10 years respectively, both hemispheres total 60 years. The dasha periods of Venus, Ketu and Mercury fall under Solar influence; the dasha periods of Mars, Rāhu and Jupiter fall under Lunar influence.

On the issue of the Viṃśottarī cycle, classical Jyotish remains silent in its allocation of unequal time periods – awarded each planet. It's possible these were based upon purely observational effects or were solely mathematical in origination. One tentative explanation of their allotment was as explained to me by my teacher, suggested equally dividing a circle into solar and lunar hemispheres, with the dasha sequence of planets arranged about it, beginning with Ketu (7 years), then Venus (20 years), Sun (6 years), Moon (10 years), Mars (7 years), Rāhu (18 years), Jupiter (16 years), Saturn (19 years) and finally Mercury (17 years). If the 19-year dasha of Saturn is split respectively into 9 and 10, both hemispheres total 60 years, which when doubled provides 120 years of a full Viṃśottarī cycle.

22.3 DASHA KĀRAKA (JUDGING EACH DASHA PERIOD)

Note: This section concludes the information presented in Section 3.2.

Of course, effects of *arising* dasha periods must be specific to their horoscope of origination; however, there are certain significations that are more than likely to manifest during their allotted period. For example, regardless of how Mars might be featured in a horoscope (for better or worse), during its dasha you would fully expect to experience typical Martian significations or activities such as conflict with competitors, quarrels with enemies, success or defeat through litigation, an increase in physical exertion, an acquisition of mineral wealth or real estate, accidents, surgeries, injury from firearms, and more. The table outlines probable Kāraka (both positive and negative) that might be experienced during the dasha period of its ruling planet.

Dasha	Positive/Negative Effects
Ketu (7 years)	*Positive:* Defeat of one's enemies, honouring of ancestors, receiving goodwill or recognition for past efforts, short pilgrimages, pursuing meditational practice or performance of devotional acts, discharging of karmic debt, acquisition of gemstones, general prosperity/monetary gains.
	Negative: Incurring surgery or injury through accidents or weapons, separation from loved ones, loss of someone close, ongoing health issues accompanied by inflammation, fever or bacterial infection, urgent surgical intervention required, mental disturbances from bhūtas (ghosts/disincarnate spirits).
Venus (20 years)	*Positive:* Marriage, birth of daughters, new partnerships (personal or business), blessing from the goddess Lakshmi, renovation of one's living space, improved home comforts, acquisition of vehicles, advancement in the workplace, improved vitality, strengthening of the immune system, pleasures of the bed, consumption of sour foods, aversion to fasting, the wearing of fine clothes and ornaments and gemstones.
	Negative: Marital problems, periods of lowered immunity, ongoing health issues (primarily centred around the kidneys, bladder and lower back), other health issues including anaemia and venereal complaints, entering into relationships with lower caste women, disturbances in home life, loss of spouse, problems with vehicles (conveyances), loss of reputation, lack of respect from co-workers, suffering scandals.
Sun (6 years)	*Positive:* Begetting progeny, blessings from Brahmins, promotion in the workplace, attains positions of authority, patronage from kings (support from governmental institutions), shielded by influential people, prosperity through one's father, receiving honours from elders, success in all business ventures, general prosperity.
	Negative: Accumulating wealth through questionable means, incurring debt from kusīda (usury), loss of one's reputation, involvement in criminal activities, long-term incarceration, estrangement of father, death of father, diseases of the eyes, heart, liver, gallbladder and small intestine, acid reflux, burning sensations in the chest, mental anguish, recurrent fevers, epilepsy, osteoporosis, broken bones (fractures from accidents).

Moon (10 years)	*Positive:* Generally an auspicious dasha – enjoying successes, performances before an audience (in the public eye), acquisition of fine silks, new clothes, the consumption of ghee, butter milk, salty foods and rice, acquiring progeny (girls), acquiring cattle, blessed by Brahmins, contentment in home life, gaining a healthy weight and cherished by one's spouse.
	Negative: Suffering a restless and troubled mind, receiving little support from spouse, enduring a difficult home life, loss of recognition and ill health coming to one's mother, wife or eldest female child, loss incurred through multiple female agents, incurring weakness or ill health via the eyes, lungs, stomach or blood, suffering severe bouts of depression, sleeplessness and mental anxiety both real and imagined.
Mars (7 years)	*Positive:* Defeating one's enemies, successes through litigation, receiving promotion in the workplace, gains in personal power and strength, obtaining wealth through minerals and gemstones, inheritance through real estate, learning new technical skills, gains through younger siblings, health promoted through strong Agnī (digestive strength), improving physical stature by exercise, discipline and/or daily regimes.
	Negative: Troubled family life, constant quarrels with spouse, injury from weapons or accidents (flying projectiles), poisoning of blood, torn ligaments, muscle fatigue and cramping, fevers, fractures, eye diseases, excess bile production, indigestion and inflammation. Engaging in cruel acts, sickness or injury to younger siblings, the loss of real-estate through fire or legal issues (including inheritance issues).
Rāhu (18 years)	*Positive:* Gains through invention or technical skill, gains through extensive research or travelling, monetary gain/general prosperity, extending one's home, fulfilment of daily desires, recognition in foreign lands, acquiring foreign acquaintances, promotion in career through resourcefulness, cunning and foresightedness, learning astrology.
	Negative: Incurring enmity from others, becoming involved in criminal activity, forming addiction to intoxicants, unable to satiate desires, losing respect, holding unpopular views or being ostracised, wandering aimlessly amidst foreigners or being forced to travel – receiving little comfort, travelling in outmoded conveyances, spurned by those not native to one's place of birth.
Jupiter (16 years)	*Positive:* Receiving high quality education, receiving many attendants, wearing new clothes and enjoying excellent and abundant food, often found in the company of influential people or receiving patronage from the wealthy, gaining independent wealth, enjoying fame, becoming renowned for religious fervour or eloquence, performing virtuous deeds (pooja) and benefiting from one's progeny.
	Negative: Loss of wealth and investment, loss through one's children, involvement in public scandal, loss of credibility, losses through education, plagued by dishonest gurus (teachers), treachery through wicked people, cursed by Brahmins, illness through biliousness, liver complaints, jaundice, prameha (diabetes), excess weight or water retention.

Dasha	Positive/Negative Effects
Saturn (19 years)	*Positive:* Rewarded for hard work, acquiring agricultural lands and other fixed assets, receiving patronage from kings, progeny of a male child, receiving bounties from the Earth, enjoying wholesome foods, losing unhealthy weight, taking regular exercise (usually walking), reaping benefits from long-term investments, achieving long-held desires. *Negative:* Incurring forced dislocation, losing one's shoes, wandering far from one's birthplace, taken in by rogues or thieves, speaking harshly of others, complaining bitterly, suffering aches and pains in the joints, becoming emaciated, suffering diseases of the face or mouth, falling of teeth, loss of hair, consuming putrid/rancid foods (mostly root vegetables), desiring to drink alcohol and consume red meat, incurring premature ageing and loss of mobility.
Mercury (17 years)	*Positive:* Developing an interest in healing or health matters, becoming successful in business, trading, travelling widely, gaining reputation through eloquence, receiving honours, knowledge from elders, seeking higher education or further instruction, developing an interest in health matters or healing, learning astrology, business law or becoming renowned in mediation or communication, gaining fame and notoriety, becoming renowned for mimicry, humorous anecdotes and wordplay. *Negative:* Incurring displeasure from one's seniors, becoming quarrelsome with friends and compatriots, losing wealth through unsound business deals, litigation or breach of contracts, becoming dull and mischievous, engaging in cruel jokes and delighting in profanity, suffering diseases of the skin, respiratory tract, nervous system and throat, living in solitude, unable to communicate (loss of voice or injury to throat).

NOTES

1. Meaning to bear fruit or accomplishment.
2. Pronounced 'vim-sho-tree'.
3. One of the *Caturyuga* (four sequentially declining world ages), Kali Yuga was said to last 432,000 human years. All Yugas reside within much greater increments of time such as Kalpas and Mahākalpas. Kali Yuga was regarded to be a time of lesser spiritual development.
4. For more information see Kirk (2012).

23

—— DṚṢṬI (Graha Aspects) ——

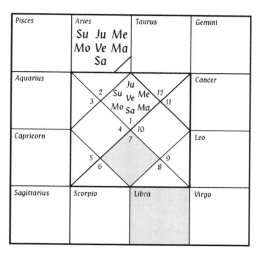

Diagram 1: All planets form a seventh house aspect (shaded grey area).

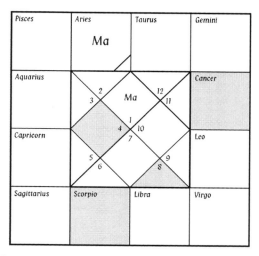

Diagram 2: Special Martian aspects 4 and 8.

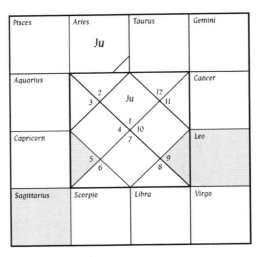

Diagram 3: Special Jovian aspects 5 and 9.

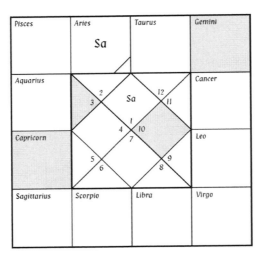

Diagram 4: Special Saturnine aspects 3 and 10.

Graha aspects are an important part of any astrological analysis, often presenting vital clues in birth-chart decryption. The word *Dṛṣṭi* (pronounced 'drishti') means 'glance' or 'give sight to', here indicating various types of angular relationships seen within the horoscope. All planets cast a 7th house aspect (assuming sign and house to be synonymous), which should be counted inclusively from the planet concerned, and forward through the sequence of zodiacal signs. For example, if Mercury occupies the 10th house, that house becomes the 1st house calculated from Mercury, the 11th house becomes the 2nd house and the 12th becomes the third house – and so on until arriving at the 4th house. This is the 7th house from Mercury and here is where he casts his 4th house aspect (refer to Diagram 1). When calculating aspects, an anti-clockwise direction is to be used for those favouring a North Indian style of chart and clockwise for those favouring a South Indian style chart.

Mars, Jupiter and Saturn all throw additional or *special aspects* from their positions. Mars aspects planets in the 4th and 8th houses from himself (refer to Diagram 2), Jupiter aspects planets in the 5th and 9th houses from himself (refer to Diagram 3), and Saturn aspects the 3rd and 10th houses from himself (refer to Diagram 4). Interestingly, there appears to be no distinction made between these various positions; that is, Jupiter's 5th and 9th aspect seem equally beneficial as much as Saturn's 3rd and 10th are to be considered trying or harmful, and so on. The main consideration, as always, appears to be the friendship or enmity felt toward the planet (or Rashi) being aspected. For more information refer to the 'Friendships, enmities and neutrality' table in Section 2.8.

Rāhu and Ketu appear to be the exception (with regard to Dṛṣṭi), seemingly unable to form aspects, only conjunctions.[1] (*Note:* Conjunctions in Jyotish are generally considered to outweigh any and all measurable effects afforded by a graha aspect.[2]) Although the nodes are in some ways inseparable (heralding from a singular entity), their actions and effects are generally fractious. Grahas found conjunct a lunar node will naturally aspect its counterpart by a 7th house aspect, yet its latter node appears not to return the aspect. It has been speculated that on some level both nodes function much like a capacitor, absorbing and storing the energy from their 'host planet' or 'sign', weakening it – before re-asserting their own agenda on the now wearied casualty. Here the conjunct node sets the agenda whereas his counterpart is merely an 'accessory after the fact'. That either node has the power to do this seems plausible, as only the nodes have the power to obscure the luminaries.

Any planetary aspect will be felt, but 'closeness' by degree produces added potency. For example, Jupiter at 1° Leo would exchange a somewhat negligible aspect with another planet tenanting 29° Aquarius. The closer the degree of aspect, the greater the intensity. It should also be borne in mind that unless planets are conjoined or in houses/signs of opposition, aspects are not mutual.

Lastly, and rather importantly, whether an aspect is to be considered favourable or not depends upon the state and strength of the planet making the aspect. That is, is the planet in question in a state of exaltation or debilitation? Is it found to be tenanting its own sign or moolatrikona (or friends) sign? Is it retrograde, combust or aspecting an enemy graha?

Note: Extensive studies of aspects (and their misunderstandings) have been explained in some detail in the excellent *Graha Sutras* (Wilhelm 2006). Readers are referred to this work for more information.

NOTES

1. Rāhu and Ketu are sometimes given to cast Jovian-like trinal aspects upon the 5th and 9th house from their position; references to this effect are supported in works such as *BPHS*. Readers are encouraged to test these aspects for themselves.
2. Planets are said to 'squabble' when occupying the same sign. Vedic Astrology generally considers it more agreeable for planets to be evenly spaced and to form favourable aspects with one another.

PART IV

THE MOON AND ITS LUNAR MANSIONS

24

── LUNAR CURIOSITIES ──

The bright fortnight of Shukla Paksha (increasing Moon phase) is considered day-time and auspicious for divine souls. Equally, the diminishing (recessive Moon phase) known as Krishna Paksha is considered their night-time. A single lunar month is then equal to a day for inhabitants of Pitru Loka or such realms. A single year as divided by Uttarāyana[1] and Dakshináyana[2] is equal to but one day of the Deva.

Manusmṛti – Laws of Manu

Earth is an oddity within our solar system, hosting a satellite almost one third its own size. From an Earthbound perspective a rising full Moon seems to dominate the horizon; from the Moon's perspective, Earth-rise would be a spectacle ten times greater.

Second only to the Sun, the Moon is our greatest and nearest luminary. Some 240,000 miles distant and 2172 miles in diameter, it dominates the stellar arena. Uniquely positioned, the diameter of the Moon is approximately 1/400 that of the Sun; however, the Sun's distance from the Earth is approximately 400 times greater than that of the Moon. Through the effect of angular diameter our Moon is perceived to be of equal circumference to that of the Sun (see Section 24.3).

Our Moon has mesmerised humanity throughout history. Early cultures were almost entirely devoted to her capricious nature as she waxed and waned her way across the heavens. It is said that the Greeks, Romans and Hebrews would all assemble at the instances of her fullness, discharging their duties of piety and gratitude for her unswerving and unwearied attendance[3] to Earth. Likewise the conspicuous nine nautical stars[4] (falling prominently along her orbit) provided ancient mariners with a means to reckon longitude at sea, enabling sustained oceanic navigation.

The Moon's sidereal month is approximately 27 days and 7 hours (fixed star to fixed star); its synodic revolution (full Moon to full Moon) is approximately 29 days and 12 hours. The Moon completes 13 such cycles during the course of our terrestrial year and all with its axial revolution almost perfectly synchronised to Earth's orbit. By an odd quirk of celestial mechanics, this manifests as a single-faced Moon (from Earth's perspective), hiding her so-called 'dark side'.[5] From the Moon's perspective its day (a full lunar month) reaches temperatures of 120°C+ and nights plummet to −120°C!

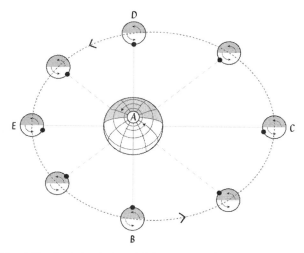

Diagram of Moon's libration in longitude with (A) representing the Earth, (B) new Moon, (C) first quarter and apogee, (D) full Moon and (E) final quarter and perigee.

Key: The dotted line shows the Moon's elliptical orbit; arrows denote the direction of orbits and rotational direction. Black dot denotes a fixed point of reference upon the Moon's surface; from the Earth's perspective this marker would be positioned at the Moon's centre. Each complete orbit sees the Moon perform one axial rotation.

Despite her outwardly fixed countenance, the Moon does subtly librate, due largely to its elliptical orbit coupled with an inequality of angular velocity. This collectively produces a rolling wobble effect, an irregularity that can be witnessed with time-lapse photography, but goes largely unnoticeable by direct observation. A libration in longitude occurs on the Moon's eastern and western limbs, alternately hiding and revealing some of the terrain nearer its northern and southern poles.[6]

As the Earth's surface area is approximately thirteen times greater than that of the Moon,[7] our reflected *Earthlight* produces a similar effect to that of Moonlight upon the Earth. This effect is magnified a dozen times, coupled with a subtle blue-green tint, bathing the lunar surface with eerie phosphorescence. During the lunar dark fortnight (approaching the Sun), our Moon enjoys two weeks of reflected Earthlight, courtesy of its companion. For the Moon, Earth exhibits similar phases of luminance, although in a contrary order. Perhaps future attempts to colonise the Moon would inevitably incur an Earth-side real estate premium, naturally demanding a higher price for this illumination as well as an Earth-rise spectacle nearer its poles. Inhabitants of Moon's so-called dark side would have to content themselves with the Sun, distant orbs of planets and of course an abundance of amazingly 'brightened stars' totally unencumbered by a thick gaseous atmosphere.

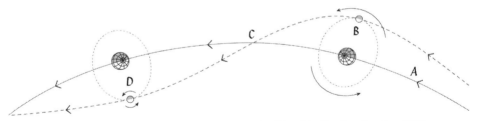

Intersection of Earth/Moon orbits: (A) Represents Earth orbit and its direction of motion. (B) The Moon, having previously crossed Earth orbit, appears to gain ground after passing full Moon. (C) Serpentine Moon orbit, threading in and out of the Earth's orbit. At its third quarter the Moon starts to lose ground to the Earth. (D) New Moon; here Earth starts to gain ground until the Moon reaches its first quarter.

With respect to Earth's orbit, our Moon pursues an elliptical pathway. This is in reality a series of large serpentine undulations, all slightly concave toward the Sun. During the course of the year the Moon regularly intercepts,[8] crosses and sweeps inside Earth orbit as both bodies hurtle about the Sun at speeds approaching 67,000 miles per hour. This additional weaving lunar motion adds an even greater capriciousness to a celestial body already associated with a fickle temperament.

In Vedic Astrology the Moon is considered to have no planetary enemies, although she does have her favourites within the royal household. This uniquely lunar attribute may be (in part) due to her regular obscuration of planets and stars during her monthly cycle. From an Earthbound perspective the rapidly advancing eastward limb of the Moon swiftly swallows both planet and star, only to have them re-emerge unscathed at her western limb. Due to the speed of the Moon and her proximity to the ecliptic, this phenomenon is a frequent occurrence. *Note:* Under greater magnification the Moon can be seen to be constantly performing the occultation of countless lower magnitude stars.

24.1 LUNAR NODES

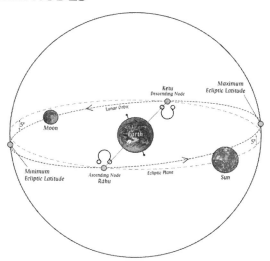

Earth-centred diagram (un-scaled): Showing the lunar nodes, lunar orbit, Moon, Earth, Sun and ecliptic. The nodal axis cuts the ecliptic at two points (see Rāhu and Ketu) inclined at approximately 5°. Every lunar month sees the Moon cross the ecliptic twice, alternately travelling northward and then south.

The route of Rāhu's circuit (Rāhumandala) is situated upon the lowest wheel of the Kāla Chakra, at an altitude of ninety thousand yojanas above the Earth and ten thousand yojanas below the path of Sûrya. The planet Ketu, with his hundred tail-like projections, resides in the same space.

Bhūgola Varṇanam

Lastly, and perhaps most pertinent to this work, are the lunar nodes and their relationship to the Earth, lunar orbit and ecliptic. The nodes are a key part of any chart interpretation, their axis[9] and graha interactions studied with great interest by astrologers. Both nodes are generally considered fully fledged planets, malefic in influence and delighting in the skewing or rarefying of planetary emissions at conjunction. Though permanently retrograde in motion,[10] neither node has any physical substance – yet collectively they produce a highly potent effect along their axis. Under the influence of the northern node, planets tend to become super-charged or uncontrollable; under the influence of the southern node, grahas may become introspective, violent or self-destructive.

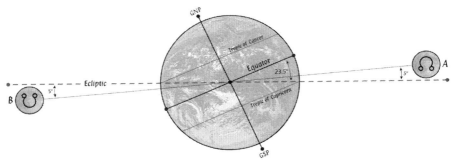

Side view (un-scaled) of the lunar orbit: Rāhu/northern node (A) and Ketu/southern node (B). Earth (centre) inclined at approximately 23.5°, GNP/GSP = the geographic poles.

The dragon/serpent iconography of the nodes appears (partly) to have originated from the constellation Hydra,[11] also known as The Water Snake. Longest of all constellations, it takes about seven hours to fully rise, stretching from Cancer to Libra.

Situated about 10° below the ecliptic, this constellation rests almost equally between the Milky Way's two points of intersection across the zodiac. Legend has it that Hydra's twisting course was inspired by the passage of the Moon (see the *Intersection of Earth/Moon orbits* image above), hence its nodes became likened to the head and tail of an enormous serpent.

This symbology of a great serpent, straddled between *Via Lactea* or *Ākāśagaṅgā* (alternative names for the Milky Way) resonate strongly in

Samudra Manthan – The Churning of the Milky Ocean, a story discussed later in Section 24.4. This tale, set in an age of gods and demons, relates not only to their quest for an elixir of immortality, but also to how their actions became a causal factor in the birth of the Moon!

Historically it is not known when the lunar nodes first made their astrological debut but their cycle appears to have been understood since antiquity,[12] with their points of intersection along the ecliptic noted to retrograde over a period of 18.7 years. This retrogressive activity may also be observed by monitoring the declination of a full Moon close to either of the solstices at a fixed latitude. When the lunar nodal axis conjuncts the equinoctial points, for example Rāhu occupying a point close to 8° 49' Pisces (current degree of spring equinox), a full Moon can be seen to reach a higher declination above the celestial equator on or near the winter solstice (northern hemisphere). When Rāhu occupies a point close to 8° 49' Virgo (current degree of autumnal equinox), a full Moon can be seen to reach a lower declination below the celestial equator on or near the summer solstice. Due to the proximity of the lunar orbit and ecliptic, winter months see an early rise/late setting lunar schedule as our Moon obligingly transits for longer, higher and apparently brighter – the reverse being true during the months of summer.

24.2 RĀHU/KETU AXIS

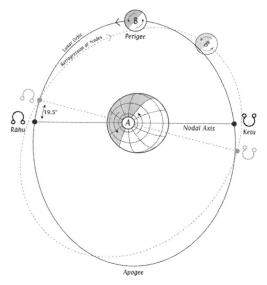

Earth-centred diagram (un-scaled): Showing the yearly 19.5° precession of the lunar nodes, completing a full revolution every 18.7 years.[13] Key: Earth (A), Moon (B).

As previously noted in Part I, there remain a generous number of explanations that attempt to model the unseen force that acts upon the celestial bodies, causing orbital instabilities such as precession. Our Moon in this regard is no different from any other in our observable solar system; however, its unique peculiarity is the rapidity of its nodal cycle. This in all probability is caused by the Earth's proximity, completing a 360° orbital wobble over a period of 18.7 years. This is in sharp contrast to Earth's rather more protracted 25,920 year orbital wobble.

24.3 ECLIPSES

> O Vipra! Whosoever is born during the solar or lunar eclipses runs the risk of sickness, sufferings, poverty and death.

Parasara

Perhaps one of the most impressive astronomical sights for an Earthbound viewer is an eclipse,[14] be it solar or lunar. To our ancestors this occurrence was seen as an alarming portent, presaging calamity or the displeasure of skyward divinities. To the ancient Jyotishi, eclipses were nothing more than a demonstration of power by the two *chhaya graha*[15] (Rāhu and Ketu), both nodes mythologically as well as intrinsically tied to the movements of the great luminaries.

Both nodes were imagined to doggedly pursue their quarry in an eternal quest for revenge, the source of their age-old enmity running something along the lines of the story in the next section.

24.4 SAMUDRA MANTHAN

Long ago, gods and demons fought repeatedly for control of the universe. As both camps were somewhat equally matched, little ground could be gained and so for the most part their ongoing struggle remained a stalemate. Frustrated, the gods finally approached Lord Vishnu for advice on how to finally defeat their enemies.

Vishnu replied, 'You must first find common ground – then pool your collective strength. When the might of deva and demon is yoked, the great milky ocean can be churned.[16] Hidden within its depths are many treasures; not least of which is *amrita* – the nectar of immortality. Once consumed it confers immortality and invulnerability – and so provides the means with which to vanquish your enemy.'

Having taken Vishnu's counsel, the deva approached the demons – who readily agreed to participate, but who secretly agreed not to share anything once the prize was theirs. Deva and demon laboured for days and after many setbacks and casualties succeeded in netting many of the ocean's bounties.[17] Finally they obtained the ultimate prize – a golden jar full of sweet nectar that granted immortality.

As soon as the jar was landed and its contents inspected, fights broke out between deva and demon over who should partake of this prize first. The demons proclaimed that their efforts had been greater and harder so naturally they should be awarded first taste. The gods retorted that it was their plan in the first place – and so they should be first to consume this prize.

And so it went on like this until – just as war looked imminent – a soothing breeze blew through them and bewitching music filled their ears. Moving through the assembled crowd, a temptress named Mohini[18] appeared and captivated their attention. As she soothed them with smiles and exotic dance, the demons were forced to their knees, entranced. Unable to tear their gaze away, the heated fury of the crowd subsided and all were lulled by her breathtaking beauty. The demons, now totally captivated, did not notice the deva edging toward the jar of amrita and starting to drink its contents.

In reality, Mohini was none other that Lord Vishnu disguised, a fact the deva had woken up to and so were freed from the spell. The demons, however, were completely bamboozled – open jawed and wide of eye. As the last of the amrita was being consumed, a particularly sly demon named Rāhu (who'd only just slithered onto the scene) realised Mohini's deception and hurriedly transformed himself into a deva. He then quietly joined their rank and file to await his chance to drink. By the time the jar reached him (he being the last deva) only one drop remained. This clung to the inner wall of the jar. Unable to control himself, Rāhu's forked tongue shot out and caught the sticky droplet, swallowing it down with great satisfaction. Sûrya and Chandra looked on in horror, now realising the serpent's deception, and raised the alarm.

Vishnu, hearing the cry of the two luminaries, dropped his guise of Mohini and let fly his Sudarśana cakrika (serrated discus), decapitating the imposter demon. As Rāhu's head and body fell to the ground they reverted to their hideous form of fangs and writhing coils, each section trying wildly to reconnect.

To the horror of all assembled, both halves of the monster remained alive! Once past the lips, amrita had conferred its gift of immortality. To compound the horror, the creature's tail transformed into Ketu – a separate entity.

In a last-ditch effort to hide their blunder, the gods tried to grab both parts; but as they grappled for each piece their hands caught nothing – as if grasping a shadow. Helpless, the deva now watched in disbelief as Rāhu and Ketu ascended into the heavens, taking their place amongst the stars, destined to circumnavigate the Rāshicakra for eternity.

Although either node is capable of causing grahana[19] (eclipses), Rāhu takes particular delight in devouring the Sun during solar eclipses, while Ketu blankets the Moon with its smoky reddish hue.[20]

24.5 SOLAR AND LUNAR ECLIPSES

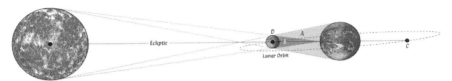

A solar eclipse occurs when the new Moon is positioned between the Earth and Sun, its orbit crossing the ecliptic close to its north or south node[21] (C and D). The Moon's umbra[22] (B) causes a focused obscuration on light; its penumbra (A) blankets a greater percentage of the Earth's surface in reduced sunlight. (Note: This image is not to scale.) A solar eclipse is partial to all positions outside of the umbra; if the whole solar disc is obscured, the eclipse is said to be total. A central eclipse occurs when the Moon is positioned exactly upon one of her nodes.

A solar eclipse appears to come on from a westerly direction, a lunar eclipse from the east. If the solar months were exactly equal to those of the lunar months, the nodal cycle would synchronise at a fixed point upon the ecliptic allowing this phenomenon to manifest during the same months of the year. As one mean lunation or synodic period[23] is approximately 29.5 days (a yearly total of 354 days), the orbiting Moon is able to pass both nodal positions but unable to accomplish its full revolution about the Sun, the consequence of which is nodal retrogression and the apparition of eclipses occurring nineteen days earlier with each passing year.

The ancients, it seems, were quite proficient in eclipse prediction, understanding the necessary conditions which brought about the phenomenon. The Chaldeans[24] used the Saros[25] Cycle – and they, knowing that the minimum interval an eclipse must repeat itself was within a period of 223 synodic months (approximately 18+ years), were able to accurately predict the forthcoming event.

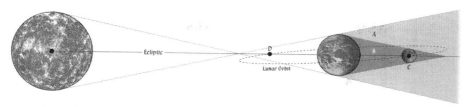

A lunar eclipse occurs when the Earth is positioned between the Sun and (full) Moon and when the Moon's orbit crosses the ecliptic close to its north or south node (D and C). As Earth's penumbra (A) passes over the Moon its surface darkens, Earth's umbra[26] (B) and atmosphere obscures the shorter wavelengths of light (blue), allowing only the longer wavelengths such as red to reach the Moon, bathing its surface in a reddish hue.

Nodal mythology neatly embeds some of the astronomical phenomena involved in a total eclipse, seeing this firstly as an assault upon the Sun by Rāhu, taking a bite out of the solar disc (called 'first contact' in astronomy). Occurring only at the new Moon, Rāhu strikes from nowhere – apparently invisible, yet hungrily devouring the solar mass until annular.[27]

It is only at this critical point that the Sun's corona becomes visible (along with the surrounding stars/Baily's Beads,[28] etc.). Though principally an Asura (demon), Rāhu's ability to obscure even the blinding intensity of the Sun (Atma) shows the hidden power behind the nodes, the universe briefly revealed through its black circle of obscuration. Rāhu has the power to obliterate our daily spectral perceptions of the world, reminding us that the stars continue to shine and influence us throughout the day even if we cannot see them.

The blue-blackened solar disc was also considered to align Rāhu to the cold energetics of planet Saturn, itself considered an achromatic sun in many of the most ancient world mythologies.[29] In contrast, Ketu's obscuration of the lunar disc presents itself quite differently. Occurring at full Moon, the lunar disc enters Earth's penumbra displaying a fractional change in luminance. Upon entering its umbra a subtle darkening from left limb occurs; like greyish smoke blown across its face. Upon reaching the midway point its advancing shadow behind the terminator starts to take on a pinkish hue. During total eclipse, the Moon's countenance becomes bathed in a deep vermilion hue, its features still discernible through its reddish glow. At this point the Moon appears almost Martian-esque,[30] looking eerily similar to the red planet having roguishly strayed far from its orbit.

Astrologically, instances of soli-lunar eclipses tend to portend dire consequences for the individual, both instances likened to a restrictive, receding forces. Typically, eclipses were considered to bring calamity, expenditure or disgrace, undermining happiness, longevity or leaving one open to disease.

Ritualistically, the advent of an eclipse seems to have been an altogether more promising event; the *Garuda Purāna* advising: 'An offering made to one's Manes at Gaya, under the auspices of Sûrya in Karkata, or under that of a solar or lunar eclipse, should be regarded as a piece of exceptional good fortune.' Other treatises allude to the auspiciousness of Sûrya grahana[31] for the performance of fire sacrifice (or the worship of Agnī), whereas Chandra grahana[32] was seen to bring an end to drought and deliver a bountiful harvest.

NOTES

1. December 21st – June 20th.
2. June 21st – December 20th.
3. Like a mother, Moon never once averts her gaze from Earth. This is perhaps one reason why Moon rules Bhanda (4th house), mother and mother's paternal line. Recent photographs by the LRO (lunar recognisance monitor) reveal the Moon's surface to have sustained a heavier bombardment of asteroids over the millennia than previously thought. Moon's close proximity and relative size to Earth may have acted like a shield protecting our world 'like a mother' in the history of the solar system.
4. The nine nautical stars are: Arietis, Aldebaran, Pollux, Regulas, Spica, Antares, Altair, Formalhaut and Markab.
5. Moon is Kāraka for emotion or 'that which hides behind a serene outward face'.
6. The rotational axis of the Moon, that is, its lunar poles, are at variance with those of Earth. The polar axis of the Moon points to within 1.5 degrees of the ecliptic pole axis. The status of the lunar pole stars changes periodically due to the precession of its rotational axis.
7. Visually, the diameter of the Moon closely matches that of the Sun. In reality our Moon is one of the smaller bodies in the solar system.
8. Approximately every 13° of Earth orbit.
9. Known collectively as the Rāhu/Ketu axis.
10. The ancients regarded the lunar nodes to be permanently retrogressive; however, modern reckoning of lunar orbital perturbations reveal its nodes to slow, become stationary and go direct. During a synodic month its nodes go direct two or three times for a period of 1–5 days, although this remains variable.
11. Also known as Al Ḥayyah (serpent) in Arabic. The Hydra constellation appears to have been astrologically significant in the past, its length watched with great interest for portents, such as comets.
12. The Chaldean Saros Cycle predicts recurrent lunar and solar eclipses after a period of eighteen years and eleven days+. Use was also made of the Draconitic Year (A Year of the Dragons), measured by the Sun's return to the north node every 346.62 days, again taking account of the node's westward movement.
13. Rāhu/Ketu mean nodes = 18 years, 7 months and 6 days.
14. Eclipse means 'to faint' or 'swoon'.
15. Shadow planets.
16. A simile perhaps of the process by which cream is churned into butter and then clarified into a golden coloured amrita called ghee.
17. These included: Kamadhenu (mother of all cows), Kalpataru (wish-fulfilling tree), Kaustubha (a magical gemstone), Shankha (Vishnu's conch shell), Airavata (king of elephants), Uchaishravas (a winged horse) and Chandra (the Moon).
18. Mohini was typically associated with temptation, desires and despair, ultimately leading to madness and one's own doom.
19. Sometimes the word grâsa is substituted for grahana, meaning 'to devour'.

20. Deeper affiliations between Rāhu/Sun and Ketu/Moon remain in dispute, however my own research was unable to find conclusive evidence either way. Both nodes are essentially the same entity, both are always implicated in their affairs of the other and both are capable of instigating solar/lunar eclipses.

21. During a partial solar eclipse, the new Moon is within a celestial longitude range of 17°–15°; likewise a partial lunar eclipse requires a full Moon to be within a celestial longitude range of 11°–9°. A new or full Moon positioned within a celestial longitude range of 5° will result in an annular or total eclipse.

22. Umbra = shadow.

23. From one full Moon to the next.

24. Indigenous Mesopotamian inhabitants (c. 600 BC), modern-day regions of Iraq, Syria and Turkey.

25. Saros = repetition.

26. Penumbra = almost shadow.

27. From *annulus* meaning 'a ring' – used to describe the total eclipse.

28. Globular iridescent phenomena, caused by sunlight shining between irregularities at the limb of the Moon.

29. See Kirk (2013, Part 2: 'Birth of Saturn').

30. Ketu is likened to Mars; this more than passing resemblance seems a fitting answer to that conundrum.

31. Solar eclipse.

32. Lunar eclipse.

25

NAKSHATRAS
(Lunar Mansions)

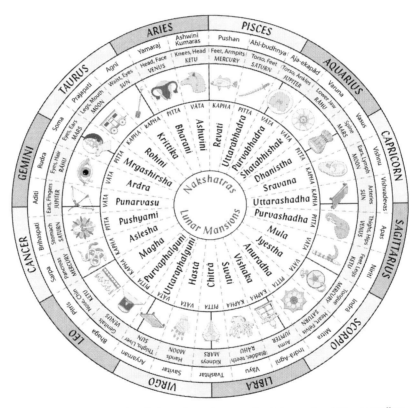

Nakshatras (lunar mansions), including information on zodiacal signs, ruling deities, controlling grahas and associated body parts, iconography and dosha.

Hindus call the current station of the Moon 'the burning one', the station it has just left 'the one left after embrace' and the station she will next enter 'the smoking one'.

India by al-Bīrūnī

Nakshatras appear to be a self-contained lunar astrology, neatly incorporating (or underpinning) the Jyotish canon. In all probability their presence represents the greater predictive power behind this system, and is certainly of some antiquity. The word Nakshatra is frequently used with reference to either junction star (Yogatârâ; see Section 1.3) or asterism[1] (the former a reference to a specific stellar coordinate).

The word Nakshatra[2] might be translated as 'protective guardians' or 'indestructible ones'.[3] Interestingly, the word *Rashi* (sign) means 'heaped together' and may well be a tell-tale reminder of an ancient merger between zodiacal signs and Nakshatras, each of the twelve 30° signs accommodating 2¼ Nakshatras.

Each Nakshatra is apportioned 13° 20' along the Moon's sidereal orbit, twenty-seven[4] in number. Each Nakshatra is overlorded by one of the planets and a specific deity or *devatha*. Nakshatras may then be categorised by number of other important attributes, including: masculine/feminine, dosha (Vāta, Pitta and Kapha), expression (active, passive and neutral), iconography, social caste, spiritual orientation (ganam[5]) and sexual compatibility (yoni dosha[6]). Nakshatras represent nothing short of an enormous inventory of qualities that help enrich and enliven any predictive venture.

Note: Any analysis of Moon ultimately places greatest emphasis upon the Nakshatra it is found to tenant, both forming an inseparable bond. Moon's transition through each Nakshatra roughly equates to a twenty-four hour period, or 1 day in the arms of each lunar bride.[7] Due to the complexities of the lunar orbit and one's Earthly latitude, transition times may appear erratic, giving extra credence to the Moon's well-observed and fickle nature.

NOTES

1. Asterisms are smaller collectives of stars that often reside within larger constellations.
2. Nakshatra is similar to Nakśate, a word meaning to co-habit. This might refer to the Moon's celestial brides with whom a day was spent with each.
3. Also referred to as 'a way to approaching the divine' see Frawley (1990). Also translated as 'the place you ascend to'.
4. *Abhijit* is considered to be the 28th Nakshatra though seldom used in Jataka (birth charts). The name Abhijit means 'great victory'; its ruler is Brahmā (see Rohini Nakshatra). Vega or α Lyrae is the fifth brightest star in our skies.
5. Ganam denotes the spiritual orientation/evolution of each Nakshatra: Deva = divine, Manusha = human and Raksha = demon.
6. The sexual compatibility of Nakshatras is considered of prime importance in long-term partnerships. Yoni types are denoted by fourteen varieties of animal. Interestingly but not surprisingly, nine of these animals also correspond to the twelve year lords favoured in comparative South Asian astrologies.
7. Moon may be either gender depending upon its situation.

26

PLANETARY RULERSHIP
—— OF NAKSHATRAS ——

Although Moon and Nakshatras are inseparable, the remaining grahas hold some dominion over Nakshatras. A system of co-rulership[1] encompasses specific Nakshatra to reflect the individual dynamics of planets. Though there are many attributes awarded each Nakshatra, its planetary rulership is clearly heightened in any overall appraisal of the asterism.

Planetary rulership of the Nakshatras is as shown in the table

Nakshatras and planetary rulership

Ketu	Venus	Sun	Moon	Mars
Ashwini	Bharani	Krittika	Rohini	Mrigashirsha
Magha	Purvaphalguni	Uttaraphalguni	Hastā	Chitrā
Mula	Purvashadha	Uttarashadha	Śravana	Dhanistha

Rāhu	Jupiter	Saturn	Mercury
Ardra	Punarvasu	Pushyami	Aslesha
Swati	Vishaka	Anhuradha	Jyestha
Shatabhishak	Purvabhadra	Uttarabhadra	Revati

Although each Nakshatra has its peculiar mythology and uniqueness of character, the rulership of the planets does seem to transcend these base attributes in some measurable way. For example, Nakshatras ruled by the Moon's north node (Rāhu) tend to be more extreme, unconventional or verbally outspoken. All Rāhu-ruled Nakshatras seem especially prone to accumulate and aggravate Vāta dosha. Conversely, Venus-ruled Nakshatras are visually captivating, alluring, forceful – yet often harbour self-esteem issues below their well-polished exteriors, much like *ven*-eer (a typically *ven-usian* inspired word).

Nakshatras form one of the most fascinating aspects of Vedic Astrology and yet remain its most mysterious. In one interview, James Braha interestingly remarked, 'I don't believe today's understanding of Nakshatras bears any resemblance to how they were used in Vedic times. Both of my mentors told me the Nakshatras were a complete system on their own, and neither of them were educated in that area (which says a lot). My own instincts, even at the very start, were that Nakshatras were entirely predictive. And by predictive, I mean how many children, what kind of illnesses, specifics about the spouse and career, and so on. About ten years after my studies in India, I heard from an astrologer who called to confirm that my instincts were correct. He said that he had studied in India with a guru who taught him the Nakshatra system that had been passed down to him orally. I do remember him giving me an example of how Nakshatras actually work. He said that in order to predict a person's specific health issues, look at the Nakshatra placement of Mercury. What I can say about Nakshatra explanations today is that they seem mostly psychological and behavioural, not predictive.'

The Nakshatra portraits in the next chapter I have derived from various sources, including classical texts, oral traditions, modern authors and collective snippets gleaned from my various teachers over the years. Though hardly the last word on Nakshatras, I hope the reader finds the following useful.

Note: The following Nakshatra portraits have been presented in categories of planetary rulership as opposed to their normal running order.

It should also be mentioned here that not all Vedic astrologers agree with the use of planetary overlords[2] for Nakshatras, considering instead their presiding deity to be exclusive. As it is almost impossible to read any interpretation of Nakshatras without some mythological reference to their assigned devatha, I feel this issue is being addressed. In truth it seems that both are of great importance and both should be given some voice in their interpretation.

NOTES

1. This system of co-rulerships may also compel the Moon to adopt a more agreeable stance toward other grahas, again underlying its lack of enmity toward any planet.
2. Planetary Nakshatra lords are considered by some to be erroneous. This association they feel has arisen because of dasha systems (primarily Viṃśottarī) where planetary sequences have become attached to Nakshatra and overridden the significance of their original (and more important) ruling deities.

— NAKSHATRA PORTRAITS —

27.1 KETU-RULED NAKSHATRAS
Ashwini 0° 00' – 13° 20' Aries (β Arietis/Sheratan)

A person born when the Moon passes through the asterism of Ashwini will be fond of ornaments, will be of fine appearance and will be popular, skilled in their work and intelligent.

Brihat Jataka by Varāhamihira

First of three Ketu-ruled Nakshatras, Ashwini notably carries the iconography of a horse's head. Ashwini affords the attributes of swiftness and precision. This Nakshatra also has great strength and stamina, yet great modesty. Noted for its special association with conveyances and travel, planet/s or ascendant degree found residing are compelled to move, both physically and geographically. Suffering from a restless yet pioneering spirit, an Ashwini person enjoys pushing themselves to the absolute limit – physically, mentally and creatively. Due to Ashwinis' informal communitive style and organisational skills, they are eagerly recruited by the less well-organised, becoming drawn into larger-than-life projects.

Ashwini individuals often gravitate toward healing or healthcare industries, where fast and decisive action can save lives. This Ketu-ruled Nakshatra has a strong affinity toward medicines that can be either naturalistic/traditional as well as the modern pharmacopeia.

Finding any excuse to get lured into a quest for knowledge, they seem adept at uncovering something interesting. This Nakshatra has a naturally inquisitive, borderline obsessive nature that refuses to quit until every stone is overturned or tree uprooted. Much akin to their writhing and decapitated planetary lord (Ketu), those of this Nakshatra are perpetually looking for a lost head! Ashwini has also a great passion for shifting huge swathes of information and unearthing golden nuggets. By applying their built-in information filters they are able to quickly sift unadulterated items from the fabricated or mundane.

Physically, Ashwini tends to accentuate one's forehead and eyes (appearing a little serpent-esque) with squared shoulders and above-average height. Their frame is often supple with subtle athletic proportions. Their hands are often long with dexterous artistic fingers. Their complexion can be slightly ruddy, given a warm look, making them appear Pitta-dominant in constitution. In truth their health is often more impacted by diseases of a Vāta/Kapha nature, aggravated by damp or cold conditions. This necessitates their need to keep active (avoiding prolonged periods of a sedentary posture). Related body parts ruled by Ashwini include knees, head (cerebral hemispheres) and the soles of the feet.

The deities of Ashwini are *Ashwini Kumaras*,[1] celestial twins depicted with horses' heads. According to legend, these twins were acknowledged for their mastery of all things medicinal and rejuvenative.[2] Legend places them upon the ancient battlefields of gods and demigods, administering to the wounded or dying with magic poultices, ointments and mantra. In addition to their miraculous pharmacopeia they lay claim to the reclamation of souls from the afterlife, reanimated by a draught of the fabled *soma*[3] drug.

The secret of the soma plant was prised from the lips of the Atharvan priest[4] Dadhyañc[5] after the twins became apprenticed to him. Dadhyañc paid with his life[6] for sharing this secret – but was himself resurrected by the twins, who administered this selfsame drug to their slain instructor. They were known to traverse both land and sky in golden chariots, yoked to horses, buffalo or eagles. Their presence is said to be marked by flocking birds.

Physically the twins were noted for their youthful appearance,[7] honey-coloured limbs and lotus flower garlands. Both are described as 'walking a red path'[8] – administering potent medicines which promote great longevity.

Later representations[9] of the twins were singular, horse-headed and solely feminine; this deity was seated upon a lotus and clothed in white garments. Typically she is shown holding a book in one hand with medicinal plants in the other.

Magha 00° 00' – 13° 20' Leo (α Leonis/Regulas)

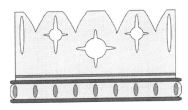

A person born on the lunar day of Magha will be possessed of great wealth and storehouses full of grain; will delight in the frequenting of hills and the performance of religious ceremonies. One will be valiant, a merchant, will feed animals and avoid the company of women.

Brihat Saṃhitā by Varāhamihira

Second of the Ketu-ruled Nakshatras, Magha notably carries the iconography of a crown, royal palanquin or palace, indicating a connection to all things regal. Symbolically this Nakshatra occupies the 'lion's heart', nested within chest of the royal constellation – Leonis.

There is an air of self-proclaimed importance to this Nakshatra. It is sometimes said that those with their natal sun in this Nakshatra 'shine as gold'. Known to the ancients as *The Mighty*, this star often affords great physical strength and keenness of intellect. If Moon, ascendant degree or planet/s tenant Magha they become greatly intensified, projecting their ambition above and beyond other considerations in a birth-chart. This they sometimes do with a disconcerting mixture of ruthlessness, tempered with strange subservience to an unseen power. There is also born-leadership quality, gaining respect and acceptance with comparative ease. If well-positioned, Magha individuals can inspire with motivational words or lead by example.

Magha individuals seem quickly to rise in their chosen career, often supported by father-like figures, guiding/nurturing their protégées, much to the frustration of their peers. Magha may also denote one supported by ancestral wealth, enjoying few financial restrictions in their adolescent years; however, some burden may be placed upon them to repay this investment (in kind) during their most productive years.

If poorly positioned, Magha individuals may become tyrannical and overbearing, preferring 'flail to crook'. Those dominated by this star often become highly religious or overly devoted to their chosen cause. Like a compass needle they often remain unswerved in the face of great adversity.

In youth, Magha individuals tend to be light and agile, giving them an athletic edge. They often gravitate to competitive environments, expending great physical reserves in an effort to win and dominate. In later years their physique may become prone to weight gain and joint inflexibility, with an underlying weakness in the chest area. Chronic heart conditions and respiratory ailments tend also to dog them in later years. Typically Magha individuals develop heavier squared features and tense jaw lines, often retaining good dexterity and hand–eye coordination well into their senior years. Their mental constitution tends toward the sharp and critical (Pitta); their physique has some Kapha qualities. Oddly enough, Magha individuals usually succumb to an underlying Vāta condition, which tends to undermine the nervous system, making diagnosis extremely difficult in its early stages.[10] Over time, Vāta's drying action reduces immunity (Ojas), instigating deficiencies of the nervous system. Other bodily parts ruled over by Magha include chin, nose, lips, spleen and spine.

The *Pitris* (or Manes) preside over this Nakshatra. Often translated as the forefathers or progenitors of mankind, the Pitris are described as immortal (primeval) deities that ward over humanity. Periodically they are called upon (usually at the close of a great world age) to revive or reseed the scattered remnants of humanity. The Law Code of Manu[11] says: 'From the Rishis came the Pitris (patriarchs), from the Pitris came both Deva and Danavas, and from Devas came the world of animals and vegetables in due order.' In India, the Pitris are generally propitiated during the sixteen lunar days of *Pitru Paksha*, an annual ritual that honours the departed (particularly one's own parents). Magha Nakshatra denotes a deep connection to one's ancestors and their wisdom. Typically, those strongly influenced by Magha not only display an aptitude for historical fact, but actively seek a reinstatement of its wisdom, reawakening an interest in *those having gone before us*.

Later descriptions of Magha portray her as solely feminine, bearing the face of a monkey and riding atop the body of a ghoul. Her thin spidery limbs support a large pot-belly while she herself carries rolled balls of dough and stems of kusha grass.

Mula 0° 00' – 13° 20' Sagittarius (λ Scorpionis/Shaula)

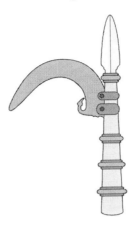

A person born on the lunar day of Mula will be a dealer in herbal remedies, flowers, roots, fruits and seeds. One will be the head of men, rich and delight in working with the land and its soil.

Brihat Saṃhitā by Varāhamihira

The third and final Ketu-ruled Nakshatra is Mula. Symbolically, Mula is portrayed as aṅkuśa (elephant goad) or the swishing tail of a lion. Both are apt symbols for latent power. Goads may be used to great effect when steering the most formidable of beasts (an elephant), as may the tail of a lion that idly flicks away annoying pests. Anything bidding for more of the latter's attention will have teeth and claws to deal with.

Mula means 'root' and is considered one of the most mysterious of Nakshatras. This asterism forms the stinger in the tail of the constellation Scorpionis, situated in the first 13° 20' of Sagittarius. Mula Nakshatra marks a point uncannily close to galactic centre, giving some credence to its substratum of epicentre/creational symbolism.[12] Of the three Ketu-ruled Nakshatra, Mula is generally considered to be its most challenging.

Associated traits of this star include darkness, calamities, violence, darkness, unrest, terror and death. Those having their natal Moon in Mula tend to be strongly intuitive with an intense probing mindset. They make excellent researchers, teachers/lecturers and natural orators. This Nakshatra can make for skilled healers, physicians or counsellors, able to intuit the root cause of dis-ease, delivering swift and lasting remedies.

Poorly positioned planet/s or ascendant degree negatively aspected in this Nakshatra may overwhelm the mind with dark imagery. It may also indicate one pulled toward violent forms of religions or occult fanaticism. On the surface this Nakshatra may appear passive or just plain laid back, but it is anything but. Like the roots of a great tree, more lies hidden from view than is in plain sight.

Health-related issues of this Nakshatra include autointoxication (addiction to stimulants), weakened immune system, blood pathogens and circulatory/arterial weakness. Related body parts of this Nakshatra include the legs and feet, lumbar vertebrae and sciatic nerve.

Those of this Nakshatra often respond well to herbal remedies, particularly those derived from the plant's rhizome. Avoidance of red meats, alcohol, pungent spices and excessive oil go a long way to strengthening their immune systems. Adequate hydration (with mineralised water) is another strong factor in health promotion for these individuals. Not so curiously, Mula individuals have an ability to transmute poison, giving them a higher than average resistance to ingested toxins. However, this adaptogenic quality inadvertently leads them toward greater experimentation, addiction and self-destructive tendencies.

The presiding deity of Mula is *Niriti*, guardian of the south-west[13] direction and daughter to *Adharma* (immorality) and *Hiṃsā* (violence). Mother to *Mṛtyu* (death), she is better known as the goddess of dissolution and destruction.

This dreaded Hindu deity is often portrayed on temple walls or reliefs – sword in hand, standing prostrate over a corpse. Thought to be analogous with the goddess *Alaskshmi*,[14] her wraithlike figure with darkened complexion is usually clad in black garments, adopting a stance that demands devotion and propitiation from any onlooker. In some instances Niriti was believed to take the form of a large owl that returns to the land of the dead at the first light of dawn. The goddess is said to preside over infertility, misery, misfortune, physical discomfort and the loss of one's children.

Later descriptions of Mula also portray her as a menacing feminine figure, her face a terrifying mixture of human and she-wolf or jackal. Often pictured standing over her victim, she holds a sword or club aloft, ready to strike a blow.

27.2 VENUS-RULED NAKSHATRAS

Bharani 13° 20' – 26° 40' Aries
(35 Arietis/Musca Borealis)

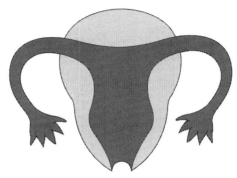

A person born when the Moon passes through the asterism of Bharani will be successful in his undertakings, truthful, free from disease, able bodied and free from grief.

Brihat Jataka by Varāhamihira

First of three Venus-ruled Nakshatras, Bharani[15] notably carries the iconography of a yoni (symbol of the goddess *Shakti*). Said to be *that which carries* or *bears away*, this Nakshatra is associated with deep primal forces that seek to break constraint and throw themselves at the world. There is a strong element of frustration and constriction in this Nakshatra as those born under its auspices seem constantly held back or denied what they feel is rightly theirs. Moon in Bharani was often considered a foreboding of childhood mortality or trauma sustained during the birthing process.

Bharani Nakshatra was also thought indicative of Jiva,[16] which sought hasty reincarnation, returning to avenge some karmic misdemeanour or injustice wrought against them in previous incarnations. There is often a pronounced fear of water,[17] drowning or the dark connected to this Nakshatra. If associated with the 12th astrological house its positioning was thought to indicate the loss of life via deep water.

The theme of karma is somewhat intensified in this Nakshatra as Saturn[18] reaches the point of maximum debilitation at 20° Aries, the middle of Bharani. Saturn's debilitation in Aries appears to relax its restrictive influence somewhat, allowing a quickening not normally associated with this most delaying of planets. Here karmas ripen with speed and rapidity, forcing great changes upon an individual in swift succession. By nature, those born under the auspices of Bharani may appear subdued and slightly introverted (even absent-minded) but beneath their outer façade deeper plots are being hatched.

Bharani is a Nakshatra with its eye firmly fixed on fast-tracking, a way to jump the queue, secure what it needs and exit the hero. This Nakshatra has also a reputation of ferocity and severity – this is not an asterism known for diplomatic skill. When cornered, antagonised or caught off guard it may well resort to violent outbursts or physical aggression to secure the upper hand.

Males born with their Moon or ascendant in Bharani tend to be slightly brash in manner or harsh in speech. They can be highly competitive, physically able or drawn toward contact sports or environments where one-upmanship is actively encouraged. Females with a well-placed Bharani Moon can be highly attractive, impulsive and career-orientated, skilfully outplaying their adversaries in situations where fast, resourceful and outspoken words are called for.

In stature Bharani tends toward a well-proportioned medium build. When pushed, their physical endurance is high and able to deliver greater efforts than might be expected. Their movement is often graceful and precise with just a hint of narcissism (not able to resist a sneak look in the mirror, affirming that outer appearances match their self-image). There is often a tendency for the face to have a somewhat soft triangular appearance, broadening at the temples and tapered toward a narrowing chin; this has the effect of making their eyes seem large in proportion to the rest of the countenance.

Health-related issues of this Nakshatra include injuries/accidents to the neck and face, as well as fevers, muscular spasm and a weakness of the body's connective tissue. Primary body parts ruled by Bharani include the head and face, pineal, pituitary and hypothalamus glands, the eyes and toes.

The presiding deity of Bharani is Yamarāja,[19] Lord of the underworld, also known as Lord of Death. Greatly feared, this deity appears in *Rig Veda*, but becomes greatly expounded upon in the *Atharva Veda* and *Vishnu Purāṇa*. According to *Rig Veda*, *Yama* and his twin sister *Yami* became the first humans to ascend to Devaloka (the realm of the gods). Born the son of Sûrya (Sun) by his second consort Chhaya[20] (shadow), Yamarāja and his sister lived a mortal life, later joining the ranks of immortals. Although initially given lordship over heaven he appears to have been denigrated to Lord of the Seven[21] Infernal Regions, saddled upon an ox, dressed in red cloth and wielding a mace.

Ancient religious texts of India speak of the soul's departure and its journeying once freed from the physical body. Here after, the dead stand before Chitrāgupta, registrar of all actions. Here they plead their case a few hours after their passing into shadow. If deemed worthy, they are escorted westward to *Svarga Loka*[22] by *Yamadutas* (servants to Yama). Conversely, the less than worthy are taken southward to face the green-skinned figure of Yama, who then asks, 'What did you do with your life?' If the individual offers some token of redemption,[23] Yamarāja may show compassion, releasing the soul from the torturous clutches of hell. If during the interim their body was unmourned and immolated, its owner faces eternal incarceration and is subjected to a torment befitting their worldly crimes. Interestingly, the soul's journey to face Yamarāja is considered to take less than one day, yet their return to *Bhu-loka* (Earth) to witness their cremation is a journey of ten days, hence the practice of delayed funerary rites.

Later descriptions of Bharani deity portray her riding atop a large buffalo, clothed in scarlet and wielding a noose and wooden staff. Typically her skin is black, her countenance a frightening mixture of human and elephant.

Purvaphalguni 13° 20' – 26° 40' Leo (δ Leonis/Zosma)

A person born on the lunar day of Purva Phalguni will delight in the dancing of young women, music, painting, sculpture and trade of exotic items. One will deal in the sale of honey, salts, cotton and fragrant oils and be forever in the enjoyment of youthful vigour.

Brihat Saṃhitā by Varāhamihira

Purvaphalguni is the second Venus-ruled Nakshatra, suitably represented by a warm glowing hearth. As might be inferred from its symbolism, this Nakshatra is cordial, nourishing and opulent, promising a restive space where one can retire from the suffering of the world, taking time to enjoy one's company and surroundings.

Called *former reddish one* or *the earlier fig tree*, this Nakshatra forms the first of three unique *pairs*[24] considered joined at the hip (so to speak) with its close counterpart *Uttaraphalguni* discussed in Section 27.3. Purvaphalguni occupies an area of conjoining stars situated close to the lion's girdle in the constellation of Leonis. Other popular icons attached to this Nakshatra include a Śiva lingam, fruiting fig tree, raised platform, hammock and the front legs of a cot.

This Nakshatra is generally considered an oasis where travellers replenish and recuperate; however, it is also accepted to be Māyā (illusory), leading the resolute off-track or away from obtaining an objective. Procrastination may be an issue for those having prominent planet/s or ascendant degree located in this Nakshatra. Alternatively this star provides an ideal environment for self-healing, particularly after prolonged periods of stresses and strain. This star can be a welcome distraction for minds engaged in tiresome research, helping to provide a fresh outlook or creative solution to break the deadlock.

Purvaphalguni is creative, resourceful and inventive, reaping some level of fame and fortune in all undertakings. Whether starting afresh or breathing new life into the outmoded or unwanted, those falling under the auspices of this asterism seem always to find the limelight and the crowd's adulation.

Purvaphalguni is visually engaging, awash with drama and a rich spectacle of colour. Able to hold the eye without tiring, those born with their Moon in this Nakshatra have great charisma as well as a natural talent to entertain and enliven the weariest of crowds, making excellent hosts at any get-together. Masters in the dissolution of cultural boundaries and customs, their talent to intermingle and conjoin helps to find common ground upon which to build relationships and understanding. Those born to this Nakshatra have excellent social networking skills.

Outwardly, Purvaphalguni individuals may appear sensual and attractive with a magnetic personality; inwardly they often crave recognition and self-glorification, never seeming to find any level of satisfaction with their accomplishments. They may also have a tendency to over-react or become hyper-sensitised to any form of criticism.

Physically their stature tends toward the shorter and lighter framed; their complexion/skin is said to be of variegated colour (meaning that the tone of the skin seems to vary across the body). Their eyes can often seem heavily lidded and the lips full. Later in life the face may appear to broaden about the jaw line, forming a double chin. Health-related issues of this Nakshatra include a higher than average risk of injury by accident,[25] and a weakness of the lower spine, hips and sciatic nerve. There is often a heightened sensitivity to the digestive tract, suffering periods of reduced immunity as well as periods of mental fatigue (depression and emotional breakdown). Related Nakshatra body parts include genitalia, inner thighs, lower spine and hips.

The presiding deity of this Nakshatra is *Bhaga*, referred to as 'Blissful Sun God', 'Dispenser of Wealth' and 'Brother of the Dawn'. Bhaga was also one of twelve Âditya.

Although a number of references are made to Bhaga in Vedic mythology, he appears more of a minor deity and if mentioned at all is only counted in the company of others, most notably his sister *Uṣas* – the dawn light. Celebrated in a number of hymns, the Âdityas are primarily concluded to be the twelve solar months. The influence of Bhaga is said to be present in the month of *Tapas* (21st December – 20th January). His appearance is duly propitiated to impart wealth, health and happiness. Bhaga is also considered to have some influence upon marital bliss.

Âdityas were not just solar deities, but also personified forms of light; whether burning in the hearth as fire (Agnī), skies lit by lightning (Indrā) or celestial wanderers (planets), these twelve deities aggregated into one universal light – Sûrya the Sun. As seen in other Nakshatra portraits, a number of Âditya preside over their fates and fortunes.

Later descriptions of Purvaphalguni portray a goddess riding a chakra (wheel or disc), her features that of an elephant, her complexion reddened. In her hands she caresses brilliantly coloured birds.

Purvashadha 13° 20' – 26° 40' Sagittarius (δ Sagittarii/Kaus Media)

A person born on the lunar day of Purvashadha will be kind and gentle in manner, fond of voyages across the sea, truthful and wealthy, delighting in work with the soil. One will be a boatman, dealing in fruits, flowers and trade across the waters.

Brihat Saṃhitā by Varāhamihira

The third and final Venus-ruled Nakshatra is Purvashadha,[26] commonly portrayed as the tip of an elephant's tusk or winnowing basket.[27] Purvashadha might be translated as 'the earlier unsubdued', symbolising its unrelenting and invincible nature; it occupies an area of conjoining stars situated between the bow and back of the centaur/archer in the constellation Sagittarii. This Nakshatra forms the second in a series of pairs; its counterpart Uttarashadha is later discussed in Section 27.3.

This Nakshatra is strongly connected to the water element, its effect, like water, observed to spread outwards in all directions simultaneously. Like water, its energetic penetrates and erodes, adapting to any or all contours. The iconography of an elephant's tusk reaffirms its subsidiary energetic, one very much connected to brute force. The strength of the elephant is undisputed in nature, even the most ferocious of predators clearing a path before it. When faced with adversarial confrontation, those that stand against this Nakshatra may face total annihilation in a show of strength.

Purvashadha combines the intellects of Jupiter (Brihaspati) and Venus (Shukra), bringing together two masterful instructors. Here, both court-advisors convene and conspire in one Nakshatra.[28] This combination is set to manifest interesting (if not conflicting) results. Both planets are benefic in status yet their end goal is diametrically opposed. Jupiter promotes the thirst for self-knowledge and enlightenment, Venus promotes self-awareness but veers sharply toward worldly self-indulgence. Overall, the states and strength of both gurus should be carefully ascertained to determine which of the two is more favourably positioned to dominate its counterpart. Ultimately both are *people-friendly* planets, meaning their goals are attained through interaction and relationship, both having an ability to enthuse and energise. When imbalanced or dominated by other malefic planets they manifest like the tusk of an elephant, their gross energy focused at the tip and brought to bear upon its quarry.

Physically, those of this Nakshatra show a narrowing of the hips and squared upper frame with longer than average arms. The whites of the eyes are often radiant, their stare becoming pronounced and penetrating. The ears may appear elongated with generous fleshy lobes; the jaw line is strong, often pronounced with evenly spaced strong, whitened teeth. Purvashadha individuals are intuitively drawn to the ocean or the need to be close to water. This element is often indicated as the preferred medium upon which their fame is spread. Those of this star often find favour in the role of close advisor or trusted friend, able to make hard decisions or stick to their guns. Their will to victory and high endurance often allows them to succeed where others fail dismally.

Health-related issues of this Nakshatra include swelling (oedema) of the tissues and imbalances affecting the body's water metabolism such as Prameha (diabetes), kidney nephritis/stones and urinary tract infections. Related Nakshatra body parts include the thighs, hips, arteries and veins.

The presiding deity of this Nakshatra is *Apás*,[29] one of eight Vasus in the service[30] of Indrā. Vasus form one in a number of Vedic triads.[31] These are distinguished in the *Brāhmanas* as Heavenly Âdityas, Rudras of Air and Earthly Vasus.

The water goddess *Apás* appears in this final category of Vasus, accompanied by Soma (Moon), Dharā[32] (the Earth), Anila (the wind), Usas (dawn), Anala[33] (fire), Dhruva (the pole star) and Parjanya (god of thunderstorms). Later hymns of the *Rig Veda* re-ordered many of these minor gods into a more comprehensive group named Viśvedevāh or all-gods, these being conveniently assigned the Purvashada's stellar counterpart – *Uttarashadha*.

Later descriptions of Purvashada portray her as solely feminine, four-handed and clothed in yellow garments. Her features are those of a shark, the colour of her skin turquoise. In her hands she typically carries a lotus flower, necklace, water vessel and rope.

27.3 SUN-RULED NAKSHATRAS
Krittika 26° 40' Aries – 10° 00' Taurus (η Tauri/Alcyone)

If born on the lunar day of Krittika one will delight in the adornment of white flowers, performance of religious ritual and be skilled in the occult arts. One will be a brahmin, priest, astronomer, a miner or one skilled in art of pottery.

Brihat Saṃhitā by Varāhamihira

First of the Sun-ruled Nakshatras is Krittika, often portrayed as an arrow in flight, a flame or edged weapon. *Kart* means 'to cut' or 'to burn away', a name taken from the eldest son of Lord Śiva, Karttikeya[34] (also known as Skanda). The primary attributes of this Nakshatra are radiance, heat and sharpness. Krittika has a strong connection to metalworking (forging) and the working of precious metals as well as weapons of warfare.[35]

Although this Nakshatra spans 26° 40' Aries to 10° Taurus, the open-star cluster Pleiades[36] is designated *Krittikās* – its six major stars thought to be representative of the wives of the *Saptarishi*.[37] These same wives suckled and reared the infant Karttikeya to manhood, in order that he might fulfil his destiny. As the fiery warrior donned his armour in readiness for battle, his would-be nurses related the story of his birth and ultimate destiny.

Once Agnī, disguised as a mythical bird,[38] stole the seed[39] of Lord Śiva and carried it away. While passing above the Himalayas he began to tire as his burden grew ever heavier and had now started to burn. As the fire engulfed him, he swooped lower and sought a place to rest and cool his feet. Spying a ravine and river he dropped his cargo into the cooling waters. Falling at the water's edge the burning seed ignited the reeds and a great fire sprang up. When the smoke had cleared and the fire died down, a young infant was revealed, lying in a bed of solidified metals and ash. Agnī retrieved the child and delivered him to the wives of the *Saptarishi* with instructions that he be nurtured and protected until such time as he would be called to face *Taraka* the demon. Due to an unwise boon from Brahmā, Taraka had been made invincible to all but the offspring of Śiva and so now his seed had been stolen in order to remove this blight from the universe. Karttikeya is portrayed as six-headed[40] and adorned in golden armour, seated upon a peacock.[41] His standard is that of a cockerel.

Any planet/s falling in Krittika become greatly illuminated. The sage Nārada (born of Brahmā) once said, 'Those who feed Brahmins with ghee and pudding on this lunar day ascend to Devaloka.' The Moon (Kāraka for mind, emotion and senses) particularly favours residence in Krittika Nakshatra, receiving its full exaltation at 3° Taurus.

The stature of Krittika individuals may be of average height but appearing to have a slight elongation of the torso and shortening of leg. Their shoulders are generally broad and sturdy, their neck heavy, their face rounded. Eyes are often large and attractive, framed with heavy eyebrows. There is a kindly 'concerned' look to them and their general behaviour is respectful.

Health-related issues of this Nakshatra include digestive ailments of the small intestine, inflammation of the liver, hypertension and enlargement of the heart. Related Nakshatra body parts include the waist, eyes, neck, larynx, tonsils and lower jaw.

Fire's nature causes it to rise and intensify with the addition of new fuel, so too this Nakshatra – delivering similar instances that raise one to new and prosperous heights, only to wane and diminish to embers. Being a Nakshatra associated with heat and burning, Krittika implicates disturbances that involve inflammation/bleeding and febrile conditions. This heating effect is accentuated in the last 3° of Aries (fire) and cooled somewhat in the ensuing 10° of Taurus (earth).

The presiding deity of Krittika is, not surprisingly, *Agnī*, the Vedic fire god. Agnī is a pivotal figure in Vedic literature, appearing in numerous texts, firstly as co-creationist[42] of the universe and later adopting a role of celestial messenger. His flame carries invocations and prayers from the world of mortals into the godly realms via yajña.[43] As a protector of Vasus, Agnī also became closely allied with Indrā, in an advisory role (see Jyestha Nakshatra in Section 27.9).

Agnī is described as a red-coloured man, black-eyed and soft of face (thought to be smeared with ghee). Agnī is sharp-toothed, wild-haired, swift-tongued and lit by a golden radiance. His vahan (vehicle) is a ram. Summoned forth by the rubbing of aranis,[44] his sudden appearance delights in devouring his parents (or any material upon which he feeds). From a small flame his growth is unprecedented; if left uncontrolled he reduces everything to ash. Even the strongest of metals yield to his intensity. It is said, 'As the Sun purifies all nature with his light and heat, so Agnī shall purify everything which enters his flames.'[45]

In terms of physiology, Agnī is better understood as 'he who converts, assimilates and burns away that which is unwanted'. In modern terms this might be equated to the selectivity of our immune system as well as healthy digestion. On a personal level, our digestive fire (internal Agnī) governs our body's ability to convert and assimilate nutritive materials. As this nutrition circulates and nourishes the deeper tissues, refined forms of Agnī continue to convert and assimilate, assigning essential vitamins and minerals to specific organs or body systems.

Agnī also maintains (and regulates) many aspects of bodily health including skin lustre, colouration of by-products (mala), generation of internal heat as well as the vitality and strength of tissues. On a mental level, balanced Agnī helps facilitate mental digestion and assimilation, promoting a keen intellect with an ability to learn (intake), retain (memory) and apply (learning by experience).

Finally, it is said of Agnī: 'His love for all is equal, he visits the hearth of all homes[46] (both rich and poor). At the close of mortal life he pays one final visit upon us as fever, purifying the spirit (burning up passions, regrets and attachments to that life) in preparation for our onward journey.'

Later descriptions of Krittika portray her as solely feminine, her complexion deep crimson, her hair wild. Seated atop a powerful white goat, her countenance is half-human, half-goat. Dressed in fine jewels, she carries a long red wooden spear.

Uttaraphalguni 26° 40' Leo – 10° 00' Virgo (β Leonis/Denebola)

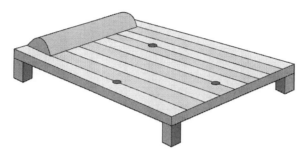

A person born on the lunar day of Uttaraphalguni will be mild, modest and generous, learned in many disciplines. One will become wealthy in the trading of grains, virtuous and reside in the company of princes.

Brihat Saṃhitā by Varāhamihira

Second of the Sun-ruled Nakshatras is *Uttaraphalguni*, commonly marked by the Yogatârâ β Leonis (Denebola), denoting the end of the leonine tail in the constellation Leonis. Commonly portrayed as a hammock, fruiting fig tree or rear legs of a cot, its symbolism is associated with tranquil spaces, healing and recuperation.

Alternative descriptions of this Nakshatra include 'later reddish one' and 'patronage star', both denoting this asterism's renown for aid or investment – when sought. Uttaraphalguni is also a prestigious star for those wishing to return health to the sick or strength in the weary.

Similarly, mirroring its counterpart *Purvaphalguni*, the energetic behind this star is more globally serving, which means providing for the individual, on the understanding they also contribute for the benefit of all. *Uttaraphalguni* is also considered a star of union, which might be in matters of business or personal relationship. Astrologers generally consider this star the most appropriate for marriage, ensuring long and rewarding marriages. It is said that Lord Śiva and Pārvatī were united under this asterism.

Those of this Nakshatra are often well organised, tenacious and sincere, generous to a fault, and more often generous with their time. Though they strive for social integration and the mutual attainment of all, they do not suffer fools gladly. Those who abuse their better nature or seek to profit from their goodwill quickly come face to face with a scorching figure of authority.

The first quarter of this Nakshatra is dominated by a powerful solar energetic, the rulership of Sun reflected on both levels, as lord of the sign and as Nakshatra lord. The latter three-quarters of this Nakshatra are positioned in service-orientated Virgo (ruled by Mercury), which helps stimulate the need to heal, nourish and serve. The influence of the latter also helps brighten their already keen intellect.

Physically, their stature may be inclined toward a taller, broad frame, their face seemingly square and the jaw line strong. Their countenance is often slightly disproportionately large for the size of the head. The nose is often straight, long and pronounced, their lips thin and cheeks slightly ruddy (in all seasons).

Health-related issues of this Nakshatra include weakness of the small intestine (ulcers), diseases of the genitalia, injury to the lower spine, severe headaches, appendicitis, thrombosis and inflammatory conditions of the liver. Related Nakshatra body parts include the genitals, outer thighs, liver, small intestine, bowel and navel.

The presiding deity of this Nakshatra is *Aryaman*, a name meaning 'devotee of Sûrya'. As one of twelve Âditya, Aryaman represents friendship, patronage and benevolence. Both Aryaman and Bhaga (see Purvaphalguni in Section 27.2) were evoked in unison and mutually complementary. Other popular deities associated with Aryaman included Indrā (king of the gods[47]) and Varuna (Oceanic God[48]). The propitiation of Aryaman at the start of a marriage ceremony is deemed auspicious, his blessings also sought during periods of personal trial or difficulty. Aryaman is mentioned by name about one hundred times in the *Rig Veda* yet little detail of this deity is recounted. As an Âditya, he maintains a supporting role to Mitra, a more prominent and influential manifestation of the Sun god (see Anuradha Nakshatra in Section 27.8 for more information).

Later descriptions of Uttaraphalguni portray her as solely feminine, white-skinned, four-armed and seated atop a cow. Her face is that of a tigress. In her hands she holds the Sun and Moon, a rope and a wooden staff decorated with an impaled human head.

Uttarashadha 26° 40' Sagittarius – 10° 00' Capricorn (σ Sagittarii/Nunki)

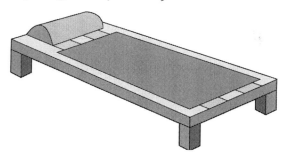

A person born when the Moon passes through the asterism of Uttarashadha will be liked generally; will be grateful and return all favours bestowed upon them. One will be learned, virtuous and obedient.

Brihat Jataka by Varāhamihira

The third and final Sun-ruled Nakshatra is *Uttarashadha*, its symbology often depicted as a rough wooden cot. This star is sometimes called 'the latter unsubdued' or 'unconquered', exemplifying its underlying strength and benevolent qualities; it also forms the second of the bridged Nakshatra. Its counterpart *Purvashadha* has been discussed in Section 27.2 and occupies an area of conjoining stars, situated between the bow and back of the Sagittarii constellation.

Greatly akin to its counterpart, high levels of endurance are also emphasised, yet the brute force and single-mindedness are comparatively subdued from those expressed in Purvashadha. This Nakshatra has a more introspective quality, channelling one toward self-accountability. This area of the heavens concerns itself with the re-apportioning of wealth and power so successfully sequestered by the former. This is also mirrored within the boundaries of the Nakshatra. Here the Sun enjoys the initial Jupitarian expanse in Sagittarius, only to enter the cooler and restrictive Capricorn, falling under the intensity of its lord, Saturn.

The wooden cot iconography of Uttarashadha aptly represents its sense of austerity. This Nakshatra cultivates an inner awareness of practical and attainable, cautious not to dilute its strength or to overextend itself. One good analogy of this asterism would be the preparation of ghee (clarified butter). Transformation of butter to ghee sees many intermediary stages, but the art of masterful preparation remains patience and diligence – its ultimate reward a liquid golden oil that remedies many ills.

Physically, their stature often manifests as a well-proportioned (erring toward taller) frame, fair in complexion and bright-eyed. They often have an appearance of being broad-faced or having widely set eyes. They often appear reserved, uninterested or chameleon-esque in nature, morphing into a multitude of surroundings. Deliberately dressing-down, they tend to avoid bright lights or trends. There is a simplicity to them that should never be underestimated, for although projecting an unattached or nonchalant demeanour, they often attain influential positions, able to attract wealth and investment. Uttarashadha individuals are straightforward and plain talking, but often take time to warm to. They are not given to casual friendships and seldom give their loyalty with ease.

Health-related issues of this Nakshatra include weakness of lymphatic vessels, the knees, skin, ears, urinary system, dysentery, typhoid, allergies or eczema. Related Nakshatra body parts include the thighs, arteries, veins, knee joints and patella.

The presiding 'deities' of Uttarashadha are *Viśvedevāḥ*, a unity of minor gods and goddesses, merged conveniently into a collective. Viśvedevāḥ were populated by such divinities as Apás (water goddess), Soma (the Moon), Dharā (the Earth), Anila (the wind), Uṣas (the dawn), Agnī/Anala (fire), Dhruva (the pole star) and Pratyūsa (pre-dawn). On occasion, their ranks were swollen to include the addition of Âdityas, Rudras, Maruts,[49] Aṅgirasas and Ṛbhus.[50] These accessions appear to have been convened so as not to exclude *any* from commendation. Overall some forty hymns have been dedicated to Viśvedevāḥ in *Rig Veda*, especially in connection to prominent sacrificial rites.

Later descriptions of Uttarashadha portray her as solely feminine, white-skinned and radiant, adorned in gemstones and wearing a crown of gold. Four-armed, she holds a serpent, nectar pot, rope and book. Wrapped in the scales of a serpent, she rides atop a large snake.

27.4 MOON-RULED NAKSHATRAS

Rohini 10° 00' – 23° 20' Taurus (α Tauri/Aldebaran)

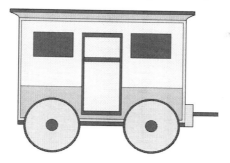

A person born when the Moon passes through the asterism of Rohini will be truthful, will not covet the property of other men, will be clean of habits, and be of sweet speech, firm views and fine appearance.

Brihat Jataka by Varāhamihira

First of the Moon-ruled Nakshatras is *Rohini*, its prominent symbology that of a carriage/farmer's cart[51] or banyan tree. This asterism is sometimes called 'the ruddy one' or 'growing one', symbolising its warm and sensual nature.

Allied to all forms of artistry, Rohini delights in visual, musical or magical performances. In her guise of Chandra's favourite consort, Rohini became a legendary figure in the conjugal arts, her husband held captivated in her Nakshatra to the exclusion of his remaining twenty-six lunar brides.

Rohini has a kindred relationship to soil, its richness and fertility – which ultimately determines the bounty of a harvest. This Nakshatra is also considered auspicious for building projects, including the laying of foundation stones. Typically, both commercial and personal dwellings are commenced under the auspices of this Nakshatra. Rohini is also considered a lucky star for all entrepreneurial projects. Moon's transition through this region of the sky was deemed fortuitous[52] for the attainment of wealth, health and longevity. Many fixed-term financial commitments are deemed to prosper under this star.

The stature of the Rohini person is inclined toward a well-balanced, somewhat athletic frame (particularly in youth), becoming fuller and rounded with age in the upper body (women) and square-shouldered and with muscular arms (in men). The neck may also appear shorter and slightly disproportionate to their limbs and trunk. Appearance is often fair, attractive and youthful, displaying large eyes and lustrous (though somewhat dry) hair. Even into advancing years their skin displays a milky quality that resists wrinkling and the effects of ageing. Horoscopes in which Rohini Nakshatra features prominently are often likely to experience more than their fair share of jealousy from others, echoing the tale of the Moon's angry lunar brides, who sought revenge upon their husband.

They are easy to engage, fun to be around and extravagant in tastes, having an adventurous sprit and outgoing nature. There is often a childlike innocence to their actions – sometimes painfully unaware of dangers they court when pursuing their headlong course toward enjoyment. When queried or corrected with regard to these actions, they are quick to anger but the tempest of these theatrical outbursts is easily subdued or, better still, side-tracked into some other creative endeavour.

Health-related issues of this Nakshatra include pain or swelling about the breast, injuries to the neck and face, irregular menses, sunstroke, high blood pressure, heart problems, fevers and aching calf muscles. Related Nakshatra body parts include the legs, mouth, tongue, palate and cervical vertebrae.

The presiding deity of Rohini is *Prajāpati*,[53] an epithet of Brahmā in the guise of *lord of all creatures*. Brahmā is an important and influential deity, effectively holding sway over one-third of the *Trimūrti*.[54] Although later Purāṇas erode his stature somewhat, his status as prime creator of the universe endures.

Yajur Veda describes Brahmā as 'the first of all gods' and 'from him all things proceed and in him pre-existed the universe'. Commonly represented as four-headed and red in colouration,[55] he dresses in white raiment and sits atop a swan.[56] His consort is Sarasvati, goddess of wisdom,[57] but in earlier tales it is Sāvitrī (descendant of the Sun god). The latter's sexual union was said to have culminated in a pregnancy term of 100 years, before giving birth to the four Vedas, various Shāstra, Rāgas,[58] Rāgiṇīs[59] and the four great world ages.[60]

Still greatly respected, Brahmā has but one minor temple dedicated to him in Pushkar, Rajasthan. According to his exploits, Brahmā constantly infuriated Śiva and Vishnu by granting boons to ever more powerful demons, who wrought havoc upon the universe. Brahmā also wrongly cursed his son Nārada, condemning him to perpetual rebirth for two hundred thousand years. After receiving a redemption from Vishnu, Nārada righted his injustice by cursing his father to endure 'a loss of all status' for three consecutive aeons, during which time humanity would turn away and forget the creator, something that indeed seems to have befallen him.

Later descriptions of Rohini portray her as solely feminine but take on a serpent-esque quality. Pale-skinned and clad in garlands of flowers, she rides atop a goose, carrying a pot of nectar and a rope.

Hastā 10° 00' – 23° 20' Virgo (δ Corvi/Algorab)

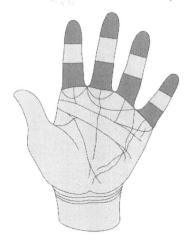

A person born when the Moon passes through the asterism of Hastā will be of active habits, full of resources and shameless, a thief and a drunkard.

Brihat Jataka by Varāhamihira

Second of the Moon-ruled Nakshatras, *Hastā* means 'hand'; its symbology is most appropriately an open hand revealing its *Rekha* or lines. This star has many attributes ascribed to it, but is more commonly associated with artisans, illusionists or those who find fame using the skill of their of hands.

Symbolically, hands are representative of many things, not least their ability to magically conjure-up or to fashion things before only imagined. The famous Āyurvedic surgeon Susrutha once asked his students, 'What is the most adaptive instrument we have at our disposal', to which his students offered a long list of important surgical aids. He then stated the correct answer to be 'the human hand', for it is the tool from which all others are ultimately crafted.

Two hands symbolise positive and negative, masculine and feminine. Four fingers and one thumb represent the five elements or five senses. Three phalanges on four fingers represent twelve zodiacal signs; the lines drawn upon the palms and fingers are its signposts to destiny.

Noted for speed and its call to action, Hastā has a strong desire to coerce, heal or trick. Hastā individuals are quiet and somewhat withdrawn, preferring open landscapes to those of urban living; but that being said, their mercantile qualities (Mercury achieves exaltation in this Nakshatra) often lead them toward centres of trade, commerce and industry, which inevitably leads to the bustle of cities. On a more negative note, Hastā has been known to inspire underhanded dealings and sleight-of-hand tricksters, infamous for their uncanny ability to part people from their property on nothing more than a handshake.

Physically, those of this Nakshatra tend toward a taller, slender frame, well-built (strong joints) but carrying a frailty in their mannerism. Calm in nature, with a pleasing smile, these individuals quickly put others at ease, playing the perfect host. Their posture is often slightly stooped with deep-set eyes. Their hands may be prominent and strong-looking, often long-fingered with a firm grip and at least one good prominent scar (usually acquired through an accident in childhood).

One hallmark of this star is their world of constant highs and lows; every day a new challenge, every turn of the page brings something new and unexpected into their lives. However, their highly adaptive nature seems always to turn a potential setback into an opportunity, reaping benefits from the most unlikely of places. Generally the first half of their life may seem hard and gritty – getting a 'firm grip' may appear to take an eternity. Later, after experimentation and experience, they settle into their chosen vocation and skill-sets, eventually achieving some notoriety. Hastā individuals quite often find themselves thrust into the public arena, parading their wares before the eyes of those who become mesmerised by their ability.

Hastā individuals are usually artistic, fast-talking, witty and inventive; they excel in the visual arts, sales, foreign trade and all types of healing, particularly those that involve a hands-on technique such as acupuncture, chiropractic/osteopathy, Bowen-therapy, reflexology, therapeutic massage or even surgery. These individuals are often gifted palmists, astrologers and fortune tellers, having a strong interest in the occult sciences.

Health-related issues of this Nakshatra include injury to the hands, weakness of bowels (constipation/diarrhoea/IBS), under-production of digestive enzymes, diseases of secreting glands, neuralgia, skin sensitivities/ diseases, nervous conditions including hysteria and hypochondria. Related Nakshatra body parts include the hands, small intestine, digestive enzymes and secreting glands and the skin.

The presiding deity of this Nakshatra is *Savitar*. Described in the *Rig Veda* as *golden eyed*, *golden handed* and *golden tongued*, known to illuminate the Earth, heavens and air. In *Śatapatha Brāhmaṇa*,[61] Savitar takes on a more protective role, associated with the birthing process or one's emergence into the world. Though closely aligned to Sûrya, Savitar performs a number of separate, important functions, such as the conveyance of souls into the afterlife or the conferring of immortality upon mortals, removing malevolence from dreams or cleansing the waking world.

Savitar was propitiated to bestow health upon the sick and ailing, driving away diseases through the action of washing or the purification of sin. Sometimes referred to as *apāṃ napāt* (child of the waters) his actions were known to *coerce* or *lead* waters; by his will their currents became intensified. Savitar was thought to reside in the middle kingdom (a region between heaven and Earth). From here the rains issued and from here he impelled Sūrya, combining forces with the Sun god to produce his warming rays.

Later descriptions of Hastā portray her as solely feminine. Pale-faced, her countenance is that of a buffalo. Thought to convey wealth, she wields a bolt of lightning in one hand, holding a rope in the other. Typically the vehicle of Hastā is a horse.

Śravana 10° 00' – 23° 20' Capricorn (α Aquilae/Altair)

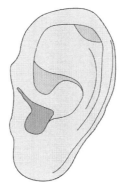

Those who are born on the lunar day of Śravana will be cunning, of active habits, efficient workmen, bold, virtuous, god fearing and truthful.

Brihat Saṃhitā by Varāhamihira

The third and final Moon Nakshatra is *Śravana*; its symbology associated with a human ear, footprints in sand[62] or the tip of an arrow, often called 'The Star of Listening' or 'learning'. Śravana individuals naturally gravitate toward centres of learning, knowledge and wisdom – driven onward by the quest for truth.

Its ear motif deeply connects this star to *Akash*, the æther/space element, the medium through which sound moves. It is through this medium that Śravana individuals very much prefer to connect, be it through voice or dance, and in some instances the absence of either. Śravana has a restive energetic, pausing often for reflection and lamentation. Positioned midway in the Saturn-ruled sign Capricorn,[63] Śravana craves re-evaluation but not before assessing details. Like the eye of a great storm this asterism breathes calm and balance into turbulent spaces, a chance to redistribute resources and put one's house in order.

Śravana individuals tend toward a smaller, lighter physique, but often well-proportioned. Somewhat outspoken in opinion, their voice has a melodious quality. Large-eyed and full-lipped, they are service orientated, gravitating toward environments which keep them constantly preoccupied by the wants and needs of others. They make excellent counsellors, lawyers, coaches, crime fighters and healers, or those who have a talent to listen – or who support a worthy cause.

Although noted for their stern demeanour, they also have a lively fun side. This, however, remains well-masked under daily duties. Above all else, Śravana individuals may be relied upon to stay professional, until the bitter end.

Health-related issues of this Nakshatra include allergies of the skin, weakness of lymphatic vessels (usually the groin area), knees, hearing loss or ear infections (or those inducing vertigo), infections of the urinary tract, low immunity/thymus gland, kidney stones and watery types of eczema. Related Nakshatra body parts include the ears, lymphatic system, immune system, reproductive system, testes/ovaries.

The presiding deity of Śravana is *Vishnu* – second of the Trimūrti. *Vishnu* means 'highest step',[64] and his presidency over this star naturally places some emphasis over its role within the collective of twenty-seven Nakshatras. Tales and deeds of Vishnu are multi-faceted and innumerable; however, some of the key points of his lordship may be noted in the following.

Rig Veda portrays Vishnu primarily as the 'god of grace', a trait similarly attributable to Sûrya (Sun god). Early accounts divine Vishnu to be the source of Indrā's great strength, and who over time absorbs many of the characteristics and mythologies of another contemporary deity, Varuna.[65] One such example is *Samudra Manthan* (see Section 24.4), the churning of the great milky ocean.

Vishnu's appearance is black; he resides in a kingdom of pure gold. He is four-handed and holds a conch, mace, lotus and flaming chakra (or serrated disc). His consort *Maha Lakṣmī*[66] rests at his feet while the stem of a lotus springs upward from his navel. Positioned at the centre of this blossoming lotus sits Brahmā (the creator). In his role as 'unconquerable preserver', Vishnu periodically awakes from his slumber, each time representing the dawning of a new world age. Vishnu is often pictured sleeping, wrapped in the coils of *Śesha-nāga* or *world-serpent*. This coiled leviathan represents the unfolding of time and precariously balances himself upon the shell of *Kūrma* (another avatar of Vishnu) in the guise of a giant turtle or tortoise.[67]

Vishnu is portrayed as ten avatars, called upon separately during ages of darkness. Each avatar sets itself against resident evil, ridding the world of corruption and evil to secure humanity's redemption. Of the ten avatars, only the *Kalki* remains to make his appearance. Prophesied to emerge during Kali-Yuga, Kalki is of brāhmaṇic caste yet takes the form of a gilded warrior, sitting upon a white horse. Bearing a conch, he is armed with bow and arrow, sword and flaming chakra. His appearance will be read in the skies and signals an *end of days* for Earthly kings and/or rulers of men.

Later descriptions of Śravana portray her as solely feminine, monkey-faced and green in complexion. Four-armed, she wields a mace, conch shell, chakra (disc) and lotus flower. The vehicle of Śravana is a horse.

27.5 MARS-RULED NAKSHATRAS
Mrigashirsha 23° 20' Taurus – 6° 40' Gemini (λ Orionis/Meissa)

Those who are born on the lunar day of Mrigashirsha will delight or deal in perfumes, dress, pearls, flowers, fruits, precious stones, wild beasts, birds and deer; will be Somayajis or singers; will be lascivious; will be good writers or painters.

Brihat Saṃhitā by Varāhamihira

First of three Mars-ruled Nakshatras, its iconography is that of a deer's head; *Mriga-shirsha* means 'head of a deer'. Known also as 'the searching star', those born under this asterism often appear to be in a state of perpetual agitation or alertness. Like the deer, there is a cautious yet playful adventurousness associated with this star. Slow-footed, timidly testing their surroundings, those of this Nakshatra can spring into action at the crack of a twig. Coupled with this flighty nature comes also the power of the deer's heart.

This Nakshatra is deeply interwoven with the legend of Prajāpati and Uṣas[68] and sits atop the small triad of stars at the apex of the winter constellation of Orionis, marking the Taurean/Geminian borders of the Milky Way; this Nakshatra could therefore be said to bridge earth (Taurus) and air (Gemini) elements. Both are wonderfully displayed in the associated traits of this star. Earth: sensate, practical and grounded on the one hand; Air: flighty, creative and temperamental on the other. During the alliance of gods and demons in *Samudra Manthan*, Mrigashirsha was said to have been prominently framed in heaven, helping provide the final impetus for the seeking of amrita (nectar of immortality).

Mrigashirsha individuals often appear slighter or shorter in frame, yet physically strong. There is generally a marked flexibility in their joints/limbs, yet often an inherent weakness of upper-back and neck. Facially there is something of the doe-eyed and innocent in their features; often the length of the jaw may seem slightly accentuated, with higher than average cheekbones. Typically their eyes are wide-set and mild. By nature, those of this Nakshatra are often suspicious, sensing ulterior motives in the most innocent of acts. They tend to prosper best in solo careers, as this freedom allows their full creativity to manifest with ease and surety. In more collaborative ventures their competitive side is awakened and may become counter-productive. The saying 'you're cramping my style' aptly suits this asterism and those born under its auspices.

Health-related issues of this Nakshatra include weakness of eyes, skin allergies, partial paralysis, diphtheria, constipation, haemorrhoids, high blood pressure/blood disorders and heart disease (all heightened Pitta tendencies). Related Nakshatra body parts include the eyes, jugular vein, neck, upper spine, tonsils, vocal cords, ears and thymus.

The presiding deity of Mrigashirsha is Soma (pronounced Sō'mā), *god of immortality*, one amongst a number of influential early Vedic deities, frequently venerated and invoked throughout *Rig Veda* and paired with the likes of Indrā, Agnī, Pūṣan and Rudra.

References to soma occur throughout *Rig Veda* (particularly Book IX), which deals in some depth with the identification of soma plants. It appears the mythos surrounding soma was indeed based upon a real plant (possibly a vine) known to the ancients and harvested for ritualistic use. Soma fell into the category called *Divyausadhis* or celestial drugs, many of which are no longer identifiable or available.[69]

Descriptions of its draught are replete with preparation and fermentation techniques yet remain sketchy about detailed identification or reliable sources to procure the plant, saying, 'Prior to the attendance of gods (who receive Sō'mā) the plant was first expressed[70] with flat stones upon a frame lined with a woollen material. The filtrated juice then flows into wooden vats and from here offered to the gods or poured upon fire or drunk by priests.'

The milky sap[71] of this planet is referred to as both food and drink and appears to have been sweetened with honey, milk or occasionally ghee. The subsequent fermented version of the draught was called *Somyam-madhu* or soma-mead.

An alternative form of soma (known as Utsa) was said to reside in a honey-well located at the highest step of Vishnu and brought to Earth by an eagle.[72] Later Indrā (king of the gods) becomes heavily intertwined with soma legends, heightening his own profile in the process – as once intoxicated he becomes fully invincible, riding into battle undaunted by any enemy.

The post-Vedic soma becomes almost exclusively inseparable with the divine nectar *amṛta*, thought to exude from the Moon. During full Moon (Shukla Paksha) this amṛta is greedily drunk by the gods who lay in wait each month to receive its bounty. During new Moon (Krishna Paksha) the Moon slowly recovers from his loss of vital fluids and begins to replenish – a process that culminates at the following full Moon.

Soma as deity takes on a variety of guises in the Vedas, named and honoured, yet less anthropomorphic than his contemporaries. Whether manifesting as divine being, luminary (Moon) or intoxicating beverage there remains great mystery surrounding this most flighty of supernatural beings.

Later descriptions of Mrigashirsha portray her as solely feminine. Three-faced, her countenances are those of snake, horse and deer. Holding a pot of nectar and carrying a rope she rides atop a vulture, her complexion akin to that of the Moon.

Chitrā 23° 20' Virgo – 6° 40' Libra (α Virginis/Spica)

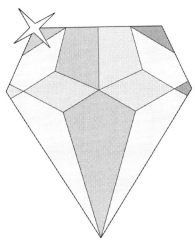

Those who are born on the lunar day of Chitrā will be dealers in jewels, precious stones, fine clothes, writers and singers, manufacturers of fine perfumes, good mathematicians, weavers, surgeons, occultists and dealers in Rajadhanya.[73]

Brihat Saṃhitā by Varāhamihira

Second of the Mars-ruled Nakshatras, *Chitrā* is commonly represented by a gemstone or perfectly spherical pearl. Chitrā is also known as 'the craftsman's star' or 'the star of opportunity'.

Chitrā Nakshatra is known to be inventive resourceful and creative, whose emphasis falls squarely upon grand design or the visually arresting. *Chitrā* means 'brilliant' or 'illuminating' and as its names suggests is identified with great works of art, breathtaking architecture or mechanisation fused with grace, beauty and precision.

Chitrā Nakshatra is marked by the bright star Spica (α Virginis; see Section 1.6), venerated throughout many ancient world cultures. Its luminance earned it the title *stunning pearl* – suspended in heaven. Like the hidden wealth of a gemstone, Chitrā is adept at revealing hidden beauty, coaxing the dull and ordinary into revealing their splendour. Like a pearl, its shell must be opened to reveal its bounty. Chitrā is said to rule over all acts of transformation such as hammering, cutting, polishing and sharpening – all very Martian-esque attributes.

Chitrā individuals tend toward a leaner and taller framed individual; their eyes are often pronounced (large) and attractive, the face can be squarish in appearance with high cheekbones and squared jaw line. Balanced and contented in mannerism, they often display a bewildering array of facial expressions in rapid succession. Upper arm and forearm are often well-developed, the hands square, strong and compact. A Chitrā persona can be magnetic, possessing charm and a flowing disposition. Pleasant to be around, they create a relaxed and easy environment that strives to keep a crowd entertained. Those of this Nakshatra always permit their contemporaries to shine but always outshine the competition if given a chance. It is said that Shukra (Venus) feels out-performed by this star, hence his debilitation in Chitrā Nakshatra.

Health-related issues of this Nakshatra include injury to the forehead, kidney stones, brain fever, diabetes, the lower part of the belly and the passage of urine, abdominal ulcers, appendicitis, hernia and lumbar region of the spine. Related Nakshatra body parts include the forehead, kidneys, lumbar vertebra and neck.

The presiding deity of Chitrā is Tvashtar, architect and artificer to the gods. Tvashtar appears with some regularity throughout Vedic texts, charged with a degree of notoriety.[74] Tvashtar is credited as both designer and fashioner, praised for his artistry and strength of hand. He is portrayed as riding a shining chariot, yoking its two steeds whilst wielding an axe. Principally this deity is renowned for paring down the circumference[75] of the Sun, using the excess to forge Indra's lightning bolts.

Tvashtar edged the iron axe of Brahmaṇaspati[76] and crafted the drinking vessels of gods and demons for the most precious of beverages – life-extending soma.[77] Tvashtar was said to have created the horse and given it the speed of the wind. He was given the title *Viśvarūpa* (omniform) for his ability to manifest any manner of beings by his will alone.[78] Much like the deity *Savitar* (see Hastā Nakshatra in Section 27.4), he was thought to reside in the middle kingdom (a region between heaven and Earth), healing the sick and conferring life extension.

Tvashtar was greatly fond of adoring worshippers; his golden hands were said to grant divine gifts to his most faithful admirers. In later Purāṇic roles, however, his status appears somewhat diminished, devolved to fashioning divine weapons or godly conveyances, later referred to as *Vishvakarma*, his artisan skills appearing more sought after by Lord Yamaraj, who commissioned hellish contrivances to punish his captives in the infernal regions.

Later descriptions of Chitrā portray her as solely feminine, her complexion white, her features those of a tiger. Four-handed, she carries a rope, a pot of nectar, a book and lotus. The vehicle of Chitrā is a buffalo.

Dhanistha 23° 20' Capricorn –
6° 40' Aquarius (β Delphini/Rotanev)

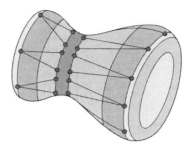

A person born in Dhanistha will be liberal in his gifts, wealthy, courageous, fond of music and greedy.

Brihat Jataka by Varāhamihira

The third and final Mars-ruled Nakshatra is *Dhanistha*, its symbology associated with the damarū (drum) or flute.[79] Known as 'the star of symphony' its iconography portrays the unrelenting beat or passage of time.

Drums are often symbolic of deeper undercurrents that move beyond normal perception, likened to the pulse of life itself. As the mridangam vibrates its rhythm into the æther it has a powerfully hypnotising effect upon its listener. Equally, the resonance of the flute conjures up a similar energetic – much like the pied-piper merrily leading his entourage under its melodious spell. The flute was also the preferred instrument and constant companion of Krishna, its melodies mesmerising the young Gopis.[80]

Those born under this star are quite often blessed with some level of notoriety or they desperately seek fame and fortune, desiring to travel or spread their name. Dhanistha Nakshatra often bestows an ability to influence large proportions of the populace, being quite often prominent in birth-charts of those whose career extends to the performing arts, particularly those which combine music and dance.[81]

Dhanistha individuals often present a typical Martian-esque physique, with good muscle tone (particularly in their younger years). Generally they do not display any great height; however, a narrowing waistline and broader shoulders may appear to accentuate the figure, giving an appearance of height. Facially their eyes appear large, the lips full, the shape of the face slightly oval. They have a keen and penetrating intelligence that remains ever watchful, despite their carefree and somewhat dishevelled demeanour. Curiously, in social situations they are not natural stand-outs, but given an opportunity (or a stage upon which to perform) they quickly take control of the assembled, stealing the show or stirring up a storm. Those of this star are often unafraid also to trespass into politically questionable arenas, often delighting in a bit of mild boat-rocking. The warrior planet Mars finds full exaltation within this asterism, heightening its passion, drive and need to conquer.

Health-related issues of this Nakshatra include weakness of the lower back, liver and urinary tract, high blood pressure, thrombosis, heart disease, neurosis, arthritis of knees and ankles, injury to the shins and the fracturing of leg bones. Related Nakshatra body parts include the spine, cerebrospinal fluid, the ankles and calf muscles.

The presiding deities of Dhanistha are the *Vasus*, an eight-fold[82] collective of important deities comprising: *Soma* (the Moon), *Dharā* (the Earth), *Anila* (the wind), *Uṣas* (the dawn), *Anala* (fire), *Dhruva* (the pole star), *Apās* (water goddess) and *Parjanya* (god of thunderstorms). Vasus fall under the overall stewardship of Agnī; however, under invocation were nearly always combined with *Indrā* (see Jyestha Nakshatra in Section 27.9). In time, both Indrā and Vasus were eventually usurped by the rising prominence of Vishnu (see Śravana Nakshatra in Section 27.4).

Later descriptions of Dhanistha portray her as solely feminine, its deity seated upon a lotus, surrounded by an assortment of gems. Her complexion is golden, her eyes large and attractive. Robed in rich red fabrics, her hands grant blessings to worshippers.

27.6 RĀHU-RULED NAKSHATRAS
Ardra 6° 40' – 20° 00' Gemini (α Orionis/Betelgeuse)

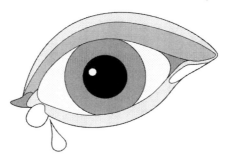

A person born when the Moon passes through the asterism of Ardra will be insincere, of irascible temper, ungrateful, troublesome and addicted to wicked deeds.

Brihat Jataka by Varāhamihira

First of the Rāhu-ruled Nakshatras is *Ardra*, portrayed as a teardrop, human head or gemstone. Although occupying the dualistic sign of Gemini, Ardra's Yogatārā (α Orionis) is actually located at the shoulder of Orion[83] in the constellation of the same name.

Ardra is commonly interpreted as 'moistening' or 'washing' in quality, highlighting its shodhana/cleansing energetic. The symbolism of this Nakshatra appears deeply rooted in the foreboding associated with darkening skies, lightning and torrential rain. However, once this tempest has abated, its passing leaves the landscape feeling cleansed, freshened and fertile.

Physically, Ardra individuals may appear shorter and lighter in stature, yet often have excellent endurance to sustained exertion. They display quick and well-coordinated gross motor skills, but overall appear somewhat erratic in mannerism. The skin is often tawny with a pronounced darkening about the eyes, giving them the appearance of being deeply set. The face is often ovular, terminating in a sharp or pronounced chin. Their hair can be lank, dark or wiry. Health-related issues of this Nakshatra include a weakness of the throat, arms, shoulders and hair, insomnia, asthma, cough, pneumonia or diseases which arise from inappropriate sexual habits. Related Nakshatra body parts include hair, eyes, throat, shoulders and the arms.

Socially, Ardra types can be extremely cordial, often having a talent for unflattering mimicry or fast-paced/quick-witted rhetoric which helps to lighten any over-seriousness pressed upon them. They often have engaging and probing personalities, but are famed for their tantrums and unsightly outbursts, all of which are luckily (like storms) short-lived. Highly skilled in problem solving, re-ordering or re-evaluation, an Ardra persona enjoys finding solutions to apparently unworkable or untenable situations, unless of course the problem has been created by themselves!

The presiding deity of this Nakshatra is *Rudra*[84] (storm god[85]), one of three important figures found presiding over an early collective of deities.[86] Known as *Rudras*[87] or *Maruts*, these were considered to be the offspring of Rudra and Pṛśni[88] (the latter a pregnant raincloud, bearing the former's lightning).

Accompanied by fierce, wide-mouthed baying hounds, Rudra was feared by all. His skill with a bow and arrow were unrivalled amongst the gods. Though principally an *Asura* (and known as a demon who seeks to slay men), Rudra was also propitiated to avert impending disasters or preserve life (both man and beast[89]). In his role of healer, Rudra was noteworthy for his persona of physician or *he who carries a thousand remedies*.[90] Rudra's physical appearance is described as 'radiant and adorned in gold, firm of limb with braided hair. Armed with bow and arrow, club and thunderbolt, his colouration is ruddy (or coppery). His belly is black and red, his throat blue, he is also beautiful of lips (speech?). Rudra is one-thousand eyed and known as "The Archer". He resides in high places (mountains) etc.'

Rig Veda portrays Rudra as violent and terrifying, showing little remorse or reason for his action. Under his alternative name *Mahādeva* he was feared as a slayer of men, horses and livestock. Unless propitiated/soothed, nothing was thought to avert his stormy maelstrom of lightning and howling wind.[91] Rudra is primarily identified as a proto-Śiva, who like his counterpart *Vishnu* underwent radical remodelling and partial fusion with his contemporary deities. Śiva later became most famed for his 'Cosmic Dance' during which the universe and time unfold; a cessation of this dance brings the dissolution of all matter. Restful and harmonic steps are known as *Ananda Tāṇḍava*. Sharp, violent or destructive steps are known as *Rudra Tāṇḍava*.

Later descriptions of Ardra portray her as solely feminine and dark of complexion. Robed in green, she displays a necklace made of human bones. Riding atop a large bull, she holds a long spear.

Swati 6° 40' – 20° 00' Libra (α Bootis/Arcturus)

Those who are born on the lunar day of Swati will be of a mild and quiet nature, will control his passion and be skilled in trade, will be merciful, unable to bear thirst, of sweet speech and disposed to do acts of charity.

Brihat Saṃhitā by Varāhamihira

The second Rāhu Nakshatra is *Swati*,[92] commonly portrayed as a polyp of coral or a sword. This Nakshatra reflects the ebb and flow of all things, a reminder that the only constant is change. Much like the coral reef,[93] those born under this star enjoy meeting challenges head-on, bracing themselves for an onslaught. This coral metaphor serves as a reminder that those born under this star draw heavily on skills perfected over time, much as coral accumulates by slowly layering on successive deposits, each reinforcing its collective framework. Swati also denotes tenacious action, literally 'a will to conquer and survive at all costs'.

Swati may also be represented by a sword, indicating sharpness and swiftness as well as conflict or violence. Swords may also be a work of art, skilfully forged from the finest material, their preparation a process of constant re-shaping and sharpening until achieving the perfect edge.

Named the 'star of self-reliance', this Nakshatra is strongly connected with self-motivation and self-creation, a focal point from which to expand or strike out. Swati is also known for the quality of independence, seeking constantly to disseminate knowledge or information as widely as possible. Those born under this star often have a pioneering quality about them, said to have a keen eye for potential pitfalls or unsound investments. Swati individuals are often highly industrious and not shy about getting their hands dirty. Always on the lookout to improve or enhance, they may seek out discarded or unwanted items, investing time and effort in restorative projects, seeing value where others lack vision.

Physically, these natives may be larger framed or broad shouldered. A narrowing of their hips can give their torso a slightly triangular shape. Often having a wild or unkempt appearance, it somehow always passes for an intentional, almost fashionable, look. Those born under this star make good strategists but periodically succumb to strong emotional outbursts that overpower reason. Though likely to extend a helping hand to anyone in need, once crossed (like a sword) they are never likely to forget injustice or being cheated.

Health-related issues of this Nakshatra include skin ailments, inflammation of the urethra or bladder, teeth and kidney stones. Related Nakshatra body parts include the jaw, chin, teeth, skin, bladder and urethra.

The presiding deity of this Nakshatra is Vāyu (god of wind). Defined as a personification of the wind (as distinguished from Vāta Dosha), Vāyu was an important deity in *Rig Veda*, most commonly evoked as the dual deity *Indrā-vāyu*.[94] Descriptions of Vāyu are indefinite, such as thousand-eyed, swift and beautiful. Like Indrā he delights in drinking soma[95] and touching the skies. Fastest of all gods,[96] he rides a golden-seated chariot, pulled by ruddy steeds yoked by his will alone. Vāyu wanders the various pathways of the air, giving breath to the gods and stirring the dust upon the Earth. It is said of Vāyu: 'One hears his roar but his form is never seen.'

Invocation of Vāyu was undertaken for fame, wealth[97]and healthy offspring. He was also propitiated for the acquisition of gold. Vāyu became a protective deity for the weak and elderly (Vāta rules the latter part of life) and, like Rudra, had strong healing abilities. It is often said of Vāyu, 'He prolongs life, having the treasure of immortality in his house.' When invoked in his more wrathful aspect, Vāyu performed in quite the opposite function, summarily dispatching any quarrelsome adversaries.

Later descriptions of Swati portray her as solely feminine, pictured riding an antelope. Her countenance is that of a buffalo, her complexion dark. Four-armed she carries a flag, a pot of nectar, a rope and a sheath of kusha grass.

Shatabhishak 6° 40' – 20° 00'
Aquarius (λ Aquarii/Hydor)

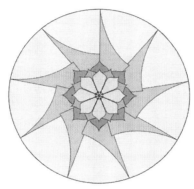

A person born when the Moon passes through the asterism of Shatabhishak will be harsh in speech, will be truthful, will suffer from grief, will conquer his enemies, will thoughtlessly engage in his work and will be of independent ways.

Brihat Jataka by Varāhamihira

The third and final Rāhu Nakshatra is *Shatabhishak*, its symbology a circled lotus or basket filled with herbs. Its circular motif (all-encompassing yet isolating) beautifully symbolises the distant and somewhat cerebral nature of those attached to this Nakshatra. Its lotus iconography symbolises evolution and personal growth.

Those born under this star are very much self-contained or self-sufficient, often preferring their own company. The lotus can be representative of *Jiva* (spirit), considered to rise from primordial depths, struggling through murky waters toward the light and self-illumination.

Shatabhishak is very much connected to health and the healing arts, its principal deity *Varuna* often evoked in matters of illness or by those who seek longevity. This Nakshatra also has some affinity to herbal remedies, or through therapies that relate to water, herbal decoctions, baths or cleansing. Accidents or sicknesses incurred whilst the Moon tenanted this Nakshatra were deemed inauspicious, likely to cause much discomfort and distress. It is said that 'health matters arising under this Nakshatra require the skills of a hundred physicians to remedy its ills.'

Called 'the veiling star', those born under this star feel themselves to be in direct opposition to an unseen force that strives to oppress and deceive the populace at large. There is a tendency to adopt socially unpopular standpoints or to engage in relentless campaigns amidst overwhelming odds, whatever the cost (be it physical, emotional or financial). Careful analysis of Rāhu may often pinpoint where that individual's personal fight or battleground will become most active. The undercurrent of these people runs deep; they are greatly insightful, but often unworldly.

Physically, those of this Nakshatra can appear large-framed, but not firm of body. Often pale in skin tone, or high in forehead, their eyes are often heavily lidded. There can be a marked frailness about them, both physically or mentally, seeming to require some deep level of self-healing. Shatabhishak often bestows ongoing health issues which challenge the individual throughout their lifetime. On a positive note, these same difficulties may inspire them to begin the self-healing process. Many born under the auspices of this star are gifted with excellent memory retention and clear thinking; they often have a youthful or somewhat brightened countenance. Notably, their speech pattern is typically accentuated or eccentric, giving them a distinct proclivity for intellectual wordplay or playful banter.

Health-related issues of this Nakshatra include weakness of the calves, injury to the chin, bilious attacks, typhoid, high blood pressure, diabetes, paralysis, bone fractures and high fever. Related Nakshatra body parts include the teeth and lower jaw, the knees, ankles and toes.

The presiding deity of this Nakshatra is *Varuna* (god of the cosmic waters, rains and ocean). Featured prominently in many Vedic poems, Varuna is described as having a countenance akin to that of Agnī. Kṣatriya in caste,[98] he was sun-eyed, fair-skinned and balding, clad in a golden mantle as if robed in ghee.[99] Like Savitar and Tvashtar he is described as beautiful-handed, thousand-eyed and seated upon the strewn grass, consuming soma in the company of Mitra.[100] Varuna's celestial mansion was of a thousand doors, supported by a thousand columns. From this heavenly seat, clasping his Nāgapāsa,[101] he was thought to gaze down upon the deeds of men, looking into their homes, hearts and beyond to deep hellish realms.

Varuna is said to have commanded myriads of spies[102] who pervade all the spaces and report back to their master.

Varuna's post-Vedic status reduced him to a kind of proto-Poseidon figure, usually portrayed riding a sea monster[103] in a triumphal posture, upon open seas. Although losing some of his earlier omnipotence, he retained his oceanic mastery as well as healing[104] and rainmaking abilities. Like Rudra, he was often invoked to intervene in matters of health. It is reported that 'Varuna can take away or prolong life, he has a thousand remedies[105] that can drive away death and releases one from sin. He is a wise guardian of immortality and the righteous hope to meet him in the next world where Varuna and Yama reign in bliss.'

Later descriptions of Shatabhishak portray her as solely feminine, bearing the face of a horse and garmented in rich red fabric. She carries a rope and pot of nectar. The vehicle of Shatabhishak is a Makara (sea monster).

27.7 JUPITER-RULED NAKSHATRAS
Punarvasu 20° 00' Gemini – 3° 20' Cancer (β Gemini/Pollux)

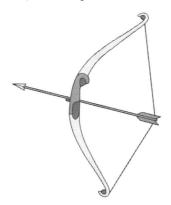

Those who are born on the lunar day of Punarvasu will be noted for truthfulness, generosity, cleanliness, respectfulness and decency, personal beauty, good sense, wealth and fame. They will also be merchants, dealing in excellent articles, will be fond of service and will delight in the company of painters and sculptors.

Brihat Saṃhitā by Varāhamihira

First of the Jupiter-ruled Nakshatras is *Punarvasu*, portrayed as a bow, quiver of arrows or building. *Punar* means 'to return' or 'to revisit', *Vasu* might be translated as 'illuminating' or 'brilliant'. After the darkening skies and storms of Ardra (preceeding Nakshatra), Punarvasu brings sunlight, illumination and clear skies.

The bow and quiver depicts the directness of this Nakshatra, its reluctance to pursue convoluted pathways; like an arrow in flight, Punarvasu is straight from the shoulder and piercing. Those born under this star enjoy challenges and the chance to overcome obstacles and setbacks, thoughtfully returning the experience (to their quiver) until again called for. One of the hallmarks of this Nakshatra is its ability to identify value from detriment, often having the patience to sift large amounts of data (in relative swiftness) before isolating its gems and carefully cataloguing them for future reference.

The symbology of a building indicates a likelihood that those of this Nakshatra are forced to wander far from their place of birth, often in search of fame, fortune or – sometimes – anonymity. Residence and integration in foreign lands often secures them some level of notoriety, achievement or in some cases infamy.

Known also as 'the star of renewal' there is a marked tendency for those born under this star constantly to reinvent themselves, perhaps physically through appearance (fashion, bodywork, etc.) or through identity with a particular ideology or a social group.

Energetically, Punarvasu may produce some highly driven individuals, often seen as a blur of motion, labouring on new projects into the small hours without any apparent fatigue. Their minds are sharp, discriminating and decisive, with a passion to accumulate knowledge, and often they find themselves in a position to put it to good use.

Physically, Punarvasu individuals may appear athletic in build, light of frame yet retaining a good muscular base, enabling them to perform with greater efficiency than might be expected. Facially, they may appear slight-featured, with an elongated narrowing jaw line. Their eyes are often small, bright but nervous looking. With the passing of years their skin can develop a dappled appearance inclining toward heat-rash, blotchiness or rosacea.

Often shrewd in business, they may develop some odd yet successful stratagems for surviving commercially. They may be thrifty yet seldom give the appearance of being bereft of comfortable endowments. They are often law-abiding and god-fearing in nature, having been exposed to a childhood steeped in religious iconography. In their latter years these religious sentiments are often rekindled or re-enacted with some fervour.

Health-related issues of this Nakshatra include fevers and headache, weakness of the heart, lungs and liver, pancreatic imbalances, inflammation of the ears and throat, damage to the shoulder blades and digestive insufficiencies. Related Nakshatra body parts include the fingers, ears, throat, shoulder blades, pancreas, liver and nose.

The presiding deity of Punarvasu is *Āditi* (mother to the gods), whose name means 'boundless' or 'infinite'. Āditi appears prominently throughout Vedic mythology; in *Rig Veda* she is invoked to release one from the bonds of physical suffering or moral guilt. In many textual references, Āditi is accompanied by one or more of her sons, the Âdityas.[106] The role-playing of Āditi in Hindu mythology appears as varied as her name 'without boundaries' suggests. Said to represent the primal mother (Devî/Shaktî) and wife to Daksha,[107] she is frequently honoured with the origination of all Devas,[108] feeding them with honey-sweetened milk. Likewise, her antithesis, *Ditî*, is responsible for the manifestation of the *Daityas* (enemies to the gods), representing all corruptive and finite forces in the universe.

Physically, Āditi is described as radiant and expansive. Seen as a supporter to all living creatures, she is said to 'belong to all men'. Protective and undecaying, she is described as the Mother of Kings. Invocation of the goddess was deemed most auspicious at sunrise, midday and sunset.

Later descriptions of Punarvasu portray her as solely feminine, bearing the face of a wild boar. Pale in complexion, she is seen to wield a lightning bolt, elephant goad and rope, her fourth hand making a gesture of fearlessness. The vehicle of Punarvasu is a wild cat.

Vishaka 20° 00' Libra – 3° 20' Scorpio (ι Librae)

Those who are born on the lunar day of Vishaka will grow trees yielding red flowers and red fruits; be dealers in gingelly seeds,[109] beans, cotton, black gram and chick peas and worshippers of Indrā and Agnī.

Brihat Saṃhitā by Varāhamihira

Second of the Jupiter-ruled Nakshatras is *Vishaka*,[110] its symbology a potter's wheel or diverging branches of a tree. Called 'star of purpose', Vishaka concerns itself with finding its place in the grand scheme of things.

Vishaka bestows a restless spirit, often manifesting as an extremely inquisitive youth, eager to explore their world, soon after taking their first tentative steps. Additionally, those born under the influence of this star feel a need to expand their horizons, journeying far from home at a relatively young age. Outwardly directed, they are always eager to test their mettle in the clamour for success.

Beneath the veneer of this asterism lies a dualistic nature – cool and mild-mannered on the one hand; sharply contrasted by an assertive, dictatorial and sometimes quarrelsome nature. This dichotomy is rooted in their need to explore and discover the truth of things. Like a spinning potter's wheel, Vishaka individuals have a restive and stable core contrasted by an intense and high-speed periphery, their immediate environment tending always to bring them more than a fair share of daily challenges. The iconography of Vishaka's diverging branches is a constant reminder of the stark choices and destiny associated with this Nakshatra, whose individuals seem forever to be faced with complex dilemmas.

This Nakshatra has a devotional side also; being Jupiter-ruled they may be attracted to various forms of worship or to the attainment of higher knowledge. However, the indulgent self-interests of Venus (two-thirds of Vishaka rest in Libra) are constantly on hand to stray the devout from their course. The final 3° 20' of Vishaka dips a toe into Mars-ruled Scorpio, inviting a final Martian-esque tint to an already full repertoire. This latter influence suffuses the character of Vishaka with a penetrating intensity (and acridity), all wonderfully echoed in its alternative names such as 'the forked' or 'dual branched'.[111]

Physically, Vishaka individuals are often of mixed constitution; Jupiter's own situation is a useful factor in determining the tendency of dosha imbalances. Overall, their frame tends toward the lighter or less physically robust. Their features may be soft, rounded and youthful. In later years there is a tendency for water retention and/or elevated blood pressure; the colouration of their skin may lean toward darkened shades, tanning easily yet resistant to creases and signs of seasonal weathering.

Health-related issues of this Nakshatra include vertigo, weakness of the arms, abdominal pains and weak kidneys, blockage of pancreatic ducts, bladder infections, haemorrhoids, enlarged prostate, bladder wall inflammation and uterine cysts. Related Nakshatra body parts include the arms, lower abdomen, pancreas, rectum, prostate gland and bladder.

Paired or collective deities are a common theme in the early Vedic period, particularly with respect to Indrā, king of the gods.[112] Rulership of Vishaka here falls to *Indrā-agnī*,[113] most venerated of all dualistic deities. Exultant hymns in praise of Īndrā-agnī intensify the roles of both warrior gods, collectively referred to as 'wielders of the thunderbolt', 'slayers of Vṛtrasura' (dragon/serpent), 'invincible in battle' and 'fort destroyers'.

Other coalescent states of Indrā include *Indrā-váruṇā*, *Indrā-vāyu*, *Indrā-bṛihaspātī* and *Indrā-sómā*. Likewise, Agnī also appears in the guise of *Agnī-sómā* and *Agnī-parjanyā*. In contrast to these highly charged and aforementioned titles, Īndrā-agnī became identified as 'sacrificial priest', 'drinker of soma' and 'wise lord of the abode', given to driving away troublesome demons, bestowing food, granting wealth, giving strength and providing cattle. These latter traits also highlight an alternative and benefic nature apparent behind the outward ferocity of their union.

Later descriptions of Vishaka portray her as solely feminine, bearing a reddish complexion and the face of a lion. She wields a thunderbolt, a spear, nectar pot and goad in her four hands. The vehicle of Vishaka is a ram.

Purvabhadra 20° 00' Aquarius – 3° 20' Pisces (α Pegasi/Markab)

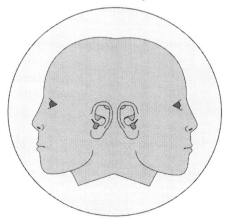

Persons born on the lunar day of Purvabhadra will be thieves, shepherds, torturers; wicked, mean and deceitful; will possess no virtues; will neglect religious rites and will be successful in fighting.

Brihat Jataka by Varāhamihira

The third and final Jupiter-ruled Nakshatra is *Purvabhadra*, symbolically represented by twins or a man bearing two faces,[114] this latter iconography reminiscent of the Roman god *Janus*, one famed for presiding over beginnings and endings. Similarly, this Nakshatra is also considered to favour opportunity and transition, introspection and extrospection.

Three-quarters of this Nakshatra reside in Saturn-ruled Aquarius; its final 3° 20' are located in Jupiter-ruled Pisces. Its Aquarian allotment (although governed by constrictive Saturn) has some renown for the slightly radical[115] or future-orientated outlook. Its latter Piscean allotment tends toward orthodoxy, is defensive and conservative in outlook. Here two faces of Jupiter are unveiled – first through Aquarian waters, distributed for mutual advantage, and latterly 'traditionalistic' Pisces. This interesting mixture of antipodal energy lays the foundation stone for some highly eccentric individuals.

Those born under the auspices of this star often find themselves a magnet for life's social misfits or those who seek to profit without thought of consequence or action. They themselves might also have a talent for yoking or manipulating the weaker-minded, their uncanny predictive abilities and synchronal good fortunes often endearing them to unscrupulous wealth-seekers or *Chaṇḍāla*.[116] Those of this Nakshatra often incline toward the simple life, appearing quite aesthetic in taste and requiring little from their surroundings. They invariably seem to derive the very best from what is at hand. The shadow side to this asterism can be its somewhat heated and stormy nature. Brandishing a cursive tongue, their words can cut people down to size with the greatest of ease.

Physically, Purvabhadra individuals may appear tall, lean or with an unusual habitus, appearing somewhat disproportionate or unbalanced in stature (although often nothing obvious to the eye). Their movements are swift and precise, with a sharp corrective eye for detail. Their overall disposition errs toward the nervous or fearful, their minds tending to dwell upon morose thoughts. On a positive note, those of this Nakshatra have a witty and insightful sense of humour, with a firm dash of sarcasm. They are excellent judges of character (able to spot fraudsters at a distance). Natural counsellors and philanthropists, they are always willing to lend a hand to those in dire need or in financial straits.

Health-related issues of this Nakshatra include weakness of the chest/lungs, mental trauma, rheumatism, liver complaints, constipation and oedema (usually a swelling of the ankles, feet or toes). Related Nakshatra body parts include the sides of torso, navel, ankles, feet and toes.

The presiding deity of this Nakshatra is *Aja-ekapād*, a name frequently taken to mean 'he who protects' or 'drinks with one foot' or 'one-footed goat'.[117] The word *Aja* may also be interpreted as 'stormer' or 'driving'; and *ekapād* as 'single-footed'. This deity appears closely connected to a number of aerial deities such as *Rudra*[118] or *Ahi-budhnya*[119] and is thought to have been just one in a host of earlier storm gods,[120] although there remains some level of conjecture over this supposition.[121]

Later descriptions of Purvabhadra portray her as solely feminine, bearing the face of a boar, with a whitish complexion. She frequently carries a pot of amrita and the severed head of a ram. The vehicle of Purvabhadra is a goat.

27.8 SATURN-RULED NAKSHATRAS
Pushyami 3° 20' – 16° 40' Cancer
(δ Cancri/Asellus Australis)

A person born when the Moon passes through the asterism of Pushyami will have control over his desires, will be generally liked, learned in shāstras, rich and will be fond of charitable acts.

Brihat Saṃhitā by Varāhamihira

First of the Saturn-ruled Nakshatras is *Pushyami*,[122] often portrayed as an arrowhead and/or a flower/herb.[123]

Arrows are symbolic of deadly force, suggesting that the bounties of this Nakshatra are not to be scorned or trifled with. The flowering stage of a plant's life-cycle is symbolic of maturity and endurance, an indicator that nectar is ready to be shared. Pushyami is also symbolised by an udder of a cow, highlighting its many nurturing qualities. Traditionally called 'the nourisher' or 'the thriving one,[124] Pushyami is indicative of spiritual wisdom, benevolence, commitment, self-inquiry or those learned in various shāstra.[125] Pushyami rewards both materially and spiritually, enabling growth, prosperity and, most importantly, the propagation of wisdom.

This Nakshatra parallels the attributes of its presiding deity, Brihaspati (great instructor). Called 'father', Brihaspati blesses individuals with health and longevity. The flowering[126]/herbal motif of this Nakshatra indicates not only a devotional nature, but also its curative potential, that is, its ability to remove affliction or disease.

Quite often bookish in nature, those of this Nakshatra are to be found loitering in libraries, centres of higher education, public parks or places where a generous spattering of nature is to be found. They are natural orators and usually enjoy public speaking, their great memories standing them in good stead as they reel off pages of impressive (or corroborative) data if and when required. There is a somewhat officious/over-responsible nature to Pushyami individuals, but once connected on a more scholarly level they expose a more liberal temperament. Those born under this star gravitate toward peaceful and reclusive havens – rowdy or fast-paced locations irritating to their sensitivities. However, when nested in relative comfort or self-cocooned in thought, even these environments may become tolerable.

Physically, they incline toward a proportioned athletic frame, shoulders often broadened and limbs slightly elongated. With the passing of forty years the lower abdomen has a tendency to distend or become herniated. Visually their eyes might appear small, but are usually sharp, quick and bright. The face may be rounded softly with a sharp pronounced chin.

Health-related issues of this Nakshatra include respiratory ailments such as asthma and tuberculosis, gastric ulcers, jaundice, fever and colic, weakness of the stomach, pancreas, ribs and mouth/gums. Related Nakshatra body parts include the mouth, stomach, gums, ribs and lungs.

The presiding deity of this Nakshatra is *Brihaspati*, teacher to the immortals (gods) and lord of sacred speech. Said to instigate the rainclouds and bring forth thunder,[127] Brihaspati was also a formidable battle deity, brandishing an iron axe and golden hatchet forged by Tvashtar. Brihaspati frequently demonstrated his prowess in battle; the tips of his arrows like diamonds struck his foe like thunderbolts. His chariot was pulled by ruddy steeds and was said to assail any demon's stronghold. Born of lightning in the heavenly realms, Brihaspati was likened to a blacksmith,[128] that is, from whom all gods were forged.

Described as beautiful-tongued and one-hundred winged, he was also seven-rayed, seven-mouthed and sharply horned. His body was the colour of ghee with a slight ruddiness. His complexion bright and pure, his voice clear and penetrating.

In earlier Vedic epics, Brihaspati and Indrā were paired on a number of occasions, both having warlike traits and each being partial to the soma elixir. Renowned as wielder of lightning, Brihaspati was considered both ally and epithet of Indrā, promoting devotional practice and penance to the king of the gods. Several hymns of *Rig Veda* are dedicated to Brihaspati in connection with Indrā's slaying of Vṛtra (the serpent/dragon[129]).

Later descriptions of Pushyami portray her as solely feminine, her body a light shade of orange, her complexion greyish (cloudy). In her hands she carries a rosary, nectar pot and chakrika (weapon). The vehicle of Pushyami is a goat.

Anuradha 3° 20' Cancer – 16° 40' Scorpio (δ Scorpii/Dschubba)

A person born when the Moon passes through the asterism of Anuradha will be rich, will live in foreign lands, will be unable to bear hunger and disposed to wander from place to place.

Brihat Saṃhitā by Varāhamihira

Second of the Saturn-ruled Nakshatras is *Anuradha*, its symbolism a flowering lotus or the rising Sun (as seen through a triumphal gateway[130]). Anurādhā means 'beloved of Krishna'.

Called 'the star of success', Anuradha boasts a wealth of organisational skills as well as an ability to form stable and lasting alliances. Individuals born under the auspices of this Nakshatra are unlikely to forget friendship, kindness or a helping hand extended to them. Often they may feel burdened by this debt until able to return in kind.

Saturn's rulership over this Nakshatra makes for a hard taskmaster (a commonality of all Saturn-ruled Nakshatra), forcing the individual to experience a number of tough setbacks on the road to success. Fortuitously, Saturn also equips that same individual with ample stamina and determination, finally delivering their reward and fulfilling his axiom 'Saturn never denies, just delays'.

Craving challenges or a call to strange lands, their pathway often unravels through a series of chance meetings and lucky breaks, their friendly disposition quickly establishing new connections or quickly rekindling previously severed connections. Greatly akin to the life-cycle of the lotus (a primary signification for Anuradha), flowering is preceded by a long upward journey through murky waters, before arriving triumphantly (and washed clean) into the light. In this way also, the later years in the life of the individual prove the most rewarding.

Physically, Anuradha can appear bright of face, radiant with an alluring stare (often quite mesmerising to the opposite sex). Their stature tends toward a strong frame, although it should be studied carefully in regard to constitution. Saturn, although cold and Vāta by nature, may become somewhat variegated in Anuradha, due to the influence of Scorpio (Pitta/Kapha in quality). The influence of Mars (Scorpio's lord) should also be ascertained before assessing dosha.

Health-related issues of this Nakshatra include a weakness of the bladder, genitals, rectum or pubic bone, chest infections, constipation, haemorrhoids, nose bleeds, menstrual problems and high fever. Related Nakshatra body parts include the heart, nasal bones, pelvis, rectum and anus.

The presiding deity of Anuradha is *Mitra*, a prominent solar deity and Âditya. His manifestation was by 'utterance of voice', and noted to ignite 'a bond of friendship between men'. Known as sustainer of gods, his role appears to have been mostly supportive, stabilising the space between heaven and Earth. Said to ignite the Sun and hold it true to its heavenly course,[131] the orb of the Sun was known as 'the eye of Mitra'. Mitra and Varuna[132] appear closely associated in various mythologies, as was Agnī, who when kindled (and radiant) was said to be 'as Mitra'.

The name Mitra generally implies friendship and passivity; it is perhaps this aspect of his character that inspired benevolent and devotional connotations ascribed to this Nakshatra. Like his contemporaries – *Indrā*, *Agnī*, *Aryaman* and *Savitar* – Mitra was an important early figure in Vedic worship; however, like his contemporaries, he was superseded by later adaptations or merged deities.

Later descriptions of Anuradha portray her as solely feminine, her face likened to a cat. Her torso is black from head to waist, and pale from the waist to her feet. In one hand she carries a thunderbolt; in the other a lotus. The vehicle of Anuradha is a horse.

Uttarabhadra 3° 20' – 16° 40' Pisces (γ Pegasi/Algenib)

Those born on the lunar day of Uttarabhadra will be Brahmins, performers of sacrificial rites; will be generous, devout, rich and observant of the rules of the holy orders; will be heretics, rulers, dealers in rice.

Brihat Jataka by Varāhamihira

The third and final Saturn-ruled Nakshatra is *Uttarabhadra*, symbolically portrayed as a sword, coiled serpent or sea monster. Although similar in disposition to its counterpart, *Purvabhadra*, this Nakshatra displays some unique attributes. Termed 'the warrior star', there is a tendency for this asterism to strike a firm and finalising blow, finishing what had begun – whatever the cost. Natives of this Nakshatra quickly mobilise in the event of necessary action, but are generally more even-tempered and stable compared with their counterpart.

Uttarabhadra Nakshatra is deemed fortunate in matters of legacy, that is, sporadic gifting from benefactors or profits from long-term investment. Real estate, heirlooms/antiques and other fixed assets should also be considered. Tendencies to accumulate or 'chance upon' wealth are typically associated serpents/nāga, that is, secured or hidden treasures. Additionally, some portion of one's income might be derived from the practice of occult arts, such as astrology, clairvoyance or divining, all deemed serpent-esque talents.

Uttarabhadra was thought to host 'the nature of soma',[133] indicating some potential for healing/rejuvenation. Though strongly intoxicating, this fabled drug also induced strong purgation, relieving bodily tissues of deep-seated toxins. Soma was also a powerful rasāyana, restoring youthful qualities to aged or injured limbs. Administration of purgation therapies or medicines under the auspices of this star were deemed highly beneficial, providing long-term health benefits.

Physically, those of this Nakshatra are of average height, light in frame, their movements smooth and precise, their overall disposition self-confident, worldly and/or slightly narcissistic. They make little discrimination of social status, seeing all as equal. Often philosophical in outlook, they are cautious, pragmatic and measured, seldom overlooking an advantage or an opportunity for advancement. With good oratory skills, excellent memories and adaptability, they quickly rise to positions of significance – even, perhaps, beyond those of their own expectation.

Health-related issues of this Nakshatra include a weakness of feet, lungs and teeth, anaemia, fevers, digestive irritability, constipation, piles and epilepsy. Related Nakshatra body parts include sides of the torso, navel, ankles, feet and toes including toenails.

The presiding deity of Uttarabhadra is *Ahi-budhnya*, known as the 'water born serpent' or 'serpent of the depths'. Ahi-budhnya is sometimes judged to be a type of atmospheric spirit, although any detailed description of its form is lacking. The word *Ahi* is generally translated as 'serpent', *budhnya* alludes to 'the deep' or 'coming from below'. Vedic scholars have concluded this deity to be a type of ribbon cloud or water spout (tornado), twisting skyward in serpent-like motion. Alternative theories align Ahi-budhnya to one manifestation of Agnī, also likened to a writhing serpent. Worshippers appear to have beseeched this deity to deliver them from injury or evil, suggesting Ahi-budhnya to be of malefic disposition. Propitiation of this deity has also been connected with the healing of venomous bites.

Seldom invoked singly, Ahi-budhnya was most commonly united with Aja-ekapād[134] or Vishvadeva.[135] In post-Vedic literature Ahi-budhnya appears synonymous with the Rudras (see Ardra Nakshatra in Section 27.6).

Later descriptions of Uttarabhadra portray her as solely feminine. In feature, her countenance is likened to that of a horse, her complexion pale. Riding a large bull, she carries a two-headed drum (damarū).

27.9 MERCURY-RULED NAKSHATRAS
Aslesha 16° 40 – 0° Cancer (ε Hydrae)

Those born on the lunar day of Aslesha will be dealers in perfumes, roots, fruits, reptiles, serpents and poisons; will delight in cheating others of their property; will be dealers in pod grains; and will be skilled in medicines of every sort.

Brihat Jataka by Varāhamihira

First of the Mercury-ruled Nakshatras is *Aslesha*, its symbology associated with the serpent (Nāgā). Known to the ancients as 'the entwiner' or 'embracer', this asterism is a storehouse of serpentine symbology.

Snakes in Indian mythology have mixed connotations, and for good reason. Historically, serpents can represent the passage of time, physical rejuvenation, paralysis, healing, toxins, seduction, protective guardians, hidden wealth, cruelty and, lastly, death. In short, the iconography of the snake is a mixture of reverence, fascination and repulsion.

Astronomically this Nakshatra corresponds to the head of *Hydrae*,[136] one of the longest constellations in the northern hemisphere.[137] Hydrae marked a troublesome portion of the sky for both Greeks and Babylonians, signifying periods of strife, plague and drought. For the ancients, Hydrae also represented a fearsome guardian who stood watch at the underworld's gateway. Interestingly, the word *nāgā* might be translated 'where no one follows', alluding to the uncanny ability of serpents to slither into the smallest of spaces, retreating into their hidden netherworld.

Natives of Aslesha generally embrace all forms of study, relentlessly digging until the unknown gives up its secret. If tasked with a conundrum, their solution is to back-engineer its pieces, in an effort to reconstruct and understand its entirety. Those born under this star also have an uncanny ability to side-step lock and key, gaining access where others fail. If attaining 'the high ground', they will often bask in their small triumphs, in plain sight of their competitors.

Armed with charisma and persuasive personality, those of this star appear far less prone to fall foul of their detractors (or outstay their welcome), ensuring (by subterfuge) that their enemies remain firmly at one another's throats, before quietly exiting the scene – slipping between the cracks and departing like a ghost.

Physically, Aslesha individuals appear larger in body, broad-shouldered and firm-limbed. Their features are often rounded or smooth, their eyes penetrating and hypnotic. In some cases there can be a marked tendency to repeatedly lick their lips or hold their mouth ajar, as if physically exerting themselves.

Often those of this Nakshatra have pronounced fondness for sweet or oily foods – addictions of one sort or another may sometimes be hallmarks of this asterism. Additionally, they are fond of adorning themselves with gems and/or precious metals. Aslesha women are often glamorous or highly fashion conscious, enjoying a certain amount of social notoriety.

Health-related issues of this Nakshatra include digestive sensitivity, weakness of oesophagus, diaphragm and pancreas, diseases of the liver, dropsy, Vāta pains, tremors, injury to the feet and hands or ailments that confound diagnosis. Related Nakshatra body parts include fingertips and fingernails, oesophagus, stomach, diaphragm and pancreas.

The presiding deity of Aslesha is *Sarpa*[138] (the snake). Counted in the ranks of the eleven Rudras or Ekādaśarudras,[139] Sarpa was also the child of Tvashtar, artificer to the gods.

Periodically shedding skins, snakes were associated with longevity and, more often than not, wealth (usually in the form of gems or precious metals). Nāga folk were rumoured to stockpile hoards of fabulous treasure in *Pātālaloka*, their subterranean netherworld. Here dwelt the Snake Lords; each of their kingdoms were illuminated by the glow of supernatural gems, embedded in their hoods. The most priceless gemstones and metals were located in Bhogawati,[140] the Nāga capital. In later mythology (Hindu and Buddhist), Nāga-folk take on a benevolent role as humanity's 'watchers' or 'overseers', monitoring our spiritual development. Alchemical treatises (from about the same period) describe serpents and dragons as custodians of longevity elixirs, vehemently protecting their secret from the uninitiated.

Serpents have rich symbolism attached to their form as well as their venom. The bite of the snake was known to invite death, yet correctly purified and administered had highly curative properties.[141] Cobra venom is particularly honoured in Āyurveda; once ingested it immediately ushers all dosha back to their bodily residences, that is, colon (Vāta), small intestine (Pitta) and stomach (Kapha). The practice of *Agada Tantra* (Āyurvedic toxicology) regards duly processed venom to be a potent counteractive agent in cases of severe poisoning, both naturally occurring and man-made.

Later descriptions of Aslesha portray her as solely feminine, her face a mixture of snake and cat, her complexion reddish. In two of her four hands she carries a serpent, in the remainder a nectar pot and mala (beads).

Jyestha 16° 40' – 30° Scorpio (α Scorpionis/Antares)

A person born when the Moon passes through the asterism of Jyestha will have few friends, will be very cheerful, virtuous, and of irascible temper.

Brihat Saṃhitā by Varāhamihira

Second of the Mercury-ruled Nakshatras is *Jyestha*, its symbology associated with an earring, parasol[142] or protective talisman. *Jyestha* means 'chieftain' or 'most senior' and in all probability harks back to the deeds (and high status) of this asterism's principal deity, *Indrā*. Known as 'the vanquisher of Vṛtra' (the dragon), Indrā's chronicles are replete with heroic exploits upon the battlefield, dispatching demonic hordes or troublesome rivals.

The combative nature of this Nakshatra may be partly attributable to its occupation of Mars-ruled Scorpio, fuelling its intensity. Both feared and revered, scorpions were venerated in many cultures for their stealth and lightning reflexes, ambushing unwary victims or repelling attack with raised stinger laced with lethal neurotoxin. Its venomous strike earned scorpions a somewhat darkened notoriety, yet its venom was highly prized, having potent curative properties.[143] The healing attributes of this Nakshatra are conferred by its ruling deity Indrā[144] and planetary lord Mercury,[145] both recognised as influential healers in their own right. The positioning of this Nakshatra within the infamous eighth sign,[146] Scorpio, amplifies its desire for occult knowledge, intoxicants, elixirs and the quest for longevity.[147]

Jyestha marks an important position in the constellation Scorpionis; its Yogatârâ, *Antares*,[148] rests squarely upon what is considered to be the heart[149] of the Scorpion. Antares is frequently mistaken for planet Mars due its intense ruddy hue, simulating the Martian glow. During his eighteen-month journey through the zodiac, Mars sometimes passes within 2–3° of Antares, bringing him into direct conflict with his competitor – Antares is Greek for 'anti-Ares' or 'that which rivals Mars'.

A spectre of inner conflict may loom large in natives of this Nakshatra, due partly to its planetary lord, Mercury, feeling ill at ease in either Martian-ruled signs. Likewise the influence of combative Mars, intertwined with the mercantile pursuits of the former, does not make for a smooth, even temperament. These juxtaposed qualities are often apparent, with individuals appearing outwardly accommodating yet prone to bouts of irritability or competitiveness, especially when challenged on matters of finance or debt obligation.

Physically, Jyestha types are endowed with great physical stamina, are firm of limb and resolute in course. They are often mild in features (yet sharp-eyed), not given to indulging in mundane or petty concerns. Those born under the auspices of this asterism were observed to show addictive tendencies to alcoholic beverages, as well as sleeping disorders or defects of the jaw,[150] teeth and throat. In mannerism they are often hot-tempered, given to defamatory outbursts or public displays. If unfavourably featured, Jyestha may cause much sorrow or financial instability in life; however, 'never one to be beaten' (often the individual's favourite motto), the power of this Nakshatra enables them to not only resist, but retaliate against oppressive or overwhelming forces.

Health-related issues of this Nakshatra include weakness of the neck, colon, anus, genitals, ovaries and womb. Related Nakshatra body parts include the tongue, colon, ovaries, womb, genitals and anus.

The presiding deity of Jyestha is *Indrā*, king of the gods, also known as 'bringer of lightning'. With over two hundred and fifty hymns dedicated to his name, this deity is often portrayed atop a white elephant, thunderbolt clasped in hand, poised to smite any who dare oppose him. Primarily a thunder god, Indrā's secondary roles included dispelling darkness[151] and removing drought through the liberation of rain. Considered an atmospheric deity (residing in the middle regions), Indrā became allied to the likes of Vāyu, Sûrya and Agnī. Of all his formidable weapons,[152] Indrā and thunderbolt (Vajra[153]) became inseparable, making it his weapon of choice.[154] Hewn from a metallic substance known as *āyasa*, his thunderbolts were bright and thousand-pointed, all skilfully crafted by Tvashtar.[155]

Indrā held some renown as a 'car-fighter', often dispensing wrath whilst riding his golden chariot, steered by Vāyu who yoked two fearsome horses, described as 'golden maned' and 'bearing eyes that blaze like the Sun'. Indrā, sometimes accompanied by his consort Indrāṇī, is most commonly described as youthful, bearded,[156] tawny-haired, golden-armed and wielding a thunderbolt. His arms are described as extending (or far-reaching), his grip of hands like iron. Overall, Indrā has a ruddy appearance, illuminates like the Sun, and has a belly able to accommodate large quantities of soma.

During the Purāṇic period,[157] Indrā's might is almost entirely overshadowed by the popularity of the emerging Trimūrti: Brahma, Vishnu and Śiva. As Indrā usurped the powerful and popular deities of his day,[158] so too was he to endure the same fate. Eventually occupying the role of Heavens King (in name only[159]), Indrā then leads a host of demi-gods until his final humiliation in the Hindu epic *Rāmāyaṇam*, eventually becoming Rāvana's captive in Lankadeepa.[160]

Later descriptions of Jyestha portray her as solely feminine, her face resembling a bear, her complexion yellow. In one hand she holds a thunderbolt; in the others, she holds a lotus, nectar pot and elephant goad.

Revati 16° 40' – 30° Pisces (ζ Piscium)

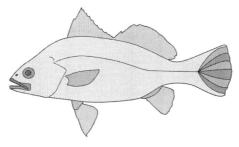

Those who are born on the lunar day of Revati will be dealers in water-flowers, salt, gems, conch shells, pearls, creatures of water, fragrant flowers and perfumes; they may also be boat-men.

Brihat Jataka by Varāhamihira

The third and final Mercury-ruled Nakshatra is *Revati*, its symbology mostly associated with that of a fish or damarū (drum). The name *Revati* might be translated as 'the wealthy' or 'winning prosperity', its status generally accepted to be a star of good fortune. As Ashwini[161] initiates the cycle of the twenty-seven Nakshatras, so Revati brings this sequence to a close, hence the association of Revati with rest, endings and returns.

The presiding deity of Revati is Pushan, commonly propitiated for assurances of safe passage or reliable guides to and from perilous (distant) lands. Prior to journeying beyond the boundaries of one's birthplace, it was traditional to make an offering to Pushan, to clear the path ahead of obstacles or malefic forces that sought to delay or harm. These observances were also deemed auspicious in helping to manifest 'hidden wealth'[162] – things which might be revealed to observant travellers. This Nakshatra also presides over misplaced items, those who lose their way or those who have departed (our ancestors).[163]

Physically, Revati individuals may be of moderate height with excellent symmetry of frame, their shoulders usually broad, their complexion fair. Those of this asterism are said to be sincere in their undertakings and pure of heart, though often suffering from low self-esteem, appearing somewhat awkward, soft-spoken or shy. Although their overall demeanour suggests an introspective/reclusive personality, quite often they are anything but, dreaming secretly of fame and fortune or an opportunity to unveil hidden talents or wares.

Those of this Nakshatra often display artistic inclinations[164] or are just in themselves creative thinkers. During childhood there can be a propensity toward non-serious yet lingering bouts of illness. These can be extremely debilitating at times, slowing their development during the formative years with transitory afflictions more akin to *curiosities*, which are almost impossible to diagnose or treat. These seemingly random bouts of reduced vitality heighten the person's feelings of inadequacy but at the same time enable them to develop strong intuitive abilities with an unbounded imagination. Once loosened from the grip of these childhood morbidities they quickly make up for lost time, finding firm footings which allow their imaginations to run wild.

Health-related issues of this Nakshatra include weakness of the feet and toes, congestive diseases of the chest, mental disorders, stomach ulcers, nephritis, lethargy, excessive bile production, genital diseases caused by excessive sexual indulgence. Related Nakshatra body parts include lymph system (axillary nodes), the armpits and feet.

As presiding deity, Pushan[165] (*Pūṣan*) was considered guardian and sustainer of cattle, overseer/protector of travellers. Referred to as the son of Sûrya and brother to Indrā, he was known also by the epithet Narāśaṃsa (meaning 'praised of all men'). Pushan was also one of twelve Âdityas (see

Punarvasu Nakshatra in Section 27.7). Though frequently in the company of Vishnu (see Śravana Nakshatra in Section 27.4) and Bhaga (see Pūrvaphalguni Nakshatra in Section 27.2), he was hierarchically superior to both.

Physical descriptions of Pushan are somewhat lacking, and if described at all seem to centre upon specifics such as his feet, recounting his trampling upon the wicked, or his goad, being used to direct lost cattle homeward. His awl,[166] it is said, was used to guide and to puncture. Like Rudra, Pushan's hair (and beard) was braided, he stood armed with a golden spear and was renowned for his charioteering skills. Pushan was all-seeing, his appearance radiant (glowing) like Sūrya. This made it impossible for him to conceal[167] himself. His vehicle was said to be given speed by a team of nimble-footed goats.

Although considered to feed and nourish, Pushan is often associated with the falling out of one's teeth. In a tale called 'Rudra punishes Prajāpati and distributes his seed', the gods attempt to remove Rudra's arrow from the body of Prajāpati (the weapon used to deter his incestuous act). Unwittingly, the removal of the arrow spills Prajāpati's seed (vital essence). In attempting to preserve this seed for sacrificial use, the gods take it to Bhaga, who duly consumes it as a pre-sacrifice. Upon ingestion, his eyes are promptly burnt from their sockets, making him blind. A second attempt is made to preserve the seed by quenching its heat and presenting it to Pushan, who also tries to ingest it. Upon consumption he is disfigured as this vital essence promptly causes his teeth to fall out, forcing him thereafter to consume only watery gruels or ground rice.[168]

In post-Vedic literature Pushan is mentioned with greater infrequency, many of his earlier deeds slowly usurped by the rising popularity of the unified Sun god Sūrya or Vishnu the preserver. If mentioned at all in later works, Pushan appears to have adopted the trimmings of a simple pastoral deity, who merely reflects the radiance of the Sun god.

Later descriptions of Revati portray her as solely feminine, her countenance that of a camel, her complexion fair, her voice powerful. Holding a nectar pot, gemstones and lotus flower she rides boldly upon an elephant.

NOTES

1. Kumaras = Princes, also known as great horsemen.
2. The Ashwinis are awarded great merit in the lineage of Āyurvedic masters, having been instructed directly by Daksha Prajāpati and indirectly by Brahmā.
3. See the author's previous work, *Rasa Shāstra: The Hidden Art of Medical Alchemy* (Mason 2014).
4. Priestly caste devoted to the worship of Agni and ritual sacrifices involving horses. The semi-divine character of Dadhyañc is reputed to have administered soma to heal the wounds of Indrā.
5. Dadhyañc, son of Artharvan, renowned for his skill in the kindling of Agni.

6. Indrā, king of the gods (see Jyestha Nakshatra in Section 27.9) had previously placed a curse on the priest lest he divulge any secret pertaining to soma.

7. Their name is suggestive of 'being in possession of horses' although they are most often portrayed as human bodies bearing horses' heads.

8. Longevity and the colour red are mutually interchangeable. A number of prominent mineral/metallic medicines display a reddish colouration: for example, FeO_2, HgS and PbO_2.

9. All subsequent personifications of the Nakshatras have been taken from *Caturvarga-chintāmani* by Himādri (13th century AD).

10. A typical Ketu trait.

11. Celebrated yet controversial ancient Indian statecraft/legal text dated to about the 3rd century AD. Indian mythology identifies Manu as the first man named Svayambhuva. In parallel with the Christian Adam, he too emerged from the body of a creator, followed shortly by the first woman named Shatarupa.

12. 6° 40' Mula Nakshatra marks a position close to the 'presumed' galactic centre. From the junction star Revati, middle of Mula Nakshatra is exactly 113° 20', that is, 100° plus the span of a single Nakshatra (13° 20').

13. Directions were: Indrā (East), Agnī (South East), Yama (South), Niriti (South West), Varuna (West), Vāyu (North West), Soma (North) and Kubera (North East). The South Westerly direction may also be given over to the Pitris.

14. Sister to Lakshmi, goddess of wealth and prosperity.

15. Bharani = she who carries. Bharani is formed by a faint triangular grouping of three stars in the tail of the ram. In the past this group had been identified as part of Musca borealis or northern fly or Lilium (fleur-de-lis). Both designations were short-lived, eventually fading into obscurity. Historically both symbols have been associated with Venus and used accordingly in occult rituals that seek to connect to the 'Morning Star'. Whether these motifs were chosen consciously or unconsciously, Vedic astrologers had seen a deep affinity to Venus within this portion of the sky, awarding that planet Bharani Nakshatra.

16. Jiva (also *Jiwa*) represents the essence or spirit or that which survives death and seeks a new body with which to experience its karma.

17. It is said that Vishvakarma constructed four pits to punish the wicked; these pits were surrounded by a moat of boiling water – heated by Agnī. The dead were made to swim across this short stretch of water to prove their innocence. The pure of heart would feel no heat, just cooling, cleansing waters, whereas sinners would be boiled alive.

18. Shani is brother to Yamarāja and both are connected to dharma, karma and judgement.

19. Yama = the restrainer (he who keeps mankind in check).

20. Alternative mythologies of Yamarāja make him the offspring of Vivasvat (morality) and Saranyu (clouds).

21. *Bhagavadgītā* and *Garuda Purāṇa* name and describe 28+ types of hell, each especially tailored to the needs of its captives, from paupers to kings.

22. One of seven planes of existence, *Svarga Loka* was an intermediate location for the pious, once released from their physical body.

23. A last show of respect for the dead includes Yagas (purification by fire), Sankirtan (eulogy) and Bhajan (song).

24. Paired Nakshatra are: Purva/Uttaraphalguni, Purva/Uttarashadha and Purva/Uttarabhadra.

25. Leo = fire Rashi, and so those under this Nakshatra are warned of injury by fire or excessive heat.

26. This Nakshatra is sometimes referred to as *Aparajita*, meaning 'the undefeated'.

27. Traditional agricultural appliance used to separate the chaff from grain.

28. Purvashada is lorded by Venus and situated at 13° 20' – 26° 40' Sagittarius (the masculine fire sign ruled by Jupiter). Vishaka Nakshatra again combines their energetics, Jupiter lording Vishaka in a sign ruled by Venus (Libra) but sees the final 3° 20' of this Nakshatra falling into Mars-ruled Scorpio.

29. Also known as *Apah* or *Devata-toya* = Water Goddess, *áp/jala* in Sanskrit means 'water'.

30. An advisory role.

31. Protective rulership of the three groups is: Varuna/Adityas, Rudra/Rudras and Indrā/Vasus.

32. Bhumi Devi = Earth goddess.

33. Agnī and Anala both represent fire; however, the Vasus collective was under the protective rulership of Agnī.

34. Known also as Subramanian or Kumar, a later Hindu war god adopting attributes of Agnī and Indrā. In some accounts Karttikeya is acknowledged as the son of Agnī who overlords planet Mars. The name Karttikeya is sometimes taken to mean 'son of the Krittikās'.

35. India is rich with iron ore. Early iron age culture in India was thought to be experimenting with this metal as early as 600–400 BC. Meteoritic iron was not unknown to the ancient world, its use catalogued in a number of artefacts from early civilisations. Examination and identification of these artefacts reveals them to have a very high carbon content, as well as increased amounts of nickel and cobalt. *Dhumaketu* (falling stars) were considered to be projectiles of remnants of godly weapons.

36. More specifically its largest and brightest star (η Tauri /Alcyone), identified as its Yogatârâ.

37. Saptarishi were: Kaśyapa, Atri, Vasishta, Viswamitra, Gautama, Jamadagni and Bhardwaja. The seven stars of Ursa Major were considered their celestial lights. The brightest stars in Pleiades represent six of their wives. The seventh wife *Arundhati* accompanies her husband Vasishta in Ursa Major in the form of *Alcor*, companion star to *Mizar*.

38. Garuda – a mythical human/eagle hybrid. Garuda are symbolic (in Indian alchemy) as holding or fixing liquid mercury. Garuda and Nāgā (serpents) are antagonistic toward one another; the latter also a synonym for mercury. The tale of Karttikeya is replete with alchemical references including the seed of Śiva (mercury), Pārvatī (sulphur) and Garuda (fixing agent); the afterbirth of the infant Karttikeya identifies an amalgam of metals, the ensuing fire on the river bank is a metaphor for the vaporisation of mercury, releasing its grip upon the amalgam. Finally, the peacock (vehicle of Karttikeya) is symbolic of transmuted poison.

39. Śiva's semen is generally acknowledged to be Pārada/mercury.

40. In order that he receive nourishment from all six of his nurses/surrogate mothers, Karttikeya is said to have grown five extra heads so that he could feed simultaneously from all.

41. A bird immune to many types of Visha (poison).

42. One *Rig Veda* creationary myth ascribes the appearance of the universe due to the powers of Indrā, Maruts and the fire god Agnī. Both Agnī and Savitar (see Hastā Nakshatra in Section 27.4) were said to have been amongst the first mortals to drink soma (principle of immortality), thus transforming all the 'early ones' into the known Vedic gods.

43. Fire rituals accompanied by offerings and mantra.

44. Wooden blocks and shaft agitated to produce a flame by friction; this procedure was known as Agnī Manthan. The *Rig Veda* attributes the first appearance of Agnī to the sage *Vivasvat* (father of both the Ashwins and Yamaraj), manifested by his efforts with the aranis.

45. The religion of Agnī in Graves (1959).

46. Agnī is considered 'protector of homes' whether a shelter (building) or within the body (that which houses Atman) and protects health via its digestive fire.

47. See Jyestha Nakshatra in Section 27.9.

48. See Shatabhishak Nakshatra in Section 27.6.

49. A number counted between 21–180, assisting Indrā in his warlike exploits.

50. Triad (or dual deities) of warlike gods evoked along with Indrā to secure the victory of men upon the battlefield.

51. Usually depicted tiling fields and pulled by oxen, squarely linking this Nakshatra to the earth element.

52. Diametrically opposite Rohini, Jyestha's ruling deity *Niriti* has been likened to Alaskshmi (goddess of misfortune). The Babylonians also considered the Rohini/Taurus–Jyestha/Scorpio axis highly pertinent to zodiacal division bifurcating the Milky Way.

53. *Maitrāyaṇī Saṃhitā* describes Prajāpati's infatuation with his daughter Uṣas/Rohini. In trying to elude her father she transforms herself into an antelope to escape. Discovering this deception; Prajāpati also transforms himself into a buck and pursues his daughter across the skies. Rudra (Śiva), incensed by Prajāpati's action, threatens to loose his arrow at the buck but deliberately misses when offered the lordship of beasts by Prajāpati. Symbolically this tale is storyboarded in the zodiac by the constellations Taurus and Orion, with special emphasis on Brahmā Hrdaya/α Aurigae (the heart of Brahmā), Lubdhak/α Canis Majoris (Sirius), Mrigashirsha/λ Orionis (deer's

head), Rohini/α Tauri (Aldebaran) and Ardra/α Orionis (shoulder of Orion, the giant). The three stars in the belt of Orion are said to represent the shaft of Rudra's arrow.

54. *Trimūrti* (three forms of the supreme being), that is, Brahmā/creator, Vishnu/preserver and Śiva/destroyer. Sectarians often promote hierarchical status within the triad, seeking to promote the merits of one over another. The triad most popular in early Vedic culture was Indrā, Agnī and Soma.

55. Perhaps another commonality displayed by the ruddy star Alderbaran/α Tauri (Rohini Nakshatra).

56. A goose may also be substituted for swan.

57. Born from the thigh of Brahmā, Sarasvati is the goddess of speech, knowledge and wisdom. She also takes rulership of music (instrumental and vocal), as well as the visual arts. Due to her point of origination, Sarasvati is also considered the daughter of Brahmā.

58. Musical scales/notes associated with the seasons and time of day.

59. Associated wives of the Rāgas.

60. Satya, Tretā, Dvāpara and Kali are collectively known as the world Yugas.

61. Associated with the ritualistic Shukla (white) Saṃhitās of Yajurveda.

62. Vishnu once appeared before the demon Bali, disguised as the dwarf Vamana. Gaining an audience before the demon he requested everything within three strides be awarded to him. Laughingly, Bali granted his request wishing to see the dwarf make a fool of himself. Whereupon the small figure transformed into a giant, crossing the known universe in three mighty steps.

63. Mythological references to Capricorn mark its zodiacal position as ending the golden age of gods and man. For more information see Kirk (2013).

64. This name is in praise of Vamana's mighty footsteps. In the Ebenezer Burgess translation of *Sûrya Siddhânta*, he suggests that 'as Vishnu is seen primarily as a solar deity', these steps mark the three pivotal solar declinations throughout the year, that is, two solstices and spring equinox.

65. See Shatabhishak Nakshatra in Section 27.6.

66. Goddess of good fortune.

67. Animals readily praised for extreme longevity.

68. See Rohini Nakshatra in Section 27.4.

69. See *Caraka Saṃhitā*: Cikitsāsathānam, Section 1.4 'Return of Sages to the Himalayas'.

70. Aṃśu (shoots or stalks) when pressed precipitate a milky exudate.

71. The sap of soma was said to be either ruddy or tawny in colouration.

72. The actions of Syena, the eagle, were usurped by garuda.

73. A species of millet, *Panicum frumentaceum Rox.*, grown in India.

74. Tvashtar was father to Indrā and Brihaspati, father-in-law to Vāyu. Tvashtar appears in *Mahābhārata* and *Bhāgavata Purāna* as a form of the Sun god.

75. Samjñā (wife of Sûrya) implored Tvashtar (her father) to re-girth her husband in order to bear his heat and radiance.

76. Another name for Brihaspati.

77. Tvashtar was thought to be one of the guardians of soma, this beverage sometimes referred to as the 'mead of Tvashtar'. Tvashtar's cup or 'bowl of the year' is thought to be the Moon undergoing its thirteen lunar cycles during the twelve solar months.

78. The offspring of Tvashtar all had some ability to reshape matter.

79. As the mridangam is indicative of Śiva, so is the flute to Krishna.

80. Those who attend cows. In Puranic literature this term is usually applied to youthful female attendants of cows.

81. This might also include singers, public speakers, broadcasters or poets.

82. Described as solar deities, Vasus were eight in number. Membership of this group varies, depending upon source.

83. Also known as the giant.

84. Rud means 'to weep'.

85. Also known as *Paśupati*, 'Lord of Beasts', due to indiscriminate attacks upon cattle wandering the hillsides. He was also identified with Agnī (fire god) due to lightning and any resulting fire.

86. Heavenly Āditya, Rudras of Air and Earthly Vasus.

87. Also known as *Rudriyas*.

88. Pṛśni: Mother to the Maruts.

89. Rudra was frequently worshipped to protect cattle or crops.

90. See Shatabhishak Nakshatra.

91. Rudra was also referred to as Howler.
92. Also known as *Nishtya* (outcast) according to *Taittirīya Brāhmaṇa*.
93. Sometimes termed 'the oceans' rainforests'.
94. Indrā rode with Vāyū in his chariot, the latter's speed and agility being employed in battle.
95. As a guardian/protector of soma – see Ashwini Nakshatra in Section 27.1.
96. Vāyu is said to have bested Indrā in drinking soma.
97. Vāyu was primarily a god of wealth, accumulated through the trading of steeds.
98. Varuna assumed a role of moral governor, ensuring ethical conduct from his worshippers; he displayed less of a warrior-god role than his ultimate successor Indrā.
99. Clarified butter for abhisheka/yagya.
100. Varuna and Mitra are often described mutually in company. It has been suggested that Varuna was lunar in his origin and Mitra a solar deity. Varuna and Mitra were two of seven Ādityas, the remaining five being Mercury, Venus, Mars, Jupiter and Saturn.
101. Fetter or shackles with which to bind and constrain guilty parties.
102. A passage taken to mean single stars (many-eyed and countless multitude). Varuna was understood to be the many-eyed firmament of night.
103. Mythological hybrid sporting the forelegs and head of a deer, the midsection of a crocodile and the tail of a fish. Makara is also the name for the astrological sign Capricorn.
104. Injury/illness occurring under this Moon is still considered a bad omen, one requiring the services of a hundred physicians.
105. Shatabhishak is also known as the Nakshatra of a hundred physicians.
106. In Rigveda Āditya were seven in number (representing the two luminaries and five known planets). In later Purāṇic mythology the number increased to twelve, said to represent the twelve solar months. These Ādityas are given as: Dhatri, Aryaman, Mitra, Varuna, Indrā, Sūrya, Pushan, Savitar, Anshu, Bhaga, Tvashtar and Vivasvat.
107. Dakṣa Prajapati – born of Brahmā. In later Purānic tales Āditi becomes daughter to Dakṣa.
108. Her original 33 children have subsequently multiplied to become 330,000,000 in totality.
109. Sesame seeds.
110. Also known as *Radha*, meaning 'beloved of Krishna', complimenting the ensuing Nakshatra *Anuradha*.
111. These names might relate to an asura named Vṛtra, dispatched by Indrā-agnī. Two-branched and forked may be references to the tongue of the serpent.
112. War god/warrior caste.
113. Indrā-agnī is the only dual deity to preside over a Nakshatra.
114. The Nakshatra may also be represented by a sword.
115. Aquarius is frequently ill at ease with worldly matters, seeing the establishment as a hotbed of secrecy or manipulation.
116. Those who reside at the edge of town, that is, outcasts, grave robbers or those who immolate the dead and perform capital punishments.
117. The allusion to a goat might be this animal's agility and speed. Lightning itself might appear similar to that of the animal's hind leg, delivering a swift and potent kick. See Oldenberg (1894).
118. In post-Vedic literature *Aja-ekapād* and *Ahi-budhnya* appear enumerated amongst the Rudras (see Ardra Nakshatra in Section 27.6).
119. Deity of the consecutive asterism.
120. A commingling of air/Aquarius and water/Pisces might also signify the qualities of this deity, that is, rain.
121. *Taittirīya Brāhmaṇa* and *Atharva Veda* support the role of Aja-ekapād as a solar deity, said to have risen in the east asserting some relationship to Agnī/Sūrya.
122. Also known as *Tiṣya* (meaning auspicious).
123. This Nakshatra also has some connection to herbal remedies.
124. The word *pusti* means nourishment.
125. Various limbs of Vedic knowledge including *Jyotish Shāstra* (astrology), *Rasa Shāstra* (alchemy), etc.
126. This deity is considered by some to be 'lord of plants'.
127. Forces of nature also attributable to Zeus and later the Roman Jupiter.
128. A skill taken from his father Tvashtar (see Chitrā Nakshatra in Section 27.5).

129. See Jyestha Nakshatra in Section 27.9.
130. The triumphal gateway is also attributable to Vishaka Nakshatra. As both were intimately linked through their symbology, that is, Krishna (Vishaka) and his consort Lakṣmī (Anuradha), the former was considered the more direct and assertive, the latter tender and yielding. In some sense both Nakshatra may be considered paired.
131. Known as Ravi-marga, the Sun's pathway (or ecliptic).
132. Varuna was associated with night, Mitra the day (further allusion to their lunar and solar origins). If propitiated in unison an abundance of rain was assured.
133. See Mrigashirsha Nakshatra in Section 27.5.
134. See Purvabhadra Nakshatra in Section 27.7.
135. See Uttarashadha Nakshatra in Section 27.3.
136. Named after the nine-headed Lernaean Hydra (offspring of Typhon), encountered in the swamps of Lerna by Heracles. The venom of the slain creature was used by the hero to dispatch a number of adversaries during his twelve labours.
137. Hydra is over 100° in length, stretching (below the ecliptic) from Cancer to Libra. The word Nāgā is synonymous with length (height) and longevity.
138. *Mahābhārata* mentions Sarpa to be the son of Sthānu, great-grandson to Brahmā.
139. According to some sources the eleven Rudras were: Sarpa, Hara, Bahurūpa, Tryambaka, Aparājita, Kapālin, Vrishâkapi, Śambhu, Raivata, Kapardin and Mṛgavyādha.
140. Literally the 'City of Nāgās'.
141. See the author's previous work, *Rasa Shāstra: The Hidden Art of Medical Alchemy* (Singing Dragon, 2014).
142. Representative of Vedic society's higher echelons, the merits of umbrellas/parasols are also extolled at some length in the medical text *Caraka Saṃhitā*. The use of a talisman was considered a necessity to guard against malefic forces. Jyestha Nakshatra is especially important for the empowerment or wearing of amulets.
143. Agada Tantra classifies visha/venom of snakes and insects (including scorpion) to have highly therapeutic properties. Some poisons may be prescribed to counteract the effect of other poisons. Some poisons restore nerve functionality in cases of paralysis or induce purgatory action in cases of digestive stagnation. Classical Chinese Medicine utilises dried scorpion for similar conditions including impaired organ functionality and/or liver cleansing. Recent studies have concluded that the venom of the death-stalker scorpion has potent anti-carcinogenic properties.
144. Indrā is generally credited as one of the divine sources of Āyurvedic wisdom. *Caraka Saṃhitā* pays tribute to Indrā saying: 'Indrā expounded the immortal and sacred science of life (Āyurveda), consisting of three principles viz. aetiology, symptomatology, and the knowledge of therapeutics.'
145. As planetary ruler, Mercury is known to emit a healing green ray; planet Mercury is also primary Kāraka for healing and medicines.
146. Scorpio and the 8th house are directly connected to death, longevity and knowledge of the occult.
147. Indrā legends are deeply entwined with the life-extending beverage soma. Jyestha Nakshatra is approximately 180° opposite the abode of Soma, that is, Mrigashirsha Nakshatra.
148. Antares (α Scorpionis) has a magnitude of 0.92 making it 16th brightest star in the northern hemisphere. Antares is thought to be one of the largest stars known. Alderbaran or α Tauri is another red giant positioned almost 180° opposite Antares. Both stars mark the ingress of the Milky Way into the zodiac.
149. Interestingly, a scorpion's heart actually resides in the abdomen, in an area known as the *meso-soma*.
150. During a battle with the demon *Vyaṃsa*, Indrā was said to have had his jaw struck from his body. Indrā is also noted to agitate his jaws (in a curious way) after the consumption of soma juice.
151. This might refer to a lessening of tamas (primal instinct as well as strong attachments to worldly pleasures). Tamas brings darkness and an inability determine right from wrong. One projection of tamas might be demons, hence Indrā was seen as a slayer of demons.
152. His other formidable weapons included a golden bow and arrow, hook and net. Rainbows were thought to be a physical manifestation of his bow.
153. Indrā's thunderbolts are also identified as having been manufactured from the bones of Dadhyañc (also Dadhichi). These bones, having been licked clean of flesh by the Kamadhenu cow, were passed to Vishvakarma to fashion them into Vajra-yudha (lightning bolts of war).
154. Indrā is described as *Vajrabhṛt* – 'he who bears the bolt'.

155. See Chitrā Nakshatra in Section 27.5.
156. When stirred into action his beard was said to become violently agitated.
157. The name Purāṇā means 'in ancient times'. These are a collection of 18 major texts written in Sanskrit and in story form cataloguing the history of the universe (cosmology), genealogies of gods, demigods, kings and the cycle of world ages. There is no agreement as to their age; however references to them have been found as early as 550 BCE. The Puranas are sometimes referred to as the 5th Veda.
158. There were a number of earlier Vedic triads including *Agnī-Vāyu-Sûrya* and *Varuna-Mitra-Aryaman* etc. Indrā replaces Vāyu, relegating him to the rank of his charioteer.
159. In the Puraṇās the name *Indrā* becomes an official title. An Indrā may reign for one divine year in heaven (an equivalent of 360 earthly years), after which time a god or meritorious mortal may bid to ascend to the throne, by either the performance of sacrifice or austerity.
160. When Ravāna conquered the celestial kingdom, Sûrya (Sun) was forced to illuminate his palace during day and Chandra (Moon) during the night. Agnī cooked at the king's hearth, while Indrā adorned his royal person with garlands of flowers. In another version of Indrā's eventual defeat, *Indrājit* (Ravana's son) overcame him in battle, taking him prisoner.
161. See Ashwini Nakshatra in Section 27.1.
162. Hidden wealth can be an allegory for 'buried within the earth', perhaps in the form of precious gems, metals or minerals.
163. The ruling deity of Revati was Pushan, a deity tasked with conducting the dead into the afterlife.
164. Venus reaches his full exaltation at 27° Pisces in Revati Nakshatra.
165. His Greek equivalent might be Hyperion, one of the 12 Titans. Father to Helios, he was also known to be watchful, illuminating and wise, tending his cattle on Thrinacia.
166. Uses of an awl include scribing or marking leather/hide. As guardian overseer to various animals (horses, cows and sheep), it seems fitting that he shows some dominion over their associated animal products. Pushan was also noted to 'weave' and 'smooth' the clothing of sheep.
167. Planets tenanting Revati Nakshatra may find it difficult to conceal their talents.
168. In desperation the gods finally approach Brihaspati, who advises they present the highly volatile seed to Savitar. In his golden hands alone this seed is quenched/stabilised, no longer able to cause harm or injury. Many Śiva/Rudra stories regarding vital essence (or semen) seem to reference some form of alchemical symbolism. In this instance Prajapati's seed (a synonym for mercury) is stated to cause blindness. Direct inhalation of mercuric fumes were known to cause the shrinkage of gum tissue and a subsequent loss of teeth. In the story, the final appearance of Savitar (a synonym of the metal gold), an amalgam of mercury and gold forms a stable amalgam with the material, finally subduing the liquid metal. Hastā Nakshatra (ruled by Savitar) lies almost directly opposite Revati Nakshatra (one of three Mercury ruled Nakshatra). During the administration of purified Pārada (mercury), ground rice, milk and ghee are recommended to be consumed, both having neutralising and cooling effects, in contrast the heating properties of mercury.

28

— NAKSHATRA QUALITIES —

Qualities of Nakshatra were broadly divided into seven groups expressing the attributes: fixed, sharp, fierce, swift, tender, sharp-tender and mutable. Each of these was then assigned preferential activities, thought favourable to be propitiated during the lunar transit of that Nakshatra.

Fixed *Nakshatras*	Sowing seeds or planting trees, royal coronations, acts of propitiation, laying of foundation stones and financial investment
	Rohini, Uttaraphalguni, Uttarashadha, Uttarabhadra
Sharp *Nakshatras*	Mantra, spells and incantations, the raising of spirits, seeking an alliance with kings, dispensation of law and the incarceration of wrongdoers
	Ardra, Aslesha, Jyestha, Mula
Fierce *Nakshatras*	Capture of wrongdoers, defeating one's enemies, working with poisons, lighting of fires, forging metals and manufacture of weapons
	Bharani, Magha, Purvaphalguni, Purvashadha, Purvabhadra
Swift *Nakshatras*	Medical treatment, healing, short journeys, trading, pleasurable pursuits, artistic endeavours, education and study, buying or wearing of fine clothes and the adornment of jewels
	Ashwini, Pushyami, Hastā
Tender *Nakshatras*	Propitiation of gods, wearing of fine clothes, adornment of jewels, artistic endeavours, musical performances, forming of friendships or sexual union
	Mrigashirsha, Chitrā, Anuradha, Revati
Sharp/Tender *Nakshatras*	Propitiation of gods and acts of devotion (see both Sharp and Tender)
	Krittika, Vishaka
Mutable *Nakshatras*	Communication, education, study, long and short pilgrimage, devotion to one's chosen deity and the offering of scented flowers, honey or ghee
	Punarvasu, Swati, Śravana, Dhanistha, Shatabhishak

PART V

THE PROPITIATION OF PLANETS AND REMEDIAL MEASURES

29

UPAYES
(Remedies and Propitiation)

The twigs of sacrificial trees or plants such as Arka, Palasha, Khadira, Apamarga, Pippali, Oudumvara, Shami, Durva and Kusha blades are to be soaked with curd, honey and clarified butter, each then cast in sacrificial fires (Homa ceremonies) celebrated for the propitiation of the planets, for even a king may derive many benefits from the worship of planets.

Garuda Purāṇa

One of the most practical and interesting areas of Vedic Astrology is its *Upayes* (means or method of alleviation), designed to enhance or mitigate planetary emanations. Planetary propitiation is nothing short of appeasing grahas identified as potentially negative[1] or embellishing those that already show a propensity to shine. The most common methods of propitiation included in this chapter are *Yantra* (sacred diagrams), *Pooja* (ritual), *Maṇi*[2] (jewels), *Aushadhi* (medicines), *Kavach* (shields), *Mantra* (sacred sounds) and *Mala* (rosary).

29.1 YANTRA

Use of yantra will be partly revisited in Chapter 32; here, however, I present in a greatly condensed form some useful information with regard to their use.

The word *yantra* simply means apparatus or device, each displaying varying complexities of geometric or numerological design. A yantra aims to reproduce a three-dimensional (inanimate yet energetic) object upon a two-dimensional surface. These designs featured heavily in the many Hindu/Tantric rituals where involvement of a higher cosmic force is required.

Navagraha design honouring all planets. Its inscription reads: 'By drawing this yantra and keeping it in an auspicious place you will pacify Navagraha'. Clockwise from top: Saturn then Sun, Moon, Rāhu, Mars, Mercury, Venus and Ketu. Jupiter's glyph is inscribed on the central pot of amrita. Outer text comprises beeja (seed) mantra,[3] starting from the position of the Sun: Hreem, La, Sreem, Kshmee, Kleem, Ēi, Aum.

Often rendered in red sandalwood paste, saffron or ground vermilion,[4] many of these ceremonies commenced with inscription of the preferred design upon a previously sanctified surface. This might be sheet metal, strips of bark, cloth or the bare earth. The most favourable and durable medium for Yantra is metal, usually in the form of thinly worked sheets of gold, silver or copper – inscribed, etched or stamped with their designs. In some instances sheets of copper may be plated with gold for added potency, durability or just enhanced attractiveness. The most suitable (non-metallic) material is *Bhojpatra* (leaf of *Betula utilis*) also known as Himalayan birch.[5] Both leaf and bark of this tree are favoured for yantra inscription, the latter bearing a startling white fascia that provides an excellent surface upon which to work. Bhoja may also be substituted by thin wooden strips/slices from mango trees[6] (*Mangifera indica*) or the leaves from the talipot palm (*Corypha umbraculifera*) called *Olla*. Strips of Olla were traditionally favoured for both manuscripts and yantra in southern India and Śrī Lankā. If stored under favourable conditions, palm leaves have the potential to survive for several centuries before replacement becomes necessary.

To their inscriber, yantra denote a consecrated area where the presence of a deity could be made to reside during ceremonial use. Indeed, the very act of yantra creation is considered a kind of visual meditation, bonding inscriber and deity into the energetics of the design.

The world of yantra design is both varied and complex, with many plays upon a singular theme. Whether constructed for ritualistic or talismanic purposes, yantra became an important technology employed for meditative/ visualisation purposes. Their availability and popularity as an alternative to gemstones has made them highly desirable in astrology.

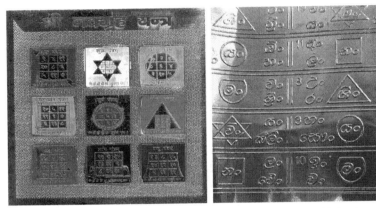

Left: Etched hand-coloured Navagraha Yantra; this particular rendition is gold-plated to protect its surface from finger marks/oxidation. Right: Close-up of Sadu Chandra Navagraha Yantra, inscribed onto a thin sheet of copper foil.

Purchase of ready-made or deity-specific yantra in such countries as India and Śrī Lankā is not a big issue; what often presents itself as being a greater issue is how one can potentise this device to produce the desired effect. In truth, all yantra should undergo empowerment prior to use. Potentiating is best achieved by one well versed in remedial astrological techniques, usually those with some family lineage in these arts. Some Hindu temples (specifically consecrated to grahas) may be able to offer this service – however, if access to this kind of facility proves difficult it should be possible to contact a Vedic astrologer to purchase or empower your yantra. It should also be borne in mind that potentiating of yantra itself is heavily dependent upon favourable astrological conditions, along with its own array of rituals, offerings and supporting mantra.

Not surprisingly, many if not all of the astrological yantra prescribed by Śrī Lankān astrologers are designs favouring a strongly Buddhist theme (see Chapter 34); these primarily focus on the removal of detrimental planetary forces. Some of these designs can be exquisitely detailed and are often laboured over for many hours by the local medicine man/shaman. Although there is some scope for personal stylisation, there remain a number of traditional rules to be adhered to when preparing yantra. Examples of these rules include the following:

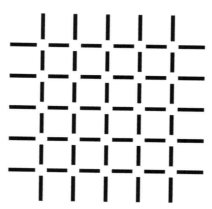

The crossing of lines on yantra is to be avoided as these spaces or points hold energy; see apparent white squares at the intersection points of horizontal and vertical lines.

1. Yantra should have an absence of intersecting/crossing lines in the design as intersections, particularly with the outer border. Empty spaces between lines are seen to focus or hold energy.

2. Some sections of the yantra are to be reserved specifically for an individual's name to be inscribed; these then become the focal point and add specificity to the overall effect.

3. Yantra are to be given *Dṛṣṭi* (sight or glances) and *consecrated* to a specific Deva (god) or Yaksha (demon). In the case of astrological yantra, this would mean alignment to benefic or malefic grahas – opening a portal in the yantra which allows direct connection to the planets in question.

4. All yantra should be opened or awakened by Pooja/Havya-váhana (see Chapter 32). Pooja favouring deva are conducted during the hours of daylight, under an auspicious Nakshatra. Flowers, milk, scented water and fruits are then offered to satiate the relevant deity/ies in question. If the yantra is attempting to honour a more demonic force, pooja is conducted after sunset with ceremonial offerings that include black cloth, animal blood and putrid foods. In some cases the carcass or skin of a dead animal might be used.[7]

5. Favourable astrological conditions are sought before potentising yantra; this usually involves Mhurta, a method for ascertaining favourable astrological conjunctions.[8]

6. During the manufacture of yantra an appropriate mantra is to be offered. This will help empower the work, further protecting the individual from harm. Yantra should always be constructed with the good of the patient in mind.

7. Yantra constructed solely for the duration of planetary dasha (see Chapter 22) are best worn around the neck, enclosed in Suraya (see Section 29.4) and hanging directly over the heart area. Generally this type of yantra will not require re-activating during its designated term.[9] All of the above being observed, a fully charged yantra can be presented to the patient, hopefully promoting *Dṛṣṭi* from benefic planets while averting unwelcome glances from malefic planets.

29.2 YANTRA SPECIFIC TO THE GRAHAS

The following designs centre more on numerological factors than geometric design. These samples are commonly used in Jyotish to propitiate grahas via specific numerology. The selections of numbers for each design are based upon the following principles.

Number 9 symbolically represents the planets as well as underpinning the 27 Nakshatras, that is, 2+7 = 9. Number 9 also represents the highest single digit attained in the decimal counting system.

Cast metal Navagraha Yantra, with mystical numbers in tables of nine-by-nine squares. This particular example is a variation on a theme but still reduces to the all-important number 9.

When unlocking the occult significance of graha yantra, the importance of 9 should always be kept in mind. Confronted with the following designs it becomes apparent that each subsequent yantra increases incrementally in the same position; that is, starting with *Sûrya Yantra* (see Section 29.3), the top-centre box displays a value of 1, the same position in *Chandra Yantra* displays number 2, and so on. This remains consistent throughout the set.

The numerical total of each yantra can be arrived at vertically, horizontally and diagonally. Each number box comprises 3 vertical and 3 horizontal lines; hence its identifying number is 6 (3+3). The total value of each yantra (for example, Sun = 15) is then multiplied by the number 6, arriving at 90 – a total that can itself then be numerically reduced to 9 (that is, 90 = 9+0 = 9).

The table illustrates all nine yantra totals and their numerical reductionism.

Yantra sequence/numerical values

No.	Yantra Deity	Value
1	Sûrya/Sun	$15 \times 6 = 90, 9+0 = 9$
2	Chandra/Moon	$18 \times 6 = 108, 1+0+8 = 9$
3	Kuja/Mars	$21 \times 6 = 126, 1+2+6 = 9$
4	Budha/Mercury	$24 \times 6 = 144, 1+4+4 = 9$
5	Brihaspati/Jupiter	$27 \times 6 = 162, 1+6+2 = 9$
6	Shukra/Venus	$30 \times 6 = 180, 1+8 = 0 = 9$
7	Shani/Saturn	$33 \times 6 = 198, 1+9+8 = 18, 1+8 = 9$
8	Rāhu/North Node	$36 \times 6 = 216, 2+1+6 = 9$
9	Ketu/Southern Node	$39 \times 6 = 234, 2+3+4 = 9$

To further impress, the unity of all 9 yantra can themselves be totalled and again reduced to the single digit 9 thus:

$$90+108+126+144+162+180+198+216+234 = 1458, 1+4+5+8 = 18, 1+8 = 9.$$

Overall, the power and symbolism contained in this form of Navagraha is considered second to none, becoming a highly popular means of graha propitiation.

29.3 YANTRA EFFECTS

Note that in the following images, equivalent digits (lower left) have also been shown.

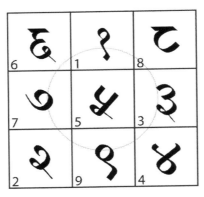

1. Sûrya Yantra: All sides add to the numerical value of 15.

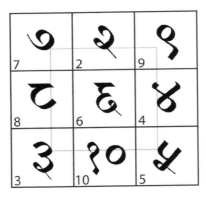

2. Chandra Yantra: All sides and diagonals add to the numerical value of 18.

Benefits of Sûrya Yantra

Protects against financial loss, accidents and damage to one's property, severe punishment, legal entanglements and overt governmental scrutiny (taxes) as well as protection against diseases that relate to the eyes, heart, bones or blood. Sûrya Yantra promotes longevity, intellect, physical strength, vitality and vigour, improves career prospects, wealth, social status and increases incidences of fame and/or governmental benefit. Use of Sûrya Yantra is advised for those wishing to strengthen a Sun weakened by malefic aspect/s, poor house/sign placement or association with a powerful malefic/s.

Benefits of Chandra Yantra

Protects against mental anxiety, watery diseases, premature ageing, insomnia, aimless wanderings, lethargy and depression. Protection against a loss of comfort (physical/home comforts) as well as emotional comfort. Chandra Yantra promotes beauty, wealth, health and longevity (this yantra is said to revive even those bordering upon death). This yantra also promotes mental clarity, positive emotion, a happy home-life and creativity (including children). Considered paramount for strong progeny, the Moon is said to fertilise and ripen/fulfil. Use of Chandra Yantra is generally safe, regardless of detrimental sign/house placements or malefic aspects. The Moon shows no enmity toward any graha and plays a pivotal part in every horoscope.

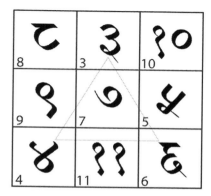

3. Kuja Yantra: All sides add to the numerical value of 21.

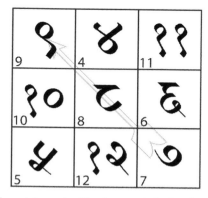

4. Budha Yantra: All sides and diagonals add to the numerical value of 24.

Benefits of Kuja Yantra

Guards against personal injury, accidents and violent attack whilst protecting one's properties (buildings) from damage (internally and externally). Reduces health conditions that relate to deep tissue inflammation and muscular strains whilst improving circulatory insufficiency and diseases of the blood. Kuja Yantra promotes healthy competition, athleticism and sportsmanship, improves relations with younger siblings, helps reduce financial burdens and increases drive, determination and courage. Use of Kuja Yantra is advised for those wishing to strengthen a Mars weakened by malefic aspect/s, poor house/sign placement or an association with another powerful malefic.

Benefits of Budha Yantra

Preserves mental faculties, improved learning abilities and greater levels of mental concentration. Reduces obstacles to study, dispels nervous conditions, speech impediments, respiratory ailments and diseases of the skin. Budha Yantra improves oration (communicative) skills, mercantile activities and career prospects, promotes a youthful demeanour and skilful dexterity (hand–eye coordination). A yantra worn to promote mercurial energies is generally safe; however, some study should be made of Mercury's sign/house placement or its receipt of malefic aspect/s. Budha graha is a mild benefic and highly impressionable, likely to mimic *any* qualities found aspecting it, both benefic and malefic.

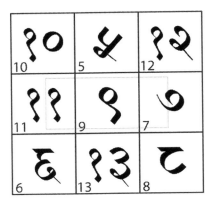

5. *Brihaspati Yantra: All sides add to the numerical value of 27.*

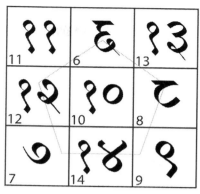

6. *Shukra Yantra: All sides and diagonals add to the numerical value of 30.*

Benefits of Brihaspati Yantra

Protects against apathy and ignorance, the loss of wisdom and obstacles to study. A weakened or poorly aspected Jupiter reduces sattvic qualities and impairs long-term health prospects (weakens immunity levels), as well as the ability to determine truth from falsehood. Brihaspati Yantra specifically improves relations with one's teachers, heightens concentration and creates opulence. Jupiter is a congenial planet and as such the use of its yantra expands one's sphere of influence, boosting social status and improving people-friendly skills. Jupiter is generally regarded as *the great benefic* and as such most likely to cushion painful life-blows. Jupiterian energetics are also beneficial for progeny, creativity and spiritual pursuits. Wearing a yantra for Jupiter is generally safe; however, study should be made of its sign/house placement and/or malefic aspect/s to ascertain its status in regard to the individual's horoscope.

Benefits of Shukra Yantra

Helps protect against over-indulgence and personal excesses (financially as well as physically), whilst removing obstacles from family/married life. Shukra Yantra, like Jupiter, improves relations with one's teachers as both are considered instructors/gurus. Shukra Yantra heightens creativity (artistic pursuits), promotes youthfulness, beauty, grace and refinement. A well-placed (and energised) Venus aids in improved longevity, stimulating immune functionality as well as fortifying the kidneys and reproductive system. Wearing a yantra to promote Venus energy is generally safe (next to Jupiter it is considered a great benefic); however, study should be made of sign/house placement or malefic aspect/s to ascertain its status in regard to the individual's horoscope.

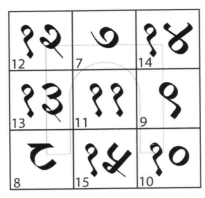

7. *Shani Yantra: All sides and diagonals add to the numerical value of 33.*

Benefits of Shani Yantra

Protects against the effects of premature ageing, stiffness of limbs, fatigue, coldness, depression/isolation and the loss of social status. This yantra helps mitigate the effects of bodily toxins and their impedance from removal. Shani Yantra improves circulation, mobility, self-confidence and resilience. The use of this yantra imparts strength to the legs and feet, promotes bone density and flexibility of joints. Shani graha is most associated with longevity and health; its positioning and strength is of prime importance in these matters. Wearing a yantra to promote Saturn energy should be given due consideration, as its energisation may also encourage the early fruition of latent karmas.

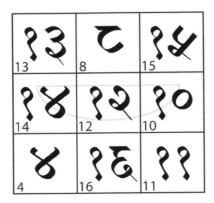

8. *Rāhu Yantra: All sides add to the numerical value of 36.*

9. Ketu Yantra: All sides and diagonals add to the numerical value of 39.

Benefits of Rāhu Yantra

Protects against mental anxiety, demonic possession, fearfulness and self-intoxication (addiction). Typically, the nodes have a deranging effect upon the nerves and senses; Rāhu shows an affinity to the hearing faculty, Ketu to the olfactory sense. Rāhu Yantra soothes and heals the nervous system, restores impaired hearing and reduces loss of balance (vertigo). Empowerment of this future-orientated graha helps one plan for the coming years, avoiding unnecessary expenses and unseen enemies (usually pathological[10]). Rāhu Yantra promotes fame, popularity and influence; it also sensitises psychic abilities. Before wearing Rāhu Yantra, its malefic potential should be fully considered prior to use. Rāhu graha has the potential to increase Vāta dosha, impair the senses and attract injuries, as well as encourage psychic disturbances. Those of a more sensitive disposition are cautioned before considering the use of this yantra.

Benefits of Ketu Yantra

Protects against sudden calamities, accidents and illnesses of a mysterious origin. Ketu Yantra is also useful in cases of allergies (such as rhinitis), slow-healing sores/bruises and auto-intoxication (poisoning). Ketu rules over biting/flying insects, wild-natured dogs and viral infections that tend to manifest as some form of inflammation (Mars natured). Ketu Yantra helps purify blood, heal deep-seated (sometimes karmic) wounds, sharpen the senses (perception), improve concentration, remove obstacles and promote moksha (liberation). Ketu, like Rāhu, has the potential to increase Vāta dosha, impair the senses and attract injuries. Those of a more sensitive disposition are cautioned before considering the use of this yantra.

29.4 KAVACH AND SURAYA

The word *Kavacha* (also *Kavach*) means 'shielded' or 'protective armour'. The concept behind Kavach (like yantra) is the use of mystical text, symbols or numbers inscribed upon metal foils and worn about the neck in Suraya. The information contained thereon can be specific to an individual's birth chart. Kavacha are crafted during favourable planetary conjunctions, ensuring the best possible outcome after their creation. In some instances Kavacha take the form of thick elongated metal pendants (engraved singularly or double-sided) with an appropriately matched metal chain. These also are recommended to be worn directly over the heart. Copper sheets are the most common medium for Kavacha; however, some prefer the precious metals silver and gold.[11]

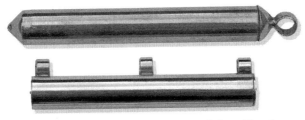

Indian-manufactured Suraya, horizontal or vertical pendants fashioned from brass.

Suraya are small, hollow pendants (favoured in Śrī Lankā) and most commonly used to carry Kavacha. Metallic contents of Suraya are lightly coated (prior to insertion) with auspicious astrological oils,[12] helping to reduce oxidisation. The use of Suraya, however, is not limited to Kavacha/yantra – a number of other materials, including Kṣāra,[13] dried herbs and bhasma,[14] also find themselves worn in these protective amulets. Gold or silver Suraya are considered best, these usually being packed with a fine cotton wick saturated in astrologically medicated oils. Recipients of these talismans are frequently warned to remove Suraya if called upon to attend funerals, or cross funerary grounds. They should also be removed when consuming meat from lower-caste animals, such as pigs. Failure to remove talismans may result in the negation of their power.

Kavacha worn for astrological purposes in Śrī Lankā are usually issued by a local astrologer or indigenous healer called *Veda Mahaththaya*.[15] After insertion into Suraya, each is then *metaphysically* sealed with a protective spell. Suraya can be worn for a period of up to seven years before renewal. In light of important transits (particularly by slower-moving graha such as Saturn, Jupiter and lunar nodes), the recipient of the Suraya may request his or her astrologer to re-potentate its contents if any ill-effects become apparent.

NOTES

1. This also includes submissive or weakened graha states present in one's horoscope.
2. Although gemstones seem to form the greater part of propitiation these days, there are far less costly (and in my opinion ultimately more rewarding) forms of planetary laudation.
3. Hreem (purification/purgation and atonement), La (seed of Lam – grounding/earth element), Sreem (health, longevity and nurturing), Kshmee (wealth, prosperity and abundance), Kleem (builds strength and potency), Ēi (speech, music and the arts), Aum (mental acuity, attentiveness, consciousness).
4. Cinnabar (HgS) or Naga Sindoora (Pb_3O_4, lead tetroxide).
5. The highly astringent nature of this bark helps draw pigment into its surface, preventing any over-saturation; Bhoja bark has medicinal renown for its styptic quality when applied to bleeding wounds.
6. Known as the king of Asiatic fruits, mango has an excellent styptic action as well as strong anti-inflammatory, antispasmodic, laxative and cardio-tonic properties. Mango is well known for its densely grained hard-wood, fruitfulness and excellent longevity; some species are known to live for more than two hundred years.
7. The latter ceremony is mentioned here for completeness/reader interest only.
8. Some of the general rules for a Mhurta include: strong 1st house and 1st lord, a well-placed 'bright' Moon (not under malefic aspect/s), favourable Nakshatras for Moon and ascendant, both Nakshatra lords should be well placed and strong. 10th house should be well-disposed along with its lord, etc.
9. Yantra made for dasha periods are usually consecrated and sealed for that period: Ketu = 7 years, Venus = 20 years, Sun = 6 years, Moon = 10 years, Mars = 7 years, Rāhu = 18 years, Jupiter = 16 years, Saturn = 19 years and Mercury = 17 years.
10. Unseen pathological enemies might be interpreted as viruses, fungal infections, bacteriological agents and intestinal parasites.
11. Both metals have a history of use to fortify the body; gold promotes strong immunity, silver was known as an anti-bacterial agent.
12. One popular oil is Henaraja Thailam. Its formulation is a closely guarded Buddhist secret, but known to contain over one hundred native herbs. Henaraja oil is particularly volatile during manufacture; its processing requires a high level of skill.
13. A highly alkalising agent, usually a plant salt extracted by calcination.
14. Bhasma here means ash collected at the close of Agnī-hotra, the source of this fire being a mixture of bilva wood (*Aegle marmelos*) or dried cow dung.
15. Veda Mahaththaya practise a healing system similar to Āyurveda with the addition of certain indigenous herbs/foods. In some instances recent generations of healers have embraced more Āyurvedic techniques, making it difficult to differentiate between the two approaches.

30

SUPERNATURAL ORIGIN
—— OF GEMSTONES ——

The following are gems: Diamond, Sapphire, Emerald, Agate, Ruby, Blood-stone and Beryl, Amethyst, Vimalaka,[1] Royal Gem, Crystal, Moon-gem, Saugandhika,[2] Opal, conch, Azure-stone, Topaz, Brahma-gem, Jyoteerasa,[3] Sasyaka,[4] Pearl and Coral.

Brihat Saṃhitā by Varāhamihira

Freshwater pearls from Lake Biwa (Shinga Prefecture), Japan. Moti/pearls are considered both a gemstone in Jyotish and medicinal animal-product in Āyurveda.

In the age of the gods, a powerful demon arose whose name was Bala.[5] In performance of gruelling penance and austerity he obtained a mighty boon from Lord Brahmā. He asked that he might defeat all challengers in single combat, effectively making him unstoppable upon the battlefield. With his new-found strength he quickly set about conquering the heaven and Earth, subjugating even the gods. Although a tyrant, he retained one good quality: he pledged unconditional support for all necessary Yagya[6]/sacrifices to be made.

This, however, proved to be his ultimate downfall as herein lay the method by which the gods were to rid themselves of their oppressor. Skilfully crafting a great sacrifice in honour of his inauguration, the gods made preparation for great yagya, except of course to not find a suitable sacrifice. At the moment of sacrifice the gods looked to one another in despair and chorused, 'Lord of all, there is no sacrifice deserving enough for this occasion. None but the lord of heaven himself is suitable.' Remembering his promise, Bala lowered his head in resignation and stepped forward and offered himself. Upon the instant of his death his lifeless body then miraculously transformed into an enormous gemstone.

Racing forward to receive this marvellous gift, the gods began arguing with one another over who should take possession. As they all pulled and tugged upon the stone it shattered into a million pieces, falling from heaven to Earth like rain. In time, pieces of the once-great gem worked themselves deep into the Earth, later to be liberated by humans in their myriad forms.

30.1 MAṆI (GEMSTONES)

Upayes dwell heavily on the use of gemstones, awarding them a superior status in regard to graha propitiation. There are, however, a growing number of astrologers who now question this premise, as these remedies have begun to spiral out of control. Today in India, it is almost impossible to have any Jyotish consultation without being bamboozled by astro-gem dealers, eager to sell their wares.

When consulting ancient and classical works, there is a decided lack of information surrounding the use of gemstones as astrological remedies. Āyurvedic alchemical texts acknowledge gemstone (and metal) usage to remedy certain health conditions, but little detail is to be found on counteracting the effects of malefic grahas seen in a horoscope.

Esteemed volumes such as the *Garuda Puraṇā* and *Brihat Saṃhitā*[7] make considerable efforts in deliberating over the qualities of gemstones, that is, their value and physical appearances – yet fail to mention any astrological application.[8] Contemporary works, however, have fully embraced this aspect of astrology, unleashing a whole swathe of planetary-gem specialists who now aim to remove any or all burdens placed upon an individual by 'unlucky stars'.

Personally, I feel this aspect of Jyotish is a real minefield, with quality gems demanding extortionate prices and stones of lesser quality passed off as higher grade specimens. Knowing a reliable jeweller or gemmologist is essential, as even the experts are sometimes fooled when caught in a hasty exchange of stones and wherewithal.

Some of the most saddening tales told are by those who are whisked through hasty impersonal analysis to be brow-beaten into a gem purchase. This type of astrology is not uncommon in Asia; especially by those who prey on excursionists. I have found myself in this position more than once, but alas it seems to be part and parcel of the territory and so 'to be forewarned is to be forearmed'.

All that being said, the use of gemstones as an astro-remedial is still unquestionably worthy. Plainly and simply, there remains something deeply alluring about the nature of gemstones, not only from an aesthetic point of view but also from the fact that the ancients held them in such high regard, something that suggests there was more to them than eye candy.

30.2 MATCHING STONES TO PLANETS

Navaratnā are to be considered Mahāranta, that is, mānikya (ruby), muktā (pearl), pravāla (red coral), tārkṣya (emerald), puṣparāga (topaz), vajra (diamond), nīlamaṇi (sapphire), gomeda (hessonite) and Vaiduryam (chrysoberyl) are ratnas related to the Navagrahas.

Rasendra Sāra Saṅgraha[9]

As briefly mentioned, little explanation on the astrological benefits of gemstones in the classics has been given, or their affinity shown toward certain planets. These associations (if mentioned at all), appear mostly within the context of iridescence, structure and colouring, failing to address why a particular example had been selected over another for its remedial properties.

One promising extract from *Rasaratna Samuccaya*[10] notes the apparent benefits of adorning the body with gemstones, saying: 'By wearing gemstones over the body, one gets relief from the bad effects of celestial bodies like the Sun etc.; long life, health, good fortune, energy and boldness. One is freed from the effects of demons and other such bad spirits.' But again this does not explain where these ideas originated, what mechanism is at work behind this effect or what properties of the gem are causing the effect.

Properties of gems: when consumed (in the form of bhasma) are sweet in taste, laxative, good for eyes/vision, cold in potency, and destroy poison; when worn on the body, these bestow auspiciousness, pleasantness of mind and remove the bad effects of grahas (planets).

Bhāvaprakāśa Pūrvakaṇḍa

A number of references are made in *Rasa Shāstra*[11] to the curative effects of gemstones, when prepared as *bhasma* (or alchemical ash). These same references mention little with regard to their various planetary associations. Gemstones in the form of an oxide are quite prevalent in these medical texts, their residual ash the end result of complex alchemical techniques. These processes aim to slowly draw an essence from their structure, converting the hardest of stones into smooth white, grey and pink powders. Bhasmas have astringency, are light, tasteless and all-pervasive, that is, their minute particle size allows them to penetrate the cellular structure of the body.

The whole process of conversion is extremely labour-intensive, taking many months to complete each step of conversion; however, the end efficacy of the remedy was considered to justify the means.

Indications of ailments best treated with gemstone[12] bhasma are important guides to diseases/doshic imbalances governed by each of the grahas. These associations might indicate how the therapeutic advantages of each helped develop the astrological portraits of planets. For example, rubies ruled by the Sun nourish the eyes, heart and blood. Pearls ruled by the Moon tonify the stomach and lungs and nourish the eyes. Red coral ruled by Mars helps build blood, muscle and ligament. Emeralds ruled by Mercury help nourish nerve, skin and lungs and promote intelligence. Yellow sapphire ruled by Jupiter helps strengthen memory and nourish the brain. Diamonds ruled by Venus strengthen ojas and immunity. Blue sapphires ruled by Saturn help promote physical strength through the muscular/skeletal system and also increase longevity. Garnet ruled by Rāhu aid in the removal of obstinate skin diseases, blood toxins and mental disorders. Cat's eye ruled by Ketu helps cleanse the blood, kills parasites and reduces inflammation.

30.3 PAIRING AND SETTING

The table lays down some popular recommendations for the pairing of planets with primary and substitute gemstones.

Grahas, gemstones and setting metals

Sun	Ruby (P) Sunstone (S) Setting metal: Gold/Silver
Moon	Pearl (P) Moonstone (S) Setting metal: Silver/Gold
Mercury	Emerald (P) Peridot (S) Setting metal: Silver/Platinum
Mars	Red Coral/Red Spinel[13] (P) Red Agate/Carnelian (S) Setting metal: Silver
Jupiter	Yellow Sapphire (P) Citrine or Topaz (S) Setting metal: Gold
Venus	Diamond[14] (P) Clear Quartz (S) Setting metal: Silver/Platinum
Saturn	Blue Sapphire (P) Blue Amethyst (S) Setting metal: Silver/Stainless Steel/Copper
Rāhu	Hessonite[15] (P) Setting metal: Silver
Ketu	Chrysoberyl/Cat's Eye (P) Setting metal: Silver

(P) = primary stone; (S) = substitute stone. All gemstones should be set 'open-backed', fully contacting the skin.

Note: Arch-malefics Saturn, Mars, Rāhu and Ketu are to be energised only under specific circumstances or if they have been severely compromised in the eyes of the astrologer. Having a strongly malefic nature, their empowerment is advised with caution; unfortunately, such detailed circumstances are beyond the scope of this book.

Primary gemstones are of course costly, not to mention difficult to acquire. It should also be borne in mind that expensive outlays in no way guarantee success. It is highly possible that a good gemstone will go some way to relieving certain types of negatively perceived karma, but you cannot just buy your way out of it – unless, of course, the horoscope indicates this to be so.

Significant purchases should always be through a trustworthy source, so it is imperative to seek advice before parting with a large sum of money. Additionally, it is worth having two astrologers analyse the same horoscope – look for points of agreement (in regard to gemstone recommendation).

Personally I would always consider a good (S) substitute stone, being not only more abundant (and affordable) but far less likely to have been enhanced.[16] If properly prepared and worn with good intent, substitute stones can be highly effective, at times outperforming their more exclusive cousins.

Setting metals are treated with equal care, every planet having some affinity to a particular metal. Gemstones are best set into gold or silver, as indicated in the table. An example of this would be ruby (sacred to Sûrya), worn primarily to enhance the power of the Sun. If the individual in question already had an *excess* of the fire in their body (high Pitta), wearing a ruby might aggravate this condition. Setting the gemstone into a cooling lunar metal such as silver helps subdue the heating nature of that stone. Cooling is achieved by referring its transmitted planetary ray through silver before absorption by the body's subtle energy field or physically via the surface of the skin. Conversely, if the same individual suffered from *low* or *variable* Agnī (digestive fire), a ruby would be more appropriately set into the solar metal, gold. The alternative metals copper, platinum and stainless steel (mentioned in the table) should also be given some brief explanation here.

Copper, though well-known and worked by the ancients, is considered a heating metal, also likely to oxidise if worn next to the skin. Salts and acids excreted by the body will cause discolouration of jewellery when worn for extended periods (although some regard the copper salts beneficial for certain medical conditions).

Platinum (from the Spanish *platina* = little silver) is a silvery-white metal that appears in the periodic table before gold and mercury. Although perceived as a 'new metal' its historical use can be traced back to 300 BC. This high-temperature metal can be worked with gold and silver using a process known as *sintering*. Platinum is non-toxic and has no known biological role. Reactions to pure forms of this metal are unlikely; however, mixtures (containing nickel) can cause skin reactions. Due to the higher cost of this metal, it is more likely that gold or silver would be used – but if preferred its energetics are thought to be more cooling.

Stainless steel is a modern alloy made from iron, chromium, nickel, copper, titanium and carbon. Fast becoming a popular metal for jewellery, its use is not encouraged for the same reasons as platinum mixes.

The remaining metals are covered in some depth in Section 30.9.

30.4 QUALITIES OF A GOOD GEMSTONE

Some qualitative tests recommended by ancient sources advocate the use of abrading wheels, strongly alkalising substances and scratch tests to be made upon gemstones of a suspect nature.

Incredibly, the manufacture of artificial gems[17] was known to antiquity and were thought to be mixtures of iron, topaz, corundum, garnet, beryl, lapis, crystal and silica. These materials (worked at very high temperatures) were often then passed off as natural, making traders extremely vigilant when it came to the authentication of gemstones.

The following ten recommendations outline desirable and undesirable qualities that should be sought or avoided when selecting good quality gemstones and actions to be taken prior to wearing. These recommendations aim to be fail-safe but should not be an absolute guarantee of a gemstone's provenance. Some enhancing technologies used in today's market appear to have been borrowed (and polished) from ancient sources – particularly those that involve dying or soaking stones at high temperatures.

1. Gemstones should be as blemish-free as possible, without abrasions, cracks, fissures, inclusions[18] or opaque clouding.

2. Gemstones should feel cool to the touch with a slightly greasy surface.

3. Gemstones should be unbleached and free from colour enhancement; that is, devoid of dyes, coatings and other methods of artificially brightening.

4. Gemstones should be as free from, or subjected to as little, high-temperature practices as possible. Traditional methods in this regard seem to be less inclined to stress or fracture the structural integrity.

5. Irradiated gemstones should be avoided at all costs.

6. Gemstones should ideally be a minimum weight of 2 carats[19] (P) primary and 3 carats (S) substitute.

7. Gemstones should be worn on the appropriate hands; that is, masculine planets on the right hand, feminine planets on the left hand.

8. Gemstones should be set into an appropriate metal to enhance their positive effects (see the table in Section 30.3 for more information).

9. Gemstones should directly contact the skin; that is, open-backed pendants, bracelets and/or rings.

10. Gemstones should be cleansed prior to use by bathing them in gangajal, salt water[20] or milk. One should also elect an auspicious time before first wearing.

30.5 WEARING GEMSTONES

There are some useful guidelines applicable when wearing gemstones, many making a lot of sense upon closer inspection.

After setting gemstones and undertaking the appropriate purification, pendants, bracelets and/or rings should be worn during the first hour after sunrise on the weekday most appropriate to their planetary lord. Selection of an appropriate finger (for rings) is also indicated (so as to honour planetary friendships and enmities), see the 'Friendships, Enmities and Neutrality' table in Section 2.8. Friendships and enmities of planets is a key factor in the consideration of gemstone wearing, as comfort of a planetary lord is essential if its benefic effects are to be felt.

Secondly, the gender of each planet should be also be considered. Here, for example, Moon and Venus are feminine; Sun, Jupiter and Mars are masculine. The remainder of planets – Mercury, Saturn, Rāhu and Ketu – are neuter and can be worn on either hand. Moon, Mars and Venus hold no dominion over a particular finger and so their positioning is to be determined by their friendship status with a surrogate finger. Mars can suitably be worn upon the ring finger (Sun), Venus upon the middle (Saturn) or little finger (Mercury) of the left hand (feminine). Moon, having no enmity with any planet, can be worn (to some degree) upon any finger, but generally gives better results upon the index finger (Jupiter) or ring finger (Sun) of the left hand.

For a more detailed account see the table.

Respective fingers/hand for the wearing of gemstones

Sun (Fire)	Ring finger (right hand)	Mars (Fire)	Ring finger (right hand)	Saturn (Air)	Middle finger (right or left hand)
Moon (Water)	Index finger (left hand)	Jupiter (Water)	Index finger (right hand)	Rāhu (Air)	Middle finger (right or left hand)
Mercury (Earth)	Little finger (right or left hand)	Venus (Water)	Middle finger or little finger (left hand)	Ketu (Air)	Middle finger (right or left hand)

There is some debate amongst astrologers as to whether gemstones perform better on the left or right hand. The left hand is feminine (open and allowing), the right hand masculine (assertive). The left hand is considered (by some) to absorb and assimilate planetary rays whereas the right hand is better able to project and manifest those same rays.

Consulting a number of astrologers in Śrī Lankā, the advice was pretty clear-cut. If you are going to wear a powerful gemstone such as ruby (Sun-enhancing), there is only one place it can go – on your right hand. If you are seeking to enhance femininity, material comforts and physical beauty, the appropriate gemstones are worn on the left hand.

Pendants positioned over the throat area project their healing upon the throat chakra (a point of reconciliation on the body between the *feeling* heart and *thinking* mind). Pendants worn lower on the chest work specifically on the heart, improving circulation, blood and overall vitality.

30.6 NAVARATNĀ (NINE GEMS)

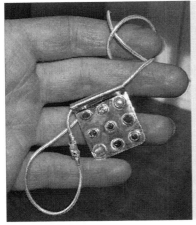

बुध Mercury	शुक्र Venus	चंद्र Moon
शनि Jupiter	सूर्य Sun	मंगळ Mars
केतु Ketu	गुरु Saturn	राहु Rahu

Navaratnā pendant (left) and planetary positions (right).

Navaratnā pendants[21] or rings seek to honour all grahas in one decorative design. These are often tailored to suit a predominant dosha, by their choice of metal. With a mixed bag of planetary strengths and weaknesses in any horoscope it can sometimes be difficult to isolate or safely empower one planet without unbalancing the remainder. When gemstone propitiation is fraught with tradeoffs it is often deemed wise to recommend Navaratnā, a kind of 'belt and braces' approach. With all bases covered, no single planet can dominate.

This nine-stone set has become a highly popular and desirable option with many astrologers today. There is also the added issue of changing dasha periods and planetary transits. As favourable planets come and go, they may lose some benefic qualities if found to be occupying a difficult sign or house. Navaratnā in this regard may be worn safely almost indefinitely with little risk of incurring planetary hostilities.

Many Śrī Lankāns wear *Navaratnā-muduwa* (nine-stone rings), I don't think I ever encountered an Jyotishi there that did not wear or own one. Typically the gem-array of these rings includes a ruby (Sun), pearl (Moon), red coral (Mars), emerald (Mercury), topaz (Jupiter), diamond (Venus), sapphire (Saturn), garnet (Rāhu) and lapis lazuli (Ketu).

30.7 BIRTHSTONES

Sign	(P) Primary	(S) Substitute
Aries	Ruby or Red Coral	Red Spinel or Bloodstone[23]
Taurus	Diamond	Clear Zircon or Quartz
Gemini	Emerald	Green Peridot or Tourmaline
Cancer	Pearl	Moonstone
Leo	Ruby	Sunstone
Virgo	Emerald	Green Peridot or Tourmaline
Libra	Diamond	Clear Zircon or Quartz
Scorpio	Ruby or Red Coral	Red Spinel or Bloodstone
Sagittarius	Yellow Sapphire	Topaz or Citrine
Capricorn	Blue Sapphire	Amethyst or Aquamarine
Aquarius	Blue Sapphire	Amethyst or Aquamarine
Pisces	Yellow Sapphire	Topaz or Citrine

Some Śrī Lankān astrologers and indigenous healers opt for *Birthstones* if pressed to make gem recommendations. Birthstones reflect choice stones most appropriate to the individual's rising sign (see table). Similar to

Navaratnā, these stones are worn to produce generally beneficial effects regardless of all planetary states and strengths in a horoscope. Wearing a Birthstone is considered a safe and sensible practice, enlivening or activating weakened grahas whilst at the same time limiting the harmful effects of malefic planets. As is the case with any gemstone recommendation, each is first worn at a pre-appointed time and given suitable purification prior to wearing.

30.8 USING GEMSTONES ĀYURVEDICALLY

> From the bones of gods came pearls – animating life in the primal waters. That I may fasten onto this life, lustre and longevity – may this amulet of pearl protect thee for the life of a hundred autumns.
>
> *Atharva Veda*

This section is partly a continuation of Chapter 20 and concerns itself with gemstone therapy, in accordance with Āyurvedic principles of dosha. The table outlines the general attributes of both primary and secondary gemstones.

Energetics of gemstones

No.	Planet	Gemstones	General Effects
1	Sun	Ruby (P) Sunstone (S)	+P (strongly), –VK, strengthens the heart and nerves, improves circulation, digestion (Agnī) and vision. Enhances intellect, discrimination and independence, improves self-esteem. Ruby is considered to have a tonifying action upon asthi dhatu (bones and teeth).
2	Moon	Pearl[23] (P) Moonstone (S)	+K, –P (strongly), –V, soothes the eyes, heart and emotions, strengthens nerves and kidney/bladder functioning. Pearl produces a sedative effect and is a general rasāyana for all bodily secretions/fluids. Pearl purifies the blood and reduces acidity; it is particularly useful for children and female reproductive ailments.
3	Mars	Red Coral (P) Red Spinel/ Red Agate/ Carnelian[24] (S)	+K, balances PV, general action is cooling. Red coral nourishes blood, reproductive and respiratory systems. Coral promotes strong connective tissue, muscular/tendon elasticity, and reduces inflammatory conditions. Red coral improves stamina and boosts energy levels.

4	Mercury	Emerald (P) Peridot (S)	+K, –PV, general rasāyana for the nervous/respiratory system, reduces inflammation, itching, skin complaints and fever. Useful for a number of childhood ailments including eczema and asthma, improves attentiveness (ADD) and tonifies blood. Emerald promotes homeostasis of rasa dhatu, the maintenance of nervous tissue and skin lustre.
5	Jupiter	Yellow Sapphire (P) Topaz/Yellow Citrine or (S)	+K, –V, slightly increases P. General action is warming and nutritive (tissue builder), good for convalescence, promotes digestion, strengthens hepatic functioning and mineral absorption. Yellow sapphire promotes vision, healthy gums and teeth, balances the hormonal/glandular system and supports the immune system. Beneficial in cases of hearing loss and vertigo.
6	Venus	Diamond (P) Herkimer Diamond/ Clear Quartz (S)	+K, –VP, said to have excellent anti-visha properties, promotes longevity and strengthens ojas. Diamond is aphrodisiac, improves kidney functioning, boosts immunity and balances water metabolism. Useful in cases of urogenital diseases, diabetes and weak pancreatic functionality.
7	Saturn	Blue Sapphire (P) Blue Amethyst (S)	+V, –PK, reduces excess Pitta and oedema, soothes painful joints and heals fractures. Useful in cases of constipation, piles and varicose veins, poor circulation, paralysis, reduced vision, hearing loss and vertigo. Sapphire helps bind and heal damaged tissue, promotes flexibility and reduces inflammation; this gemstone is generally considered to promote longevity.
8	Rāhu	Garnet/Cinnamon Stone (P)	+P, –V, slightly increases Kapha. Calms vitiated Vāta, increases appetite and promotes vitality. Soothes the nerves, reduces depression, allays fears and protects against external negative forces. Generally known to promote prosperity and success but also likely to encourage addiction.
9	Ketu	Chrysoberyl/Cat's Eye (P)	+PV, –K, strengthens immune system, protects against external pathogens (including psychic attack), unexpected accidents and injury. Helps reduce inflammation and paralysis and tonifies the nervous system. Cat's eye promotes astrological/occult power and psychic ability.

In contrast to the above, there are also a number of primary and substitute gems (inclusive of setting metals) employed by indigenous healers in Śrī Lankā expressly for the pacification of vitiated dosha. The next table outlines common recommendations.

Pacification of dosha with gemstones (Śri Laṇkā)

Dosha	Primary Stones	Secondary Stones
Vāta	Ruby, blue sapphire, yellow sapphire, topaz and pearl	Moonstone, opal and lapis lazuli
Setting	Ruby set in silver on the right ring finger.	Moonstone set in sliver on the right ring finger.
	Blue sapphire: set in sliver on either middle finger.	Opal set in gold on the left ring finger.
	Yellow sapphire: set in gold on the right index finger.	Lapis lazuli set in a gold necklace.
Pitta	Blue sapphire, emerald, pearl, jade and red coral	Moon stone, peridot or clear quartz
Setting	Blue sapphire set in sliver on right middle finger.	Moonstone set in sliver on either index finger.
	Emerald set in silver on either little finger.	Peridot set in silver on either little finger.
	pearl set in silver on either ring finger.	Clear quartz set in silver on either ring finger.
	Jade set in silver on right index finger.	
	Red coral set in silver on either ring finger.	
Kapha	Diamond, ruby and garnet	Chrysoberyl, opal, lapis lazuli and red agate
Setting	Diamond set in gold on right ring finger.	Chrysoberyl set in gold on the left index finger.
	Ruby set in gold on left index finger.	Opal set in gold on right index finger.
	Garnet set in gold on right index finger.	Lapis lazuli set in a gold necklace.
		Red agate set in a gold necklace.

30.9 PROPERTIES OF METALS

Nine breadths with nine he combines, in order to lengthen a life for one hundred autumns; in the yellow (hárita), three; in silver (roupya), three; in iron (áyas), three – enveloped with fervour.

Atharva Veda

Metals have been briefly covered in Section 30.3 but there are a number of additional properties attributed to their native form as well as that of bhasma.

Metals (known in general as *loha*) were commonly divided into four groups: *Pārada* (mercury), *Sudha* (pure), *Puti* (impure) and *Misra* (mixed);

what we today would recognise as liquid, precious, non-ferrous and alloyed. Metals were also subject to caste: gold and silver = royal caste, tin and copper = brahmanic caste, iron = warrior caste, lead and alloys = servant caste.[25] Mercury (in its planetary guise) was of royal blood, but his namesake metal remains beyond caste as mercury forms an amalgam with all metals except iron.[26] Despite his royal birth, Mercury maintains cordial relations with planet Saturn – whose metal (lead) he frequently ingests and transmutes into gold.

References to caste appear almost certainly astrological, seemingly related to planetary hierarchy; that is, Sun/gold/king, Moon/silver/queen, Jupiter/tin/minister, Venus/copper/minister, Mars/iron/commander-in-chief, Saturn/lead/servant and the lunar nodes, brass/bronze/militia. The following table outlines the individual curative potential of metals. *Note:* All medicinal effects given here refer to their oxide forms or bhasma, having undergone suitable purification techniques as advised by Rasa Shāstra (Vedic Alchemy).

Energetics of metals

Metal	Effect
Swarna Gold (Au)	Gold primarily represents masculine solar energy (heating), Pitta dosha and the fire god Agnī.[27] Its tastes are astringent, bitter and sweet, its essence oily. Gold promotes digestive strength, heals bones, gives strength to the heart and small intestine, improves vision, counteracts the effects of poison, is an aphrodisiac and general rasāyana. Known as the King of Metals, gold was deemed perfected or sudha.[28] Its ability to remain untarnished over time conferred longevity and wisdom upon its wearer. Gold was thought to be of five types, all precious, if converted from lower/base metals (such as lead) it became suitable to rejuvenate the human body. The nature of gold was considered sattvic.
Rajata Silver (Ag)	Silver represents feminine lunar energy (cooling), Kapha dosha and Lord Śiva.[29] Its tastes are sour, astringent and sweet, its essence is oily and lekhana.[30] Silver reduces VK, increases digestive strength, heals gastric mucosa and the stomach. It gives strength to the respiratory system and nourishes the eyes (improving vision). Silver counteracts the effects of poison, is aphrodisiac and rasāyana for the body and mind. Known as the Queen of Metals, silver was also deemed sudha and, like gold, its wearer would be spared the effects of old age and granted wisdom/intelligence. Silver was considered a sattvic metal.
Tamra Copper (Cu)	Copper is representative of the war god Karttikeya. Its tastes are astringent, bitter and sweet, its essence is heating, oily, heavy and lekhana. Copper reduces PK and promotes digestive strength. Copper feeds upon āma, is anti-bacterial and anti-fungal. It digests fat, improves mobility and elasticity, heals connective tissues, promotes vision, is emetic and counteracts the effects of poison; it also kills pathogens (krimi[31]). Copper was deemed to be sudha (pure) but also harboured tamasic qualities.

Metal	Effect
Loha Iron (Fe)	Iron is representative of Tvashtar,[32] architect and artificer of the gods. Its tastes are astringent, bitter and sweet, its essence firstly cooling then heating. Iron reduces PK, is dry and heavy, yet promotes the formation of healthy blood. Iron destroys anaemia, strengthens spleen and gives lustre to the skin. Iron counteracts the effect of poison, is aphrodisiac and rasāyana for blood. It confers a compact and robust nature. Known as the Marshal of Metals, iron instils the will to succeed and a love of victory. Iron was deemed sudha but also harboured rajasic qualities.
Pārada* Mercury (Hg)	Mercury (known also as Pārada) is representative of Lord Śiva.[33] Its dosha is V-P-K, its guna rajasic, it displays all six tastes.[34] It is yoga vāhin (a vehicle for other metals) and strongly heating. Liquid at room temperature, its solidification is achieved by forming an alloy with gold, silver, copper, lead, tin and zinc. If united with sulphur, mercury converts into HgS, a stable black sulphide called Kajjali. This combination is frequently used to make Pottali,[35] a semi-metallic ball of mercuric sulphide. Pottali are commonly worn in a pouch about the neck as a talisman. Mercury's uniqueness places it in a class of its own. Considered the Master Metal, it is readily combined with a large number of metals, minerals and gemstones to make potent remedies in the medicinal science of Rasa Shāstra.[36]
Vanga Tin (Sn)	Tin is representative of Indrā (King of Heaven). Its taste is bitter and astringent, it aggravates V and reduces K, its long-term effect is drying. Tin promotes intelligence, heals diseases of the skin and urogenital system. It is considered an esteemed remedy in cases of diabetes, anaemia, vertigo, depleted ojas, auto-immunity issues, digestive instability (such as abdominal bloating) and hearing loss. Low levels of tin in the body usually manifest as nerve sensitivity, hair loss, hearing loss, depression, low self-esteem and loss of bone density. Both tin and zinc have similar medicinal properties; both metals have a low melting point and both resemble mercury (Hg); hence both were noted to have powerful healing abilities. Tin was deemed puti (impure) and also harboured rajasic qualities.
Yasada Zinc (Zn)	Rulership of zinc appears jointly administered by Jupiter and Venus, although it could be said to favour the latter. Zinc reduces PK but aggravates V; its taste is bitter yet sweet and cooling in post-digestion. Zinc promotes healthy vision, strong teeth and bones, nourishes majja dhatu (nerves and higher brain functioning) and gives bala (strength). Low levels of zinc in the body usually manifest as pancreatic imbalances, depression, throat infections, inflammation, ulcers, bruises, stomatitis, low immunity (reduced ojas) and low libido. Zinc was deemed puti (impure), harbouring rajasic qualities.
Naga* Lead (Pb)	Lead is representative of Vasuki (serpent deity). Lead is known as Naga (snake) due largely to the hissing sound it produces when purified/processed. Inference to a snake is also equated to its toxicity. Lead was considered puti (impure) and a lower caste metal. Its guna is tamasic. Lead reduces VK but aggravates P (long-term its effects are heating). Lead promotes digestive strength, healthy joints and the elimination of toxins. Naga bhasma is frequently found in rasa formulae that attempt to treat diseases of the urogenital system, including diabetes. Lead is also favoured in the treatment of auto-immune diseases such as rheumatoid arthritis and eczema. Lead (Pb) is highly toxic, accumulating in the brain, nervous system, blood and kidneys.

Pittala Brass (Cu+Zn)	Brass is ruled by Rāhu; it is considered mishra (an alloy). It is bitter, cold and drying, reducing PK but increasing V. Its guna is tamasic. Brass promotes liver function and healthy blood; it is a hepatic rasāyana. Brass is also beneficial for the spleen, circulatory system and skin; its cleaning and scraping action helps remove Āma (undigested food), parasites and accumulated dosha. Brass is considered to have important yoga vahin properties for other remedies in Rasa Shāstra.
Kansya Bronze (Cu+Sn)	Bronze is ruled by Ketu and has similar properties to Pittala. Both are mishra loha (alloys) and bitter in taste. The long-term action of bronze is heating and light; its guna is tamasic. Bronze reduces PV but can aggravate V with prolonged use. Bronze promotes strong vision, purity of blood and hepatic/digestive strength. Bronze is also useful for the removal of toxins, intestinal parasites and inflammation. Bronze is considered to have excellent anti-bacterial properties.
Additional Loha Alloys	
Pasloha[37] Varta Loha (Cu+Sn+Zn +Fe+Pb)	Pasloha is an alloy used to propitiate Ketu. This combination of five metals is frequently cast into pendants or worn as a bracelet made from the five entwined wires. Pasloha is very popular in Śrī Lankā; its Indian counterpart is is Varta loha. There are slight discrepancies in the two mixtures; however, the general consensus of mixture appears to be brass, bronze, copper, iron and lead (in equal proportions). Pasloha reduces PK, is tamasic in guna, pungent, sour, yet cooling in long-term action. Medicinally this metal has good anti-parasitic properties, aids in the removal of skin diseases, reduces constipation, heals urinary disorders and promotes bala (strength).
Tri-loha (Au+Ag+ Cu)	An alloy of gold (25pts), silver (16pts) and copper (10pts). Tri-loha is sweet in taste, sour in post-digestion and has excellent rasāyana properties. Tri-loha promotes circulation and heart functionality. It increases digestive function and promotes longevity. This alloy's properties are likened to gold (but with reduced strength). Its actions are +P, –VK. No guna is indicated for this metal but is presumed to be largely sattvic in nature due to its combination of three sudha metals.

* Toxic by ingestion, vapours or prolonged contact with skin.

30.10 DHATU AND *DHATU*

Metal-crafting is an ancient practice and nowhere was it more skilfully undertaken than in the Vedic culture. It is not exactly clear how the practise of shodhana (purification) first arose in the metallurgy of the day, but evidently residual forms of molten metal had been tested for latent medicinal properties.

The word 'loha' (a broad synonym for all metals) is believed to be derived from root *luh*, meaning 'extractable essence'. Later the word *Dhatu* was adopted for metals; this again may have astrological undertones due to a correlation made between the seven bodily tissues, also called Dhatu, and the seven primary planets, both seen as primary factors in the long-term maintenance of health and strong bodily cohesion.

Dhatus – bodily and metallic

Planet	Dhatu	Tissue	Metal
Sun	Asthi	Bone	Gold (Au)
Moon	Rakta	Blood	Silver (Ag)
Mars*	Māṃsa	Muscle/tendons	Iron (Fe)
Mercury	Rasa	Plasma	Mercury (Hg)
Jupiter	Medas	Fat	Tin (Sn)
Saturn*	Majjā	Nervous system	Lead (Pb)
Venus	Shukra	Reproductive fluid	Copper (Cu)

* Note: Mars and Saturn's rulership over Dhatu are often interchangeable; that is, imbalances in muscle/tendons and nervous system may be attributed to the handiwork of either graha. As Rāhu and Ketu preside over alloys they are not considered here.

NOTES

1. Unknown category of stones mentioned in the *Kauṭilīya Arthashāstra*. These are described as white or red in variety.
2. Unknown subsidiary gem believed to resemble the colour of a well-known flower.
3. Unknown, mentioned in the *Kauṭilīya Arthashāstra*, described as white or red in variety.
4. Vibrant blue stone known as Sasyaka/copper sulphate ($CuSO_4$).
5. Bala = strength.
6. Ancient fire ceremonies/sacrifices desiring a loss of negatively accrued karma.
7. Authored by *Varāhamihira*.
8. A number of astrological works (such as *Brihat Parasara Hora Shāstra*) make mention of gemstones, but more in relation to their bestowal of fortune/gain on an individual. For example, during Shukra Maha Dasha one sees gains in white clothes, conveyances, gemstones (such as pearls) and beautiful damsels.
9. Famous alchemical text compiled by Śrī Gopalkrishna Bhatt, c. 14th–15th century AD.
10. Compiled in the 13th century by Vāgbhaṭāchārya.
11. A Vedic science broadly equated to medical alchemy.
12. These indications are found also in the bhasma of associated planetary metals and animal products, that is, pearls, coral, etc.
13. Red Spinel ($MgAl_2O_4$) is found in Śrī Laṅkā and used as a substitute for red coral.
14. Rulership of Diamond relates to colour imperfections. If clear, diamonds are given to Shukra (Venus). Otherwise: Sun = copper coloured, Varuna = blue, Indrā = brown, Agnī = yellow, Lord of Pitris = white and the Maruts = green coloured specimens. Those with a colouration similar to conch are said to be worn by Brahmā.
15. Hessonite/Garnet ($Ca_3Al_2(SiO_4)_3$ known also as Cinnamon Stone.
16. Gem enhancement typically includes bleaching and dyeing (pearls are particularly prone to this type of enhancement). *Coating* (also known as *backing*) introduces colour pigments or metal oxides to tint gemstones. Synthetic resins may also be applied to the calcium carbonates such as corals and pearls. Gemstones can be exposed to high temperature to remove porosity or crystalline fracturing. Typically these gems will be coated in a paste made from boiled rice and powdered limestone. When dry they can be exposed to very high temperatures for short periods. Encasing them in this mixture allows gems to be heated without incurring cracks. Heating them in this way also prepares their surface to receive dyes (ironically added to hide imperfections). Some types of wax application were also known to the ancients, these again being used to hide blemishes in gems.
17. Geuda are classified as milky white corundum combined with small amounts of rutile (TiO_2). When heated to temperatures of 1500°C+ a variety of different colours (including reds, yellows and blues) is achieved.

18. All gemstones exhibit tiny blemishes or inclusions; these occur during assemblage. A total absence of blemishes should be viewed with suspicion.
19. 1 carat = 0.2g/200mg.
20. Rock salt dissolved in warm water.
21. *BPHS* makes mention of a set of nine gems or *navamin-vraja*.
22. Also known as Rudhirakhya.
23. Pearls are often graded on a four-tiered system: (A) = low grade, misshapen; (AA) = ovular, 20 per cent or surface blemishes; (AA+) = oval, 90 per cent blemish-free; (AAA) = spherical, high lustre, 95 per cent blemish-free metallic surface. Pearls suitable for astrological purposes should be AA+ or AAA grade.
24. Carnelian (SiO_2 + Fe) or Spinel (also known as Balas Ruby) $MgAl_2O_4$ can be used.
25. The lunar nodes are sometimes awarded servant caste, but are more commonly associated with the king's militia (recruited for war en masse from the populace).
26. A more complete list would also include platinum, tantalum, tungsten and molybdenum.
27. Gold is known as *Vahnisambhuta*, meaning 'that which originated from fire'.
28. Sudha means 'pure' or 'without blemish'.
29. Śiva is intrinsically linked to all Moon/Soma legends as Chandra adorns his head as a waning crescent.
30. Cleaning/scraping action.
31. Krimi might be interpreted as parasites, pathogens, bacteria or viruses.
32. Brihaspati is also considered as having some rulership over iron (see Pushyami Nakshatra in Section 27.8).
33. Pārada is considered the sexual emissions or 'shukra' of Lord Śiva.
34. Āyurveda recognises six rasa (tastes). These are: sweet, sour, salty, pungent, bitter and astringent.
35. Pottali = to contain or condense (solidify).
36. See the author's previous work, *Rasa Shāstra: The Hidden Art of Medical Alchemy* (Singing Dragon, 2014).
37. Also known as Pañca Loha.

31

RUDRĀKṢA

Having obtained a mighty boon from Brahmā a demon called Tripurasura conquered the universe and overcame all. The gods sought the help of Lord Śiva, who meditated on a solution for a thousand years. Stirring from this meditative state he confronted Tripurasura, reducing the demon to ashes with the fiery sight from his third eye. A few tears from this eye fell upon the Earth and magically transformed into Rudrākṣa trees.

Śiva Purāṇa

Seeds from the Rudhir[1] tree were and are traditionally collected and prepared as meditation (mala/ rosary beads).

Rudrākṣa *mukhi* (dried seeds) of the Rudhir tree are found throughout the Himalayan region, Bhutan and Nepal. Rudrākṣa, also known as Rudra's Tears, have become highly venerated totems, prized for invoking that deity's protective power. Rudrākṣa are deemed particularly potent in matters of health, good fortune and the removal of obstacles or enemies.

Mythologically there were thought to be 38 variations of Rudrākṣa, twelve said to have emanated from the right eye of Śiva (solar) and sixteen from his left (lunar) eye. Ten additional types emerged from his Ajna (third or hidden eye).

Rudrākṣa from the solar eye are blood-red in colour, those from the lunar eye are white. The blackened variety are said to be from the third eye of the God. Red Rudrākṣa are likened to Kṣatriya (warrior caste), white to Vaiśya (merchant caste) and blackened varieties to Śūdra (servant caste). Seeds which have been purified[2] are considered Brahmanic in caste.

Generally Rudrākṣa are all of a brownish-red colouration, although a number of shades and mixtures are sold. These can range from a blackened tan to deep red, orange/red and on occasion a bleached whitish variety. All are deemed acceptable for talismanic/ritualistic use. Most aficionados naturally favour the striking red variety with an appropriate number of faces. The seed's façade is highly decorative and intricately grooved, each division about its radius said to constitute a face. Some Rudrākṣa seeds are known to display over twenty[3] faces, but these are rare. Numerically, divisions between one to ten are common, with odd numbers less likely to occur. Every 'face' denotes an allegiance toward a particular sub-deity or action. The table outlines some of the most popular variations.

Faces	Deity	Planet	Action
1	Śiva	Sūrya	Freed from one's sins
2	Śiva/Pārvatī	Chandra	Known as Gauriśaṅkara, this Rudrākṣa promises remission of all sins, known and unknown
3	Agnī	Sūrya	The sin of strīhatyā[4] is removed
4	Brahmā	Shani	The sin of narahatyā[5] is removed
5	Kālāgnirudra	Brihaspati	Removal of sins obtained by over-indulgence in food and sex
6	Kārttikeya	Kuja	Remission of sins pertaining to conflict and war
7	Kāmadeva	Shukra	Freed from the sin of theft (especially connected to the theft of another's gold)
8	Vināyaka[6]	Ketu	Absolution from theft, treachery and deception
9	Bhairava[7]	Rāhu	Attainment of liberation and absolution from murderous acts
10	Janārdana	Budha	Success and liberation from Earthly sins, relief from malefic grahas, ghosts and demons
11	Ekādaśarudras	Kuja	Obtains merits equal to great yagas
12	Ādityas	Sūrya	Freed from disease, worry and Earthly ills, obtains the blessings of the Sun god and absolution of sin
13	Kārttikeya	Kuja	Enjoys pleasure and luxury, obtains sweetened medicines (rasāyana) and benefits from rasa (mercury)
14	Paramaśiva[8]	Ketu	Attains ultimate liberation (mokṣa)

Some Rudrākṣa bear hidden motifs (if studied with enough care). Clear examples of the *Om* symbol, Śiva lingam, yoni, trishul, elephant's trunk[9] or sarpa/serpent greatly increase desirability.

A seed of good quality should be hard and greasy to the touch. It should display deep segregations with a protruded natural opening that bisects the seed. Those lucky enough to acquire a genuine, well-presented Rudrākṣa are further advised to bathe it in salt water (or fresh milk) prior to use. Specimens that have become damaged (chipped, scratched) or contaminated by tiny burrowing insects are deemed to be of little value.

Rudrākṣa seeds (like gemstones) can be subjected to clever levels of forgery. Replicas fashioned from betel (areca) nuts, lotus seeds, nutmeg and a whole array of wild seedpods currently flood the marketplace. A resurgence of interest in this humble seed has awakened the temptation for counterfeit, known to fool even the experts. Those wishing to purchase Rudrākṣa are advised to exercise caution and take advice prior to purchase. There are a number if high-profile dealers who guarantee authenticity as well as boasting scientifically tested stock.

NOTES

1. Also Utrasum Bead-tree (*Elaeocarpus ganitrus* Roxb.).
2. Typically, Rudrākṣa are first soaked in coconut water. Seeds are then removed, pasted and powdered. Rudrākṣa Churna can be mixed with sesame oil and applied externally for conditions such as asthma, pneumonia and chest pains. Rudrākṣa Churna can be mixed with coral bhasma and honey, making them useful in cases of paralysis, skin diseases, hypertension and nervous disorders.
3. Instances of thirty eight divisions have been mentioned in the Purāṇas, although these are attributed to previous Yugas (world ages).
4. Murdering one's wife.
5. Murdering one's husband.
6. Lord of hosts/great armies, sometimes taken to be another form of Ganesha.
7. A blackened emanation of Lord Śiva.
8. Formless aspect of Śiva.
9. Relating directly to Ganesha.

32

—— POOJA ——

Brahmin performs Navagraha Pooja, honouring the nine planets.

Raksha seeking to disrupt Yajna, Yagya and Kratu rituals, aim to halt the flow of Havish (divine foods) from reaching the realm of Devas. Through the sacrificial arts – ghee, saffron, jaggery, grain etc. (offered into transformative flames) are at once transported to the heavenly realm.

Deprivation of Earthly essence (nectar) emaciates the Deva, who tire, become weak and are unable to protect human life from calamity. In this condition, attacks by Raksha upon the heavenly kingdom also increase.

Śiva Purāṇa

One of the most elaborate and specialised forms of planetary propitiation is undoubtedly pooja[1] (or pūjā). One variation of this ritualistic ceremony *invites* all nine grahas into a pre-prepared sacred space to attend a private celebration of their divinity. The ceremony is usually performed by a

Brahmin (priest) and at some point during the proceedings the individual who requested the service may be instructed to act as an attendant. Typically the date and time of the pooja will be elected by an astrologer using Mhurta[2] techniques.

In recent years, pooja (like most things) has become somewhat commercialised;[3] however, that being said it is still possible to find an appropriately trained individual willing to perform the necessary ritual. Sometimes a little legwork on the part of the querent may also unearth a treasure trove right in your own neighbourhood as it is always possible that your locale harbours a Hindu temple or one well versed in these matters. Temples can usually be approached with a request to hire the services of their *Yajat* (one who performs pooja) on your behalf.

Navagraha-sthapana inclusive of Ganesha, betel leaves/nuts, saffron, milk, ghee, yoghurt, rice and kavacha, and so on.

Most Hindus perform some type of pooja on a daily basis, with varying levels of complexity. These can be conducted with a bewildering array of ancillaries, including ghee, saffron, turmeric and flowers. Intensive fire sacrifices called *Ahuti* may also be enacted, ceremoniously casting ghee, grains, new cloth, kushmanda,[4] coconuts or cooked foods into flames. It is believed that foods offered into fire are devoured by the Agnī and borne away to the godly realm. This act is known as *Havya-váhana*. Agnī's alternative functioning as dispeller of evil spirits doubly intensifies his inclusion in the ritual.

Perhaps one of the most effective methods of alleviating planetary affliction is *Navagraha-sthapana*,[5] the ceremony enacted to honour all nine grahas. This subtle *metaphysical* approach to propitiate malefic planets should not be underestimated. Planetary pooja can, under the right circumstances, deliver excellent results, particularly where the individual concerned becomes instrumental in its organisation and sources all materials required to perform that ritual. The following represents an outline of what might take place during Navagraha-sthapana.

Ahuti (fire sacrifice); in this case a ceremonial coconut is offered at the close of a pooja.

32.1 SUITABLE MATERIALS

Listed below in two categories are a number of materials that might be required during pooja:

- *General items* include foods, herbs, flowers, betel leaves/nuts.

- *Ritual items* include kadai (iron), wood kindling, cows' urine and dung (the latter is obviously prepared in advance by drying in sunlight). Cow dung cakes are extremely auspicious for fire rituals, burning with great intensity and producing a slightly aromatic smoke. Cow dung is considered to produce a superior order of flame. It is believed that any or all cow produce has a cleansing, sattvic energetic. Likewise, cows' urine is deemed equally auspicious when cast upon open flames (for purification purposes).

General items

No.	Item	No.	Item
1	whole coconut or banana	9	saffron
2	turmeric	10	coloured flowers: orange, white, red, lime green, yellow, pale blue and dark blue/purple
3	yoghurt	11	mint
4	jaggery	12	sandalwood
5	nara-dhanya, that is, bengal, red, black, horse, and green gram, white rice, black-eyed peas, wheat and sesame seeds	13	ghee
6	honey	14	cardamom
7	betel leaves/nuts	15	camphor (incense)
8	milk		

Ritual items

No.	Item	No.	Item
1	cotton wick (for ghee lamp)	4	wood kindling
2	cows' urine	5	cow dung cakes
3	white cotton cloth	6	iron kadai or fire pit for Ahuti

Prior to pooja a small ghee lamp[6] is lit and a bowl of water poured. A sacrificial coconut (or banana) is placed atop a copper/ceramic pitcher called a *Kalasha*[7] (usually nested upon betel leaves). The coconut itself is painted with bands of turmeric paste mixed with sandalwood – these adorn its girth. Next a beverage named *pañca amrita*[8] is prepared from *dahi* (yoghurt[9]), *dugdha* (milk), *ghee* (clarified butter), *madhu* (honey) and *jaggery* (palm sugar). These ingredients are pasted and used to entice the grahas to attend the ceremony.

Note: Saffron, basil, mint and cardamom are sometimes included or substituted for any unobtainable ingredients.

A brass dish with spoon is filled with water kept close to hand, this being used throughout the ritual for purification purposes, drunk from the hand and sprinkled in each cardinal direction. A plain cotton cloth (square) is spread upon the central working area, supporting a raised bed of nara-dhanya (nine grains); this is sometimes topped with an additional tier of unbroken white rice. The grains are fashioned into a circular design that is roughly divided into eight quadrants with a central depression (one for each graha). Betel leaves (tips facing outward) mark each eighth leaving a space at the centre to accommodate a final leaf representative of the Sun – centre of the solar system. Whole betel nuts are then used to represent the nine planets.

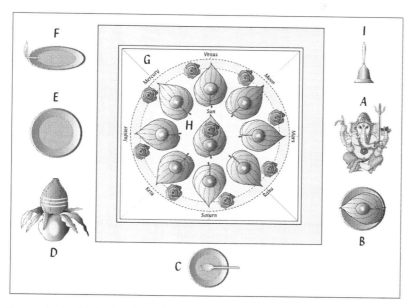

Planetary Pooja: (A) Figurine of Ganesha, (B) betel leaf/nut for Ganapati pooja, (C) copper dish (filled with water) and spoon, (D) kalasha, (E) akshata (unbroken rice grains), (F) ghee lamp, (G) white cotton cloth (square), (H) nara-dhanya raised circle, (I) brass bell.

32.2 NAVAGRAHA-STHAPANA

At the appointed time the pooja commences with its first act, the propitiation of Lord Ganesha. This is done to remove all obstacles and to clear a space in which to receive the planets. Each of the planets is honoured in turn, enunciating their status/hierarchy, directional strength, birth data and lineages.

This introduction follows the sequence of the weekdays: Sunday = Sun, Monday = Moon, Tuesday = Mars, Wednesday = Mercury, Thursday = Jupiter, Friday = Venus and Saturday = Saturn. Lastly the lunar nodes are introduced with reference to their dual rulership over Saturday for Rāhu and Tuesday for Ketu. At the close of each introduction each of the nine betel nuts is duly decorated with turmeric and sandalwood paste, fed pañca amrita, placed back upon its appropriate betel leaf and adorned with a relevantly coloured flower: Sun = orange, Moon = white, Mars = red,

Mercury = lime green, Jupiter = yellow, Venus = pale blue and Saturn = dark blue/purple. Again, the lunar nodes are decorated with colours akin to their natures, that is, Rāhu = dark blue/purple (Saturn) and Ketu = red (Mars).

32.3 POORNA

The complete form of pooja (called Poorna) should include Ahuti/fire sacrifice at its close, during which the decorated coconut (or other substitute fruit) used in the service is immolated. Typically a small brick-lined fire pit or iron kadai is stacked with dried cow dung cakes on a bed of dry sand with the offering stacked atop. During this sacrifice, cows' urine and akshat are additionally thrown onto the flames. This final act is dedicated to Lord Rudra,[10] totally reducing the sacrificial object to ash. During Poorna, selected verses from Śrī Rudram[11] (Namakam[12] and Chamakam[13]) are recited before the ritual's conclusion.

NOTES

1.   Pūjā, an offering of flowers and an awakening through the recitation of god's name.
2.   Electional astrology.
3.   Through the medium of the internet, poojas are now being offered live from India by webcam; however, delivery of priestly services via cyberspace seems impersonalised and clinical, both parties distanced and dispassionate, their bond purely mercantile. In the author's opinion it seems more appropriate that the individual participates in the ritual in order to directly commune with any or all of the honoured deities.
4.   Also known as ash pumpkin.
5.   Navagraha-Sthapana = to fix/subdue the nine planets.
6.   Sesame seed oil infused with Dattura (Datura Stramonium) seeds.
7.   Kalasha pitcher symbolises the seven sacred rivers ie: Yamuna, Ganga, Saraswathi, Godavari, Narmada, Sindhu and Kaveri.
8.   Pañca = five, amrita = nectar.
9.   Usually buffalo curd.
10. An epithet of Śiva; see Ardra Nakshatra in Section 27.6.
11. Taken from the Krishna Yajur Veda and dedicated to Lord Rudra.
12. Comprising eleven anuvāk (chapters) from Śrī Rudram, each chanted for immediate/specific results. The first anuvāk seeks the absolution of all sin, alleviation from droughts and famine, the protection of one's cattle, the removal of evil spirits and monsters, the loss of disease and the abating of malefic rays from the grahas and stars.
13. Comprising eleven anuvāk from Śrī Rudram; chanted for long-term wishes and fulfilment of desires, that is, longevity, moksha, worldly contentment and the cessation of suffering.

33

PACIFYING GRAHAS
(Daily Routines and Rituals)

The evil effects of malefic aspects may be warded off by the worship of gods and the intervention of Brahmins, by propitiatory ceremonies, Japa (the recitation of holy mantra), observances, gifts, self-control and speaking to or association with Brahmins.

Brihat Saṃhitā

The following represents a kind of 'belt and braces' approach to planetary propitiation but is nonetheless an important aspect of this work. There are literally hundreds of recommended devotional acts, both passive and interactive, advised for the appeasement or attentions of a planetary lord – far more than can be enumerated here. Those wishing to explore this fascinating area of astrological techniques are advised to consult such accomplished works as *Lal Kitab* (also spelt Laal Kitaab).

Perhaps the most effective part of a daily routine is its focus on creating a bond between the individual and a particular planet. Pooja and Yagyas often have an initial 'dramatic' result but their effect, like sound waves, eventually dissipates over time, requiring a periodic top-up. The focus therefore of the daily routine/ritual is to preserve that harmonic, making sure it continues to be broadcast over greater periods, albeit of lower intensity.

Pacifying grahas

Grahas/ Planets	Activity and Day
Sûrya/Sun	*Sunday:* Charitable acts, fasting, Agnī hotra, offerings of wheat, saffron, red roses, jaggery or honey in a golden-coloured vessel. Construction of a small shrine dedicated to Sûrya in the southern corner of the home should be decorated with orange coloured fabric. Meditation/prayer should be observed at 12 noon. Scented water in a copper vessel may also be presented. *Promotes:* Absorption of prāṇa and the enkindling of digestive fire (Agnī). *Strengthens:* The heart, small intestine, blood vessels, bones and eyesight. *Mantra:* AUM SURYAYA NAMAHA or AUM GHRINI SURYAYA NAMAHA – chanted 108 times at sunrise on Sunday.
Chandra/ Moon	*Monday:* Devotional acts, fasting, food donations, offerings of milk, white rice, honey or white roses. In some instances Sindoora[1] will be offered along with a conch shell. Construction of a small shrine dedicated to Chandra in the northern corner of the home decorated with light blue fabrics, meditation or prayer at sunset, the wearing of silver, pearls or moonstone. Kheer[2] is also recommended to be made and offered during puranmashi.[3] *Promotes:* Longevity, rejuvenation and peace of mind. *Strengthens:* Blood, eyesight, stomach, lungs and digestive system. *Mantra:* AUM SOM SOMAYA NAMAHA – chanted 108 times at sunrise on Monday.
Kuja/Mars	*Tuesday:* Physical training, fasting, offerings of barley or masoor dal. Construction of a small shrine dedicated to Kuja in the southern corner of the home decorated with vermilion-coloured fabrics, meditation, prayer at sunrise, the wearing of magnetic iron ore, silver, red coral, red agate, carnelian or spinel. *Promotes:* Wound healing (reduces scarring), physical prowess (speed and agility), cunning, courage and strength. *Strengthens:* Muscle, haemoglobin, marrow, ligaments and sinew. *Mantra:* AUM KUJAYA NAMAHA or AUM KRAN KRIN KRON SAH BHAUMAYA NAMAH – chanted 108 times at sunrise on Tuesday.
Budha/ Mercury	*Wednesday:* Astrology, fasting, offerings of mung dhal, millet, green lentil, tulsi[4] leaf or pumpkin seeds. Construction of a small shrine dedicated to Budha in the eastern corner of the home decorated with emerald-green fabrics, meditation or prayer at sunrise, the wearing of silver, platinum, emerald, peridot or jade. *Promotes:* Intellect, discrimination, quality of speech (eloquence and vocabulary), lustre of skin, dexterity of hands and general rasāyana. *Strengthens:* Nervous system, lungs, skin and mucus membranes. *Mantra:* AUM BUDHAYA NAMAHA or AUM BRAN BRIN BRON SAH BUDHAYA NAMAH – chanted 108 times at sunrise on Wednesday.

Brihaspati/ Jupiter	*Thursday:* Study of scripture, pooja, fasting, offerings of rye, saffron, turmeric gram dhal or ghee. Construction of a small shrine dedicated to Jupiter in the eastern corner of the home decorated with yellow/orange silks or fine yellow fabrics, meditation or prayer at sunrise, the wearing of gold, yellow sapphire, topaz or citrine.
	Promotes: Wisdom, intelligence, devotion and physical endurance, reduction of negative astrological forces (Jupiter is the great benefic), lubrication and lustre of the tissues.
	Strengthens: Liver, gallbladder, glandular system, synovial joints and cartilage.
	Mantra: AUM BRIM BRAHASPATYA NAMAHA – chanted 108 times at sunrise on Thursday.
Shukra/ Venus	*Friday:* Music or art therapy, offerings of oats, cream, yoghurt, jaggery, misri (crystallised sugar) and white sesame seeds. Construction of a small shrine dedicated to Shukra in the northern corner of the home decorated with fine white silks or white fabric, meditation or prayer in the evenings, the wearing of silver, platinum, diamonds or clear quartz.
	Promotes: Fertility (both male and female), beauty and strength of eyes, youthful looks, supple limbs, lustre of skin and ojas.
	Strengthens: Reproductive secretions (semen/ovum), kidneys and urinary systems, eyesight and general immunity.
	Mantra: AUM SHUKRAN SHUKRAYA NAMAHA – chanted 108 times at sunrise on Friday.
Shani/ Saturn	*Saturday:* Work upon the land (sowing/harvesting), fasting and service to the elderly, devotion to Hanuman, offerings of black sesame, mustard seed, urad dal, gangajal[5] or soot, the feeding of crows and burning of sarsoon oil[6] and the donation of goods to charitable causes. Construction of a small shrine dedicated to Shani in the western corner of the home decorated with dark blue or heavy coarse fabrics, meditation or prayer at sunrise, the wearing of stainless steel, pañca loha, blue sapphires or amethyst. Sesame oil/ghee lamps, the wearing of dark clothing.
	Promotes: Endurance, strength, tolerance, detachment, devotion and relief from suffering and pain.
	Strengthens: Colon, teeth, bones, joints and ability to expel āma from the body.
	Mantra: AUM SHAN SHANAISCHARAYA NAMAHA – chanted 108 times at sunrise on Saturday.
Rāhu and Ketu	*Rāhu (Saturday), Ketu (Tuesday):* For propitiation of the lunar nodes see Saturn for Rāhu and Mars for Ketu. Service or devotional acts given to the nodes will also strengthen any associated planet/s. As both nodes are airy in nature their propitiation will tend to have the most effect upon bodily systems and organs dominated by Vāta dosha.
	Offerings of special note: Foods cooked in a black iron pan, jau (barley) dough balls, Krishna dattura, a mirror and dark blue cloth (for Rāhu).
	Ganesha Puja: Black and white til (sesame seeds) mixed or conch shell (for Ketu).
	Mantra for Rāhu: AUM RAM RAHAVE NAMAHA – chanted 108 times at sunrise on Saturday.
	Mantra for Ketu: AUM KE KETAVE NAMAHA – chanted 108 times at sunrise on Tuesday.

NOTES

1. Sindoora might be a number of materials including mercuric sulphide (HgS), red lead oxide (Pb_3O_4) or quicklime and turmeric.
2. Milk pudding made from white rice, wheat or tapioca.
3. Full Moon day.
4. *Ocimum tenuiflorum*.
5. Water from the Ganges.
6. Mustard seed oil.

34

—— BALI/SHANTI KARMA ——

Ceylon 1925: Malkaruge, a man of some influence in his village, was blessed with the birth of a son. Wishing to ascertain the child's fate in the world he decided to consult a well-known astrologer. Having never required this service himself (and being of a sceptical nature) Malkaruge resolved to test the astrologer by substituting his son's birth-time for that of a cat which had recently given birth. Pondering the horoscope presented to him, the astrologer queried Malkaruge saying, 'Such a time is not possible for a human – this moment has been reserved for an animal.[1] The time you have given me is incorrect – do you seek to test me?'

Recollections of Malkaruge by his great-grandson

Mitigation of negative forces emitted by planets is called *graha-apala* and is dealt with in some considerable depth by Śrī Lankān astrologers. This unwanted attention force is commonly addressed through a ceremony known as *Bali*[2] (pronounced Ba-lī) a word meaning 'offering to god'.

Bali is curious mixture of indigenous folk-religion and Theravada Buddhism, combined in such a way as to ward off negative planetary influences. The outcome of this alliance is a type of *folk-Buddhism* with its fusion of karma, rebirth and nibbāna. Many (if not most) of the island's supernatural demons, be they animal sprits or demigods, have been yoked and in some cases recruited into the Buddhist pantheon, elevated to the role of a bodhisattva.[3]

Astrology is a highly popular subject with the Śrī Lankān population, many of whom wear some order of astrological gemstone or protective talisman. This has in no small way allowed the planets to fall under the influence of Buddha,[4] who is primarily called upon during Bali to oversee the planets' invocation and manifestation during the ceremony.

The actual Bali ceremony consists largely of blessings and the recitation of Buddhist stanzas,[5] accompanied by the wearing of bright costumes, anklets, headdresses and decorative jewellery – along with rhythmical hypnotic percussion. Ancillary offerings introduced during the ceremony include coconuts, coconut oil, palm leaves, rice, plantain stems, betel nuts/leaves, roasted foods and limes.

Performed at dusk in a specially constructed pavilion, Bali usually requires the attendance of immediate family and/or close friends.[6] The patient or *āturaya* sits close to the officiate or *bali-edura* while he extols salutary Buddhist verses and introduces the planets most prevalent in the coming ritual. It is explained to the assembled that due to various misfortunes the patient has requested Bali to help appease the malefic forces responsible for his or her miseries. He then unveils beautifully painted clay/bamboo effigies representative of each graha (constructed anew each time for individualised ceremonies). Each of these life-size figures is dressed, coloured and decorated with its respective planetary yantra, astride its common *vāhan* (vehicle) and brandishing its preferred weapon. To one side of these figurines a live cock is ceremonially bound by its feet and tied close to the deities; it is believed that any negative influences exorcised from the patient will be transferred into the animal.[7]

Flaming torches illuminate the proceedings with intermittent flares produced by rosin powder thrown onto open fires called graha-puṭa along with various food offerings. A number of highly aromatic oils are also burnt during the proceedings in preparation for the exorcism of the patient. One of the principal aims of these ceremonies is to collectively alleviate the patient from the dreaded cohorts of *sora*, *hora*, *saturu* and *bhaya*, that is, thieves, robbery, enemies and fear.

Bali ceremonies can take a number of days to complete, each time abating just before the dawn. Upon conclusion its figurines, pavilion and altars are disassembled and removed to a locale known to be frequented by evil spirits. Here they are left to degrade and return to the ground from which they sprang, absorbing any remaining negativity.

Bali is almost exclusively performed for the pacification of malefic grahas[8] boasting some 13,000+ different forms, each variation designed to tackle the most challenging and complex of astrological configurations.

The following nine tables outline appropiate Bali ceremonies, yantra, mantra and items of propitiation awarded each planet during *graha-apala*.

Ravi – Sun

1	Bali/Shanti Karma	Sûryawansa Baliya
2	Protective Deities	Śiva/Mahā Bhairava Devata
3	Sacred Flowers	Moonamal (Indian medlar[9]) and rathu nelum[10] (red lotus)
4	Graha Dhana (offerings)	Ruby, orange/red cloth, red sandalwood paste, red lotus, gold metal fashioned into a lotus, jaggery, wheat and lentils
5	Metals	Swarna (gold) and Pittala (brass)
6	Gems	Padmaraga (ruby) and Sûryakānta (sunstone)
7	Herbs	Ela, devadaru, yastimadhu, raphu nelum, savandara, kumkumapu, kumbuk and sapumal
8	Mineral	Manah Sila (realgar)
9	Yantra	Śiva-Sûrya Mandala, Sûrya Mandala Yantra
10	Sacred Tree	Kapu-imbul (red cotton tree)
11	Day/Direction of Rulership	Irida (Sunday) and East
12	Planetary Mantra	'Om Ravivare Sûrya avatare murtunjaya siddhi siddhī eswaha'

ඕම් රවි වාරේ සූර්ය අවතාරේ මුර්තුන්ජය සිද්දි සිද්දි ඒස්වහඃ

Sandhu – Moon

1	Bali/Shanti Karma	Somaratna Raksha Baliya
2	Protective Deities	Maha Brahmā, Chandā Bhairava Devata
3	Sacred Flowers	Saman pichha (jasmine), sudu nelum (white lotus) and sudu attana (white dattura)
4	Graha Dhana (offerings)	Silver fashioned into a bo-leaf, mother of pearl, conch, elephant tusk, cows' urine, camphor, white rice, ghee, yoghurt, milk, buttermilk and white cotton cloth
5	Metals	Swarna (gold) and Rajata (silver)
6	Gems	Muthu (pearl) and Chandrakānta (moonstone)
7	Herbs	Shatavari, bala, saman pichha, sudu nelum and sudu aptana
8	Mineral	Calcite (surama sapheda), godanti haritala (selenite), gouripashana (white arsenic) and sudha (calcium carbonate)
9	Yantra	Sadu Chandra Navagraha Yantra, Chandra Mala Yantra and Ratana Yantra
10	Sacred Tree	Kapu-imbul (red cotton tree)
11	Day/Direction of Rulership	Sandhuda (Monday) and North West
12	Planetary Mantra	'Om Somavare Chandra avatare murtunjaya siddhi siddhī eswaha'

ඕම් සෝම වාරේ චන්දු අවතාරේ මුර්තුන්ජය සිද්දි සිද්දි ඒස්වහඃ

Budha – Mercury

1	Bali/Shanti Karma	Pārvatī Kalyana Baliya
2	Protective Deities	Vishnu, Samhāra Bhairava Devata
3	Sacred Flowers	Tala (sesame) and nāmal (cobra saffron flowers)
4	Graha Dhana (offerings)	Dark green cloth, elephant tusk, perfumes, ghee, paddy rice, goats milk and mung dhal
5	Metals	Pārada (mercury), Swarna (gold), Rajata (silver) and Lokada (bell metal)
6	Gems	Tarksya (emerald), puttikā (peridot) and vaikranta (green tourmaline)
7	Herbs	Tala, nāmal, gotu kola, tulsi and bhringaraj
8	Mineral	Pirojaka (turquoise), pīlu (green jade), malachite and ilmenite (green sand)
9	Yantra	Budha Vishnu Mandala Yantra, Vishnu Agora Yantra
10	Sacred Tree	Castor tree
11	Day/Direction of Rulership	Badada (Wednesday) and North
12	Planetary Mantra	'Om Budhavare Brahmā avatare murtunjaya siddhi siddhī eswaha'

ඕම් බුධ වාරේ බුහ්ම අවතාරේ මූර්තුන්ජය සිද්දි සිද්දි ඒස්වහඃ

Kuja – Mars

1	Bali/Shanti Karma	Kuja Dosha Bhuma Naga Baliya
2	Protective Deities	Kataragama, Beeshāna Bhairava Devata
3	Sacred Flowers	All red flowers
4	Graha Dhana (offerings)	Sugandhikam,[11] dark red cloth, sorrel, barley, jaggery and red lentils
5	Metals	Loha (iron), Kantapashana (black magnetic iron ore) and Tamra (Copper)
6	Gems	Pravala (red coral) and spinel
7	Herbs	Beli, bala, hingu, jatamansi, kurundu, rukmal, gammiris, moonamal, guggulu and kaneru (karaveera[12])
8	Mineral	Akika (agate), Rudhiram (carnelian), Gaireeka (red iron oxide)
9	Yantra	Abisambidana Yantra, Skandakumara Yantra
10	Sacred Tree	Kolon[13] tree (haldu)
11	Day/Direction of Rulership	Angaharuada (Tuesday) and South
12	Planetary Mantra	'Om Kujavare Antara avatare murtunjaya siddhi siddhī eswaha'

ඕම් කුජ වාරේ අංතර අවතාරේ මූර්තුන්ජය සිද්දි සිද්දි ඒස්වහඃ

Brihaspati – Jupiter

1	Bali/Shanti Karma	Abhaya Kalyana Baliya
2	Protective Deities	Śiva, Shanta Bhairava Devata
3	Sacred Flowers	Beli, all yellow flowers
4	Graha Dhana (offerings)	Horses, elephants, ivory, yellow cotton cloth, jaggery, honey, turmeric, yellow pulses and onion flowers
5	Metals	Vanga (tin) and Swarna (gold)
6	Gems	Peela pukhraj (yellow sapphire), pushparaga (topaz), spaṭika (yellow quartz/citrine)
7	Herbs	Saman pichha, sudu aba, idda mal leaves, yastimadhu, ashwaganda and tala
8	Mineral	Kaharuba (amber)
9	Yantra	Narasiha Yantra
10	Sacred Tree	Bodhi[14] tree
11	Day/Direction of Rulership	Brahaspatinda (Thursday) and North East
12	Planetary Mantra	'Om Guruvare archarya avatare murtunjaya siddhi siddhī eswaha'

ඕම් ගුරු වාරේ ආචාර්ය අවතාරේ මූර්තුන්ජය සිද්දි සිද්දි ඒස්වහඃ

Sikuru – Venus

1	Bali/Shanti Karma	Deva Mangala Baliya
2	Protective Deities	Pārvatī Devi, Unmatta Bhairava Devata
3	Sacred Flowers	Kesharamal, all fragrant flowers
4	Graha Dhana (offerings)	Gemstones, brightly coloured clothes, white rice, ghee, jaggery and perfumes
5	Metals	Tamra (copper), Yasada (zinc) and Rajata (silver)
6	Gems	Hiraka (diamond), sudha pukhraj (white sapphire) and spaṭika (clear quartz)
7	Herbs	Elā, kumkuma, shatavari, nelli (amalaki), sudu rosa and safed musali[15]
8	Mineral	Manah Sila (realgar), rasaka (calamine)
9	Yantra	Sanjeewani Yantra, Navanata Yantra
10	Sacred Tree	Karanda[16] tree
11	Day/Direction of Rulership	Sikurāda (Friday) and South East
12	Planetary Mantra	'Om Shukravare kivi avatare murtunjaya siddhi siddhī eswaha'

ඕම් ශුක්‍ර වාරේ කිවි අවතාරේ මූර්තුන්ජය සිද්දි සිද්දි ඒස්වහඃ

Shani – Saturn

1	Bali/Shanti Karma	Dasakroda Raksha Baliya
2	Protective Deities	Vishnu, Kala Bhairava Devata
3	Sacred Flowers	Lokmal, all blue flowers
4	Graha Dhana (offerings)	Blue gems, metal vessels, coarse black/dark blue cloth, loksumbhulu (soot/coal dust), buffalo milk, kalu tala (black sesame seeds) and kollu (horsegram); for special effect feed red rice cooked in milk and ghee to crows
5	Metals	Naga (lead) and Loha (iron)
6	Gems	Nilama (blue sapphire), katella (blue amethyst), pachcha padian (aquamarine)
7	Herbs	Satakuppa, tala, babila, triphala and guggulu
8	Mineral	Lapis lazuli, shilajit, jet and black tourmaline
9	Yantra	Maha Vishnu Mandala Yantra, Nila Mandala, Vishnu Āgoraya Yantra
10	Sacred Tree	Nuga[17] tree
11	Day/Direction of Rulership	Senasurāda (Saturday) and West
12	Planetary Mantra	'Om Shanivare sarpa avatare murtunjaya siddhi siddhī eswaha'
		ඕම් ශනි වාරේ සර්ප අවතාරේ මුර්තුන්ජය සිද්දි සිද්දි ඒස්වභඃ

Rāhu – North Node

1	Bali/Shanti Karma	Krishna Raksha Baliya
2	Protective Deities	Śiva, Rûdaya Bhairava Devata
3	Sacred Flowers	See Saturn
4	Graha Dhana (offerings)	A serpent made from gold, elephant tusks, black horses, meat from a black goat, kasturi (musk gland), camphor, buffalo milk, goats milk, coarse black/dark blue cloth and iron vessels
5	Metals	Pittala (brass) and loha (iron)
6	Gems	Gomeda (garnet/hessonite)
7	Herbs	Eethana, tala, kolon leaves, kalanduru, vaccha and sandalwood
8	Mineral	As Saturn
9	Yantra	Nāgārjuna Yantra
10	Sacred Tree	Vetaḱe (a type of tall reed used in basket making)
11	Day/Direction of Rulership	As Saturn (Saturday) and South West
12	Planetary Mantra	'Om Rāhuvare ausura-Indrā avatare murtunjaya siddhi siddhī eswaha'
		ඕම් රාහු වාරේ අසුරේන්ද අවතාරේ මුර්තුන්ජය සිද්දි සිද්දි ඒස්වභඃ

Ketu – South Node

1	Bali/Shanti Karma	Asura Mangla Baliya
2	Protective Deities	Vishnu, Patāla Bhairava Devata
3	Sacred Flowers	As Mars
4	Graha Dhana (offerings)	A serpent made from gold, sesame oil, tala seeds, kasturi, cows' urine, goats' milk, clothes made from goats' skin/fur, copper vessels
5	Metals	Kansya (bronze) and Pasloha (5 alloys)
6	Gems	Vaiduryam (beryl/cat's eye)
7	Herbs	Tala, eethana (conch grass), kolon leaves, kalanduru (musta), vaccha (calamus), ginger and bhringaraj
8	Mineral	See Mars
9	Yantra	Aghora Yantra, Nagamala Yantra, Pātāla Mrityunjaya Yantra
10	Sacred Tree	Plantain tree
11	Day/Direction of Rulership	As Mars (Tuesday) and South West
12	Planetary Mantra	'Om Ketuvare kitravarṇa avatare murtunjaya siddhi siddhī eswaha'
		ඕම් කේතු වාරේ කිතුවර්ණ අවතාරේ මූර්තුන්ජය සිද්දි සිද්දි ඒස්වහඃ

In instances of extreme affliction (even life-threatening emergencies) it may be deemed necessary to propitiate all nine planets in a ceremony known as Nava Graha Baliya. Its corresponding mantra reads:

'Om namagraha mandale navagraha murtunjaya siddhi siddhī eswaha'

ඕම් නමෝ නමගුහ මන්ඩලේ නවගුහ මූර්තුන්ජය සිද්දි සිද්දි ඒස්වහඃ

For corresponding yantra see the image on the following page.

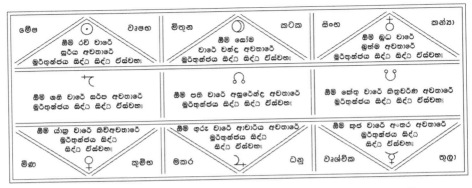

Navagraha Yantra: Top (left to right) SUN – MOON – MARS; middle (left to right) SATURN – RĀHU – KETU; bottom (left to right) VENUS – JUPITER – MERCURY. The twelve Rashis sequence appears either side of the planetary glyphs (upper and lower row), starting with Aries top left and finishing with Pisces lower left.

NOTES

1. Sarvartha Chintamani (shining thoughts, regarding all matters) c. AD 1300 notes that 1st and 4th lords in mutual reception or 1st or 4th lords situated with either of the lunar nodes denote a yoga for animal birth.
2. Bali-ya ceremonies are more popular in the island's southerly regions.
3. One who aspires to Buddhahood.
4. The planets became more prominent in Buddhism during the 8th–9th century AD (see Tejaprabha Buddha, Lord of Constellations).
5. Poetical verse commonly arranged in a recurring metrical unit.
6. Young girls close to puberty, or those that have recently fallen pregnant, are excluded from these ceremonies. It is thought that exorcised malefic spirits lurk in the vicinity and attach themselves to the youths or foetus.
7. In some instances animals/birds are sacrificed, their blood offered during the ceremony.
8. Bali and Tovil (devil dancing) are believed to rout ghosts, demons and other nefarious nature spirits.
9. *Mimusops elengi* Linn.
10. *Nelumbo nucifera.*
11. Another name for red spinel ($MgAl_2O_4$).
12. *Nerium oleander* (Indian oleander).
13. *Haldina cordifolia.*
14. *Ficus religiosa.*
15. *Chlorophytum borivilianum.*
16. *Carissa carandas.*
17. *Ficus benghalensis* (Indian banyan).

IN CONCLUSION

Recent decades have shown a surge of interest in all areas of occult sciences; perhaps none more so than in astrology itself, deemed Queen of occult sciences. This reawakening has also stirred considerable curiosity in Vedic teaching, not only Jyotish but in all of its sister-sciences such as Āyurveda, Vāstu, Rasa Shāstra, Yoga and more. Each year, high-street and cyber bookshelves increasingly expand with new gems on these very topics, feeding an ever hungrier (and discerning) audience of knowledge seekers.

In this book I have tried to give some account of the astrological richness embedded in Jyotish. I am therefore hopeful that the information contained herein may inspire others to explore mankind's first revelation of our true place amongst the stars. I leave the reader with a final inspirational quote from *Yajur Veda*:

Explore the sky and be blessed with good fortune.

APPENDIX

1. QUICK REFERENCE GUIDE – PLANETS AT A GLANCE

Quick Reference I

Planet	Celestial Court	Element	Dosha	Guna	Gains Strength
Sun	King	Fire	Pitta	Sattvic	South
Moon	Queen	Water	Kapha/Vāta	Sattvic	North
Mercury	Regent	Earth	Tri-dosha	Rajas	East
Mars	Commander-in-chief	Fire	Pitta	Tamas	South
Jupiter	Minister	Æther	Kapha	Sattvic	East
Venus	Minister	Water	Kapha/Vāta	Rajas	North
Saturn	Servants	Air	Vāta	Tamas	West
Rāhu	Militia/outlaws	–	Vāta	Tamas	–
Ketu	Militia/beggars	–	Vāta	Tamas	–

Quick Reference II

Planet	Direction	Character	Kāraka	Health/Body	Metal
Sun	East	Dignified, regal	Atma/soul	Prāṇa, heart, small intestine, bones, teeth and eyes	Gold
Moon	North-west	Mild and gentle	Mind/emotions	Blood, stomach, breast, lungs, eyes and bodily secretions	Silver
Mercury	North	Communicative yet humorous	Speech/intelligence	Nervous system, skin and lungs	Mercury
Mars	South	Martial yet philanthropic	Courage/strength	Muscle, ligaments, tendons, blood (haemoglobin)	Iron
Jupiter	North-east	Generous, learned and expansive	Wisdom/fortunes	Fat, liver, gallbladder, pancreas, circulatory system	Tin

Venus	South-east	Flattering yet pleasure seeking	Desires/ yearnings	Reproductive tissues, bladder, kidneys and pancreas	Copper
Saturn	West	Hardworking, mean and uncompromising	Sorrow/ misfortune	Marrow, skeletal frame, joints (large and small), colon and excretory organs	Lead
Rāhu	South-west	Future orientated and irreligious	Addictions	As Saturn	Brass
Ketu	South-west	Reclusive, rebellious and reckless	Non-attachment	As Mars	Bronze

Quick Reference III

Planet	Deity	Complexion	Glances	Season	Time Period
Sun	Śiva/Rudra/ Agni	Blood red	Upward	Summer	Solstial (6 months)
Moon	Gauri/Apas	Tawny	Forward	Monsoon	48 minutes (1 muhūrta)
Mercury	Narasimha/ Narayana	Grass green	Sideways	Autumn	Seasonal (2 months)
Mars	Karttikeya/ Hanuman/ Bhumi	Reddish	Upward	Summer	1 day (dina)
Jupiter	Brihaspati/ Brahmā/ Indrā	Tawny	Forward	Pre-winter	1 month
Venus	Lakṣmī/ Shachi (Indrānī)	Variegated	Sideways	Spring	15 days (paksha)
Saturn	Yamaraj	Dark or indescribable	Obliquely	Winter	1 year
Rāhu	Sarpa	As Saturn	Downward	As Saturn	1 year
Ketu	Ganapati/ Chitrāgupta	As Mars	Downward	As Mars	–

Quick Reference IV

Planet	Gemstone	Grains/Seeds	Motifs	Taste	Height
Sun	Ruby, sunstone	Wheat	Circle	Bitter	Average
Moon	Pearl, moonstone	White rice	Square	Salty	Short
Mercury	Emerald, peridot, green tourmaline	Millet/mung beans	Arrow	Shad-rasa	Average

Planet	Gemstone	Grains/Seeds	Motifs	Taste	Height
Mars	Red coral, red agate, carnelian	Barley	Triangle	Pungent	Short
Jupiter	Yellow sapphire, topaz, yellow citrine	Saffron	Rectangle	Sweet	Tall
Venus	Diamond, clear quartz	Oats	Pentagram	Sour	Average
Saturn	Blue sapphire, blue amethyst, aquamarine	Black sesame seeds/maize	Archway	Astringent	Tall
Rāhu	Red garnet (known as cinnamon stone)	As Saturn	Winnowing basket	–	Tall
Ketu	Chrysoberyl (known as cat's eye)	As Mars	Flag	–	Average

Quick Reference V

Planet	Means of Death	Abodes	Structures	Planetary ages	Planetary inclinations
Sun	Fevers, fires or weapons, death in governmental state/owned buildings, etc.	Wooden framed and/or thatched buildings, airy, with well-lit interiors.	Palaces, temples, royal gardens and parks.	50 years of age	Vedas, medicine, alchemy, statistics and law.
Moon	Cholera, nephritis and tuberculosis. Death connected to fluids (excess phlegm) or water (drowning), etc.	Terraced or walled enclosures artistically rendered with decorative brickwork. Buildings have multiple access points.	Lakes, ponds, wells and marinas.	70 years of age	Fine art, fictional literature, decorative arts and textiles, etc.
Mercury	Nervous system, lungs, leprosy or madness, injury to neck or spine, death occurs whilst travelling or engaged in business matters, etc.	Tidy accommodation, airy or minimalist with multiple labour saving devices.	Market places, ports, centres of trade, etc.	Teenager	Science, medicine, astrology/astronomy, geography, economics, communication, trade and law.

Mars	Blood poisoning, fevers, weapons, inflammation, witchcraft and accidents, death during surgery or in places of conflict.	High-walled (strong) buildings with few windows and minimal access.	Forts, keeps, vaults, barracks and surgeries.	Young child	The art of war, weapons, martial arts, metalcraft, minerals, law, code-breaking, survival and hunting.
Jupiter	Obesity, high cholesterol, watery diseases and choking, etc. Jupiter gives a quick and painless death in good company.	Strong wooden construction, with ample light and comforts. Spaces may contain religious artwork or sculptures, etc.	Sites of pilgrimage, places of worship, temples and sanctuaries.	30 years of age	Religious works, classics (fiction and non-fiction), grand architecture, administration (civil servants).
Venus	Ojaksaya (failure of immune system), syphilis, diabetes, etc. Death in comfortable or luxurious property surrounded by loved ones.	Terraced or walled enclosures artistically rendered with decorative brickwork. Buildings have multiple access points.	Luxury apartments, country estates, walled gardens, beauty parlours and brothels.	20 years of age	Fine art, poetry, romantic fiction, occult/magic, decorative, fashion, perfumes and textiles, etc.
Saturn	Necrosis of tissue, injury from falling, accidents in the workplace, industrial accidents, etc. Death occurs in solitary or rundown surroundings, etc.	Heavy stone construction subject to cracking or damp. Dark interiors, smelling slightly of decaying food.	Graveyards, morticians, ghettos, sewers, slaughter houses, agricultural lands.	100 years of age	Old books, iron goods, agriculture, survival techniques, underworld activities, theft, cremation of the dead, graveyards and worldly renunciation.

Planet	Means of Death	Abodes	Structures	Planetary ages	Planetary inclinations
Rāhu	Poisoning, snakebite, falling from great heights, beheading (capital punishment), death in foreign lands, etc.	As Saturn	As Saturn	100 years of age	Science, chemistry, poisons, forbidden knowledge (alchemy), hieratical religious works, prophecies and astrology, etc.
Ketu	Poisoning, insect bites, infection from animal bites, hanging (capital punishment) beatings, death in foreign lands, etc.	As Mars	As Mars	100 years of age	Occult knowledge and renunciation, chemistry, plagues, catastrophes and rebellion.

2. NAKSHATRA YOGATÂRÂ

The Nakshatra/Yogatârâ table complements the information presented in Section 1.4. This table details Nakshatra attributes and symbology, degrees of individual Nakshatra and associated stars within that asterism.

Nakshatra/Yogatârâ table

Nakshatras' Attribute and Symbol	From	To	Yogatârâ	Asterism
Ashwini/Swiftness (horse's head)	0° Aries	13° 20' Aries	β Arietis/Sheratan	β and γ¹ Arietis
Bharani/ Bearing away (womb)	13° 20' Aries	26° 40' Aries	35 Arietis/Musca Borealis	35, 39, 41 Arietis
Krittika/To cut (arrow in flight)	26° 40' Aries	10° 00' Taurus	η Tauri/Alcyone	η, 27, 23, 20, 19 and 17 Tauri
Rohini/The ruddy one (carriage)	10° 00' Taurus	23° 20' Taurus	α Tauri/Aldebaran	α, θ1, θ2, γ, δ and ε Tauri

Mrigashirsha/ Searching star (deer's head)	23° 20' Taurus	6° 40' Gemini	λ Orionis/Meissa	λ, φ1, φ2 Orionis
Ardra/Moistening (teardrop/head)	6° 40' Gemini	20° 00' Gemini	α Orionis/ Betelgeuse	α Orionis and 134/135 Tauri
Punarvasu/Star of renewal (bow)	20° 00' Gemini	3° 20' Cancer	β Geminorum/ Pollux	β and α Gemini
Pushyami/The nourisher (arrowhead/flower)	3° 20' Cancer	16° 40' Cancer	δ Cancri/Asellus Australis	δ, γ, θ Cancri
Aslesha/Entwiner (serpent)	16° 40' Cancer	30° Cancer	ε Hydrae	ε, δ, σ, η, ρ, ζ Hydrae
Magha/The Mighty (crown or throne)	0° Leo	13° 20' Leo	α Leonis/Regulas	α, η, γ1, ζ, μ, ε and o Leonis
Purvaphalguni/ Former reddish one (Fireplace/hammock)	13° 20' Leo	26° 40' Leo	δ Leonis/Zosma	δ and θ Leonis
Uttaraphalguni/ Latter reddish one (hammock)	26° 40' Leo	10° 00' Virgo	β Leonis/Denebola	β and 93 Leonis
Hastā/The hand (a hand)	10° 00' Virgo	23° 20' Virgo	δ Corvi/Algorab	δ, γ, ε, α, β and η Corvi
Chitrā/Craftsman (pearl/jewel)	23° 20' Virgo	6° 40' Libra	α Virginis/Spica	α and ζ Virginis
Swati/Self-reliance (coral polyp)	6° 40' Libra	20° 00' Libra	α Bootis/Arcturus	α and ε Bootis
Vishaka/Star of purpose (potter's wheel)	20° 00' Libra	3° 20' Scorpio	ι Libræ²	ι, α, β and σ Libræ
Anuradha/Star of success (lotus flower)	3° 20' Scorpio	16° 40' Scorpio	δ Scorpii/ Dschubba	δ, β1/β2, and π Scorpii
Jyestha/Most senior (talisman/earring)	16° 40' Scorpio	30° Scorpio	α Scorpionis/ Antares	α, σ and τ Scorpionis
Mula/Root (elephant goad)	0° Sagittarius	13° 20' Sagittarius	λ Scorpionis/ Shaula	λ, υ, ι, κ, θ and η Scorpionis
Purvashadha/Earlier unsubdued (elephant tusk)	13° 20' Sagittarius	26° 40' Sagittarius	δ Sagittarii/Kaus Meridionalis	δ, ε, η and λ Sagittarii
Uttarashadha/Later unsubdued (wooden cot)	26° 40' Sagittarius	10° 00' Capricorn	σ Sagittarii/Nunki	σ, ζ and τ Sagittarii
Śravana/Star of listening (an ear)	10° 00' Capricorn	23° 20' Capricorn	α Aquilae/Altair	α, β and γ Aquilae

Nakshatras' Attribute and Symbol	From	To	Yogatârâ	Asterism
Dhanistha (damarū)	23° 20' Capricorn	6° 40' Aquarius	β Delphini/ Rotanev	β, α, γ and δ Delphini
Shatabhishak/ Veiling star (lotus)	6° 40' Aquarius	20° 00' Aquarius	λ Aquarii/Hydor	λ, τ, δ, η, ζ, γ and α Aquarii
Purvabhadra/Former auspicious one (two-faced man)	20° 00' Aquarius	3° 20' Pisces	α Pegasi/Markab	α and β Pegasi
Uttarabhadra/Latter auspicious one (sword)	3° 20' Pisces	16° 40' Pisces	γ Pegasi/Algenib	γ Pegasi and α Andromedae
Revati/The wealthy (fish or drum)	16° 40' Pisces	30° Pisces	ζ Piscium/Zidadh	ζ, ε and δ Piscium

Abhijit – intercalary Nakshatra (Śṛṅgāta[3])	α Lyrae/Vega	α, ε and ζ Lyrae

3. PLANETARY SIGN GLYPHS

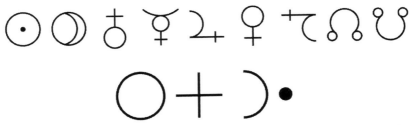

Planetary glyphs from left to right: Sun, Moon, Mars, Mercury, Jupiter, Venus, Saturn, Rāhu and Ketu. All are constructed from a circle, cross, curve and dot. Glyphs are also ordered into four pairs of opposites, that is, Sun/Moon, Mars/Venus, Jupiter/Saturn and Rāhu/Ketu. Mercury's configuration is unique, incorporating three of the four building blocks, perhaps reflecting its Tri-doshic nature and outstanding alchemical significance as 'Master Metal' (Hg).

Although not traditionally used in Jyotish, I have made use of the astrological glyphs[4] throughout the book and feel some reference to them was appropriate. All planetary glyphs are composed of four basic elements: circles, crosses, crescents and a dot. One interpretation of these key features might be:

- Circle denotes the spirit. They have been used nine times in total: once each for Sun, Moon, Mars, Mercury and Venus, with two circles for Rāhu and Ketu.

- The crescent denotes mind. This is used six times: once each for Moon, Mercury, Jupiter and Saturn with two crescents for Rāhu and Ketu.

- Crosses denote matter and are used five times: once each for Mars, Mercury, Venus, Jupiter and Saturn.

- The dot is used singularly at the Sun's centre, denoting Atman.

Rashi glyphs in order are (left to right): Aries, Taurus, Gemini, Cancer, Leo, Virgo, Libra, Scorpio, Sagittarius, Capricorn, Aquarius and Pisces.

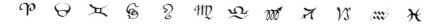

Note: Special thanks to Andrew Kirk for the use of his artistically stylised Rashi glyphs in this section.

4. STELLAR PREFIX

Many of the stellar designations used in modern astronomy are a mixture of Latin, Greek and Arabic names/letters; the following table lists the popularly used Greek alphabet along with equivalent English letters and phonetic sounds. The practice of using lower-case Greek to prefix stars was pioneered by Johann Bayer[5] (1572–1625) whose book *Uranometria* (published in 1603) promoted this particular nomenclature for star identification.

The Greek alphabet

Upper Case	Lower Case	English	English Letter	Phonetic
A	ά	Alpha	a	Al-fah
B	β	Beta	b	Bay-tah
Γ	γ	Gamma	c	Gam-ah
Δ	δ	Delta	d	Del-tah
E	ε	Epsilon	e	Ep-silon
Z	ζ	Zeta	z	Zay-tah
H	η	Eta	e	Ey-tay
Θ	θ	Theta	th	Thay-tah
I	ι	Iota	i	Eye-otah
K	κ	Kappa	k	Cap-ah
Λ	λ	Lambda	l	Lamb-da
M	μ	Mu	m	Mew
N	ν	Nu	n	Neu
Ξ	ξ	Xi	x	Zz-eye
O	o	Omicron	o	Omah-cron
Π	π	Pi	p	Pie
P	ρ	Rho	r	Row
Σ	σ	Sigma	s	Sig-ma
T	τ	Tau	t	Taw-h
Y	υ	Upsilon	u	Op-silon
Φ	φ	Phi	ph	Fye
X	χ	Chi	ch	Key
Ψ	ψ	Psi	ps	Sigh
Ω	ω	Omega	o	Omay-ga

5. RITU (SEASONAL CALENDAR)

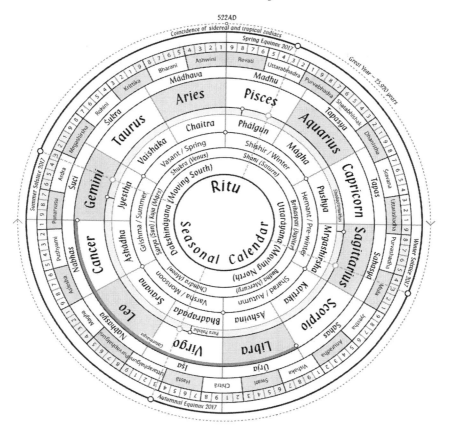

Key from the centre outwards: Uttaráyana and Dakshináyana (sun's apparent northward and southward movement toward the solstices). Planetary rulership of seasons. Six Indian seasons. Chándramása (twelve lunar months), Shaḍaçítimukhas and Pitru Paksha (set aside for civil observances). The twelve zodiacal signs. Cáturmâsya (four months set aside for Vishnu to rest). The twelve solar months, Nakshatras and Navamsha (ninth division of the 30°). The four spoked dotted lines (emanating from the centre outward) show the current positions of the solstices and equinoxes. Final outer dotted line (marked with directional arrows) indicates The Great Year (a supposed period of 25,920 years).

In India, Ritu/seasons are broken into six distinctive periods with associated planetary rulers, these being:

Shishir/winter: cold period being ruled by Saturn.

Vasant/spring: brightening period ruled by Venus.

Grishma/summer: heating period ruled by Sun and Mars.

Varsha/monsoon: rainy period ruled by Moon.

Sharad/autumn: ripened period ruled by Mercury.

Hemant/pre-winter: drying/cooling period ruled by Jupiter.

Each season encompasses two months of the year but more importantly sees the sun traverse two zodiacal signs (see calendar above). Shishir marks the start of the sáura year (sáura denoting one solar day, i.e. 1° along the ecliptic). This yearly progression not only delineates ravi-sankránti (solar transmigration through zodiacal signs) but also the solstices (ayana), equinoxes (vishuvat) and civil observances such as shadaçîtimukhas.[6] A solar year is further divided into two distinctive periods; Uttaráyana[7] and Dakshiṇáyana,[8] the former signifying the sun's six-month ascension from winter to summer solstice before starting its southern descent.

NOTES

1. γ1 (also known as Mesarthim) is the brighter of the binary pair; the combined magnitude of γ1 and γ2 is 3.8 mv.
2. Zubenelgenubi/α Libræ – α1/α2 (binary) is also considered a possible Yogatârâ for Vishaka. Both α and ι Libræ are close to the ecliptic (ι Libræ 1° 50' S and α Libræ 0° 20' N), the latter having the greater visibility. ι Libræ is thought to be a later adaptation by Hindu astronomers.
3. Triangular/pyramidal form, perhaps symbolising a special plant (soma).
4. Sanskrit letters are traditionally used in Jyotish, as Sanskrit is revered for its sacred resonances (sounds). Some modern Vedic astrologers prefer the use of astrological glyphs, as these appeal to Western tropical astrologers and are a kind of shorthand, thus are convenient.
5. The protestant lawyer from Augsburg, who remained closely aligned to the work of Tycho Brahe, tinctured with occult undertones of planetary influences upon Earthly inhabitants.
6. Shadaçitimukha – *Shadaçîti* = eighty-six and *mukha* = mouth or opening. These curious arcs of 86° commencing at the start of Libra, reoccurring at each of the dual signs: 26° Sagittarius, 22° Pisces, 18° Gemini and 14° Virgo. The remaining 16° of Virgo were considered highly auspicious for patriarchal observances. See *Pitru Paksha* within the calendar diagram.
7. Also known as Devayana (path of the Devas).
8. Also known as Pitrayana (path of the fathers).

RESOURCES

OPEN SOURCE ASTRONOMICAL SOFTWARE
Stellarium

Free open source astronomical software, Stellarium is a planetarium for your computer. It shows a realistic sky in 3D, just like you see with the naked eye, binoculars or a telescope. Stellarium runs on Windows, Linux and Mac OS X. *www.stellarium.org*

Celestia

Free open source astronomical software that lets you explore the universe in three dimensions. Celestia runs on Windows, Linux and Mac OS X. *www.shatters.net/celestia*

VEDIC ASTROLOGY SOFTWARE
Kala (Ernst Wilhelm)

Kala means 'time' the astrological force that brings events to pass. Kala is quickly becoming the premier Jyotish software, due to its greatest accuracy, ease of use and unique features. Kala has extensive calculations and easily customisable features. Kala runs in English, German, Russian, Spanish and Hungarian. *www.vedic-astrology.net*

Sri Star Jyoti Pro 7 (Andrew Foss)

Shri Jyoti Star is a powerful and elegant piece of Vedic Astrology software for both beginners and professionals, used by virtually all the leading Vedic astrologers in the West. *www.vedicsoftware.com*

Haydn's Jyotish (Haydn Huntley)

A Jyotish program that's fast, easy to use and gives you what you want. This is the software that many professional Jyotishi, including James T. Braha and Pat Hayward, actively use. There's also an option to run directly online, so no need to install. *www.hjyotish.com*

Solar Fire (marketed by Roy Gillett)

Version 9 is the world's most popular astrology software. It covers a vast range of Western techniques and many of the key Vedic ones, including six sidereal zodiacs, whole sign houses and natal and divisional Vedic charts in southern or northern square styles with dasha/bukti listings. Obtainable from Roy Gillett at www.crucialastrotools.co.uk or Astrolabe Inc. at *www.alabe.com*

VEDIC ASTROLOGERS OFFERING CONSULTATIONS

James T. Braha
jamesbraha@gmail.com

Ernst Wilhelm
ernst@vedic-astrology.net

Vaidya Ātreya Smith
contact@atreya.com

Edith Hathaway
edith@edithhathaway.com

Andrew Foss
andrew@vedicsoftware.com

Philip Weeks
philip@philipweeks.org

ĀYURVEDIC STUDY/CONSULTATIONS AND POOJA SERVICES

Dr Mauroof Athique (College of Āyurveda UK)
www.ayurvedacollege.co.uk

Dr Venkata Narayana Joshi
www.croydonayurvedacentre.co.uk

Vaidya Ātreya Smith (Āyurvedic Training)
Offering a three-level training programme to anyone interested in learning Āyurveda through advanced learning methods on an E-learning platform. Ātreya has been teaching since 1989 and his programmes are available for students all over the world.
www.atreya.com

BIBLIOGRAPHY

Adel, G.H., Elmi, M.J. and Taromi-Rad, H. (eds) (2013) *Historical Sources of the Islamic World*. London: EWI Press.

Agarwal, G.S. (1998) *Practical Vedic Astrology: A Complete Self Learning Treatise*. New Delhi: Sagar.

Agnihotri, V.K. (ed.) (2010) *Indian History (With Objective Questions and Historical Maps)* (26th Edition). New Delhi: Allied Publishers.

Allen, R.H. (1899) *Star-Names and Their Meanings*.

Angadi, R. (2014) *A Text Book of Rasa Shāstra (Iatro-Chemistry and Ayurvedic Pharmaceutics)*. Varanasi: Chaukhamba Surbharati Prakashan.

Ariyaratna, D.H. (1976) *Gems of Sri Lanka* (Seventh revised edition). Colombo: Author.

Bagnall, P.M. (2012) *The Star Atlas Companion – What You Need to Know About the Constellations*. New York: Springer Praxis.

Ball, Sir R.S. (1904) *Popular Guide to the Heavens*.

Bartlett, R.A. (2008) *The Way of the Crucible*. Lake Worth, FL: Nicolas Hays.

Béguin, G. (2009) *Buddhist Art, an Historical and Cultural Journey*. Bangkok: River Books.

Bentley, J. (1823) *A Historical View of Hindu Astronomy from the Earliest Dawn of that Science in India to the Earliest Time*.

Bhagat, S.P. (ed.) *Saravali by Kalyana Varmas*.

Bhardwaj, H.C. (1979) *Aspects of Ancient Indian Technology*. New Delhi: Motilal Banarsidass.

Bhasin, J.N. (trans.) (2002) *Sarvartha Chintamani*.

Bhat, M.R. (2013) *Fundamentals of Astrology* (Third edition). New Delhi: Motilal Banarsidass.

Birla, G.S. (2000) *Destiny in the Palm of Your Hand – Creating Your Future through Vedic Palmistry*. Merrimac, MA: Destiny.

Braha, J.T. (1986) *Ancient Hindu Astrology for the Modern Western Astrologer*. New York: Hermetician Press.

Braha, J.T. (2001) *The Art and Practice of Ancient Hindu Astrology (Nine Intimate Sessions between Teacher and Student)* (Revised edition). New York: Hermetician Press.

Brāhma Sphuṭa Siddhânta by Brāhma-Gupta (1966).

Brill, B.G. (2013) 'Mercury in Ayurveda and Tibetan Medicine.' *Asian Medicine, Traditional and Modernity, Special Issue 8.1*. Leiden: Brill.

Burgess, E. (2011) *The Sûrya Siddhântikâ – A Textbook of Hindu Astronomy*. New Delhi: Cosmo Publications.

Burritt, E.H. (1835) *Geography of the Heavens*. New York: Huntington and Savage.

Central Chinmaya Mission Trust (1983) *Symbolism in Hinduism.*

Chandra Hari, K. (1985) 'Ayanāṃśa Controversy.' *Indian Journal of History of Science* 20.

Charak, K.S. (1994) *Essentials of Medical Astrology.* Kuala Lumpur: Uma Publications.

Charak, K.S. (1999) *Sūrya – The Sun God.*

Charak, K.S. (2008) *Laghu Jātakam.*

Chatterjee, B. (English commentary) (1970) *Kaṇḍa-Khâdyaka of Brāhmagupta.*

Chawdhri, L.R. (1989) *Scientific Analysis of Horoscope based on Hindu Predictive System.* New Delhi: Sagar.

Chidambaram Iyer, N. (trans.) (1884) *Brihat Samhita of Varaha Mihira.* Madura: South Indian Press. Accessed on 15/11/2016 at https://ia601405.us.archive.org/24/items/bihatsahitvarah00iyergoog/bihatsahitvarah00iyergoog.pdf

Chidambaram Iyer, N. (trans.) (1885) *Brihat Jataka of Varaha Mihira.* Madras: Foster Press. Accessed on 15/11/2016 at https://ia902700.us.archive.org/1/items/brihatjatakavar00iyergoog/brihatjatakavar00iyergoog.pdf

Chitty, S.C. (1834) *The Ceylon Gazetteer, Containing an Accurate Account of the Island of Ceylon.*

Clough, Rev. B. (1892) *Sinhalese English Dictionary.* Colombo: Wesleyan Mission Press.

Cole, G.H.A. and Woolfson, M.M. (2002) *Planetary Science, The Science of Planets around Stars.* Bristol: Institute of Physics.

de Santillana, G. and von Dechend, H. (2014 [1969]) *Hamlet's Mill: An Essay on Myth and the Frame of Time.* Boston, MA: Nonpareil Books.

Deeson, A.F.L. (ed.) (1973) *The Collector's Encyclopaedia of Rocks and Minerals.*

DeFouw, H. and Svoboda, R. (1996) *Light on Life: An Introduction to the Astrology of India.* London and New York: Arkana.

DiCara, V. (with Kishor, V.) (2012) *27 Stars, 27 Gods – The Astrological Mythology of Ancient India.* London: Author, via Createspace Independent Publishing Platform.

Dikshit, S.B. (1969) *Bharatiya Jyotish Shāstra – History of Indian Astronomy. Part I: History of Vedic Astronomy during the Vedic and Vendanga Periods.*

Dikshit, S.B. (1969) *Bharatiya Jyotish Shāstra – History of Indian Astronomy. Part II: History of Vedic Astronomy During the Siddhāntic and Modern Periods.*

Dissanayake, C.B. and Rupasinghe, M.S. (1993) 'A prospectors' guide map to the gem deposits of Sri Lanka.' *Gems and Gemology (USA)* 29, 3, 173–181.

Dowson, J. (1888) *Classical Dictionary of Hindu Mythology and Religion, Geography, History and Literature.*

Dowson, J. (1928) *Hindu Mythology and Religion, Geography, History and Literature* (Sixth edition). London.

Dreyer, R.G.(1997) *Vedic Astrology.* Newbury Port, MA: Weiser Books.

Duncan, J.C. (1927). *Astronomy – A Textbook.*

Fernando, M.S. (2000) *Rituals, Folk Beliefs and Magical Arts of Sri Lanka.* Sri Lanka: S. Godage and Brothers.

Flood, G.D. (1996) *An Introduction to Hinduism.* Cambridge: Cambridge University Press

Frawley, D. (1986–1999) *Astrology of the Seers Correspondence Course in Vedic Astrology Workbook.* Twin Lakes, WI: Lotus Press.

Frawley, D. (1990) *From the River of Heaven, Hindu and Vedic Knowledge for a Modern Age.* Salt Lake City, UT: Passage Press.

Frawley, D. (1990) *The Astrology of the Seers: A Comprehensive Guide to Vedic Astrology.* Twin Lakes, WI: Lotus Press.

Goravani, D. (2014) *Kārakas.* The Goravani Foundation.

Graves, R. (ed.) (1959) *Larousse Encyclopaedia of Mythology.* London and New York: Paul Hamlyn.

Harness, D.M. (1999) *The Nakshatras, the Lunar Mansions of Vedic Astrology.* Twin Lakes, WI: Lotus Press.

Hathaway, E. (2010a) *Graha Yuddha: Testing the Parameters of Astrology and Astronomy.* Available at http://edithhathaway.com/graha-yuddha-testing-the-parameters-of-astrology-and-astronomy, accessed on 17 March 2017.

Hathaway, E. (2010b) *Corporate Conglomerates vs. Nation States: Which Nations Will Survive and Thrive?* Available at http://edithhathaway.com/corporate-conglomerates-vs-nation-states-which-nations-will-survive-and-thrive, accessed on 17 March 2017.

Hathaway, E. (2012) *In Search of Destiny: Biography, History and Culture as Told through Vedic Astrology.* San Diego, CA: Vintage Vedic Press.

Hockey, T. (ed.) (2007) *The Biographical Encyclopaedia of Astronomers.* New York: Springer.

Holay, P.V. (1990) *Vedic Astronomy (Vendaanga Jyotisha): A Prehistoric Puzzle.*

Holden, R.W. (1977) *The Elements of House Division.* Romford, Essex: Camelot Press.

Kapoor, G.S. (2014) *Gems and Astrology: A Guide to Health, Happiness and Prosperity.*

Kapoor, G.S.(trans.) *Mantreswara's Phaladeepika.*

Kariyawasam, A.G.S. (1995) *Buddhist Ceremonies and Rituals of Sri Lanka.* The Wheel Publication No. 402/404. Kandy: Buddhist Publication Society.

Kelleher, J. (2006) *Path of Light, Volume I: Introduction to Vedic Astrology.* Ahimsa Press.

Kelleher, J. (2006) *Path of Light Volume II: The Domains of Life.* Ahimsa Press.

Ketkar, V.B. (1921) *Indian and Foreign Chronology.*

Khot, S.G. (1993) *Astrology and Diagnosis.* New Delhi: Sagar.

Kirk, A. (2012) *Making Sense of Astrology.* Colombo, Sri Lanka: Lifelight 365.

Kirk, A. (2013) *The Seven Ages of Man.* Colombo, Sri Lanka: Lifelight 365.

Knot, S.G. (1993) *Astrology and Diagnosis.*

Krishnamurti, G. (1975) *The Adventures of Rama.*

Lokamanya (Bal Gangadhar Tilak) (1925) *Vedic Chronology and Vedanga Jyotisha.*

MacDonnell, A.A. (1897) *Vedic Mythology.* New York: D. Appleton.

Mackenzie, D.A. (2008/1913) *Indian Myths and Legends.* Glasgow: Geddes & Grosset.

Madhayan, S. *Muddle of Ayanamsa.*

Mani, V. (1964) *Purāṇic Encyclopaedia – A Comprehensive Dictionary with Special Reference to the Epic and Purāṇic Literature* (Volumes I–III). New Delhi: Motilal Banarsidass.

Marshall, H. (1846) *Ceylon – A General Description of the Island and Its Inhabitants.*

Mason, A. (2014) *Rasa Shāstra: The Hidden Art of Medical Alchemy.* London: Singing Dragon.

Mason, A. (2017) *Vedic Palmistry: Hastā Rekha Shāstra.* London: Singing Dragon.

Mishra, K.K. (1995) *World of Nakshatra.* New Delhi: Cbs Publishers.

Mukerji, K. (1969) *Popular Hindu Astronomy.* (Foreword by N.C. Lahiri.)

Murthy, K.R.S. (trans.) (2003) *Vāgbhaṭa's Aṣṭāñga Hṛdayam.*

Murthy, S.R.N. (1997) *Vedic View of the Earth (A Geological Insight into the Vedas)*. New Delhi: D.K. Printworld.

Murthy, V.B. (trans.) (1989) *Bhūgola Varṇam by Sri Vadiraja Tirtha*. Madras: Akhila Bharata Madhava Maha Mandali.

Naik, S. *Roots of Naadi Astrology: A Comprehensive Study*. New Delhi: Sagar.

Nath Seth, K. and Chaturvedi, B.K. (2001) *Gods and Goddesses of India*. New Delhi: Diamond.

O'Flaherty, W.D. (trans.) (1975) *Hindu Myths*. Harmondsworth: Penguin.

Oldenberg, H. (1894) *Die Religion des Vega*. Berlin: W. Hertz. Accessed on 15/11/2016 at https://ia902706.us.archive.org/2/items/diereligiondesv00oldegoog/diereligiondesv00oldegoog.pdf

Orzech, C.D., Sørensen, H.H. and Payne, R.K. (eds) (2011) *Esoteric Buddhism and the Tantras in East Asia*. Leiden: Brill.

Pandya, H. (ed.) (1995) *Issues in Veda and Astrology*.

Ponde, S. (1939) *Hindu Astrology*. New Delhi: Sagar.

Power, A. (2005) *Island – Land of the Pharaohs, The Quest for our Atlantean Legacy*. Peninsula Print.

Pulippani, U.S. (2011) *Gochar Phaladeepika: Torch on Transit of Planets*.

Pundit Bapu Deva Sastri (1861) *Translation of The Sûrya Siddhântikâ by Pundit Bapu Deva Sastri and of the Siddhânta Siromani by the late Lancelot Wilkinson*. Calcutta: Lewis. Accessed on 16/11/2016 at http://www.wilbourhall.org/pdfs/suryaEnglish.pdf

Raman, B.V. (trans.) (1947) *Bhavartha Ratnakara*.

Raman, B.V. (trans.) (1992) *Prasna Marga (Parts I and II)*.

Ramavijaya – The Mythological History of Rama (1891). Bombay: Dubhashi. Accessed on 21/11/2016 at https://ia800500.us.archive.org/8/items/ramavijayathemyt00unwkuoft/ramavijayathemyt00unwkuoft.pdf

Rao, R.R. (1994) *Jyoutisha-Siddhanta-Sara*. Bangalore: Kalpatharu Research Academy.

Roebuck, V.J. (1992) *The Circle of Stars*. Shaftesbury: Element.

Roy, P.C. (1965) *Mahabharata of Krishna-Dwaipayana Vyasa* (Vol. 5, *Bhisma Parva*).

Sachau, E.C. (1910) *Alberuni's India (An Account of the Religion, Philosophy, Literature, Geography, Chronology, Astronomy, Customs, Laws and Astrology of India)* (Volumes I & II). London: Kegan Paul.

Sachs, M. (1999) *Ayurvedic Beauty Care, Ageless Techniques to Invoke Natural Beauty*. Twin Lakes, WI: Lotus Press.

Saha, M.N. and Lahiri, N.C. (1992) *History of the Calendar in Different Countries through the Ages*. New Delhi: Council of Scientific and Industrial Research.

Saha, N.N. (1976) *Stellar Healing (Cure and Control of Disease Through Gems)*. New Delhi: Sagar Publications.

Salomon, R. (1998) *Indian Epigraphy*. New York: Oxford University Press.

Sastri, P.S. (2004) *Textbook of Scientific Hindu Astrology (The Ancient Wisdom of Seers to Unlock the Doors of Destiny)*. New Delhi: Ranjan Publications.

Sastri, P.S. (trans.) (1996) *Uttara Kalamrita by Kalidasa*.

Sastri, P.S.V. (trans.) (1937) *Sripati-Paddhati*.

Sastri, P.S.V. (trans.) (1950) *Phaladeepika*.

Sastri, V.S. *Vaidyanatha Dikshita's Jataka Parijata* (Volumes 1–3).

Sato, T. (1990) *Kūkai Tō Renkinjutsu*. Tokyo: Shuppan.

Sato, T. (1997) *The Gods of Shingon Mikkyō*. Tokyo: Shuppan.

Schomp, V. (2010) *Myths of the World: Ancient India*. New York: Marshall Cavendish

Shashi, U. (2009[1978]) Vedic Astrological Calculations (Revised by S. K. Duggal). Delhi: Sagar Publications.

Shubhakaran, K.T. (1991) *Nakshatra (Constellation) Based Predictions (With Remedial Measures)*. New Delhi: Sagar.

Shukla, K.S. (trans.) (1976) *Āryabhaṭīya of Āryabhaṭa*.

Siddhânta Śiromani by Bhāskarācārya (1980).

Sircar, D.C. (1966) *Indian Epigraphical Glossary*. New Delhi: Motilal Banarsidass.

Sivapriyananda, Swami (1990) *Astrology and Religion in Indian Art*.

Smith, V.A. (2009a) *Ayurvedic Medicine for Westerners. Vol. 1: Anatomy and Physiology in Ayurveda*. European Institute of Vedic Studies: www.atreya.com.

Smith, V.A. (2009b) *Ayurvedic Medicine for Westerners. Vol. 2: Pathology, Diagnosis and Treatment Approaches in Ayurveda*. European Institute of Vedic Studies: www. atreya.com.

Smith, V.A. (2009c) *Ayurvedic Medicine for Westerners. Vol. 3: Clinical Protocols and Treatments in Ayurveda*. European Institute of Vedic Studies: www.atreya.com.

Smith, V.A. (2009d) *Ayurvedic Medicine for Westerners. Vol. 4: Dravyaguna for Westerners*. European Institute of Vedic Studies: www.atreya.com.

Smith, V.A. (2009e) *Ayurvedic Medicine for Westerners. Vol. 5: Application of Ayurvedic Treatments*. European Institute of Vedic Studies: www.atreya.com.

Sparrow, C. (2006) *Cosmos (A Field Guide)*. London and New York: Quercus.

Suckling, H.J. (1876) *Ceylon – Ancient and Modern, a General Description of the Island, Historical, Physical, Statistical*.

Tennant, Sir J.E. (1850) Christianity in Ceylon with an Historical Sketch of the Brahmanical and Buddhist Superstitions.

Tennant, Sir J.E. (1869) *Ceylon – An Account of the Island, Physical, Historical, and Topographical*.

The Liṅga-Purāṇa (1973) New Delhi: Motilal Banarsidass.

Thibaut, G. and Sudhakar Dvivedi (1889) (2011) *Panchasiddhantika of Varaha Mihira*. New Delhi: Cosmo Publications. Accessed on 15/11/2016 at https://archive.org/ stream/PanchaSiddhantika/Panchasiddhantika_djvu.txt

Thomas, P. (1961) *Epics, Myths and Legends of India*. Bombay: Taraporevala.

Tobey, C.P. (1973) *Astrology of Inner Space*.

Toki, R. (2006) *Remedies in Astrology*.

Trainor, K. (2004) *Buddhism: The Illustrated Guide*. New York: Oxford University Press.

Upadhyaya, A.K. (trans.) (1998) *Siddhânta Darpaṇa* (Vol. II, 1899).

Usha-Shashi (1978) *Vedic Astrological Calculations*. (Revised and edited by S.K. Duggal, 2005.) New Delhi: Sagar.

Vaṭeśvara Siddhânta by Vaṭeśvara (1985).

Wayman, A. (1997) *Untying the Knots in Buddhism: Selected Essays*. New Delhi: Motilal Banarsidass.

Weeks, P. (2012) *Make Yourself Better*. London: Singing Dragon.

White, D.G. (1996) *The Alchemical Body, Siddha Traditions in Medieval India*.

Whitney, D.W. (trans.) (1905) *Atharva Veda Saṁhitā Part 1* (Books 1–7). Cambridge, MA: Harvard University.

Whitney, D.W. (trans.) (1905) *Atharva Veda Saṁhitā Part 2* (Book 8). Cambridge, MA: Harvard University.

Wijesinghe, Y. (1994) *Plants of Sri Lanka: A Checklist of Woody Perennial Plants of Sri Lanka.*

Wilhelm, E. (2001) *Vault of the Heavens.* San Diego, CA: Kāla Occult Publishers.

Wilhelm, E. (2001) *Core Yogas.* San Diego, CA: Kāla Occult Publishers.

Wilhelm, E. (2003) *Classical Mhurta – Vedic Electional Astrology.* San Diego, CA: Kāla Occult Publishers.

Wilhelm, E. (2006) *Graha Sutras.* San Diego, CA: Kāla Occult Publishers.

Wilhelm, E. (n.d.) *Brihat Parasara Hora Shastra.* Accessed on 21/11/2016 at http://wwwvedic-astrology.net

Wilhelm, E. (n.d.) *Mystery of the Zodiac.* Available at www.vedic-astrology.net, accessed on 21 November 2016.

Wilkins, W.J. (1913) *Hindu Mythology, Vedic and Purānic.* Calcutta.

William, H. (1950) *Ceylon – Pearl of the East.* London: Robert Hale.

Williams, G.M. (2003) *Handbook of Hindu Mythology.* Santa Barbara, CA: ABC CLIO.

Wilson, H.H. (trans.) (1896) *Vishńu Puráńa, Book 6.* London: Trübner.

Wujastyk, D. (2003) *The Roots of Ayurveda* (Revised edition). London: Penguin Classics.

ABOUT THE AUTHOR

Andrew Mason is an expert in Eastern Astrology and Alchemy. He started studying holistic medicine 20 years ago and completed his training as an Āyurvedic practitioner in 2006. He then undertook a unique and intensive apprenticeship in the east, learning astrological techniques and the closely guarded processes involved in the manufacturing of ancient alchemical remedies.

For more information please visit www.neterapublishing.com.

INDEX

31159595R00221

Printed in Great Britain
by Amazon